The Value of Arts and Culture for Regional Development

In this new volume, 28 Scandinavian researchers and others who are active in arts and culture seek to answer the questions: What has been the effect of regional and local investment in arts and culture? And what positive and negative experiences have there been? This book describes and analyzes the extent to which cultural investments at local and regional levels have stimulated development and led to essential processes of change for the community in general.

Of special interest is how different places manage to 'turn the tide'. What do their development processes involve? Which ways and means do they use to go forward in order to change their paths and start anew? These are just a few of the important questions addressed in this book. One of the most important findings is that while you can never transfer the successful renewal of one place to another like a blueprint, certain common patterns in the cultural processes are discernible.

The contributors to this book show the breadth of theoretical tools that can be used to increase awareness of the significance of culture for regional development. Throughout the book readers will find a multitude of theoretical concepts, from entrepreneurship theory, organizational institutionalism and cultural economy, to cultural planning and art management. This book will appeal to scholars and practitioners of urban and regional studies, and cultural and creative economics.

Lisbeth Lindeborg is Guest Professor at Linnæus University, Sweden. She has published extensively on regional and cultural development, regional co-operation, regional organizations and the arts.

Lars Lindkvist is Professor in Business Administration, Organization and Leadership at Linnæus University, Sweden, and is also Adjunct Professor at Copenhagen Business School, Denmark. He has published more than 50 books and scientific articles, mainly about social economy, self management and leadership in public and non-profit organizations, and cultural and creative industries.

Regional Studies Association

THE GLOBAL FORUM FOR CITY AND REGIONAL RESEARCH, DEVELOPMENT AND POLICY

Routledge
Taylor & Francis Group

Regions and Cities

In today's globalised, knowledge-driven and networked world, regions and cities have assumed heightened significance as the interconnected nodes of economic, social and cultural production, and as sites of new modes of economic and territorial governance and policy experimentation. This book series brings together incisive and critically engaged international and interdisciplinary research on this resurgence of regions and cities, and should be of interest to geographers, economists, sociologists, political scientists and cultural scholars, as well as to policy-makers involved in regional and urban development. For more information on the Regional Studies Association visit www.regionalstudies.org

There is a **30% discount** available to RSA members on books in the ***Regions and Cities*** series, and other subject related Taylor and Francis books and e-books including Routledge titles. To order just e-mail alex.robinson@tandf.co.uk, or phone on +44 (0) 20 7017 6924 and declare your RSA membership. You can also visit www.routledge.com and use the discount code: **RSA0901**.

1. **Beyond Green Belts**
   Managing urban growth in the 21st century
   Edited by John Herington

2. **Retreat from the Regions**
   Corporate change and the closure of factories
   Stephen Fothergill and Nigel Guy

3. **Regional Development in the 1990s**
   The British Isles in transition
   Edited by Ron Martin and Peter Townroe

4. **Spatial Policy in a Divided Nation**
   Edited by Richard T. Harrison and Mark Hart

5. **An Enlarged Europe**
Regions in competition?
Edited by Louis Albrechts, Sally Hardy, Mark Hart and Anastasios Katos

6. **The Regional Imperative**
Regional planning and governance in Britain, Europe and the United States
Urlan A. Wannop

7. **The Determinants of Small Firm Growth**
An inter-regional study in the United Kingdom, 1986–90
Richard Barkham, Graham Gudgin, Mark Hart and Eric Hanvey

8. **The Regional Dimension of Transformation in Central Europe**
Grzegorz Gorzelak

9. **Union Retreat and the Regions**
The shrinking landscape of organised labour
Ron Martin, Peter Sunley and Jane Wills

10. **Regional Development Strategies**
A European perspective
Edited by Jeremy Alden and Philip Boland

11. **British Regionalism and Devolution**
The challenges of state reform and European integration
Edited by Jonathan Bradbury and John Mawson

12. **Innovation Networks and Learning Regions?**
James Simmie

13. **Regional Policy in Europe**
S. S. Artobolevskiy

14. **New Institutional Spaces**
TECs and the remaking of economic governance
Edited by Martin Jones and Jamie Peck

15. **The Coherence of EU Regional Policy**
Contrasting perspectives on the structural funds
Edited by John Bachtler and Ivan Turok

16. **Multinationals and European Integration**
Trade, investment and regional development
Edited by Nicholas A. Phelps

17. **Unemployment and Social Exclusion**
Landscapes of labour inequality and social exclusion
Edited by Sally Hardy, Paul Lawless and Ron Martin

18. **Metropolitan Planning in Britain**
A comparative study
Edited by Peter Roberts, Kevin Thomas and Gwyndaf Williams

19. **Social Exclusion in European Cities**
Processes, experiences and responses
Edited by Judith Allen, Goran Cars and Ali Madanipour

20. **Regional Development Agencies in Europe**
Edited by Charlotte Damborg, Mike Danson and Henrik Halkier

21. **Community Economic Development**
Edited by Graham Haughton

22. **Foreign Direct Investment and the Global Economy**
Corporate and institutional dynamics of global-localisation
Edited by Jeremy Alden and Nicholas F. Phelps

23. **Restructuring Industry and Territory**
The experience of Europe's regions
Edited by Anna Giunta, Arnoud Lagendijk and Andy Pike

24. **Out of the Ashes?**
The social impact of industrial contraction and regeneration on Britain's mining communities
Chas Critcher, Bella Dicks, David Parry and David Waddington

25. **Regional Innovation Strategies**
The challenge for less-favoured regions
Edited by Kevin Morgan and Claire Nauwelaers

26. **Geographies of Labour Market Inequality**
Edited by Ron Martin and Philip S. Morrison

27. **Sustainable Cities**
Graham Haughton and Colin Hunter

28. **Regions, Spatial Strategies and Sustainable Development**
David Counsell and Graham Haughton

29. **Clusters and Regional Development**
Critical reflections and explorations
Edited by Bjørn Asheim, Philip Cooke and Ron Martin

30. **Regional Competitiveness**
Edited by Ron Martin, Michael Kitson and Peter Tyler

31. **Regional Development in the Knowledge Economy**
Edited by Philip Cooke and Andrea Piccaluga

32. **The Rise of the English Regions?**
Edited by Irene Hardill, Paul Benneworth, Mark Baker and Leslie Budd

33. **Geographies of the New Economy**
Critical reflections
Edited by Peter W. Daniels, Andrew Leyshon, Michael J. Bradshaw and Jonathan Beaverstock

34. **European Cohesion Policy**
Willem Molle

35. **Creative Regions**
Technology, culture and knowledge entrepreneurship
Edited by Philip Cooke and Dafna Schwartz

36. **Devolution, Regionalism and Regional Development**
The UK experience
Edited by Jonathan Bradbury

37. **Intelligent Cities and Globalisation of Innovation Networks**
Nicos Komninos

38. **Whither Regional Studies?**
Edited by Andy Pike

39. **Business Networks in Clusters and Industrial Districts**
The governance of the global value chain
Edited by Fiorenza Belussi and Alessia Sammarra

40. **China and Europe**
The implications of the rise of China as a global economic power for Europe
Edited by Klaus Kunzmann, Willy A. Schmid and Martina Koll-Schretzenmayr

41. **Globalizing Regional Development in East Asia**
Production networks, clusters, and entrepreneurship
Edited by Henry Wai-chung Yeung

42. **Manufacturing in the New Urban Economy**
Willem van Winden, Leo van den Berg, Luis de Carvalho and Erwin van Tuijl

43. **The Impacts of Automotive Plant Closures**
A tale of two cities
Edited by Andrew Beer and Holli Evans

44. **The Futures of the City Region**
Edited by Michael Neuman and Angela Hull

45. **Migration in the 21st Century**
Rights, outcomes, and policy
Kim Korinek and Thomas Maloney

46. **Leadership and Place**
Edited by Chris Collinge, John Gibney and Chris Mabey

47. **Beyond Territory**
Edited by Harald Bathelt, Maryann Feldman and Dieter F. Kogler

48. **The Recession and Beyond**
Local and regional responses to the downturn
Edited by David Bailey and Caroline Chapain

49. **Cultural Political Economy of Small Cities**
Edited by Anne Lorentzen and Bas van Heur

50. **Just Growth**
Inclusion and prosperity in America's metropolitan regions
Chris Benner and Manuel Pastor

51. **Industrial Policy Beyond the Crisis**
Regional, national and international perspectives
Edited by David Bailey, Helena Lenihan and Josep-Maria Arauzo-Carod

52. **Promoting Silicon Valleys in Latin America**
Luciano Ciravegna

53. **Regional Development in Northern Europe**
Peripherality, marginality and border issues
Edited by Mike Danson and Peter De Souza

54. **Creating Knowledge Locations in Cities**
Innovation and integration challenges
Willem van Winden, Luis de Carvalho, Erwin van Tujil, Jeroen van Haaren and Leo van den Berg

55. **Complex Adaptive Innovation Systems**
Relatedness and transversality in the evolving region
Philip Cooke

56. **Innovation Governance in an Open Economy**
Shaping regional nodes in a globalized world
Edited by Annika Rickne, Staffan Laestadius and Henry Etzkowitz

57. **Creative Industries and Innovation in Europe**
Concepts, measures and comparative case studies
Edited by Luciana Lazzeretti

58. **Community-based Entrepreneurship and Rural Development**
Creating favourable conditions for small businesses in Central Europe
Matthias Fink, Stephan Loidl and Richard Lang

59. **Regional Development Agencies: The Next Generation?**
Networking, knowledge and regional policies
Edited by Nicola Bellini, Mike Danson and Henrik Halkier

60. **Leadership and Change in Sustainable Regional Development**
Edited by Markku Sotarauta, Ina Horlings and Joyce Liddle

61. **Networking Regionalised Innovative Labour Markets**
Edited by Ulrich Hilpert and Helen Lawton Smith

62. **Re-framing Regional Development**
Evolution, innovation and transition
Edited by Philip Cooke

63. **The University and the City**
John Goddard and Paul Vallance

64. **The Value of Arts and Culture for Regional Development**
A Scandinavian perspective
Edited by Lisbeth Lindeborg and Lars Lindkvist

The Value of Arts and Culture for Regional Development

A Scandinavian perspective

Edited by Lisbeth Lindeborg and Lars Lindkvist

Routledge
Taylor & Francis Group
LONDON AND NEW YORK

First published 2013
by Routledge
2 Park Square, Milton Park, Abingdon, Oxfordshire OX14 4RN

Simultaneously published in the USA and Canada
by Routledge
711 Third Avenue, New York, NY 10017

Routledge is an imprint of the Taylor & Francis Group, an informa business

First issued in paperback 2014

British Library Cataloguing in Publication Data
A catalogue record for this book is available from the British Library

Library of Congress Cataloging-in-Publication Data
The value of arts and culture for regional development: a Scandinavian perspective/edited by Lisbeth Lindeborg and Lars Lindkvist.
p. cm.
Includes bibliographical references and index.
1. Cultural industries–Scandinavia. 2. Arts–Economic aspects–Scandinavia. 3. Cultural property–Economic aspects–Scandinavia. 4. Regional economics–Scandinavia. 5. Regional planning–Scandinavia I. Lindeborg, Lisbeth. II. Lindkvist, Lars.
HD9999.C9473S348 2013
306.30948–dc23
2012038209

ISBN 978-0-415-63837-1 (hbk)

ISBN 978-1-138-84265-6 (pbk)

ISBN 978-0-203-38565-4 (ebk)

Typeset in Times New Roman

by OKS Prepress Services, Chennai, India.

Contents

Illustrations

Figures

Tables

Contributors

Tommy D. Andersson PhD, is a Professor in Business Administration at the School of Business, Economics and Law at the University of Gothenburg and at the University of Stavanger. His main research interests and publications are in economic impact analysis, tourism, event and festival management, cost-benefit analysis and managerial economics of the hospitality industry.

John Armbrecht has a PhD from the School of Business, Economics and Law at the University of Gothenburg. His PhD thesis 'The Value of Cultural Institutions' was published in 2012 and his major research interests are cultural tourism, culture management, cultural economics and economic impact studies.

Peter Aronsson PhD, is a Professor in Cultural Heritage and Uses of the Past at Linköping University and a Professor in History at Linnæus University. He has studied the history of democracy, theory of history and has run several comparative European projects on the implications of uses of the past for contemporary society.

Trine Bille PhD, is an Associate Professor at Copenhagen Business School, Department of Innovation and Organizational Economics, and Program Director for BSc (Business Administration and Service Management). Her main research interest is cultural economics and she has published numerous books and articles within this field. She served as a deputy chairman on the executive board of Cultiva, 2001–2009, and is member of the executive board of ACEI (Association of Cultural Economics International).

Per Frankelius PhD, is an Associate Professor in Business Administration at Linköping University. His research started in the 1980s at a research programme sponsored by Apple, IBM and Swedish Post. Most of his *c.*400 publications examine the interface between innovation and marketing. Integrating nature in economic models – in the spirit of Carl Linnæus – is also a recurrent theme in his research.

Hans Gelter has a PhD in Genetics from Uppsala University. After a NSERC postdoc at Queens University, Kingston, Canada, he got a position as Senior

Lecturer in Biology at Luleå University of Technology. He then moved to the Department of Culture, Communication and Education at Luleå University of Technology where he now holds a position as Associate Professor in Experience Production, and does research in polar nature tourism and experience production.

Jennie Gelter has an MS in Experience Production from Luleå University of Technology and is now a Lecturer in the Experience production programme. Her interests lie in the anthropology of tourism and experience production, and she plans to start her PhD studies in the near future.

Anne-Britt Gran is a Professor in Cultural Policy and Cultural Theory at BI Norwegian Business School, where she is in charge of the Arts Management programme. Throughout her career she has been doing research on different topics such as theatre history, postcolonialism/multiculturalism, cultural policy and arts management, and she has published several articles and books about these subjects (see www.annebrittgran.com). She is now working on a research project concerning digital consumption of music, films and e-books in Norway.

Astrid Huopalainen is a PhD researcher in Management and Organization at Åbo Akademi University, Finland. As part of Creatin', a research project on creative industries, creative cities and on Turku as European Capital of Culture in 2011, she is writing her PhD thesis on the aesthetic economy of fashion.

Nina Kivinen is Dr Sc. (Econ.) and Lecturer in Organization and Management at Åbo Akademi University, Finland. Her research focuses on questions of space and identity in relation to work practices and particularly branding and knowledge work.

Niina Koivunen is an Associate Professor in the Department of Management at the University of Vaasa, Finland and Docent at Turku School of Economics, Finland. Her research focuses on leadership, organization culture, management education, art organizations and expert communities. She has mainly worked on discursive, aesthetic and ethnographic research approaches.

Lisbeth Lindeborg is a writer and has a PhD in Political Science from the J.W. Goethe University in Frankfurt/Main, a BA in Arts Studies and is affiliated as Guest Professor at Linnæus University, Sweden. She has published extensively on regional and cultural development, regional cooperations, regional organizations, arts, theatre and film, having had commissions as a film festival juror. She has a past as a stage actress/singer (USA) and as a broadcaster for Swedish Radio from the UK, Germany and France. She lives in Marburg.

Lars Lindkvist has a PhD and dr.merc from the Department of Organization, Copenhagen Business School where he also is an Adjunct Professor. He is a Professor in Business Administration, Organization and Leadership at

Linnæus University in Sweden. He has published more than 50 books and scientific articles, mainly about social economy, self management and leadership in public and non-profit organizations and cultural and creative industries.

Anne Lorentzen PhD, is a Professor in Geography at the Department of Planning and Development, Aalborg University, Denmark. She has published extensively on local and regional economic development and the experience economy, and on new technology and innovation in local and regional development.

Lise Lyck is an Associate Professor and Centre Director for the Center for Tourism and Culture Management at the Copenhagen Business School. Her main interests are in tourism (all dimensions, especially related to economic development), regionalization and management of culture, events and meetings. For publications see titles in the Copenhagen Business School library.

Erica Månsson is Director of Culture and Leisure Services in the municipality of Växjö. She has introduced cultural planning in Sweden and carried out Master Plan development based on cultural planning in Kronoberg County. Erica was CEO of the cultural heritage organization Kulturparken Småland which was rewarded the Museum of the Year in Sweden 2012.

Mika Mård is a PhD researcher in Organization and Management at Åbo Akademi University, Finland. As part of Creatin', a research project on creative industries, creative cities and on Turku as European Capital of Culture in 2011, he is writing his PhD thesis on authenticity within the creative industries rooted in subcultures.

Tobias Nielsén has a Master's Degree from Studies at the Stockholm School of Economics, and Columbia Business School. He is the CEO and Chief Analyst at the research-based consulting firm Volante, Sweden. Tobias' work includes mapping the creative industries, financial and management control in creative SME's economic effects of live events, and work on cultural and industry policies.

Alf Rehn likes coffee, comics and corny pop culture. He is also a dedicated fan of Ethel Merman and the divine Patsy Cline. When he can spare the time, he also works as the Chair of Management and Organization at Åbo Akademi University. For more info, see www.alfrehn.com.

Hilmar Rommetvedt is Dr.Polit., Head of Research in Political Science at IRIS – International Research Institute of Stavanger, and Adjunct Professor at the University of Stavanger, Norway. He was the manager of a major research project on Stavanger as European Capital of Culture in 2008 and has published numerous books and articles on parliamentary government, organized interests and public policies.

Sunny Sandström is Manager of Arts and Culture at the County Council in Kronoberg County, Sweden. She has worked with cultural planning and the regional cultural policy in a new model of cooperation 'Kultursamverkansmodellen'.

Katriina Siivonen PhD, works as Senior Lecturer in Nordic Ethnology at Åbo Akademi University. She is Adjunct Professor in Cultural Heritage Studies, especially in applied cultural research at the University of Turku. Previously she has worked as Research Director in Nordic Ethnology at Åbo Akademi University. Her research interests are cultural sustainability, cultural identities, local development and participatory futures studies.

Wilhelm Skoglund PhD, works as a Senior Lecturer at Mid Sweden University and a Researcher at the Regional Council of Jämtland County. His doctoral thesis concerned entrepreneurial development in rural communities and he has been working with research on the cultural and creative industries for the last four years.

Jon Sundbo is a Professor in Business Administration and Innovation at Roskilde University, Denmark. Throughout his career he has been conducting research on innovation and entrepreneurship and has published articles and books (including *The Theory of Innovation* and *The Strategic Management of Innovation*) on these topics. In particular he has studied innovation and entrepreneurship in services and the experience economy.

Saara L. Taalas is IKEA Professor in Business Studies at Linnæus University, and Head of Media Futures Network at Turku University. Saara's work on creativity includes academic articles, hands-on cultural entrepreneurship, and collaborative projects like 'Economy of Culture in Europe' (2006).

Jutta Tailas is a PhD researcher in Organization and Management at Åbo Akademi University, Finland. As part of Creatin', a research project on creative industries, creative cities and on Turku as European Capital of Culture in 2011, she wrote her master's thesis on the sensemaking of being part of a European Capital of Culture and her PhD thesis discusses the organization of places in cities.

Stig Westerdahl PhD, is Associate Professor in Business Administration at Malmö University, Sweden. His research interests are organizational studies in combination with accounting, voluntary organizations and regional development. At present he is researching real estate.

Lisa Öberg is Manager of Arts and Culture at the Regional Council in Kronoberg County, Sweden. She has worked in cultural planning since 2005.

Acknowledgements

The basis for this edited volume is the anthology called *Kulturens Kraft för Regional Utveckling* that was published in 2010 by the Swedish publishing company SNS Förlag, www.sns.se/forlag/kulturens-kraft-regional-utveckling. In that book, 22 Swedish researchers present mainly Swedish and some non-Scandinavian examples of the power of culture for regional development. So far nearly all of the copies of this book have been sold.

Instead of releasing a new edition we, together with researchers from other Scandinavian countries, have decided to put together a new book in English, with examples from all over Scandinavia, for the international market. We soon found that Routledge suited us best to establish cooperation with.

As editors we wish to extend our gratitude to Simon Holt and Robert Langham at Routledge for nursing this manuscript into book form, to Michelle Mello for her remarkable attention to detail in finding more useful words and synonyms in her proofreading of the manuscript and to Anders Olsson for help with the standardization of the manuscript. The editors also want to thank the Dean at the Linnæus University for financial support with finishing the book.

Lisbeth Lindeborg and Lars Lindkvist

1 En route in the cultural society

An introductory dialogue

Lisbeth Lindeborg and Lars Lindkvist

Lisbeth Lindeborg: Do you remember the British economist Mark Blaug and the book he edited, *The Economics of the Arts*? I think it was published some time in the mid-seventies.

Lars Lindkvist: Yes, yes – I remember. It was in 1976. He was early with his theories, like David Throsby's and Glenn Withers' *The Economics of the Performing Arts* which was published around the same time and Tibor Scitovsky's *Subsidies for the Arts*: *the Economic Argument* which came a few years later.

Lisbeth: Yes. It was Blaug who wrote about a *cultural lag* – a state of affairs and a state of mind, which characterized our societies for quite a long time after the Second World War. At that time cultural activities and the arts were marginalized within the framework of planning and development. Cultural policy was not high on the agenda and, when mentioned, it was often seen as a luxury commodity. For artists struggling to survive that was insulting.

Lars: Also, that view of culture changed in the late seventies with the publishing of the *Journal of Cultural Economics* and the founding of the Association of Cultural Economics International. Real pioneers – of course – were William Baumol and William Bowen who wrote about the economic dilemma of performing arts back in the sixties.

Lisbeth: That's it – you had the artists themselves and some economists who knew of the different great values – including the financial ones– of arts and culture. But it has taken time to get politicians involved in the issue. And we know from the chapters in this book that it is crucial to have support from politicians when promoting arts. When influential politicians finally came out and proposed investments in cultural infrastructure it meant a lot. In France, for example, the Minister of Culture Jack Lang was one of the first European ministers to really push cultural politics. Another great political personality at the time was the famous political author and politician Jean-Jacques Servan-Schreiber. In an article for *Le Figaro* in 1988 he proposed that the cold war powers should be replaced by creative powers, literally. A great idea.

Lars: Yes – thanks to personalities like that, today we are en route in an existing cultural society. There is no doubt about that. We only have to look at concepts which were dismissed and that caused controversy 20 years ago, like cultural infrastructures, creative industries and cultural investments – they are fully accepted today.

Three fictitious cultural maps

Lisbeth: And the development of more and more European regions, cities and villages prove the significance of culture as a development factor. In order to grasp what has happened in Europe over the last forty years we need our imagination to draw up three fictitious cultural maps representing 1970, 1990 and 2010, and then conduct a quantitative and qualitative comparison. The first map would be dominated by the European capitals complemented by traditional cultural cities like Edinburgh, Oxford, Amsterdam, Avignon, Montpellier, Salzburg, Barcelona, Roskilde, Munich, Heidelberg, Florence, Pisa, Geneva, etc.

Lars: One could add several more – Cambridge, Nancy, Odense, Cologne, Venice, Ravenna and others. These were the cities where visitors from other countries went to festivals, museums, magnificent opera performances and famous universities. In a way, these places have – for hundreds of years really – always been visited because of their high standard of arts and culture.

Lisbeth: Exactly. If we now look at a map from 1990 we will observe that it has been expanded with both other large, medium and small cities as well as with some villages including Holstebro and Hultsfred. These two places are both analysed in this book. Other places are Unna, Ulm, Frankfurt am Main, Limoges, Poitiers, Charleville-Mézieres, Monticiello, Sestri Levante, Maastricht, Basel, Glasgow – just to mention a few.

But – it is when we imagine a cultural map of 2010, that we become aware of the really dramatic differences. Today, Europe is densely populated with cultural places – I would say that they shine and sparkle in their diversity. I see them as stars on earth. It is not just the abundance that strikes us but also the variety of new and unexpected places. Just imagine how former run down port cities, that were categorized as hopeless cases, have now managed to reverse the decline and to achieve renewal. Excellent examples of this are two cities in the Ruhr Region, Dortmund and Essen. And look at the new fashion city of Antwerp. In Italy, Genoa and Turin have polished themselves up and in Britain, Newcastle/Gateshead and Liverpool/Merseyside have turned into popular places for tourists and students. In France, the same has happened to Marseille, Lille and Lyon and in Spain, Bilbao has become a tourist magnet.

Lars: I would love to be able to stay there a little longer and describe its development with the Guggenheim Museum in focus.

Lisbeth: I knew you would bring up Bilbao, but before that I just want to finish my monologue and add some other cultural places to the latest map, for example the formerly so-called dull mid-sized cities like Norrköping and Trollhättan in Sweden. Trollhättan is now internationally known as Trollywood, a new centre for filmmaking. Lars von Trier has made films there. In Germany you have Mannheim as well as Bochum and Gelsenkirchen in the Ruhr Region and in Britain, Huddersfield could be mentioned. And then you have the small towns in rural areas like Virserum in Sweden, Lich and Weil am Rhein in Germany and Swiss Vrin as well as neglected suburbs like Botkyrka in Stockholm and Neukölln in Berlin. These places are all cases which we, or our colleagues have studied. On the map of 2010 there is also an increasing number of regions – many more than the twelve *creative districts* listed by the World Creativity Forum.[1] Some of the most creative regions are cross-border cooperations like the Barents Euro-Arctic Region and Jämtland-Tröndelag – they are both described in this book. Saar-Lor-Lux-Wallonie-Rheinland-Pfalz and Dreiländereck, that are made up of the border regions in France, Switzerland and Germany are other prominent cross-border regions. It is really thrilling and I would look forward to seeing what the map will look like in 2030! Bilbao – you said – is one of the most interesting places… Why is that so?

Lars: Why… well – their culture-led regeneration has been so successful that terms like the 'Bilbao Effect' or the 'Guggenheim Effect' emerged. And that, in short, is the concept of iconoclastic architecture revitalizing a rundown city.

Lisbeth: And that is the famous Guggenheim Museum…

Lars: Exactly. But you must not forget that many other economic factors and urban planning efforts have contributed to Bilbao's revitalization (studied by Siemiatycki 2005; Plaza 2008; Plaza and Haarich 2009). In his book *Citydesign* (2005), Denmark's Steffen Gulmann shows us what we can learn from Bilbao's transformation and what arts and culture can contribute to regional development. Bilbao, with a population of over 350,000 changed over the course of fifteen years. Once it was a dirty harbour and industrial city whose residents were moving away because it was seen as an unsuitable place to live. Today it is a clean city with magnificent architecture, new jobs and good accessibility to both high-tech and service companies. At the same time unemployment has decreased from 35 to about 10 per cent.

Lisbeth: This is similar to what has happened in Antwerp, Lille and Marseille.

Lars: The goal of the transformation process that was started was to create a metropolis with the highest level of service. Service companies were to be drawn there. The idea was to make use of the existing skills of the city's workforce and translate those skills to service jobs, which then did not require highly educated personnel, and thus create new jobs. In Bilbao, the well-being of its residents was the starting point for the transformation and it was implemented in four stages – first it was necessary to create the physical frame, with infrastructure including IT capacity in the city's centre. The second stage was to create a real urban environment. Finally, the third and fourth stages were to increase social capital and to create a good environment for sports and art. €1.2 billion were to be invested in a new metro, €600 million in a new harbour and €160 million in what is today the world famous Guggenheim Museum Bilbao.

Lisbeth: That is a lot of money. Who was behind the financing? Most of it came from the EU I presume.

Lars: Yes, even if large investments were made by the private sector and the Basque region, it would never have been accomplished without support from the EU. Bilbao had no modern museum so the politicians made contact with Thomas

Krens, Director of the Guggenheim in New York, who showed himself to be interested in a collaboration. There was a great opposition to a new art museum among Bilbao's residents, however; the opposition even went to the election with the promise that they would tear the museum down if they won the regional election. If it had been up to the popular vote there would never have been a museum. Only a few enthusiastic driving spirits in the political system understood that it was 'now or never' for Bilbao. They saw the Guggenheim Museum as Bilbao's crowning achievement. Later, however, even those who were against the project changed their opinion.

Lisbeth: Yes, I remember the discussion. There were a lot of prejudices about Bilbao and that is something that many of the new cultural places have had to fight against. The perception of a place shows itself on a *mental map* which has to be changed not only within a region, within a city and within a village but also from the outside. In their excellent book *Mental Maps*, Peter Gould and Rodney White (1992) emphasized that politicians and other people in influential positions should be aware of their own biased thinking when they make decisions about places. When hopeless cases like the Ruhr area, for example, signalled that it was going to be a cultural space, nobody believed it in the beginning, but Ruhr was lucky enough to have planners and politicians with unorthodox visions of the future. Another thing is that these places that are being transformed must keep a hold on their past – parts of their earlier mental maps – their history, no matter how it is, is a part of their identity. So what has happened to the museum?

Lars: At the time of its start-up, the costs for the now world famous Guggenheim Museum Bilbao totalled €166 million. This included the cost of construction (€73.10 million), land (€7.21 million), artwork (€32.31 million), payment for the star architect Frank Gehry (€8.70 million) and the executive architect (€4.68 million), the Guggenheim Foundation New York twenty-year franchise fee (€13.30 million) and other Guggenheim services (€4.64 million), taxes (€7.21 million), and other operative costs (€14.87 million) (Plaza 2006). Even if this was a lot of money, the museum has generated enough jobs, related sector development and tax revenues to recoup the Basque Authorities' initial investment (Plaza *et al.* 2011).

Today, the museum is a symbol for Bilbao and annually attracts one million tourists who spend approximately €128 million in the city. If we add the museum's sales, which a few years ago were €163 million, to these €128 million, it would correspond to the creation of 5,000 new jobs, according to Gulmann (2005).

Lisbeth: That is impressive. I've yet to visit Bilbao ... I feel I have to go and have a look...

Lars: I've been there; the Guggenheim Museum Bilbao is fantastic. Plaza (2006) used input-output tables and discounting of cash flows to calculate the multiplying effect of museum visitors on the Bilbao economy and found the net present value of the museum to be €4,836,852 per year, on average. By the end of 2011, the Basque region has cut the unemployment rate by half of the Spanish national average of 20 per cent. To sum up, the Guggenheim Museum Bilbao stands today as one of the most famous examples of such an instrument for urban regeneration. It helped turn the polluted, industrial town into a global city. Let's move from Bilbao and the Basque region to Scandinavia. Do you see this as one big or many small regions?

A 'new' Scandinavian model?

Lisbeth: Scandinavia perceived as one entity is a myth. There is no question about that. And at a time like ours, when cultural diversity is seen as a condition for pluralism, heterogeneity and economic success the myth of a homogeneous Scandinavia can not be allowed to persist – it has to be abolished once and for all. When Scandinavia is perceived of as *one* cultural entity the rich regional and local diversity becomes marginalized. And that is one purpose of this anthology – to show the diversified Scandinavia. In a way Scandinavia is being rediscovered by its own inhabitants as well as by visitors in terms of new and old 'hidden' cultural assets. Most of the places discussed in this book, that were up until recently considered to be insignificant, are now establishing themselves as culturally attractive.

Lars: One of these places is the city of Holstebro in Denmark with its remarkable development. Others are the Kronoberg region in Sweden and the old industrial Kotka-Hamina region in Finland. Take the traditionally structurally weak southern Swedish Kronoberg region, for example, with its new cultural vision developed in 2007. It started out with the realization that culture and arts are basic amenities necessary in order to have a good society, which in turn is the platform for successful economic development.

Lisbeth: If I may interrupt – the examples shown here could very well serve as inspiration for other parts of the world – not as blueprints because in this context blueprints never work, but as inspirational sources. Scandinavia has often been held up as a model if we look at different developments in the society here, like the welfare state, womens' emancipation, and non-hierarchical horizontal decision structures. Maybe now is the right time to put the spotlight on Scandinavia's cultural assets, and without just focusing on the nations' capitals. The cultural planning concept which was developed in Kronoberg, for example, is well worth paying attention to . . .

Lars: That's right. Among the strategic issues which were dealt with were: How can our region be competitive enough in an increasingly globalized society? Which kind of economy should we favour? What is unique in our region and how can we use it? How can we foster a creative cultural climate enhancing tolerance and innovation? How can our region become more attractive for its inhabitants and its visitors? And it should be emphasized that it was and is important that every part of the Kronoberg society is aware of the new cultural vision and will be willing to stand up for it. It is a kind of consciousness-raising process.

Lisbeth: It could serve as a model for many structurally weak regions in Europe. This localization of cultural investments and the growth locally of cultural industries is very typical for Scandinavia where there are many small towns and municipalities and vast areas of countryside.

Lars: Exactly. An early study from 2004 of the situation in Norway shows the growing strong connection between the cultural industries and other industries. Culture-based companies also exist in the tourism and manufacturing industries. And at the same time there is a restructuring and concentration of ownership in the cultural industry's distribution links. In the line of production there is an increasing amount of small businesses and freelancers. Teams are put together to solve various project assignments. We also observe the increasing importance of networks. Within the cultural industry, public funding and voluntary efforts are of great importance for the development of ideas and talent. This then generates income in the more commercial parts of the cultural industries (Haraldsen *et al.* 2004).

Lisbeth: May I interrupt again – the expression 'voluntary efforts' is of course controversial when you think of the exploitation of people in the arts. Most artistic talents cannot earn a decent living with their art alone. In Germany and France it is catastrophic. Most of these artists are highly educated people with both academic merits and an additional education in their artistic work. In Germany their average income is €950 a month. 57 per cent of those highly qualified people have to apply for social benefits and when they get older they will get a pension of €400 monthly. You cannot possibly live on that. In this case the situation in Scandinavia is better. There are many ways to get project money and the social system works.

Lars: Yes, but it can be much better. The Norwegian study that I mentioned before (Haraldsen *et al.* 2004), points out the need for investment in culture for local development, which for many is a good thing. The companies within the cultural industries create products that contribute to other products' substance, a style or a symbolic value, something that makes them seem special. This is particularly important for business competitiveness in a high-cost country like Norway. This also applies to the geographic competition. The study highlights a number of political implications, for example, that the majority of businesses in the cultural industry are highly innovative learning organizations and they often interact with other businesses in a flexible network. As you can see, they have many of the characteristics that the business community in general is looking for and can learn from. Another thing is that many of the companies are locally place-bound and will not be moved to other countries. And many of their products are time and location specific (consumed here and now). And they are relatively labour-intensive industries that can contribute to new jobs (not 'jobless growth'). Employment in the cultural industries is increasing.

Lisbeth: I wrote about the increasing labour market a few years ago (Lindeborg 2007). At that time there were more people employed in Sweden and Finland (3.2 per cent) than in Norway (2.2 per cent) but the labour market is increasing everywhere.

Culture and the arts – concepts and terminology

Lisbeth: After my report 'Culture as a Location Factor' was published in the early 1990s, I was invited to give almost 400 lectures, mainly in Scandinavia, until the end of the decade. A question which was often put to me was how I defined culture. What most people wanted to know was: should culture as a concept be limited to fine arts or could other areas like sports be included. Another issue, which led to heated discussions, was, how far culture and art could be commercialized or instrumentalized for other purposes. When it came to the use of the word culture in an anthropological sense everybody consented. Today, the concept of culture is discussed from other points of views – tomorrow it will be another still, and so on. Concepts of culture and art move with the time – they are *zeitgeist*-phenomena – and we move with them. That's life. To give a precise definition would be a disastrous endeavour . . .

Lars: One way to characterize the cultural and creative industries is the 'concentric circles model' utilized by Throsby (2008a, 2008b). In this model, cultural goods and services give rise to two types of values: economic and cultural. The industries at the core are those with the greatest cultural content relative to commercial content and, as you move out from the centre, the industries' commercial values rise relative to cultural value. In the centre of the circle are the arts: literature, music, performing arts and visual arts. The outer ring includes related industries such as advertising, architecture, design and fashion. Throsby has found this model useful in analysing the impact of the cultural industries and applies it to several countries.

Lisbeth: There is another issue which has to be clarified. Very often – too often – you read about or hear people who express the notion that culture per se is something good, something positive. The consequence would then be that it must be subsidized. This kind of thinking is totally wrong. Culture is not something absolute in the meaning of good, as we know; culture and arts can be quite bad and evil things – like creativity, which is another word that is misused. Creativity, for example, is no good when it is criminal. And who defines what is good or bad culture? There is a very good saying by the German philosopher Dirk Baecker: 'culture is a continuous observation whereby every value also has a contrary value. Culture means having reasons prepared, which makes it possible for someone to criticize that what someone else celebrates' (Baecker 2003).

Lars: Another issue is cultural quality.

Lisbeth: That is also being discussed and there is no absolute answer to that either. When measuring quality you use all kinds of soft factors like experience, intuition, subjectivity, sympathy or antipathy, sense of beauty, certainly not a simple notion. You can measure the revenues from museums and festivals, and the income from creative industries and tourism but you can not measure quality.

Lars: There is also a difference how you use the terms culture and arts in different languages.

Lisbeth: Yes, absolutely, in Scandinavia as well as in Germany you have the word *culture* which covers every kind of artistic creativity – high and low – as well as cultural politics, and culture in an anthropological sense. In English, on the other hand, the word 'arts' is also used. In the arts supplement of a newspaper you find all kinds of culture represented. In this book both culture in its anthropological sense and arts implying artistic creativity are being used.

Regional diversity

Lisbeth: The other concept which we use is region – regional development. It is interesting how our authors conceive of it. When, for example, someone would call Scandinavia a region, this is the interpretation which you find in American research. There, a region is a limited amount of states which are loosely connected in one way or another – it is a global area like NAFTA, OAS, EU, etc.[2] Very often the common denominator for these states is a common market factor (Nye 1968; Haas 1975; Fawcett and Hurrell 1995; Telo 2001).

But in Europe a region is the third level of four: the EU as a supra-state structure is the first level, the nation states make up the second, the regions the third and the local communities the fourth. To really understand the third level you can look at the map Tabula Regionum Europae published by the Assembly of European Regions (AER).

Lars: Yes. I have seen the map – it is an interesting and unusual view to see the regions instead of the countries.

Lisbeth: What is really thrilling is that there is a regional taxonomy – there is a regional diversity (Weihe-Lindeborg 2001/2005). If we refer to the AER definition of *region*, which is, and I quote:

> A region is the first substate formalised entity – an administrative territory directly under the level of the state – with an established public rule of law and an elected political representation.

This is the first paragraph in the Declaration of Regionalism in Europe and it is the accepted definition in the EU. So territoriality is the first criterion of a region. In our book, Kronoberg region is such a region.

Lars: It is an administrative unit and has been so since Sweden was divided into counties (län) in the seventeenth century.

Lisbeth: But that is not enough. Beside regions there is the concept of a microregion. They are normally smaller regional contexts – although larger than local authorities – which can vary. They are territories within. Compared to the basic region, the territory and the existence of a microregion is determined by geographic-topographic factors – like the island Furillen in our book, or historical-cultural factors like Turku or Stavanger, or economic factors like Roskilde, or administrative factors like Holstebro.

Lars: And the cross-border regions?

Lisbeth: That is a third category emerging from intensified cross-border cooperations in neighbouring states. Our two examples in this book are Jämtland-Tröndelag and the Finnish archipelago. A kind of cross-border regions are macroregions which are mostly transnational being made up of regions in two or more neighbouring states, for example the Barents Euro-Arctic Region (Lindeborg 1995).

Lars: And what about the other cases in the book like Dalhalla, Hultsfred, Piteå, Kristiansand, Stiklestad, Horsens, Skagen and Fredrikshavn?

Lisbeth: Well they are cities or towns – that is local communities – but they are part of a regional context.

The book

Lisbeth: In this book we wanted to show how quite a few places – no matter how small, no matter how tedious – manage to 'turn-the-tide' from an unsuccessful status quo to something new. So how do they proceed? What do their development processes involve? Which ways and means do they use to go forward in order to change their paths and start anew? How long do these processes take? When can one expect to see results of the efforts, etc.?

Lars: And we wanted to show the breadth of theoretical tools that can be used to increase the awareness of culture's significance for regional development, instead of concentrating on one or two theoretical perspectives. In the various chapters you will find a multitude of theoretical concepts, from entrepreneurship theory, organizational institutionalism and cultural economy (where the authors calculate the value of, for example, Vara Concert Hall and the Watercolour Museum in Skärhamn, Sweden, for the region's residents) to cultural planning and art management.

Lisbeth: Among the most important findings is the basic fact that although you can never transfer the successful renewal of one place to another – like a blueprint – certain common patterns in the cultural processes are distinguishable. One of these findings is that cultural development is an ongoing process, which never ends.

Lars: The guideline for each chapter includes a portrayal of one or more cultural ventures and in-depth analyses of why certain projects were started and how they proceed, and an evaluation of their results for regional development thus disclosing practical and theoretical know-how for the benefit of other places. And we discuss the mechanisms triggering this cultural revolution and how awareness of culture as a building block in our societies has grown. Culture as a growth factor can be found everywhere – not only in urban contexts but also in the countryside and small villages.

Lisbeth: The book and the examples also show the significance of the Europeanization and regionalization processes as driving forces for cultural development in any one place. That leads on to the fact that there is increasing competition between regions, between cities and between villages. Is there a risk that they outdo each other? A second issue is the instrumentalizing of culture for commercial reasons. Where is the limit to be drawn? At the same time we discover that there is a growing polarity between an event-based versus art-based culture.

Lars: There are lots of questions that have been raised by our authors, 28 Scandinavian researchers, and others who are active in arts and culture. What has regional investment in arts and culture led to? What are the positive and negative experiences? We also show a few places where the cultural assets were not taken care of, and where the possibility of an outstanding cultural profile was lost.

Lisbeth: Yes, and in comparison to the positive experiences, the negative or unhappy ones are few. I think that has to do with at least two things. First of all – if you are researching a city or a region – making a field study – you tend to choose a place where the effects on the whole are positive. For most cases it is an up-and-down process. Hultsfred is a good example of that. Another reason that our cases are positive is that most of them are fairly new – they are still on their way up – and forward. That is why Holstebro is so interesting, having succeeded for almost fifty years – it is a veteran among our cases – and you want to know the reason for its success.

Lars: Another important issue is how we have chosen to organize the book. The book is organized with cases from the four Nordic countries, Denmark, Finland, Norway and Sweden as the starting point. The book could have been organized based on different themes with, for example, festivals as one chapter heading and museums as another. However, we felt it would be more valuable to present the chapters according to the respective countries. We have made our selection so as to illustrate as many cultural expressions as possible.

Lisbeth: We wanted to present Scandinavia. And there is also the notion today, with so much virtuality around us, that people need places which they can refer to. Although culture and the arts are immaterial resources – 'software of the mind'[3] – they require spatial frameworks and cultural infrastructures in order to develop. Finally, before we get into the content of the book's different chapters, don't you have a good quote that is said to be by Winston Churchill?

Lars: Yes, it is not confirmed that he really said it, but it is a good statement. In many Nordic and European debates, investments in culture are pitted against investments in other areas of the public sector, with the argument that it is better to invest in the care of the elderly than in the theatre. Lars Nordström, President of the Cultural Affairs Committee in Sweden's Västra Götaland region (which is spending three times as much on investments in arts and culture than other Swedish regions) responds to this in the region's annual report (Franck 2005), by quoting Churchill. During the First World War there were many who wondered if it wasn't time to cut cultural spending and instead invest in defence at a time when England was so beset by the Germans. Churchill disagreed, when it was suggested to him that he needed to make cuts in arts and culture, he allegedly asked: 'Then what are we fighting for?'

The chapters

Starting out is *Peter Aronsson* with the historical background. He shows the Nordic culture as an asset with many faces. The chapter argues that the persistent political viability of Nordic culture in new political settings is dependent on its foundation as a plastic construction originating outside politics.

In the first section with cases from Denmark, *Lisbeth Lindeborg* analyses the development in Holstebro. In order for Holstebro and its surrounding region to survive, the maxim of culture and arts as a growing development factor was adopted. Which strategy was developed? What risks had to be evaded and how did Holstebro proceed in its endeavour, steadily going forward from one milestone to the next? These are some of the questions that are answered. *Anne Lorentzen* explores and discusses one of the most spectacular culture projects developed in a small city in Denmark, the Days of Tordenskiold in Frederikshavn. A response to severe industrial decline, its aim was to establish a new urban identity, based on a maritime – and heroic – history. While in itself a great achievement, the developmental impact of the festival is considerable. *Lise Lyck* analyses two places, Skagen and Horsens, where arts and culture have been the main driver for economic and regional development. Both are success stories that have similarities and differences, presenting perspectives on how the arts including design can be a generator of economic development and regionalization. *Jon Sundbo* analyses the importance of a rock festival for the town of Roskilde, particularly its importance for industrial development. The festival has developed from a social and musical event to something that is also business, innovation and regional development.

In the Finnish section *Niina Koivonen* describes and analyses Tampere – the Manchester of Finland – which has undergone a painful transformation from textile and mechanical engineering industries to an international hub of ICT and creative industries. *Alf Rehn et al.* discuss what forms of expectations arose when the city of Turku arranged a cultural mega event, i.e. acted as the European Capital of Culture in 2011. They have also looked closer into the complex issues involved in managing contemporary expectations 'on the power of culture'. *Katriina Siivonen* analyses two regional development projects in the Southwest-Finland Archipelago. She raises the question: Why didn't local culture as a resource ensure socio-cultural well-being in the region? *Saara L. Taalas* focuses on the Kotka-Hamina Region in Finland as a case for exploration of creativity connected to industrial production processes and sites that have become to some degree redundant. The analysis suggests an alternative reading to creativity that is not focused on the original and novel but on the reinterpretation of production set-ups and industrial sites for the future.

In Norway *Trine Bille* examines a very special case of using culture and creativity to develop a region, namely the foundation Cultiva in Kristiansand, Norway. The case is special in the sense that a lot of money has been allocated to the foundation and the returns on this capital must be invested in projects that develop the region in economic and social terms by using arts, culture and creativity as the instrument. *Anne-Britt Gran* takes a closer look at one example of the local and regional upswing represented by the theatrical genre of the historical play and the way these plays are sponsored. Combining theories of theatre anthropology, theories of cultural sponsorship and theories about globalization provide new insight about cultural power in local and regional development. *Hilmar Rommetvedt* analyses the beliefs in culture as an instrument for regional development among the citizens, leading politicians, civil servants and business managers in the Stavanger region, both before and after the European Capital of Culture event in 2008.

Representing the biggest country in regards to geographical size and number of inhabitants, there are more Swedish chapters. The underpinning of *John Armbrecht's* and *Tommy D. Andersson's* chapter is that rational decisions about cultural institutions cannot only be based on cost analysis but must also consider the value created. Furthermore, if value created can be measured in monetary units, as costs are, it will be possible to compare value created to costs of producing culture. Contingent valuation methods are used to assess user as well as non-user values of a concert hall and a watercolour museum. *Per Frankelius* analyses the creation of an opera arena, Dalhalla, in an old limestone quarry. The main conclusion is that nature, if managed right, can very well be part of art. Such combinations, in turn, can result in novel phenomena that can have a huge impact on regional development. A model is developed describing critical factors in making ideas like this come through. *Hans Gelter* and *Jennie Gelter* tell the true story about an innovative dream of an Ice Dome Concert Hall made completely of snow and ice in Piteå, northern Sweden. An ice artist's dream and desire to produce great art soon met the reality of cultural projects and the accompanying slow bureaucracy of financing and project planning. This chapter illustrates the problem of how creative and innovative ideas cannot always be transformed into local and regional development projects. *Lars Lindkvist et al.* describe how the cultural planning method in the Kronoberg County is about looking from a bottom-up perspective at which cultural resources can be found in a region and how they can be used to develop the area and strengthen its identity. In the next chapter *Lars Lindkvist* describes the development of Furillen, a small island just outside Gotland in Sweden, and analyses the value of art and culture in terms of cultural entrepreneurship, the creation of meeting places, a design hotel and a 'culture cube', which can be used by people who want to work alone, or work with others in different cultural and creative projects. *Tobias Nielsén* draws lessons from the rise and fall, and rise again, of Sweden's biggest rock festival. He raises the questions: Who should be responsible for taking the risks with the outcome of cultural events being uncertain? Should it be the passionate social and cultural entrepreneur alone, or do other organizations and the public sector have responsibilities? Can some support, however, be counterproductive? He finds the answers in Hultsfred – a small town with an internationally famous rock festival as a platform for a 'creative cluster'. After thirty years of existence, the rock festival faced serious economic problems and the organizers were forced into bankruptcy but after one year the festival started up again.

The last two chapters are on the cross-border regions of Barents Euro-Arctic Region and mid-Scandinavia. Among the many thrilling and intriguing cultural hotspots in Scandinavia, *Lisbeth Lindeborg* sees the Barents Euro-Arctic Region (BEAR), founded in 1993 with the participation of thirteen regions in the four countries around the North Pole, as the most exotic. With 600 cultural projects in its first five-year period it increased the cultural activities in the area by 240 per cent. One objective of the cultural cooperation is to strengthen the common identity of the Barents Region in order to further regional development. In their chapter, *Stig Westerdahl* and *Wilhelm Skoglund* focus on the role of arts and culture in two mid-Scandinavian regions: Jämtland, Sweden and Tröndelag, Norway. These border regions try to strike a balance between a long history of cross-border cooperation and loyalties to the nation state. Several cultural projects illustrate the tension.

Notes

1 According to World Creativity Forum the twelve *districts of creativity* are: Flanders, Baden-Württemberg, Rhone-Alpes, Nord-Pas-de-Calais, Lombardy, Catalonia, Scotland, Tampere, Oklahoma, Quebec, Shanghai and Karnataka (India).
2 NAFTA stands for North American Free Trade Area, OAS stands for Organization of American States, EU stands for the European Union.
3 The expression 'software of the mind' was used by the Dutch management researcher Geert Hofstede in the title of his book, *Cultures and Organizations: Software of the Mind* (1991).

References

Baecker, D. (2003) *Wozu Kultur?*, Berlin: Kadmos.
Baumol, W.J. and Bowen, W.G. (1966) *Performing Arts: the Economic Dilemma; a Study of Problems Common to Theatre, Opera, Music, and Dance*, New York: Twentieth Century Fund.
Blaug, M. (ed.) (1976) *The Economics of the Arts*, London: Martin Robertson.
Fawcett, L. and Hurrell, A. (eds) (1995) *Regionalism in World Politics. Regional Organization and International Order*, Oxford: Oxford University Press.
Franck, A. (ed.) (2005) *Kultur Västra Götaland 2004/2005*, Uddevalla: Kultursekretariatet Västra Götalandsregionen.
Gould, P. and White, R. (1992) *Mental Maps*, London and New York: Routledge.
Gulmann, S. (2005) *Citydesign – byudvikling for borgere*, Copenhagen: Gyldendals forlag.
Haas, E. (1975) *The Obsolence of Regional Integration Theory*, Berkeley: Berkeley University Press.
Haraldsen, T., Flygind, S.K., Overvåg, K. and Power, D. (2004) *Kartlegging av kulturnaeringene i Norge – økonomisk betydning, vekst- og utviklingspotential*, Lillehammer: øf-rapport: 10/2004.
Hofstede, G. (1991) *Culture and Organizations: Software of the Mind*, London: McGraw Hill.
Lindeborg, L. (1991) *Kultur som lokaliseringsfaktor*, Stockholm: Industridepartementet, Ds 1991:22.
——— (1995) *Regionalt samarbete i Europa – med tyska erfarenheter, Rapport 87*, Stockholm: Expertgruppen för forskning om regional utveckling.
(Weihe-) Lindeborg, L. (2001/2005) *Zum regionalen System. Stellenwert der Versammlung der Regionen Europas*, Marburg: Tectum Wissenschaftsverlag.

Lindeborg, L. (2007) 'Kulturen som arbetsmarknad expanderar kraftigt', in B. Ayata (ed.), *Kulturekonomi. Konsten att fånga osynliga värden*, Lund: Studentlitteratur, 105–139.

Nye, J. (ed.) (1968) *International Regionalism: Readings*, Boston: Harvard University Press, Center for International Affairs.

Plaza, B. (2006) 'The Return on Investment of the Guggenheim Museum Bilbao', *International Journal of Urban and Regional Research*, 30(2): 452–467.

——— (2008) 'On Some Challenges and Conditions for the Guggenheim Museum Bilbao to be an Effective Economic Re-activator', *International Journal of Urban and Regional Research*, 32(2): 506–517.

Plaza, B. and Haarich, S.N. (2009) 'Museums for Urban Regeneration? Exploring Conditions for their Effectiveness', *Journal of Urban Regeneration and Renewal*, 2(3): 259–271.

Plaza, B., Galvez-Galvez, C. and Gonzalez-Flores, A. (2011) 'Testing the Employment Impact of the Guggenheim Museum Bilbao via TSA', *Tourism Economics*, 17(1): 223–229.

Scitovsky, T. (1982) *Subsidies for the Arts: the Economic Argument*, Santa Cruz: University of California Press.

Siemiatycki, M. (2005) 'Beyond Moving People: Excavating the Motivations for Investing in Urban Public Transit Infrastructure in Bilbao Spain', *European Planning Studies*, 13(1): 23–44.

Telo, M. (2001) *European Union and New Regionalism*, Aldershot, UK: Ashgate.

Throsby, D. (2008a) 'The Concentric Circles Model of the Cultural Industries', *Cultural Trends*, 17(3): 147–164.

——— (2008b) 'Modelling the Cultural Industries', *International Journal of Cultural Policy*, 14(3): 217–232.

Throsby, D. and Withers, G.A. (1979) *The Economics of the Performing Arts*, New York: St Martins.

2 Nordic culture

An asset with many facets

Peter Aronsson

Norden as reality and concept

Norden (as the five Nordic countries are referred to in Denmark, Finland, Iceland, Norway and Sweden) is a well-recognized mega region. In significant ways this political mega region, however, represents just one version of a historical and contemporary imagery of what the culture of the North has and can accomplish.

The idea of a Nordic region is at least as old as written history. Publius Cornelius Tacitus (AD 56–117) attributed values to people of the region in contrast to a degenerating Roman empire (Tacitus 1473). Monasteries ransacked by Northern savages, Vikings of the ninth century, did not care if they were Danish or from other parts of the North when asking God to have mercy on them. These early images of the North were created from the outside to act on threats from within and without. Usually they vary between identifying specific traits of certain and describing a broader Nordic culture, be it out of admiration or fear.

Thinking about culture and regions has a long trajectory. The notorious fluidity of both the concept of region and the delineation of their actual essence and territorial scope is likewise a longstanding trait. The much more debated concept of nation is a dream of clarity and consensus compared with region. The general dynamics of cultural and historical construction of community (Anderson 1983) are however shared. This interaction is enhanced over time and applied to various political, cultural and economic entities.

To create a strong regional distinction in general, a series of measures need to be taken regardless of regional level. Besides, naming the regional concept needs to be embedded in narratives, made easily accessible and mundane in symbols, and recognized by others as part of a larger system (Paasi 1986). These cultural, symbolic and semiotic investments are of course related to more functional values interacting with the worlds of economy, political power and social interplay.

Academics, for good reasons, usually struggle to make clear-cut analytical divisions. The necessity for this in the endeavour to bring reason to observations must however not hide the possible existence and actual utility of floating borders, hybridity and ambiguities in dealing with mobilization, conflict resolution and dynamic negotiations. Hence the interaction between several layers of regional interaction and identification testifies to their long-standing cultural, social and political utility rather than an inability to think straight. This is a first theoretical position with relevance to Norden as an asset (Aronsson 2001; Olwig and Jones 2008; Aronsson and Gradén 2012a).

The second argument is to affirm *the power of interaction between silent and explicit traits of regional culture*. All cultural exchange is not explicated and can be referred to as anthropological culture. When Tacitus refers to the rustic culture or when world value studies show that contemporary Nordic countries combine extreme levels of distributed social trust with extreme valorization of individual self-development (Inglehart and Welzel 2005) these qualities are not necessarily recognized as Nordic values, even less so as virtues. They have the potential to be acknowledged and framed as such and hence move from silent to explicit traits of regional culture, with repercussions to the actual value of these assets that can be investigated and assessed.

I prefer this distinction rather than real and imagined, reality and myth that are often used to make similar distinctions. On unclear epistemological ground they tend to label one part of reality as more real than another. Instead the nature and power of, in this case the region, can be investigated: at times the idea of Nordic culture might mobilize politics and material exchange, at times the inverse might be the case. Cultural ideas can be compensatory or falsely claim to represent social fact and still be a real social force. If they act on the behaviour of people, make them prefer certain economic exchange and political coalitions, then myth is as real as the stock exchange. This means that cultural representations of regional values in symbols, art, history, politics and popular culture are not merely to be looked upon as representing reality. They are acting upon and performing actions with consequences. The interaction between the culturally explicit and the culturally implicit is too important for their relative power to be decided upon beforehand. The idea of Norden has a long history where its importance and role has varied substantially.

The first two theoretical statements are thus made to be able to assess the dynamic nature of supra-regional concepts in Northern Europe and their interaction with various other national and regional bodies and the more silent, anthropological realities of these cultures. The need to understand the interplay between cultural elements as assets and hindrances for development needs to be explored more systematically. Let us note that Norden has both for outsiders and insiders been predominantly regarded as a good thing (but for the monks raided by Vikings and not saved by God's grace).

There are however important exceptions to this that need to be mentioned to put a critical frame around the choir of hope and goodness that might emerge out of a Scandinavian discourse. At the far end of the evil possibilities are, on the one hand, the capacity of any inclusive rhetoric to become exclusive, for example the Nazi use of the term 'Übermensch' in reference to the Aryans, a race best preserved in Scandinavia. And on the other hand, the tight social control expressed in the form of the Law of Jante, *Don't think you're anyone special or that you're better than us* (Sandemose 1936). Both a too high appreciation of the culture at one end and a negative attitude toward individuality at the other, can be a substantial hindrance to innovation and creativity.

The old history of empires, domination and subjugation also throws long shadows. Many people in new states like Norway still nourish the suspicion that Scandinavia is just a fake name used for old ambitions to dominate the country by Denmark and Sweden. Historically, this is not without grounds.

As Friedrich Nietzsche has argued, the uses of history are damaging if it locks the will to act into a narrative of absolute determination. It has however on rare occasion the power to act inspiring either by critique, by presenting positive ideals and virtues or through the very act of creating a community between the reader and the object (Nietzsche 1874, Nietzsche 1980). This chapter presents how persisting ideas of a shared Nordic culture have been utilized as a resource in a series of different contexts and discusses the mechanisms and consequences of these dynamics.

Learning from Nordic peace

Some of the early conceptions of Nordic culture were violent and brutal. This was a source of pride and example for the ambitious and belligerent states of Denmark and Sweden in the seventeenth century. They competed over being the legitimate heir of a heroic Nordic heritage, and owner of heritage treasures like the monumental graves of former warrior kings and the Saga manuscripts, to prove it. The battle fought was to restore the just ancient and heroic state of art to contemporary Europe. An ambition shared by many states also mobilizing transnational identities (Burrow 2007: 235).

Other elements of Nordic culture are already present in these images, however. They contain stories of a proto-democratic Thing society, where all free peasants are also armed citizens with rights and a voice in decisions. The women were held in high regard, strong and apt to take full care of work, household and property (Aronsson and Gradén 2012b).

These elements came to be more emphasized as active virtues on which to build in the nineteenth century, and the old more brutal evidence of culture was historicized – not into a source of regret, but as a past state of civilization, and hence not a pattern for behaviour to be reproduced. Nostalgia as an emotion, evolution as theory and progress as an everyday Utopia bridged the gap between the glorious past and present day community and created a new historical consciousness framing Norden.

The remarkable transformation of similar elements that motivated aggression into an ideology that promoted ideas of communality and brotherhood that made violent solution of conflicts unthinkable is extremely interesting. Things can be very different. German, Italian, Slavic, Arab and Chinese projects of national and regional collaboration are other examples with more varied consequences in the two last centuries.

Hence there has been a lot of scholarly interest and ideological use of the Nordic examples manifested above all in the capacity to overcome conflicts over the dissolution of the Swedish-Norwegian Union in 1905 and the Åland example of 1921 where the League of Nations' resolution solved the disputes after the independence of Finland (Aronsson 2005; Björk and Eliaeson 2000). Václav Havel, the first president of the Czech Republic directing the dissolution of the Communist state, as well as Kofi Annan, the former General Secretary of the UN, have expressed the high esteem of these Nordic conflict resolutions as positive role models. The fact that the Nordic countries have not fought with each other since then is a historic fact, and has become a continuous source of pride among the Nordic countries themselves as well as an ever more important part of the values counted as Scandinavian virtues in the world. As we will see this can also be used to cover up more ambiguous actions.

The transformation of Nordic imagery from a source of aggressive action to peaceful ideals was not a quick fix but made through a series of complicated negotiations and cultural investments that will now be briefly mapped.

From a medieval Nordic union to nineteenth-century nationalism and Scandinavism

The idea of kingdoms were apparent in the ninth century, most explicitly so perhaps at Jellinge in Denmark. Jellinge's grave mounds and runic inscriptions that state the existence, Christianity and unity of Denmark. The runic stones in Jellinge, one of which is depicted in the Danish passport, were raised by Harald Blåtand (Bluetooth), whose name is now used for the technology to connect electronic devices – inspired by his success in uniting Denmark and Norway, Jellinge is a World Heritage Site, part of the official cultural canon and endowed with a brand new visitor centre. The past and future of Denmark is defined by this monument (Wienberg 2008; Aronsson 2012a).

State-building in the medieval period was however as fragile as a bluetooth connection might be: working best on short feudal distances often interrupted and reconnected with another body. Scandinavian history was similar to the rest of post-Roman Europe, but shaped by a regional urge to mobilize otherwise fragmentized Nordic local kings, aristocrats and communities in the making, against the powerful urban Hanseatic network of German traders. A Scandinavian union was formed in 1397, the Kalmar Union headed by Queen Margareta, formally persisting until 1523.

Historically this has been viewed as the 'bad old days' in Sweden, 'good old days' in Denmark, and as not too important in Finland, Norway and Iceland since they continued to suffer under the dominance of Sweden and Denmark respectively, the two multicultural and conglomerate imperial states of Scandinavia. In the early modern period Finland was as an integral part of Sweden and several Baltic and German provinces added to the conglomerate state. Denmark, although having lost important territories in southern Scandinavia to Sweden in the seventeenth century, continues as a conglomerate state even today. In 1920 the German border was finally settled to the disadvantage of Denmark which lost a comparable part of the nation that Sweden gave up to

Russia a hundred years earlier. Iceland, through successive moves, became autonomous in 1944. Greenland and the Faroe Islands are still autonomous and self-governing parts of the kingdom of Denmark. Norway, which became part of Denmark already in medieval times, was swapped into a personal union with Sweden in 1814 and declared independent in 1905.

In the nineteenth century, after 200 years of internal struggle for hegemony, it was the emerging European superpowers of Germany and Russia that gave the immediate political context for Scandinavian countries to start collaboration once again. The cultural context changed dramatically at the same time. From a framework of values drawn from Christianity on the one hand and on the legacy of antiquity on the other, the atmosphere of Enlightenment, belief in the reason and welfare of the individual, started to search for meaning in history and the nation.

Nationalism, Enlightenment and market economy were then radically threatening ideas of universal values and exchanging them with ideas of history and progress. But it was not self-evident how to delineate the true nation and its history. Was it perhaps rather the Kalmar Union that was the true nation to be reborn out of the political and economic turmoil in the early nineteenth century? A cultural and intellectual movement of Scandinavism became a prominent force (Almqvist 1846; Hemstad 2008). It was then that the term Skandinav became prominent, as was the invention of the Viking as a label to enhance the cultural value of these ravaging bandits to an asset for political and cultural distinctions (Wallette 2009).

Actions taken by many intellectuals build on stories of Gothic descent formatted from the medieval period and a material heritage starting to be assembled and protected as such already from the seventeenth century (Widenberg 2006). When the romantic national movement gained momentum in the Scandinavian countries there was rich material to make use of in the whole of the North.

In an atmosphere of urgent historical change, threat by external political forces as well as more diffuse but fundamental changes in agricultural competition, industrial revolution and demographic explosion, ideas of historically grounded community became a much needed asset. This was enhanced by the example of the revolutionary army of Napoleon: the power of citizens, enrolled as soldiers in a mass army was hard to stop. To meet these challenges, political reform and economic development enhanced the call for citizen rights and the need to recreate community by arguing stable nations with long roots in a history cut loose from its biblical and antique sources and founded in the archaeology, ethnology and history of the nation (Berger 2010; Aronsson 2012a).

But where was the nation? The loss of territories in Denmark and Sweden called for Scandinavian mobilization already in the 1810s. Associations to save the Nordic heritage were founded and interest in prehistory became ever more important to demonstrate the long roots of an autonomous culture. Language studies became central as the languages were interpreted as remnants of independent and related cultures – Indo-Germanic, Baltic-Ugric – and were conceptualized and seen as proof of cultural relations, hence indicating communities to be built upon. The affinity of Scandinavian language, history and culture became institutionalized as knowledge, heritage and culture that resulted in repercussions for ideology, politics, architecture and aesthetics that still exist today (Molin 2003).

Most of this heritage moved in a dynamic zone in-between being identified with the actual nation state and to a broader Scandinavian culture. This was easy enough since the culture that needed preserving was older, more vernacular, more authentic and more important – and hence it was from an era before the state existed and political history became prominent, i.e. prehistoric times.

Stories and sayings told by adults as moralities for the next generation, tales passed on from grandmothers to children as entertainment, old tools and forgotten songs were transformed from heresy, gossip, past-time or rubbish into cultural assets which needed to be collected, displayed and published, and thereby symbolizing national values to be promoted and enhanced into a collective heritage.

In Denmark, the absolute monarch who was chocked by the threats which Copenhagen faced in the first decade of the nineteenth century, commissioned an investigation into the need to mobilize heritage and museums. In 1819 the Royal Museum for Nordic Antiquities (Det Kgl. Museum for Nordiske Oldsager) opened in Copenhagen as a response to Napoleonic bombardments of the city in 1801 and 1807 (Zipsane 2011). In Norway, the university was an important home to a growing collection of Nordic antiquities. And, in Sweden, Skansen opened in 1891 and the Nordic museum (Nordiska museet) was relocated to a purposely built romantic cathedral inaugurated in 1907, born out of the Scandinavic Ethnografic Collection (Skandinavisk-etnografiska samlingen) founded in 1873 and renamed in 1880 by Artur Hazelius (Hillström 2006; Aronsson 2011; Aronsson and Gradén 2012b; Aronsson 2010, Aronsson 2012a; Bäckström 2012; Hillström 2010). The latter did of course relate both to Scandinavism as ideology and the contested union between Norway and Sweden until 1905. Oscar Montelius, the leading Swedish archaeologist, stated at Hazelius' funeral at Skansen on 4 June 1901:

> It was a great and true idea by Artur Hazelius to create a museum not only for the Swedish people but for the memories of *all* the Nordic peoples. For the culture, which grew up on a Scandinavian foundation, is in principle one and the same, whether it is called Swedish or Finnish, Norwegian or Danish. They are the branches of a tree spreading out in different directions, but growing from the same stem and forming a coherent entity.
>
> (Levart 1901)

In Finland the national institutions opened before the state was established during the period between 1809 and 1918, when she moved from an integrated province of Sweden to become the Grand Duchy of Finland as part of the Russian empire. The national art gallery was named Ateneum and opened to the public in 1888, connecting directly to the European classical tradition. The national cultural historical museum opened in 1916 and had an explicit focus on the prehistory to be found before the Swedish Crusades made it part of the realm. The architecture however shows definite affinities with Nordic religious and baroque secular aesthetics and marks a distance from both Russian and classical traditions. Hence a nation in the making uses both European and Nordic elements to promote and negotiate the direction of its political aspiration (Aronsson 2012c; Pettersson 2011).

The system of international fairs was an extremely powerful mediator of knowledge, ideology and markets from 1851 and at least up until digital mass media became an alternative. They conferred representations of the achievements of nations and regions in both machinery, design and culture to an international audience, and also set the agenda for entertainment and exhibitions all over the world (Sandberg 2003). The Scandinavian countries were often presented close to each other even in the midst of national movements in the nineteenth century, and for Norway and Sweden in the same showcase (Brenna 2002).

More dominant however was the spread of aesthetics associated with Scandinavia, for example the Viking Dragon style and other variations of national romantic architecture even when ambiguously labelled Nordic, Scandinavian or national. Landscape painting and later modern functionalism and contemporary concepts such as Nordic light testify both to nationalism and a persistent proximity in expression among the Scandinavian countries that invites collective representation (Grandien 1987; Burch 2010).

Students in Scandinavia picked up on these ideas, emphatically demanding collaboration. For Denmark, that was resisting the expansion of Germany in southern Jutland in the 1860s, the hope for a political union was vital. The Swedish king promised to side with Denmark, but when war broke out 1864 he, and Scandinavian solidarity, failed to deliver.

The middle way – revisited

The idea of a shared Scandinavian culture has, as we have seen, at times been coupled with ambitions for political community and concessions to the brotherhood of the states. The pendulum passes from high ambitions over more pragmatic, important but limited achievements to disappointments. The year 1905, with the dissolution of the union of Sweden and Norway, was a temporary setback for cooperation, but soon after World War I, Scandinavian networks started to work again. After World War II important agreements on the road to a Nordic union were achieved with free movement of people, labour and goods, but overrun by the success of the EU (Hemstad 2008; Stråth 1993; Stråth and Henningsen 1997).

In a similar vein, following the release of three books by Marquis Childs in the 1930s, the most well known of which in Sweden is *The Middle Way*, a whole new genre of international assessment of the Nordic countries was born. Childs was not alone. At a time when America was looking for roads out of the Depression with a New Deal, and Europe struggled with totalitarianism of two kinds, communism and fascism, the democracies of Norden seemed to be able to find a middle way, which entailed taking care of all citizens and negotiating peaceful collaboration between contradictory forces in society while still making use of the vitality and freedom of both market and democratic rights (Childs 1936; Stadius 2012, in prep).

Gunnar Wetterberg (2010) argues for a Nordic federation, mainly on political grounds, to give voice to values of justice, equality and democracy internationally. In light of the EU's troubles, it may prove to be important to promote Scandinavian cooperation once again. It tends to be a recourse in-between the national and the global level when other options prove too complicated or disadvantageous (Wetterberg 2010; Björkman *et al.* 2011).

This initiative might interact with the latest liberal turn in the history of the Nordic welfare states. If the liberal leaders learned from Blair's turn to the right in the 1990s, now Cameron is mimicking the successful reinterpretation of the concept pursued by the New Conservatives (Nya Moderaterna) (Eklund *et al.* 2011).

Dark Norden

The major turning point in the working of the region is the turn from being a reason for aggression to a motivation for collaboration. The major turn within Norden itself appeared in the late eighteenth century, but a latent aggressive use was once again mobilized by the Nazi regime and was prevalent among xenophobic right-wing movements. If you search for Norden and white power on the internet the use of right-wing extremism will be obvious. The tricky issue is to assess if this is only a hostile takeover, or to any extent inherent of the values of the Nordic ideals themselves.

In the self-righteous Nordic light it is easy to suppress the fact that not only did the Nazis mobilize Norden as the core area for the race to rule the world, but Sweden was also the home to early and persistent racist science and forced mass sterilization of citizens deemed less suitable to breed. The instrumental side of pragmatic welfare state ambitions are not so far from the totalitarian as we would like to think (Runcis 1998; Tydén 2002).

The shield of Nordic democracy, neutralism and peacemaking corps might also be a cover up for aggressive marketing of weapons to regimes criticized for their disrespect of human rights (Burch 2012; Aronsson and Gradén 2012b).

My own view is that Nordic culture in both its explicit and implicit cultural existence has demonstrated strong positive powers, but can be turned into totalitarian implementations or used as a hypocritical shield, if not utilized with good judgement (Aronsson 2012b). There is no safe haven – not even in Norden.

A rooted asset adjusting to new uses

In the early modern period the Gothic version of Nordic values became the legitimizing foundation for claims to supremacy in Scandinavia and for a major role in the European arena. This battle was fought by the two major political forces coming out of the medieval Kalmar Union, Sweden and Denmark, with military and cultural means (Aronsson 2009; Henningsen 1997). From the nineteenth century onwards the idea of a shared culture instead of a battlefield became part of each nation's self-understanding and a reservoir for political collaboration and international marketing was labelled the Nordic model and respectively appropriated as the Norwegian, Danish, Swedish in each country (Stråth and Sørensen 1997). Interestingly enough the egalitarian and collective forms of social organization associated with this model have been recently challenged with a new interpretation of the Nordic model as a contract between an extremely individualistic Nordic citizen, in need of a pact with the state to support his or her individualism (Berggren and Trägårdh 2006; Eklund *et al.* 2011).

The material for narratives of a Scandinavian community are as manifold as any building of a region: there are aspects of similarities in language and attitudes that might account for an *homogenous region*, both with historic conditions as well as language similarities, and findings from contemporary world value surveys to support such an articulation.

A *functional region* can be argued in many ways: exchange in trade, labour, culture. It is also easy to argue that exchange in all kinds of markets, for many actors in this globalized era, is still centred on a Nordic core. Workforce might not travel to Sweden as it did in the 1960s, but rather from Sweden to Denmark and Norway, but Nordic exchange still prevails and makes Scandinavia a viable functional region.

Administratively Scandinavia is part of an infrastructure with both government bodies, NGOs and commercial organizations to give a clear image of this region as a reality. The Nordic Council with its flag is only one of them – reaching beyond the Scandinavian peninsula to Iceland and the three autonomous regions of the Faroe Islands, Greenland and Åland to make eight flags or dots in its symbolic representation (Björkman *et al.* 2011).

In this chapter however the most important aspect has been how these regions interplay with both an *identity of the region*, which could be easily argued, and the capacity of adding a layer of *regional identity* to actors identifying with Scandinavia or Norden (Paasi 1986). The purpose has been to understand how these traits might work as an asset not only on the Scandinavian scale, but also in a local, sub-regional, national and transnational setting. The dimensions of these historically delivered utilities will now be summarized, where I will also point out the fact that many values that have a positive side also have a flip side, where things can go bad. This way of reasoning is in debt to ethics of virtues in the Aristotelian tradition. Virtues are values incorporated into the identity of the subject, used with situational judgement (Taylor 1989; Aronsson *et al.* 2001, Aronsson 2012b). It is not a mechanical morality.

Scandinavia as an anthropological asset (homogenous and functional region)

The relative poverty and late modernization of the Scandinavian societies can be associated with strong valuation of equality, flat organization, a high degree of intrapersonal trust resulting in low transaction costs in both politics and economics, stable institutions and a high degree of predictability. Far-reaching secularization, rapid modernization and welfare provisions have released the individual from family and neighbourhood constraints to pick the association as best suited to a higher degree than in most societies in the world.

The flip side of these virtues includes low utopian levels, stress on cultural homogeneity and collective consensus resulting in a slow pace of change in need of much negotiation in traditional local communities while in communities more open to late modernity a restructuring of the individual identity has released a great deal of uncertainty and the other side of freedom is filled with psychic diagnoses in need of a cure.

Scandinavia as ideology and brand – explicit tales and symbols (identity of the region)

Vikings and the welfare state are perhaps the most well-known symbols. A few decades ago in the light of the Swedish/Danish sexual liberation, sin would have been another. The rural character has also found aesthetical expression in art as landscapes in late nineteenth century, melancholic films by Ingmar Bergman, a clean and white functional design by Alvar Alto and films by Lars von Trier. The brand of Nordic light has been used to introduce Nordic art internationally for the past 100 years (Burch 2010).

Literature and music provide signs of various kinds. In their novels August Strindberg, Astrid Lindgren and Vilhelm Moberg create images of Sweden as HC Andersen, Sandemose, Ibsen and Runeberg and Väinö Linna do for other Scandinavian nations. There is no Scandinavian literature within Scandinavia, but read side by side they provide a Nordic atmosphere. A new, post-welfare atmosphere is provided by the crime novels of Stieg Larsson and Henning Mankell. Tourism and cultural industries draw on all these images and use them as material for creating experiences and revenue.

Most of the images are positive, provide examples to be inspired by, attract visitors and new talent. On the flip side is that these positive tales of peace and democracy can hide hierarchical practice, cowardly actions, corruption and armament deals. Sweden and Norway are some of the great exporters of lethal weapons which do not really fit into the image of the lovely landscape of Norwegian fjords or the villages of Emil of Lönneberga and Pippi Longstocking.

Scandinavia as a political option (mobilizing for action)

The first political utility of the narrative of Scandinavia as a shared culture was to make the threshold for violence steep and the will to negotiate and support neighbours closer at hand. This helped turn Scandinavia into a positive example for Czechoslovakia during its dissolution, the lesson can of course not be taught in any easy way, but the cost of regional breakdown became horribly clear in the Balkans when Yugoslavia broke up in the 1990s. Engagement in the third world peace-keeping missions and negotiations are often assigned to Scandinavian leaders.

The two utility levels above feed into and are supported to a degree by Scandinavian organizations. The recognition of a shared culture makes negotiation easier than otherwise would have been the case and several important political achievements show the viability of Scandinavia even if it has yet to reach the level of a state. Or rather, because it is a cultural dimension, it has the advantage of being more fluid and mainly positively charged. When the power of nations are more restricted by global networking, communication and migration this level might be useful in new ways already signalled by the regionalization of Europe and the creation of cross-national regions and exchange in Scandinavia.

Is there a flip side to these openings? Besides the anti-democratic abuses motivated by Nordism mentioned above there is a more subtle loss or risk at play when regionalization gains momentum. It seems regionalization is part of a trend where we all have to actively choose ever more aspects of our own interaction with the surrounding world. A more fluid identification gives opportunity for self-expression new leeway, and individuals can relate to the Scandinavian heritage in new ways, while national community is withdrawing from former responsibilities. This reflects the logic of flexible capitalism, and has a possible negative side which can include loss of security, loss of traditional community protection and losing the hold on your own identity construction (Sennett 1998).

Scandinavia has contributed to a cultural reservoir that is delivered as a possibility to be articulated and used with care and judgement. All three dimensions of its utilities need to be addressed with both individual and collective judgement. It has been and can be used to inspire and include but also to hide atrocities and build a fence against neighbours. It is a tool, but one in which we live and hence we cannot manipulate mechanically. Nordic values need to be explored with the virtue of judgement to become a resource for positive assets (Aronsson 2012b).

References

Almqvist, C.J.L. (1846) *Om Skandinavismens utförbarhet: Föredrag, hållet i det Skandinaviska Sällskapet den 4 Februarii 1846*, Köpenhamn.

Anderson, B. (1983) *Imagined Communities. Reflections on the Origin and Spread of Nationalism*, London: Verso.

Aronsson, P. (2001) 'The Nature of States and Regions. Reflections on Territory in Swedish Historiography', in F.-E. Eliassen, J. Mikkelsen and B. Poulsen (eds), *Regional Integration in Early Modern Scandinavia*, Odense: Odense University Press, 14–40.

——— (2005) '1905 – unionsupplösning att glömma eller att stoltsera med?', in T. Nilsson and Ø. Sørensen (eds), *Goda grannar eller morska motståndare? Sverige och Norge från 1814 till idag*, Stockholm: Carlsson, 216–248.

——— (2009) 'National Cultural Heritage – Nordic Cultural Memory: Negotiating Politics, Identity and Knowledge', in B. Henningsen, H. Kliemann-Geisinger and S. Troebst (eds), *Transnationale Erinnerungsorte: Nord- und Südeuropeische Perspektiven*, Berlin: Berliner Wissenschafts-Verlag, 71–90.

——— (2010) 'Introduction: Uses of the Past; Nordic Historical Cultures in a Comparative Perspective', *Culture Unbound. Journal of Current Cultural Research*, 2: 553–563.

——— (2011) 'Identity Politics and Uses of the Past with European National Museums', *Nordisk Museologi*, 1: 117–124.

——— (2012a) 'Exhibiting Scandinavian Culture: The National Museums of Denmark and Sweden', in S. Berger, C. Lorenz and B. Melman (eds), *Popularizing National Pasts. 1800 to the Present*, London: Routledge, 169–195.

——— (2012b) 'Omdömet och historien', in M. Lindstedt Cronberg and E. Österberg (eds), *Dygdernas renässans*, Stockholm: Helsingfors: Atlantis.

——— (2012c) 'Performing the Nordic in Museums: Changing Ideas of Norden and their Political Implications', in P. Aronsson and L. Gradén (eds), *Performing Nordic Heritage. Everyday Practices and Institutional Culture*, London: Ashgate.

Aronsson, P. and Gradén, L. (eds) (2012a) 'Introduction: Performing Nordic Heritage: Institutional Preservation and Popular Practices', in P. Aronsson and L. Gradén (eds), *Performing Nordic Heritage. Everyday Practices and Institutional Culture*, London: Ashgate.

——— (eds) (2012b) *Performing Nordic Heritage. Everyday Practices and Institutional Culture*, London: Ashgate.

Aronsson, P. *et al.* (2001) *Dygder som drivkraft och föredöme*, Stockholm: City University Press.

Bäckström, M. (2012) *Hjärtats härdar: folkliv, folkmuseer och minnesmärken i Skandinavien, 1808–1907*, Möklinta: Gidlund.

Berger, S. (2010) 'History Writing and National Identity Formation', Paper to session National Identity and Hegemonic Memory, CISH conference in Amsterdam 25 August 2010.

Berggren, H. and Trägårdh, L. (2006) *Är svensken människa? Gemenskap och oberoende i det moderna Sverige*, Stockholm: Norstedt.

Björk, R. and Eliaeson, S. (eds) (2000) *Union & Secession. Perspektiv på statsbildningsprocesser och riksupplösningar*, Stockholm: Carlsson.

Björkman, J., Fjæstad, B. and Harvard, J. (eds) (2011) *Ett nordiskt rum. Historiska och framtida gemenskaper från Baltikum till Barents hav, Göteborg*, Stockholm: Makadam.

Brenna, B. (2002) *Verden som ting og forestilling. Verdensutstillinger og den norske deltakelsen 1851–1900*, Oslo: Unipub.

Burch, S. (2010) 'Norden, Reframed', *Culture Unbound. Journal of Current Cultural Research*, 2: 565–581.

——— (2012) 'Banal Nordism: Recomposing an Old Song of Peace', in P. Aronsson and L. Gradén (eds), *Performing Nordic Heritage. Everyday Practices and Institutional Culture*, London: Ashgate.

Burrow, J.W. (2007) *A History of Histories. Epics, Chronicles, Romances and Inquiries from Herodotus and Thucydides to the Twentieth Century*, London: Allen Lane.

Childs, M.W. (1936) *Sweden: The Middle Way*, New Haven: Yale University Press.

Eklund, K., Trägårdh, L. and Henrik, B. (2011) *Shared Norms for the New Reality: The Nordic Way / World Economic Forum, Davos 2011*, Stockholm: Global utmaning.

Grandien, B. (1987) *Rönndruvans glöd: nygöticistiskt i tanke, konst och miljö under 1800-talet*, Stockholm: Nordiska museet.

Hemstad, R. (2008) *Fra Indian summer til nordisk vinter. Skandinavisk samarbeid, skandinavisme og unionsøpplosningen*, Oslo: Akademisk Publisering.

Henningsen, B. (1997) *Die schwedische Konstruktion einer nordischen Identität durch Olof Rudbeck*, Berlin: Humboldt-Universität zu Berlin.

Hillström, M. (2006) *Ansvaret för kulturarvet. Studier i det kulturhistoriska museiväsendets formering med särskild inriktning på Nordiska museets etablering 1872–1919*, Linköping: Dept. of Culture Studies Linköpings univ.

——— (2010) 'Contested Boundaries Nation, People and Cultural History Museums in Sweden and Norway 1862–1909', *Culture Unbound. Journal of Current Cultural Research*, 2: 583–607.

Inglehart, R. and Welzel, C. (2005) *Modernization, Cultural Change, and Democracy: The Human Development Sequence*, New York: Cambridge University Press.

Levart, J. (1901) *Skansen och Arhur Hazelius. Enn skiss- och minnesbok*, Stockholm: Geber.

Molin, T. (2003) *Den rätta tidens mått. Göthiska förbundet, fornforskningen och det antikvariska landskapet*, Umeå: Institutionen för historiska studier Univ.

Nietzsche, F. (1874) *Unzeitgemässe Betrachtungen. Zweites Stück: Vom Nutzen und Nachtheil der Historie für das Leben*, Leipzig: E.W. Fritzsch.

——— (1980) *On the Advantage and Disadvantage of History for Life*, Indianapolis, Ind.

Olwig, K.R. and Jones, M. (eds) (2008) *Nordic Landscapes. Region and Belonging on the Northern Edge of Europe*, Minneapolis: University of Minnesota Press.

Paasi, A. (1986) 'The Institutionalization of Regions: A Theoretical Framework for Understanding of the Emergence of Regions and the Constitution of Regional Identity', *Fennia*, 164(1).

Pettersson, S. (2011) 'National Museums in Finland', in P. Aronsson and G. Elgenius (eds), *Building National Museums in Europe 1750–2010. Conference proceedings from EuNaMus, European National Museums: Identity Politics, the Uses of the Past and the European Citizen, Bologna 28–30 April 2011*, Linköping: LiU E-Press, 315–348.

Runcis, M. (1998) *Steriliseringar i folkhemmet*, Stockholm: Ordfront.

Sandberg, M.B. (2003) *Living Pictures, Missing Persons: Mannequins, Museums and Modernity*, Princeton, NJ: Princeton University Press.

Sennett, R. (1998) *The Corrosion of Character: The Personal Consequences of Work in the New Capitalism*, New York: W.W. Norton.

Stadius, P. (2012 (in prep)) 'Happy Countries: Appraisals of Inter-War Nordic Societies', in J. Harvard and P. Stadius (eds), *Communicating the North: Media and Marketing in the Making of the Nordic Region*, London: Ashgate.

Stråth, B. (1993) *Folkhemmet mot Europa: ett historiskt perspektiv på 90-talet*, Stockholm: Tiden.

Stråth, B. and Henningsen, B. (1997) *The Cultural Construction of Community in the Process of Modernization: Sweden and Germany in Comparison: A Cooperative Research Project, Florens: European University Institute*, Berlin: Humboldt-Universität zu Berlin.

Stråth, B. and Sørensen, Ø. (eds) (1997) *The Cultural Construction of Norden*, Oslo: Scandinavian University Press.

Tacitus, P.C. (1473) *Germania: De situ, moribus et populis Germaniae*, Nuremberg: Friedrich Creussner.

Taylor, C. (1989) *Sources of the Self: The Making of the Modern Identity*, Cambridge, MA: Harvard University Press.

Tydén, M. (2002) *Från politik till praktik: de svenska steriliseringslagarna 1935–1975*, Stockholm: Almqvist & Wiksell International.

Wallette, A. (2009) 'Sweden and Scandinavia: History-writing as an Identity Project in the Early Modern Period', *Scandia*, 75(2): 87–91.

Wetterberg, G. (2010) *Förbundsstaten Norden*, Stockholm: Föreningen Norden.

Widenberg, J. (2006) *Fäderneslandets antikviteter. Etnoterritoriella historiebruk och integrationssträvanden i den svenska statsmaktens antikvariska verksamhet ca 1600–1720 [Antiquities of the Fatherland: The Use of History and the Striving for Ethnic Integration in the Antiquarian Sector of the Swedish State ca 1600–1720]*, Uppsala: Acta Universitatis Upsaliensis (AUU).

Wienberg, J. (2008) 'Kanon, mindesmærker og oldtidsfund', in L.-E. Jönsson, A. Wallette and J. Wienberg (eds), *Kanon och kulturarv. Historia och samtid i Danmark och Sverige, Göteborg*, Stockholm: Makadam i samarbete med Centrum för Danmarksstudier.

Zipsane, H. (2011) 'On the Development of National Museums in Denmark', in P. Aronsson and G. Elgenius (eds), *Building National Museums in Europe 1750–2010. Conference proceedings from EuNaMus, European National Museums: Identity Politics, the Uses of the Past and the European Citizen, Bologna 28–30 April 2011*, Linköping: LiU E-Press, 257–278.

3 Turning the tide with 'Woman on a Cart'

The amazing case of Holstebro

Lisbeth Lindeborg

Prelude

Despite pouring rain, over 400 people have gathered in the square at Sognekirke in Jutland's Holstebro. It is 10 March 1966 and Holstebro has just been named Denmark's most boring city. A visiting painter hit the nail on the head when he emphasized that he dreaded exhibiting his paintings in Holstebro: there was no place as hopeless as this provincial nest.[1]

Among the shivering people there in front of the church, the mood is tense – sceptically they look at a tall object under a shroud in the middle of the square. They know that the object is a sculpture to be unveiled by the city mayor, Kai Nielsen. Inspired by an exhibition at the Louisiana Museum in Helsingör, Nielsen was lured into an impulse purchase and bought Alberto Giacometti's 'Woman on a Cart'. Only later, he realizes that the purchase is not likely to go over well with voters and he decided to hide the artwork until the upcoming municipal election was over. Some reporters got wind of it, however, and a date was set for the unveiling.

Under the cover of his big umbrella and with the installation speech on a flapping piece of paper in his right hand, the mayor is aware that the people are waiting to see what had cost the municipality 150,000 and the sponsor Carlsberg Foundation 60,000 Danish crowns. The situation is more than unpleasant when the veil falls and the skinny grey-black figure on a cart comes into view. The people in the square cannot believe their eyes: so much for so little! Well, you don't get a lot for your money these days (Skot-Hansen 1998)! They don't realize then, no one can in fact imagine, that the strange figure in the pouring rain and the mayor's first – seemingly pathetic – attempt to make the city more attractive, will be the most positive turning point in Holstebro's history (Figure 3.1).

Whereas the citizens of Holstebro write to the local paper to complain over the expensive sculpture, which 'does not even look like a woman', the nationwide Danish press and some foreign newspapers report about the curious undertaking of placing a Giacometti in the square of a little hole like Holstebro, with its 40,000 inhabitants. The venture, however, gets good press, and for the first time Holstebro is being talked about in positive terms. When the mayor is interviewed he explains that his goal is to bring art and culture to the people. Both he and his

Figure 3.1 The unveiling of Giacometti's 'Woman on a Cart', Holstebro, 10 March 1966.

colleagues are confident of the value of culture and the arts as a development and localization factor for the future. The tourists who suddenly show up to be photographed next to the artwork before they go into a cafe to soak up the experience with a cup of coffee and a pastry, are an unexpected sight.

The event also has a signalling effect among people who are active in culture and the arts. That same year, the Odin Theatre, one of Europe's most famous avant-garde theatre ensembles, moves from Oslo to Holstebro and establishes itself as a Nordic theatre laboratory. At the same time the municipal's governing body decides on an expanded investment in the arts – the whole city is to be embellished with sculptures and new architecture in public places. In this way they want to develop and strengthen the image of Holstebro (McNulty *et al.* 1985).

So begins the 'fairytale' of Holstebro and Maren, which is the genuine Danish name that the 'Woman on a Cart' was bestowed with by the Holstebro inhabitants. Since then Holstebro has been on a winning streak. The benefits of culture were already noted on 17 March 1989 by the Danish Stock Exchange News Analysis:

> Holstebro has been playing all their cards right in terms of the economy. And that has paid dividends ... the largest employment increase in Danish industry throughout the 1980s. In Holstebro the recipe for success reads as follows: create an exciting cultural life... a wide range of leisure activities and ample opportunities for education. Then the new job opportunities will more or less appear by themselves.[2]

Today, with more than 57,000 inhabitants, the Jutland town is an expanding municipality, an internationally noted cultural city with new theatres, libraries, museums and cultural centres, populated by people who are proud of their city.

New rooms for world culture

> I can take any empty space and call it a bare stage. A man walks across this empty space whilst someone else is watching him, and this is all that is needed for an act of theatre to be engaged.
>
> (Brook 1968)

In the 1960s there were many empty spaces in Holstebro. Except for some local music and arts associations there were virtually no cultural infrastructures, no cultural institutions and very few activities which could be called cultural. In 1961 there had been a highlight when twelve painters had dared to organize a week of culture. With a turnout of more than 2,000 the week was an unexpected success but there was nothing to follow up this first initiative.

Although the de-industrialization trends had been stopped through some new investments started by the leading industry in town, Faerch tobacco manufacturer, Holstebro was suffering from a severe image problem. People with aspirations left the town as soon as they could. That was the situation when Maren arrived. She brought the change. In Holstebro the empty spaces would be filled with art characterized by high quality and expertise. This was to be one remarkable feature for culture and arts in Holstebro.

Holstebrohallen: the world on stage

One of the first important milestones on the way to becoming a cultural city was the opening of Holstebrohallen in 1966 with space for performing arts, concerts, workshops, etc. As the biggest performance space in West Jutland the audience came from all over the region. When the famed Italian theatre couple Dario Fo and Franca Rame visited with their success 'La signore è da buttare' in 1968 Fo underlined that the audience in Holstebro was unusual – they also pondered what they saw and heard.[3] They were not spoilt. Daniel Barenboim, Arthur Rubinstein and Leonard Cohen as well as famous pop groups like Country Joe & the Fish and Savage Rose were among other early star performers. It even happened that an international star on a North European tour also appeared on stage in Holstebro besides Stockholm, Oslo, Copenhagen and Hamburg. Between 1969 and 1985 regional theatre companies used Holstebrohallen for their plays around seventy times a year. Together with the guest performances Holstebrohallen attracted an audience of between 80,000 and 100,000 people annually.

In 1990, Holstebrohallen changed its name to Holstebro Music Theatre. After a thorough renovation in 2006, with a new architectural outfit it is considered to be one of the most spectacular theatres in Denmark. With room for 1,200 spectators the theatre is not only home to original musical productions but also to touring theatre and international performances like it always was. Today the theatre further encompasses the Black Box Theatre with some of the best rehearsal facilities countrywide. The screen on one outdoor wall is the largest in Denmark. In 2009 another venue close to the Music Theatre and incorporating the River Storån was established, Town Space, Stream and Culture.

In both theatre buildings the Opera in the Centre presents opera for all including small children as well as youth. The aim of this regional company is to create modern musical dramas based on a classical subject matter. In 2011 the Opera in the Centre even made a small profit – of 125,000 Danish crowns.

An art museum with 'world class art and art from all over the world'

In 1967 the municipality decided to open an art museum. One of the most beautiful houses in the city, an old white villa (1906) in a park, that had been the home for the tobacco manufacturer Faerch and his family, was for sale and the municipality decided to pay the cost of 1.5 million Danish crowns. With the commissioning of the well-known art expert Poul Vad as director for the museum, Holstebro again started out on an unorthodox path. Vad suggested that the museum's permanent exhibition should primarily be composed of Danish art from after 1930.

But contrary to other provincial art museums with their fragmented mixture of many works by many painters, Vad's idea was to single out a few really good painters and sculptors and exhibit a selection of their works representing different stages of their development. But that was not enough. A work of art, according to Vad increases in interest when seen in a greater universal context. Thus the inspirational sources or fellow works of art, e.g. works of other artists created in a similar vein – or style – are also exhibited. In this way an associative chain appears, that, when required, also includes ethnic art (African, American and Asian), photography and craft objects resulting in a story evolving around the painter. Why should a more universal, contextual and theoretical outlook only be on show in the big cities, argued Vad.[4] Through this approach the Holstebro art museum also assembled an impressive collection of works by Giacometti, Picasso, Matisse and Chagall. For the visitor of this flexible museum, the effect is a thrilling widening of horizons.

Vad is no longer director but his vision of Holstebro art museum is carried on by the new leadership. In addition, the museum has always been lucky in getting money from sponsors and from funding. Like the leadership of all other cultural institutions in Holstebro the leadership of the art museum has a high level of expertise and so they know when to buy high quality art before it gets too expensive. The stimulation to acquire something new should be there before there is an expressed need for it. It is a general experience in cultural politics (Kramer 1996). Since its opening the museum had to be further expanded twice, in 1981 and 2011.

The Odin Theatre: a Danish world theatre

In 1966 the mayor of Holstebro sent a letter of invitation to Oslo. The recipient was a young upcoming theatre director with an international reputation and many extraordinary ideas about the role of theatre in society. Maybe the mayor felt a certain similarity with the young director – they were both avant-garde in their different ways. The director was Eugenio Barba the manager of the New Odin Theatre in Oslo.

Unorthodox as he was, Eugenio Barba accepted the invitation and so he and his then mainly Norwegian company moved down to Holstebro in 1966. There they rented an old farm house on the outskirts of the city and started to renovate the house and adjoining stables at the same time as they were rehearsing. Again, many citizens of Holstebro found the new cultural investment to be as unnecessary as 'Woman on a Cart', but they were impressed by the hard work and discipline of the actors turned manual workers.

The following year in 1967 the Odin Theatre was invited to participate at the Biennale of Venice. There Barba's experimental theatre had its international break through. From then on, the word about the Odin Theatre in Holstebro spread around the world. Considering that the world's most famous avant-garde theatres are located in the capitals, people outside Denmark thought that Holstebro was the capital of Denmark. For the people of Holstebro many golden days lay ahead when Barba and his theatre were visited by other great avant-garde theatre directors and companies, for example Dario Fo, Jerzy Grotowski, Jean-Louis Barrault and Japanese Kabuki and No Theatre ensembles.

The aim of the Odin Theatre is to examine the art of theatre, and develop new theatrical forms which involve daily life. The main interest is to analyse the actor's own technique in an intercultural dimension, finding out how new bridges can be built to reach the human beings in the surrounding life, wherever they are. For that purpose the whole ensemble or parts of it go on tour. So far they have brought eighty productions on stage in sixty-three countries on five continents. The theatre is constantly branching out, organizing courses, workshops, festivals in the framework of their Nordic Theatre Laboratory. With the later founded International School of Theatre and Anthropology (ISTA), the theatre cooperates with universities.

In the Odin Theatre the director carries the role of the dramatist. Barba creates and composes together with the actors. Today the actors come from different countries in the world; but in order to be accepted they have to know one Scandinavian language. In the theatre buildings there are, the White Hall and the Red Room, for performances. In one of the old stables are bedrooms for guests researching the theatre. So far the Odin Theatre gets 5.5 million Danish crowns from the municipality and an additional 40 per cent of that amount from the state except from funding from funds, etc. Every three years the Odin Theatre organizes a Holstebro Week with performances and guest appearances.

The Odin Theatre is a great asset for Holstebro but the future is uncertain. Who will take over when Barba steps down? So far there is nobody to follow.

Holstebro as a creative city: a coordinated heterogeneity

The Music Theatre, the art museum and the Odin Theatre are three creative spaces replacing the old empty spaces – each of them with an radiant aura making Holstebro a creative city. According to Siebel (2008) a creative city must be characterized through density and a certain concentration in order to produce innovative milieus. Very often – in big cities – you find certain parts of the city where the creative industries are located: you have clusters of advertising bureaus, architects and designers, etc. Since Holstebro is a small city this kind of city development is not on the agenda. In Holstebro the diversified cultural spaces are near each other.

There, the issue is another – is there a danger that every creative space – every institution – turns inward? There is a risk, because in Holstebro the institutions are autonomous. They decide themselves about their policies and how to handle their tasks. There is no meddling from municipality or the civil servant responsible for culture.

On the other hand (Siebel 2008), you need a balance between the heterogeneity that exists among different cultural spaces and a homogeneous common orientation. That is the case in Holstebro. The person responsible for culture and arts has a coordinating and a fundraising task, thus giving the diverse institutions their necessary framework. In addition, the institutions themselves meet regularly at least twice a year. Several of them meet more often. With the vision of making and keeping Holstebro a culturally attractive place they 'stick together'. There are no rivalries between the institutions, instead they help and inform each other. That is one part of the so-called Holstebro Cultural Model and one important reason that this city has so far succeeded. This is quite unusual. In most cases the development of a cultural city has its ups and downs. But there is still another and quite a similar example to Holstebro – the city of Unna in the Ruhr region (Lindeborg 1991). Both cities were known to be small and dreary places. One motivation for them to start investing in cultural infrastructures was that they wanted to show the world around them that they too could become attractive. I have called this the 'Cinderella principle' (Lindeborg 2010).

Art in the streets: a mirror of transparency and openness

In 1966 the mayor had underlined that he wanted to bring the arts to the people. That also implied that people should not have to go inside a cultural institution to be able to enjoy artistic work; the art should also go to them. The promise is fulfilled – for example, everywhere you go in the city, you meet with sculptures and statues in public places.

In the centre, opposite the Music Theatre and the Black Box, the Royal Hotel is situated at the Red Square, so called because of its red paving. It is crowned with thirty-six bronze sculptures (1995–2000) with the joint title the 'Tobacco Workers' Dream'. The sculptures depict myths and legends from all parts of the world and are eye-catching. So is 'The Citizens of Holstebro' (2004), six life-size men and six life-size women standing on a rock. They want to tell future generations about our day and age. The title refers to the work by Auguste Rodin (1886) the *Burghers of Calais*, telling the story of the English siege of Calais in 1347. The intention of the sculptor Björn Nörregard is to build a bridge between the past, present and future. Most spectacular is the 'Chaos Temple' a 400 square metre construction of iron like a metal grid on four 18 metre high masts. It is lit up by laser beams; it was the first permanent outdoor laser construction in Denmark. One laser sends a beam across the city with the help of a mirror at the top of the construction.

A foyer ties the new town hall, that was inaugurated in 1986, to the new library opened in 1981. Both buildings are full of art. One of them has the symbolic inscription on the outer wall of the council chamber. It was hand carved by the American artist Lawrence Weiner: 'Some of This + Some of That Gently Placed under the Light of Polaris'. Weiner saw the rounded shape of the council chamber's outer wall as the bow of a ship with the council members as ships' captains needing some means of navigation when making their decisions. That is the reason for the reference to the North Star.

Inside the chamber there is another symbol. In the round empty space in the middle of the chamber there is a bronze sculpture in the shape of an irregular cube on the floor. Like Lego blocks, this sculpture could be taken apart and then put together again. For any citizen coming into the chamber the sculpture will tell the outcome of the latest meeting. If the parts are spread out all over the floor, this implies that the councillors could not unite in their decision making. If the sculpture is put together, the chamber agreed and parted in unity.

In many ways the sculptural works in Holstebro send out messages. Most of the messages are about the participation of all its citizens, of transparency and of an open climate between politicians, citizens and all sectors of the Holstebro society. The mental map (Gould and White 1992) in Holstebro is characterized by an identity of participation. Everybody should feel that he or she belongs to this city and that what they say – their opinions – will be heard. Lisbet Gormsen, the director for arts and culture describes it as a communication at eye level.[5] A policy is laid down paving the way for an open communication.

The Holstebro policy of communication

There are three rules of communication or rather messages from the Holstebro politicians to their citizens:

- We tell everybody what we are doing and will be doing and we do what we say.
- We use our common sense.
- We have our eyes open for that which goes against conventional thinking.

The third rule is particularly significant for the cultural development of Holstebro.

The primary target areas for these rules are the digitalization of the municipality, the profiling of Holstebro city, internal communication, marketing and contacts with the media. Further the policy underlines that the responsibility for the communication is in the hands of the person who has the responsibility for the issue in question. Likewise everybody is responsible for making sure that there is a good communication. 'That implies that we try to identify with the respondent and that we communicate at the right time and in the right place.'

To increase the affinity between the residents, the municipality has initiated a so-called Holstebro partnership with participants from most sectors of society. The partnership operates through working groups and holds meetings to work on different programmes. The idea is that participants inform each other about what they're doing and thereby contribute to increased local awareness and the strengthening of democratic structures. This way the residents get involved in the city's development according to the so-called empowerment principle (Wagner 1997). It has been shown that success is reduced in cities that invest in culture without including the population in the process.

As regards the marketing of Holstebro, within the city as well as outside of it a so-called Profile Book is issued every year. In the richly illustrated book all kinds of activities are presented; industries, some local authorities, service entrepreneurs, schools and education as well as cultural institutions and initiatives. Started in 2007, this is an excellent project; it shows the citizens and the visitors practically all relevant aspects of living in Holstebro.

A hotbed for talent

Holstebro is known for its investment in young artistic talent and the city offers all kinds of arts education of a very high quality. A result of this is that parents with talented children try to find a way to move to Holstebro. Besides Holstebro there is only Copenhagen – with its soaring costs of living – that can offer similar opportunities for young talents.

As early as 1967, Holstebro established the first music school in Denmark. It was founded by the first composer in residence in Holstebro, Jörgen Plaetner, a pioneer of electronic music in Denmark. The then public relations manager in Holstebro, Olaf Sielemann, emphasized that when children and youth had been working on the violin five hours a day they would not go out and break up parking meters.[6] Many professional musicians started out as pupils in the music school that today has 2,200 students of all ages.

In 1976, the music school expanded its operations with a higher conservatory education. The following year, the initiative was followed up with a musical dramatic theatre that today, under the name of the Opera in the Centre, contributes to the further development of opera in the country. The focus on music encompasses the whole of Holstebro, as all students are eligible to attend the school's music classes. Furthermore, the so-called Colour Strings School was established in 2007, with an even greater emphasis on music education. In addition to regular school education a four-hour-a-day musical education is incorporated in the school day. It is the only school of its kind in Denmark outside Copenhagen.

Another milestone was the Danish Royal Ballet's sole *dépendance* outside of Copenhagen, which was established in Holstebro in 1996. Here, thirty new dancers are trained a year; the education is jointly funded by Holstebro Municipality and the Royal Ballet. It requires the same tough audition and the same pressing courses for the pupils at the *dépendance* as in Copenhagen. In addition, the Ballet School has another 100 pupils being educated in modern dance, step, etc.

Since 2005 Holstebro is also home to a talent centre, the Danish Talent Academy, incorporating all art forms: music, art and design, dance, musicals and theatre and writing. The Academy is open to students who are between 15 and 25 years old. The education is part time, can be combined with a Danish High School Education and lasts three years. In order to be accepted, the ten to fifteen students in each subject have to go through tough auditions. Most of the teachers in the Talent Academy, as well as in the ballet school, come from Copenhagen. They do not live in Holstebro.

This is a dilemma. It has become evident that Holstebro is a 'talent smithy' for young talents giving them training with the highest reputation. But after they are trained, they go away. There is not enough audience capacity for a ballet theatre of international reputation. The only performance institution of an international kind is the Odin Theatre. Although they perform every new performance in Holstebro for a while, having an audience that also comes from the region and other nearby cities, they also have to go to other places to perform, for example in Copenhagen.

'A drop of culture in all that we do'

> The right timing is a key factor in cultural politics.
>
> (Knud W. Jensen)[7]

Looking at Holstebro from the outside it seems as if arts and culture make up a roof over the municipality and all its activities. The motto for the municipality reads: 'There is a drop of culture in all that we do'; it is a driving force for the economy, for education and for health. In fact, Holstebro is the only Danish city where the cultural administration is combined with the health administration. The basic funding for the building and maintenance of the cultural institutions and other projects come from the municipality. In addition there is secondary funding from the state for the theatres, museums and the music school. A third source is several funds and sponsors.

In comparison with most other cultural places, Holstebro has succeeded in keeping its position for almost fifty years. That is amazing. It managed to turn the tide at the right time and since then Holstebro has worked on its cultural development and cultural image step by step in a most pragmatic way.

It is evident that it takes a lot of effort to turn the tide especially when confronted with the principle of 'path dependence'. The expression originates from the history of economics where scholars discovered that accepted technologies, although more and more inefficient, cannot easily be ousted by new and efficient ones. Experience has shown that there is a 'lock-in effect' when earlier established options block out new developments. The historian Paul A. David, who studies the development of technologies, came to the conclusion that 'history matters'. The history of any technology decides its future.[8]

This principle of path dependence can be found in any area of human activity, for example in institutions. The German political scientist Gerhard Lehmbruch (2000) has investigated path dependence in political systems and shown that the only way to break the vicious circle of the old path may well be through a catastrophe. Cities and regions are just as path dependent. Not until they are on the verge of complete breakdown with no other choice do they turn the tide. The Ruhr region is a brilliant example from Germany. In Britain there is Glasgow and Liverpool, in France there is Lille and in Denmark there is Holstebro.

Culture as a location factor

> In many ways Holstebro has shown itself to be a pioneering city. I am quite sure that the cultural investments will pay off in many other sectors.
>
> (Lise Östergaard, Minister of Culture 1981)[9]

What positive effects have the major investments in culture had on Holstebro so far?

The answer is: several. The transformation into a culture city has meant a growing appeal, an increased quality of life, a new identity and a winning image. This has led to a significant boost to the economy with new investments, new industries and new residents. In addition, more and more visitors come to Holstebro to take advantage of the high quality cultural activities and to shop. The range of goods is of high quality and is so abundant as to accommodate 250,000 people's shopping needs here. In 2008, Holstebro was chosen as Denmark's most attractive shopping city for the second time; it has also been elected the city of the year twice.

Throughout the year there are all kinds of events taking place in Holstebro, for example the Danish Culture Day every second year and the Days of Classical Music every year.

The former city mayor, Arne Laegaard, emphasized that what is particularly gratifying is how fast the population is growing:

> In Holstebro, we have no problem attracting new residents. We sell more houses and plots than ever:
>
> Our cultural life works like a locomotive – and even has a spill-over effect for communities outside Holstebro. One of the reasons that highly skilled people settle in neighbouring Thy, is because they have access to the excellent cultural attractions in Holstebro.[10]

More and more companies – including logistics companies – of which many are start-ups, are also coming to Holstebro. In Nupark, a big industrial park with several attractive buildings in the outskirts of Holstebro, there are no less than ninety new companies. Close by there is the biggest ethanol/biogas manufacturer in the world, Maabjerg, that started its production in 2012.

In January 2012 civil servants from the Ministry of Labour visited Holstebro in order to get information about the successful cooperation projects between local employers and the municipality to cut unemployment. In Holstebro, the number of people on social welfare went down by 0.8 per cent between 2010 and 2011. That is more than the Danish average and means a savings for the municipality of 35 million Danish crowns.

In particular, families choose to settle in Holstebro; they are attracted by the variety of cultural activities for their children and a population of which 30.3 per cent are employed in the creative sector. This is a remarkable number in a city of Holstebro's size.[11] In 2012 Holstebro Creative Community was founded. That is a network for entrepreneurs. The development of talent in arts and culture is supposed to serve as a model for all kinds of industrial enterprises.

The cultural entrepreneurs work either on their own or in small companies with a maximum of five persons. They are not only part of the cultural infrastructure, through their mere presence they show that culture as a location factor works. According to Wiesand (2008), however, the terms cultural, or creative, industries are often misused; these entrepreneurial endeavours should rather be characterized as micro businesses. Kunzmann (1995) shows that most cultural entrepreneurs want to stay where they are, they are mostly highly qualified people and they integrate easily in the society. They constitute a great asset for a city.

Evolution and revolution

Summary, conclusions and perspectives

In Holstebro, we see an amazing and long-lasting example of culture's power as an identity creation factor, a development factor, a localization factor and as a source for creative catalysators. Although we are well aware that the development strategy in one place can not be replicated in another, we can learn some fundamental lessons from the Holstebro example. These lessons are of significant value because Holstebro is an early, almost historical, example of a city that managed to halt its devastating developmental decline by, at the last minute, forging a new courageous path that led to success. Since then unorthodox thinking is a first 'rule' for municipal policies. Holstebro's history from 1966 shows us creativity in action, a place bursting with ideas where limits are exceeded and boundaries are transcended.

Another lesson is how crucial it is to not instrumentalize culture and art specifically for economic purposes. The first act that will always be of paramount importance – the purchase of Maren – was an almost defiant and emotionally laden attempt by the mayor and the local government leaders to show the world that Holstebro also understood culture of quality. It is on the path of high-quality that Holstebro has moved forward. Thus the separate institutions have only settled for highest competence as regards their leadership. The cultural managers in Holstebro are highly professional and of a kind that you usually only see in big cities.

Still another reason for the success of Holstebro is that the separate institutions cooperate. They stick together. They are friends and not rivals for financing or funds. Multilaterally they meet at least twice a year and in between, spontaneous meetings between some of the institutions occur again and again. The climate is one of transparency, openness and confidence.

The involvement of the citizens in the development of Holstebro, to make them participate in cultural life, is of paramount importance and is significant for the Holstebro Cultural Model. The citizens voice their opinions and they are being heard.

The fact that the process in Holstebro is pragmatic is also important. A city like Holstebro cannot afford to make mistakes. It's a tough job that goes forward step by step, seen from the outside it is not particularly spectacular. However, when we examine every milestone, we discover that each time has involved filling empty space with revolutionary content. We also observe an exciting dialectic between an external evolutionary process and an internal revolution. Holstebro was the city that dared when others hesitated. There the powers that be went against the current.

There are, however, some shadows 'lurking' over the city. In 2009 a SWOT-analysis was made in connection with the role of Holstebro and other cities in Jutland because of the application of Århus as a European Capital of Culture in 2017.[12] The assets of Holstebro were all listed as well as its weaknesses: emigration of talent and youth causing a shrinking creative class; lack of improvisational cultural facilities for young people – there are no subcultures; not enough activities in the institutions; in the evenings when there are no events, the city is dead; Holstebro as a cultural city cannot afford to be slack, it can not sit back and be too self-asserted – the spirit of turning the tide must not be lost.

Epilogue

In August 2012 I visit Holstebro again. A quarter to nine in the evening I walk to the Old Town Hall where 'Woman on a Cart' – Maren – is standing. She looks the same as usual. I know that some people now and then have put a sandwich on her socle but she is as thin as ever. She is the most beloved 'official person' in Holstebro. I know that she was damaged a few years ago. Subsequently she was put indoors.

For a time people visiting the Louisiana museum in Helsingör could enjoy her presence there. In the meantime the politicians in Holstebro discussed her future. They decided that she must be kept outside and so they invested one million Danish crowns in a small elevator and dug a hole in the ground in order that Maren could be hoisted up and down. On her 40th birthday, a hymn was written in her honour and she now has her own friendly association – a kind of order with 'knights'. The significance of Maren is not that she has gained in financial value (100 million Danish crowns); but rather more importantly is that she has become a symbol for Holstebro.

At 9 o'clock, two night watches in medieval costumes appear and the hymn is played from the church. Some thirty persons have gathered to experience the unique moment of Maren being lowered down. Down under she is covered with a glass armour plate and we gather around it to stare down at the top of her head through the glass. She is safe. And we know that she will be with us again, elevated up to the earth at 9 o'clock in the morning.

Notes

1 Quoted in Skot-Hansen, D. (1998) *Holstebro i Verden, Verden i Holstebro*, p. 24.
2 Translation by the author from Börsens Nyhetsanalys.
3 Quoted in Jyllands Posten, 25 September 1989.
4 Quoted in Skot-Hansen, D. (1998) *Holstebro i Verden, Verden i Holstebro*, p. 41.
5 In an interview with the author, August 2012.
6 This he told the author at a joint seminar in Härnösand, Sweden 1992.
7 Jensen, the former director of the Louisiana Art Museum in Helsingör, wrote this in his biography *Mit Louisiana liv*.
8 David, P. (1985), 'Clio and the Economics of QWERTY', in *American Economic Review, Papers and Proceedings* 75, pp. 332–337.
9 From her speech at the opening of the new library in Holstebro, 28 August 1981.
10 Quoted in the journal *Danske Kommuner*, 2 June 2005.
11 According to the research of Steffen Gulman in his article, 'Kröllede hjerner er lokomotive', in the journal *Danske Kommuner*, no. 18, 2005.
12 SWOT (Strengths, Weaknesses, Opportunities, Threats) is an instrument for the strategic planning for businesses and organizations.

References

Barba, E. and Kaergaard, D. (eds) (1989) *Vor By igår idag imorgen*, Holstebro: Odinteatrets Förlag.

Brook, P. (1968) *The Empty Space*, London: Penguin Books.

David, P. (1985) 'Clio and the Economics of QWERTY', *American Economic Review, Papers and Proceedings*, 75, 332–337.

Gould, P. and White, R. (1992) *Mental Maps*, London and New York: Routledge.

Gulman, S. (2005) 'Kröllede hjerner er locomotive', in *Danske Kommuner*, no. 18.

Jensen, K.W. (1985) *Mit Louisiana-liv*, Copenhagen: Gyldendal.

Kramer, D. (1996) *Handlungsfeld Kultur*, Essen: Klartext Verlag.

Kunzmann, K. (1995) 'Strategien zur Förderung regionaler Kulturwirtschaft', in T. Heinze (ed.), *Kultur und Wirtschaft*, Opladen: Westdeutscher Verlag.

Lehmbruch, G. (2000) 'Bundesstaatsreform als Sozialtechnologie', in *Europäisches Zentrum für Föderalismusforschung Tübingen, Jahrbuch des Föderalismus 2008*, Baden-Baden: Nomos.

Lindeborg, L. (1991) *Kultur som lokaliseringsfaktor*, Industridepartementet, Ds 1991:22, Stockholm: Allmänna Förlaget.

McNulty, R., Jacobson, D. and Penne, L. (1985) *The Economics of Amenity*, Washington: Partners for Liveable Places.

Siebel, W. (2008) 'Was macht eine Stadt kreativ', *Kulturpolitische Gesellschaft, Jahrbuch für Kulturpolitik 2008*, Essen: Klartext Verlag, 275–284.

Skot-Hansen, D. (1998) *Holstebro i Verden, Verden i Holstebro*, Århus: Klim.

Wagner, B. (1997) 'Modernisierungsprozesse im Kulturbereich', in B. Wagner and A. Zimmer (eds), *Krise des Wohlfahrtsstaates – Zukunft der Kulturpolitik*, Essen: Klartext Verlag, 87–106.

Wiesand, A. (2008) 'Götterdämmerung der Kulturpolitik?', in *Kulturpolitische Gesellschaft, Jahrbuch für Kulturpolitik 2008*, Essen: Klartext Verlag, 61–72.

4 The role of culture festivals in regional development

The Festival of Tordenskiold in Frederikshavn

Anne Lorentzen

Introduction

Many small cities are in search of new roles in today's globalized and post-industrial world. Their economic bases are under pressure from global competition for people, investment and jobs, which are increasingly concentrated in metropolitan regions. This is due to an overall industrial transformation characterized by a decrease of employment in agriculture and manufacturing on the one hand and an increase in service sector employment on the other hand (Schroll and Søgaard 2011). As the latter are concentrated in cities, while the former were traditional strongholds of small cities, it is no wonder that cities grow and rural areas and small cities decrease in terms of population. This can be seen in Denmark, where cities below 50,000 citizens have shrunk in terms of population between 2001 and 2011, while the capital area and big provincial cities have growing populations. This means that the Danish population is continuously leaving small cities and rural areas.[1]

For decades big cities have applied culture-led regeneration strategies as a response to industrial decline (Bianchini 1993; Evans 2001; Hall 2001). More recently smaller cities have also embarked on soft urban development strategies based on distinctiveness regarding culture and experience consumption opportunities (Bell and Jayne 2006; Lorentzen and van Heur 2012; Miles 2006). The challenges they are facing however, can hardly be compared to those of big cities. Big cities benefit from agglomeration advantages including culture economy clusters, variety as well as specialization of the culture supply, accessibility, large audiences, and inherited reputations among other things. In comparison, small cities have their smallness, their natural environment and their local cultural heritage to offer (Lorentzen 2009). As an offspring of smallness they have the advantage of transparency and proximity among creative actors (Hall and Donald 2012). Culture planning is characterized by a considerable degree of entrepreneurialism. Entrepreneurialism regarding culture involves private as well as public and civic urban actors and takes the form of urban culture projects (Albrechts *et al.* 2003; Healey 2007).

The balance between different types of actors seems to change with the size of the city. The smaller the city the more voluntary, civic work is involved. It has been shown how culture is mobilized in three different ways in small cities, depending on their size (Duxbury 2012). The smallest cities focus on quality of life enhancements and projects which aim to stimulate tourism. Medium-sized small cities focus on cultural activities and aim to make the cities liveable for highly skilled labour (the creative class (Florida 2002)). The larger small cities tend to connect cultural investments to the overall development of the city in a strategy which entails substantial municipal support (Duxbury 2012). In comparison the smaller cities need to 'dig civic gold' by mobilizing volunteers to work with culture projects (Stevenson 2004), because public money is scarce.

Culture planning of small cities is developed in a tension between welfare and growth agendas (Lorentzen 2012a, 2012b), and culture projects often emerge independently of city governments. This chapter deals with the culture development in a rather small city of the Danish periphery, Frederikshavn, in which a multitude of culture projects have emerged from the 'civic goldmine'. The city is too small to have a genuine agenda of culture planning. Rather it has experienced a host of civic bottom-up initiatives aimed at enhancing the quality of life, and at attracting tourists. Many of these initiatives have taken the form of festivals, understood as 'artistic events which last several days' (Karpinska-Krakowiak 2009). One such festival is a historic festival, which has grown to be the largest festival of North Denmark.

The Days of Tordenskiold is the focus of this chapter. The chapter situates the festival in the region and the city, after which it proceeds to explore different dimensions of the festival. What were the ideas behind it? What goes on during the festival, and what does it take to prepare such a big festival? How has the festival developed from 1998 up to today, and what were the drivers behind this development? Has the Tordenskiold Project any commercial value, and how has the subtle balance between welfare and growth evolved? A final section discusses the role of the Tordenskiold Project in urban and regional development, after which it concludes on the perspectives for other cities.

The challenges of Frederikshavn

Frederikshavn is a remarkable small city in the Danish periphery. It is well known in a Scandinavian context as a tourist hub due to its ferry lines to Norway and Sweden and due its proximity to Skagen, a small fishing town, which has served as a hotspot of cultural tourism since the nineteenth century, which was the golden age of Danish painting. The city of Frederikshavn has got 23,339 inhabitants. Since the administrative reform in 2007 by which the number of municipalities were reduced to almost one-third (from 275 to 98), Frederikshavn has also been the name of the municipality in which the city of Frederikshavn is the capital. This municipality has got 61,576 inhabitants, and it belongs to the smallest region of Denmark, namely North Denmark, with only 0.58 million inhabitants (Statistics Denmark).

The city of Frederikshavn has got a glorious past as host to important shipbuilding industries, which started in 1870 with the foundation of

Frederikshavn Shipyard and Floating Dock (virk-info.dk). The shipbuilding and related industries formed the city for more than 100 years in terms of income basis, labour market, education and qualifications, urban planning and culture. The fishing industries, and later tourism, were other important sources of income, but the industrial culture prevailed as the identity of the city. No wonder, since between 2,000 and 2,500 workers were employed there up through the 1990s (Ugebrevet A4 nr. 35). When increased global competition (Ugebrevet A4 op. cit.) resulted in the closing down of the most important shipyard, Danyard, in 1999, and Orskov yard dismissed most of its employees shortly afterwards, the crisis that followed was not only a matter of serious job loss, but rather it also represented a complete loss of urban identity. Add to this the reduction in fishing quotas and the decline of tourism due to the abolition of tax-free sales on ferry boats in 1999. The result was a triple crisis which swept the city in 1999–2000.

However, located in the Danish periphery, Frederikshavn, as well as the whole region of North Denmark (see Figure 4.1), has been used to levels of unemployment well above the Danish mean. This explains why the region has been the object of regional development backed by the Danish government as well as from the EU structural funds, among other things in terms of a 'strategy plan' from 2004 (Ugebrevet A4 op. cit.). Demographic decline is also among the hardships of the city, in line with the general trend for Danish small cities. In particular, because young people seek education in bigger cities (Lorentzen and Krogh 2009). North Denmark is characterized by a traditional industrial economic

Figure 4.1 Map of North Denmark.

paradigm, while the big cities, and in particular Copenhagen, are developing within knowledge intensive and expanding industries like medical, IT and the media industries (Lorentzen 2012a: 110). Compared to Denmark as a whole, employment in the region is thus well above the mean in primary industries, food processing, machine building and construction, which are traditional sectors under pressure from global competition. On the other hand the knowledge intensive services such as business services, and to a lesser extent culture provision employ a smaller share of the population (Lorentzen and Krogh 2009).

While the position of Frederikshavn as the location of manufacturing has been challenged during the last decade and a half, what other potential does the city possess? It has been shown that, in terms of liveability, the city has considerable potential (Nordjyllands Amtsråd 2003). In an analysis of 45 cities of North Denmark, Frederikshavn actually ranked as number one. This is due to the beautiful location of the city at the open sea, surrounded by green hills. It is very accessible by way of train, ferryboats and highway. It has a nice city core, with remarkable historic qualities, including a powder magazine, a castle and big historic park. It has a particular urban character due to the combination of the hilly landscape, the industrial harbour and the historic buildings. It has a good supply of public and private services (upper secondary school, technical college) and culture, in fact the best outside of the regional capital. The image of the city is in particular connected to sports (ice-hockey), some famous fellow townsmen in fashion and media and some well-known companies. These historic qualities and the location at Kattegat both serve as background for the 'Days of Tordenskiold'. The 'Days of Tordenskiold' is an annual historic festival that started in 1998, just before the structural crisis of Frederikshavn peaked.

The Days of Tordenskiold

The idea

The Days of Tordenskiold is an annual historic festival, which has taken place in Frederikshavn since 1998. In 2010 the attendance at the festival had grown to 42,000 visitors. It was started by what proved to be a fiery soul in the development of the city, namely a deputy director of the production school, which is a training institution for unskilled and unemployed youth. The school was discussing meaningful work for the trainees to do in the workshops of the school. Inspired by articles by Rolf Jensen, and later by his books (Jensen 2006, Jensen 2002),[2] who prophesizes a new phase of human history in which narratives and myths will play a key role to firms, individuals and societies, the deputy leader posed the question of how to develop a new narrative of the city now that the industrial identity had become undermined?[3] The response to this became the setting up of a historic festival depicting a heroic past of the city. The trainees produced costumes and pieces of scenery, while the deputy director together with other people wrote a play. When the Tordenskiold Project started, little was known about the historic past, so people set out to construct one, based on various sources.

The historic core of the festival is a naval history of the locality of Fladstrand (the name of the then fishing village), as it evolved during part of the Great Nordic War between Denmark and Sweden between 1709 and 1720. Peter Wessel was a successful Norwegian naval officer employed in the Danish–Norwegian navy and ennobled in 1716 by the name of Tordenskiold. Tordenskiold is the most well-known Danish sea hero, and the name of Tordenskiold is well known to this day, in particular because his copperplate portrait decorates matchboxes in Denmark. The historic evidence of his whereabouts, deeds and experiences are documented in sixty-two letters which he wrote while his fleet was located in Fladstrand and Skagen from 1716 to 1717 to protect convoys going to Norway with supplies (Marineforeningen 2010). One letter in particular from January 1717 served as inspiration for the first play written, and the letters actually continue to inspire new events at the Days of Tordenskiold.[4] As such the name of Tordenskiold was able to serve as an efficient starting point for developing and communicating a new narrative.

The impression

The Days of Tordenskiold in June 2011 was the 14th festival of its kind. It took place over three days from Friday afternoon at 3 pm to Sunday evening at 10 pm. It was, as every year, located at the wharves, which are no longer as busy industrially as they once were. The wharves had been transformed into eighteenth-century sceneries including castle, cannon posts, marketplace, stages, and so on. Most important was perhaps the twelve big wooden sailing ships in the harbour from many different countries which represent a particularly picturesque scenery. The ships were open for visitors for some hours every day, and their staff was part of the party, dressed in costumes. The many volunteers, dressed in eighteenth-century costumes, were equally picturesque, part of the scenery and of the entertainment.

Most important of all the activities of the Days of Tordenskiold included a theatre play that takes place every night during the festival, inspired by Tordenskiold's use of Fladstrand and Skagen as a naval outpost. Special effects such as light, smoke and sound contributed to the spectacle, making it very impressive. In 2011 the play was written by Hans Nygaard, who is an acknowledged Danish author. The arrival of the King – an actor dressed as the Danish King Frederik IV – has been a key symbolic event of the festival every year. The King was, as always surrounded by noblemen, while he ceremoniously inspected 'his' ships. He also hosted a drinks reception for the 'nobility' – the city council and the like, on one of the ships. A spectacular performance which took place in the open water at Frederikshavn in 2009 was a vast open water 'sea battle' among ten historic wooden sailing ships. This year a video-recording from 2009 was shown on large screens.

In 2011 a long list of other activities were part of the programme. Not only were the inevitable cannon fire repeated daily along the waterfront, the traditionally dressed 'Soldiers of Tordenskiold' demonstrated their drill now and again during the three days. For the 2011 event the soldiers had even developed a whole tattoo performance, following the arrival of 'Tordenskiold' to his troops. The children were invited to 'go to school' as children did in 1717, and a particular theatre play for children was shown every day during the festival. Children were also invited to take trips on small sailing ships. Concerts of folk music played by known, as well as less known, artists were given several times every day. Also literary events were offered in a 'public library ship' arranged in 'Fulton', an earlier training ship, where daily readings and talks were offered in relation to local history and culture, and to Danish naval history. In between performances it was possible to buy food and drinks made from old recipes, and to buy eighteenth-century costumes and souvenirs. During the festival, local as well as foreign historic groups performed traditional dance and music and visited each other. Through these gatherings bonds were maintained with the European partner cities. The city was decorated to welcome the many potential customers, and a big procession on Saturday linked the central city with the wharf.[5]

The preparation

The preparation of the festival has, since its start in 1998, been at least as important as the realization of it. Working groups consisting of volunteers, work all year round with the preparation of costumes and activities. The number of volunteers has grown from about 50 in the start to close to 1,000 for the last couple of years (Marineforeningen 2010: 15). They are organized in a number of civic organizations, of which the Soldiers of Tordenskiold Fladstrand, is the most important with its 250 members.[6] In addition, the city has three historic societies dealing with shipbuilding, the maritime history and family histories.

In parallel, the professional management of the Foundation of Tordenskiold deals with the financial issues, to raise money for the event. The budget of the event is around 3.3 million Danish kroner (DKK). The municipal budget spends 1.1 million DKK annually, and entrance fees and sales plus sponsor contracts create around 2 million DKK. In 2011 the two private main sponsors were a local marine offshore service company and a regional bank.[7] Further revenues are generated by 'exportation' in the form of events organized and partly manned in other cities, so that in total the balance for 2010 was 4.4 million DKK.[8] There is no personal profit to be gained from the festival, as the year's generated surplus, including the exported activities, is invested in new activities the following year (Marineforeningen 2010: 15). Several sailing ships arrive at the festival at their own costs basically because they want to be part of the Tordenskiold Days. Local firms contribute with materials, equipment and technical knowledge, enabling among other things the impressive special effects of smoke, sound and light. Local restaurants and catering companies organize the food supply service at the festival.[9] The preparation of the festival thus includes volunteers, the port of Frederikshavn, and the local business community, and preparations take place during the year.

The organization today still relies on volunteers as its main body. It is divided into two parts, which are the Foundation of Tordenskiold consisting of a board, a coordination committee and a director (the only salaried staff) plus a great number of working groups on the one hand, and the soldiers of Tordenskiold Fladstrand, consisting of thematic working groups (such as the Children of Tordenskiold, the King's Life Guard, and so on) on the other hand (Madsen 2011). The organization is relatively complex and at the same time non-hierarchic with a large degree of autonomy for the volunteer groups. This is required to maintain the creativity and enthusiasm of the volunteers, which is the main driver of the project (Figure 4.2).[10]

The development of the festival

The development of the festival has taken place over the last 14 years and June 2012 was the 15th anniversary of the festival. During this period the organization has been gradually changed, but its core focus is still the same as it was in the beginning, to engage the citizens in the production of a new and positive narrative of the city. The first festival in 1998 was small. It was a project for the production school, attended by some citizens and a visiting group from Norway. It was a small evening event that took place for two nights. However, many locals watched the show and wanted to participate. They started the society called 'the Soldiers of Tordenskiold, Fladstrand' in 1999.[11] Every year the festival has grown in terms of number of volunteers, guests and participating wooden sailing ships. While the first festival received 1,200 guests, in 2010 the number of visitors that arrived was 42,000 (Marineforeningen 2010: 15). Famous historic ships, like *Georg Stage* (Denmark) the *Endeavour* (the Australian replica of Cook's ship), the *Standard* (Russia) and more recently the recovered and rebuilt *Göteborg III* (Sweden) have participated in the event.[12] The role of the production school as host and key producer of the activities has been changed, as the event became too big and complex for it to handle. Instead a separate organization, the Foundation of Tordenskiold and a voluntary unit, the Soldiers of Tordenskiold, have taken over the organizational responsibility.

In the beginning all work was voluntary, but with a base in the production school, now volunteer groups represent the body of the project and the work. A certain amount of commercialization and professionalization has also developed alongside the expansion. In 2003 the Foundation of Tordenskiold employed its first permanent director. The Foundation was established with a professional board of directors and a permanent address at the wharves. The Foundation represents a platform for the development of partnerships in terms of sponsorships. Sponsor contracts have been made with different local and regional companies in arrangements of co-branding for the benefit of the companies, the Festival and the locality. The establishment of a professional board has implied an increase of the knowledge and network assets accessible to the Festival. Thus the author of *The Dream Society*, Rolf Jensen (Jensen 2006), a Danish PR expert, a

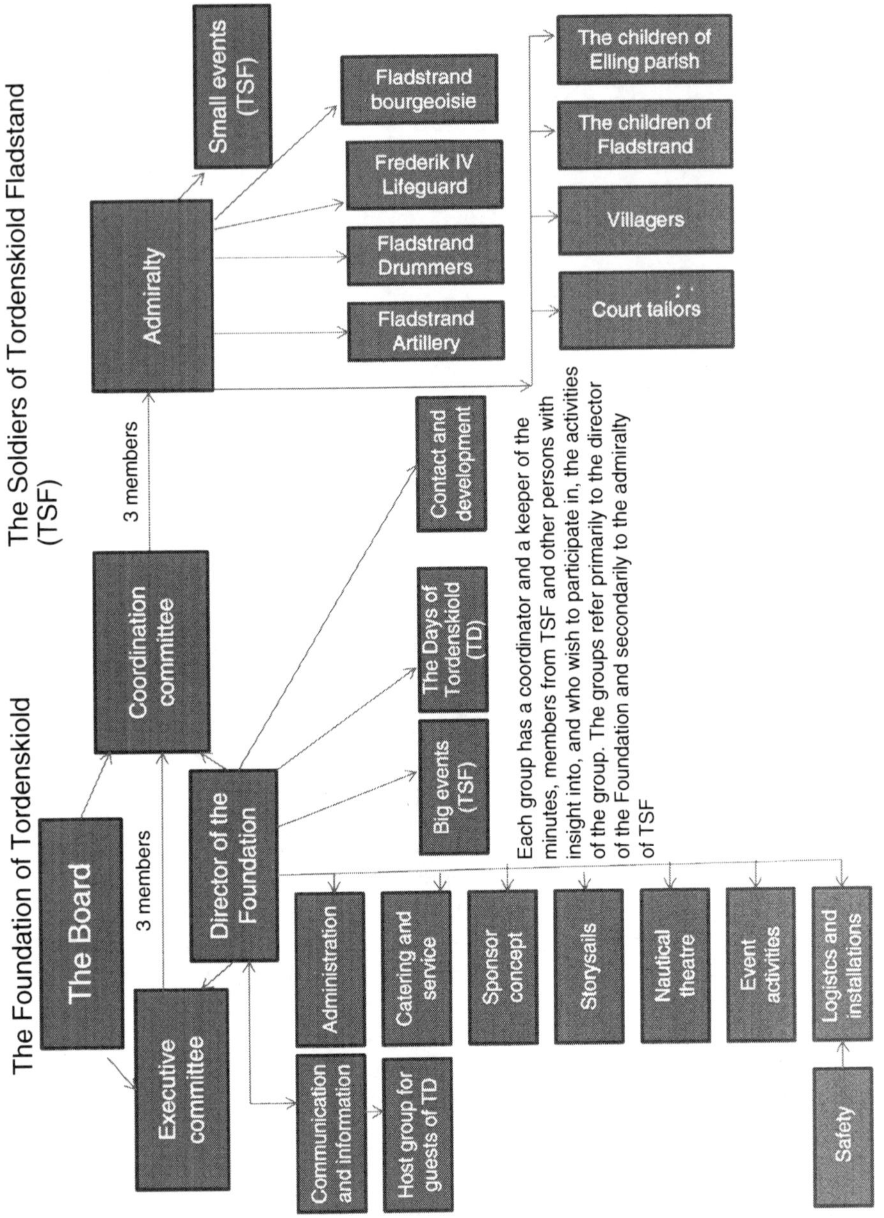

Figure 4.2 Organization chart of the Tordenskiold Project.
Source: Courtesy of the Foundation of Tordenskiold.

director of a regional bank, a representative of the port and of the municipality became members of the board, providing it with professional knowledge, new visions and access to physical and other resources.[13]

The Soldiers of Tordenskiold has become a well-organized voluntary association, consisting of several working groups, a newsletter and of course a home page.[14] They organize local events throughout the year, such as an annual celebration in honour of Tordenskiold's birthday, that takes place in the autumn, and they produce big events abroad such as the Tordenskiold event in Göteborg in August 2011.[15]

They have also been working on the development of commercial services. 'Dining with the King' was developed as a commercial service, which could be purchased by companies who wanted special entertainment at, for example, a conference dinner. The volunteers would perform as soldiers serving food for the conference guests on a sailing ship. The size and complexity of these commercial experience offerings has grown, and most recently the Soldiers of Tordenskiold arranged the 500th anniversary of the Royal Danish Navy at the naval base of Frederikshavn (2010) and the Jubilee of Aalborg Airport in the House of Arts in Frederikshavn (2011). In both cases the celebrations were developed as total theatre experiences.[16]

Not only the management has been professionalized, but also the artistic content. So far this can be seen in relation to the core event of the festival, the theatre play, which today is written by a professional playwright, directed by a professional director, and involves professional actors in the principal parts.[17]

In connection with the 2011 Festival, the Foundation of Tordenskiold published a songbook with Nordic folk songs, heroic poems and tales about Tordenskiold and his time. Singing together at parties is a tradition in Denmark, and the new song book was intended to fulfil a need among the many parties during the Festival. The aim was to strengthen the community among the Nordic participants and the locals.[18] At the same time the book would educate the locals about their history, or at least arouse their interest in learning more about it.

Another new development in 2010 and 2011 was the children's culture project, which enabled the development of a theatre play with child actors. Professionals from the Belgian Commedia dell' Arte in Belgium were contracted to develop an impressive play in a historic scenery within a huge tent.[19]

The Festival as brand and export project

The Festival is developing into an export product and a brand, not only for Frederikshavn but recently also for Denmark. Its key point is the maritime identity connected to the historic past, the industrial development, the naval base, international ferryboat connections, as well as to the outdoor recreation opportunities of Frederikshavn.

The festival groups have performed on several occasions as part of other events. As mentioned in 2010 the Foundation of Tordenskiold organized the celebration of the 500th anniversary of the Danish Navy. The event was enabled by 10,000 DKK from the municipal budget, which was considered an investment in branding as well as in networking among actors of the maritime sector.[20] From the perspective of the local government, the event can be seen as an effort to keep the base of the Danish Navy located in Frederikshavn, as this location is frequently discussed by the Danish Parliament.

In 2010, 2011 and 2012, Visit Denmark, the national Danish tourist organization, included 55 Soldiers of Tordenskiold and three sailing ships as part of a big marketing event in Oslo, promoting important tourist attractions of Denmark which included among other things Legoland. The soldiers performed in a historic scenery with booths, folk music and a naval battle. More than 100,000 people visited the event according to the organizers.[21]

In 2010, through the network of the Association of Festivals and Events (FED), the director of the Foundation of Tordenskiold was invited to South Korea to talk at a conference about the combination of citizens' involvement, cultural heritage, cultural identity and tourism related to the Days of Tordenskiold. Actually there was mutual inspiration, as the Danish speaker heard about the work of the Koreans in establishing a permanent historic City of the King, while the Koreans were keen to learn about civic involvement in cultural projects.[22] The balance for 2010 was that the 'project export' of Tordenskiold amounted to 955,000 DKK (Madsen 2011).

The future

The Days of Tordenskiold has been established as an annual event with a permanent organizational basis, and it has become part of the local identity of place. Locals are quoted as saying that they are proud of the city's ability to develop such an important event.[23] While a few years back a certain tension between a commercial approach and a civic approach was recognizable, for example, between ideas and intentions of branding versus civic identity-building, or between a focus on new commercial service products versus a focus on learning, today it seems that the growth of the festival itself has solved the contradiction by developing all aspects of it simultaneously. The original intentions of the Tordenskiold projects were actually to address both aspects.[24] Proof that the commercial focus has not become dominant is that during the last few years the cultural content of the festival has been strengthened considerably with the above-mentioned children's projects and the library and book projects respectively.

At present the Foundation together with the Soldiers of Tordenskiold are working to raise money for a permanent facility for performances, workshops and storage. The City of Tordenskiold is the name of the planned facility to be developed in a number of existing buildings on the wharf. The facility would enable the volunteers to focus more on their creative work and less on the hard work of moving around props and technical installations. It would also enable performances and events all year round (Madsen 2011).[25] According to the applicants, it can be regarded as a regional development project with the prospect of generating more than 12 million DKK in increased income to the region, equal to a multiplier effect of 3.3 (Madsen 2011).

This is to be connected with an organizational development. 'The Triangular Hat' is the name of an organization which includes citizens, business life and the municipality in a triangular umbrella organization within which all sorts of Tordenskiold initiatives can evolve with different purposes and leadership (civic, municipal or business) (Madsen 2011).[26]

The role of the Days of Tordenskiold in the locality

In 1998 the Days of Tordenskiold pioneered a long list of local festivals in Frederikshavn to be developed in the years that followed. Today the list of big annual events with regional and even international appeal is quite impressive for a small city. The list includes a couple of annual music festivals such as Rock in Frederikshavn, since summer 2003, and the Blues Festival of Frederikshavn, since winter 2006. Both were initiated by local civic groups and sports clubs. A Nordic Film Festival (since winter 2003) was initiated by a local fiery soul.[27] The Festival of Light, since 2004, was initiated by the local technical school and is now embedded in a public–private network (Freire-Gibb and Lorentzen 2011), a Festival of Icelandic horse riding (since winter 2010) was created by creative public servants.[28] A couple of bigger sports tournaments continue to attract many athletes and spectators.

The role of the Tordenskiold Project, and in particular the Days of Tordenskiold in the locality can be seen on different levels (Lorentzen 2007, Lorentzen 2008). It serves as a symbol of the change of the city from a traditional industrial city to an experience city. It symbolizes citizen involvement, and creativity. It motivates the formation of multiple networks on different geographic scales and experiments with new forms of governance (public–private–civic partnerships) and organization forms. It entails a great deal of learning for the volunteers. It generates economic value for the city, directly and indirectly, and it generates innovation in the form of new commercial service products. It can be argued that it has transformative power in challenging the discourses and practices prevailing in the city, thus paving the way for new development.

The role of culture festivals in local development

Festivals have become frequent in small cities, but what is their role more precisely? This role can be seen, on the one hand, as a qualitative change and, on the other, in terms of economic impacts. Karpinska-Krakowiak (2009) reflects on the more qualitative impacts that festivals may have. According to her, festivals offer a variety of forms of celebration and possibilities to both animate and dramatize the worlds around them (Karpinska-Krakowiak 2009: 338). Festivals act as urban image devices. They also integrate people and establish new networks among them. Because they induce commonly shared experiences, and encourage a feeling of excitement and pleasure, this common feeling can be transferred to other subjects or places such as the city. Therefore the festival enables the development of positive urban images (Karpinska-Krakowiak 2009: 338). This is not only a matter of pleasure, but also of socialization and even education (Karpinska-Krakowiak 2009: 441).

This analysis applies nicely to the Days of Tordenskiold. The Festival animates the wharves and dramatizes the local history. It has a high degree of civic involvement, shared experiences and pleasure. It creates a sense of belonging to the community and it educates the audience and the participants in local history and customs. The atmosphere contributes to the image of Frederikshavn as a pleasurable place to be for guests as well as locals and stimulates the emergence of new social and professional networks.

What if festivals produce images that are not historically correct? This is what happened in a Polish festival in Lodtz. This festival aimed at creating a picture of the city as one which integrated four different cultures (Russian, German, Jewish and Polish), in spite of the fact that they had not all been manifest in the development of the city and more particularly that they had in no way been integrated with each other (Karpinska-Krakowiak 2009). Nevertheless the Festival of Four Cultures became a success for the city of Lodtz by producing a new perception of the city as open, hospitable, creative and versatile. It can be argued that this new image is produced by and actually reflected in the festival, even if its referential authenticity is not historically correct. Experiences such as festivals may thus have enough transformative power to change the urban image and the identity of place.

Days of Tordenskiold does not entirely reflect a correct referential authenticity either, because much of the narrative is made up by the volunteers. This lack of referential authenticity does not seem to disturb the experience that guests and volunteers have. On the contrary it adds to the quality of the narrative that it is a result of the imagination and creativity of the participants. In this way the Days of Tordenskiold is not just an experience offering (Pine II and Gilmore 1999: 165) to entertain the public for a few days. It reaches into the lives of the volunteers, the residents and the guests, and even the city, both before and after the event by engaging them in preparations and networks. As such the Days of Tordenskiold can be categorized as a transformative event (Pine II and Gilmore 1999: 166ff.), and that is exactly what the original idea of the Days of Tordenskiold was about in 1998 – and what it continues to be.

Festivals as a tool for local economic development are connected with the increase of the demand for local products and services, and job creation in local businesses, community and business entrepreneurship, and to artistic creativity and innovation. In economic geographic terms this relates to the possible multiplier effects, spillovers, and increased competitiveness through innovation which can be generated with festival activities as points of departure. Empirically it is of course hard to isolate and document such effects, but statistical reference can be given to short-term effects on the demand side measured by an increase in overnight stays and audience expenditure, and long-term effects in terms of industrial structural change such as emergence of experience industries or clusters, and job creation.

The economic impact of festivals have recently been documented in consultancy reports from Denmark and the UK (BOP consulting 2011; NIRAS 2010; Visit Denmark 2011). NIRAS and Visit Denmark focus on music festivals while BOP covers many kinds of culture festivals. For example, NIRAS suggests that Skanderborg Festival (Denmark), a popular rock festival which lasts for four to five days and hosts more than 25,000 guests, generates 42 million DKK in additional tourism turnover at the regional level and 0.8 million DKK at the national level (NIRAS 2010). This festival is comparable in size to Tordenskiold Days, and the figures from Skanderborg thus suggest a considerable economic importance of the Days of Tordenskiold. Similarly BOP consulting (2011) analyses the Edinburgh festivals and not surprisingly finds that there are considerable economic gains from the increase in tourism (overnight stays, audience expenditure). Apart from a boost in tourism incomes, BOP points out another quite important economic perspective, namely that the volunteers increased their skills and thus their employability. They increased their self-esteem and their willingness to try new things (BOP consulting 2011: 54–55). This latter finding suggests that the organization of festivals helps transform local economies by creating new dynamics of learning.

The idea that festivals may create new dynamics of learning is the topic of Freire-Gibb and Lorentzen (2011). They have documented the emergence of a new cluster in connection with a local festival, involving the creation of an innovative network and educational activities. That festivals and other culture and experience offerings may merge into a new regional development pattern is observed by Scott (2010) who has documented the long-term economic transformation of a British rural region, based on the local culture and experience offerings.

Whether festivals generate wider impacts in terms of the localization of firms and population is an interesting question, which is difficult to answer. Bradley *et al.* (2002) have studied the role of urban images in location decisions by meeting organizers in two British towns. They show that urban image was one of several factors taken into consideration, but not the most important one. While their findings justify the use of place branding in urban development strategies, branding cannot be regarded in isolation (Bradley *et al.* 2002: 69). Hansen and Niedomysl (2009), based on evidence from Sweden, have shown that highly skilled labour (the creative class) is not very focused on cultural amenities when they settle. This is contrary to what could be expected according to the creative class hypothesis. Other location factors seem to be more important. This suggests that festivals such as the Days of Tordenskiold cannot be expected to generate important indirect impacts (location of firms and population) on the local economy.

In sum, festivals such as the Days of Tordenskiold can be seen to have a number of important *direct* effects on the local economy and society. They transform the urban image and the identity of place. They generate a growth of demand for local services, particularly tourist services. They stimulate learning and the development of new competencies among the labour force. They serve as point of departure for new localized innovative networks, and they may contribute to the development of a regional culture and experience economy through forward and backward linkages and spillovers. They cannot, however, be shown to lead to substantial *indirect* impacts in terms of extended location dynamics related to firms and population.

Conclusion and perspectives

Faced with the pressure from big cities functioning as magnets of people and investment in new growth sectors, small cities have embarked on soft urban development strategies focused on their distinctiveness regarding experience consumption opportunities. The organization of festivals is frequently used as a way to join forces and produce spectacular experience offerings with a broad appeal. Danish small cities are no exception, and this chapter has highlighted one of the most spectacular culture projects developed in a small city in Denmark: the Days of Tordenskiold in Frederikshavn. This project was a direct response to severe industrial decline, and its aim was to establish a new urban identity, based on the maritime – and heroic – history of the locality. Fiery souls and 'civic gold' have been the main ingredients in the project which has evolved in size and complexity over its fifteen years of existence. Living history – or story living – was the approach by which up to 1,000 locals have involved themselves in preparations for the annual event in permanent working groups. History, urban landscapes and seascapes are mobilized by the activities in theatre plays, readings, performances, sales, visits to sailing ships and social gatherings in the temporary experience space at the wharves.

The local government and private sponsors support the Tordenskiold Project, which has also established itself with a Foundation, a permanent board and a large number of working groups in a complex and flexible organization. This organization produces the continuously growing three-day festival, as well as an increasing number of more commercial experience services for regional as well as extra regional partners. The scale of the market and of the cooperative linkages has outgrown the regional level and today reaches as far as South Korea. The Tordenskiold Project seems to maintain a subtle balance between commercial and welfare objectives. Earnings are thus recycled in the Project, enabling investment into future activities. At present a major concern is how to facilitate the voluntary working groups better by purchasing permanent facilities for storage, workshops and small events.

Festivals such as the Days of Tordenskiold and the Tordenskiold Project hold the potential to induce qualitative as well as economic urban change. They act as urban image devices, and contribute to establish new images of the city among locals and visitors. These images are often used in branding campaigns, but they also form the identity of place, the connection that people feel to the place where they live. Festivals enable people to socialize, to learn and to enjoy a better quality of life. By engaging people to a large extent, festivals can also have transformative roles at different levels.

From the perspective of local economic development, festivals such as the Days of Tordenskiold, generate income based on direct demand and multiplier effects, which are far from negligible, at local, regional and even national levels.

The many creative activities of the volunteers entail the learning of and openness towards new things and this competence is in high demand in the labour market and in entrepreneurial endeavours, and can be seen as a precondition for the much-needed industrial transformation. The social networks may also transform into business or even innovative networks, and the social capital is enhanced, for the benefit of the local and regional economy. The enhanced urban image translates into growth in tourism-related trades. More far-reaching industrial transformation is however not an immediate result of better urban images of small cities as many other factors than culture offerings determine where people and capital settle geographically.

Acknowledgements

I would like to thank the director of the Foundation of Tordenskiold, Jan Michael Madsen, for letting me interview him on several occasions and for his help in getting the factual information provided in this chapter right. Also Steen Heftholm from Frederikshavn Municipality has on several occasions been very helpful, with interviews and otherwise, and I owe him my thanks. Without the support of both, this chapter would not have been possible.

Notes

1 Statistics Denmark: Nyt fra Danmarks Statistik nr. 171, 12 April 2011: Byopgørelsen, 1 January 2011.
2 Interview with Jan Michael Madsen, director of the Foundation of Tordenskiold, 12 December 2011.
3 Interview with Jan Michael Madsen, director of the Foundation of Tordenskiold, 17 September 2007.
4 Interview with Jan Michael Madsen, director of the Foundation of Tordenskiold, 12 December 2011.
5 See also the official webpage http://tordenskiold.dk.linux10.unoeuro-server.com, accessed 26 November 2011.
6 Interview with Jan Michael Madsen, director of the Foundation of Tordenskiold, 12 December 2011.
7 Source: www.tordenskiold.dk/stoetter/hovedsponsorer, accessed 26 November 2011.
8 Interview with Jan Michael Madsen, director of the Foundation of Tordenskiold, 12 December 2011.
9 Interview with Jan Michael Madsen, director of the Foundation of Tordenskiold, 17 September 2007.
10 Interview with Jan Michael Madsen, director of the Foundation of Tordenskiold, 12 December 2011.
11 Interview with Jan Michael Madsen, director of the Foundation of Tordenskiold, 12 December 2011.
12 Interview with Jan Michael Madsen, director of the Foundation of Tordenskiold, 12 December 2011.
13 Interview with Jan Michael Madsen, director of the Foundation of Tordenskiold, 17 September 2007.
14 The homepage address of the Soldiers of Tordenskiold is http://tby.dk.
15 Source: www.tordenskiold.dk, accessed 26 November 2011.

16 Interview with Jan Michael Madsen, director of the Foundation of Tordenskiold, 12 December 2011.
17 Nordjyske, 22 June 2011.
18 Nordjyske, 22 June 2011.
19 Nordjyske, 26 June 2011; Nordjyske, 17 June 2010.
20 Source: www.frederikshavn.dk (accessed 5 December 2011).
21 Interview with Jan Michael Madsen, director of the Foundation of Tordenskiold, 12 December 2011 and kanal Frederikshavn at www.kanalfrederikshavn.dk/vis/nyhed/tordenskiolds-soldater-indtog-aker-brygge-i-oslo (accessed 16 December 2011).
22 Source: http://nordjyske.dk/artikel/10/5/2/3708104/3/sydkorea-har-bud-efter-tordenskioldsdagene (accessed 16 December 2011).
23 Interview with Jan Michael Madsen, director of the Foundation of Tordenskiold, 17 September 2007.
24 Interview with Jan Michael Madsen, director of the Foundation of Tordenskiold, 12 December 2011.
25 Interview with Jan Michael Madsen, director of the Foundation of Tordenskiold, 12 December 2011.
26 Interview with Jan Michael Madsen, director of the Foundation of Tordenskiold, 12 December 2011.
27 Source: www.byportalfrederikshavn.dk/index.php?ID=11&lang=da&hid=6, accessed 26 November 2011 (but no longer available).
28 Interview with Steen Heftholm, public servant of Municipality of Frederikshavn, 22 April 2009.

References

Albrechts, L., Healey, P. and Kunzmann, K. (2003) 'Strategic Spatial Planning and Regional Governance in Europe', *Journal of the American Planning Association*, 69(2): 113–129.

Bell, D. and Jayne, M. (2006) *Small Cities. Urban Experience Beyond the Metropolis*, 1st edn, Abingdon: Routledge.

Bianchini, F. (1993) 'Remaking European Cities: The Role of Cultural Policies', in F. Bianchini and M. Parkinson (eds), *Culture Policy and Urban Regeneration*, 1st edn, Manchester: Manchester University Press.

BOP consulting (2011) *Edinburgh Festivals Impact Study. Final Report*, BOP consulting.

Bradley, A., Hall, T. and Harrison, M. (2002) 'Selling Cities', *Cities*, 19(1): 61–70.

Duxbury, N. (2012) 'Shifting Strategies and Contexts for Culture in Small City Planning: Interlinking Quality of Life, Economic Development, Downtown Vitality, and Community Sustainability', in A. Lorentzen and B. van Heur (eds), *Cultural Political Economy of Small Cities*, 1st edn, London and New York: Routledge.

Evans, G. (2001) *Cultural Planning. An Urban Renaissance?*, 1st edn, London and New York: Routledge.

Florida, R. (2002) *The Rise of the Creative Class – and How it's Transforming Work, Leisure, Community and Everyday Life*, New York: Basic Books.

Freire-Gibb, L.C. and Lorentzen, A. (2011) 'A Platform for Local Entrepreneurship: The Lighting Festival of Frederikshavn', *Local Economy*, 26(3): 157–169.

Hall, H.M. and Donald, B. (2012) 'Clarifying Creativity and Culture in a Small City on the Canadian Periphery: Challenges and Opportunities in Greater Sudbury', in A. Lorentzen and B. van Heur (eds), *Cultural Political Economy of Small Cities*, 1st edn, London and New York: Routledge.

Hall, P. (2001) *Cities in Civilization*, New York: Fromm International.

Hansen, H.K. and Niedomysl, T. (2009) 'Migration of the Creative Class: Evidence from Sweden', *Journal of Economic Geography*, 9(2): 191–206.
Healey, P. (2007) *Urban Complexity and Spatial Strategies*, London: Routledge.
Jensen, R. (2002) *Heartstorm*, Viby J: JP Bøger.
——— (2006) *Dream Society*, 2nd edn, København: Børsens Forlag.
Karpinska-Krakowiak, M. (2009) 'Festivalization of the City. Contemporary Examples', *Urban People*, 11(2): 338–350.
Lorentzen, A. (2007) *Frederikshavn indtager 'The Global Catwalk'*, Aalborg: Department of Development and Planning.
——— (2008) *Knowledge Networks in the Experience Economy. An Analysis of Four Flagship Projects in Frederikshavn*, Aalborg: Department of Development and Planning.
——— (2009) 'Cities in the Experience Economy', *European Planning Studies*, 17(2): 829–845.
——— (2012a) 'Sustaining Small Cities through Leisure, Culture and the Experience Economy', in A. Lorentzen and B. van Heur (eds), *Cultural Political Economy of Small Cities*, 1st edn, London and New York: Routledge.
——— (2012b) 'Yderområder I Danmark. Hvad er problemet?', in J.L. Christensen (ed.), *Nordjyske udviklingsperspektiver*, Aalborg: Aalborg University Press.
Lorentzen, A. and Krogh, R. (2009) *Oplevelsesøkonomi, udvikling og planlægning i nordjyske kommuner*, Aalborg: Department of Development and Planning.
Lorentzen, A. and van Heur, B. (eds) (2012) *Cultural Political Economy of Small Cities*, 1st edn, London and New York: Routledge.
Madsen, J.M. (2011) *Tordenskiold som ramme*. Frh 2.0. Ref Type: Slide.
Marineforeningen(2010) 'Tordenskiolddagene i Frederikshavn', *Marineforeningens Tidsskrift Under Dannebrog*, 97(3): 12–15.
Miles, S. (2006) 'Small City – Big Ideas: Culture-led Regeneration and the Consumption of Places', in D. Bell and M. Jayne (eds), *Small Cities. Urban Experiences Beyond the Metropolis*, 1st edn, London: Routledge.
NIRAS (2010) *Analyse af danske musikfestivaler*, NIRAS.
Nordjyllands Amtsråd (2003) *Bykvaliteter og bosætning i nordjyske byer*, Aalborg: Nordjyllands Amt.
Pine, II, J.B. and Gilmore, J.H. (1999) *The Experience Economy*, Boston: Harvard Business School Press.
Schroll, S. and Søgaard, V. (2011) *Knækker Danmark – eller knager det bare?*, Esbjerg: Center for Landdistriktforskning.
Scott, A.J. (2010) 'The Cultural Economy of Landscape and Prospects for Peripheral Development in the Twenty First Century: The Case of the English Lake District', *European Planning Studies*, 18(10): 1567–1589.
Stevenson, D. (2004) "Civil Gold" Rush. Cultural Planning and the Politics of the Third Way', *International Journal of Cultural Policy*, 10(1): 119–131.
Virk-info.dk available at: www.virk-info.dk.
Visit Denmark (2011) *Festivalen som trækplaster*.

5 Culture as a generator of regional development and economic growth

Skagen and Horsens

Lise Lyck

Introduction

This chapter presents and analyses two cases in Denmark where culture has been the main driver of change and economic development. The first case is about the city of Skagen in Northern Jutland. The transformation began at the end of the nineteenth century when painters were attracted to Northern Jutland by the light, the local fisherman life and the village itself (Gyldendal 2012a). The painters settled down in the city of Skagen and attracted authors and other artists to join (Region Nordjylland 2012). It is a story about using art and culture to transform a village into a city and to develop a region's economy through art and tourism. It is also a story about creating a fashionable holiday destination and using the name Skagen as a brand to increase regional economy by adding a design product to the complex.

The second case is about the city of Horsens. At the end of the twentieth century Horsens was a city primarily known as the location of the Danish state prison. There was zero economic growth in the region and its citizens were moving to other places. The municipality council and some engaged local citizens decided to change the situation by using events and experience economy. Today, the state prison has become a hotel which is a tourist attraction and Horsens and the surrounding region have developed into a centre for culture and events that attract people from other parts of Denmark as well as internationally. Furthermore, it has become a location where the Danish state hosts international meetings.

These two success cases are presented and compared, with the aim of identifying similarities and differences. This chapter ends with a conclusion of what is needed for culture to create change as well as generate economic development and economic growth.

Two decisive questions on the perception of the relation between culture and economics have for many years been the following:

- Is culture mainly an *expenditure* (consumption), implying that culture is a part of private and public consumption?

- Is culture a *production factor* implying that culture is a necessary factor in order to create output in a society?

These two perceptions are found in research and in politics. Looking at culture as a part of consumption is the most common, however, the perception of culture as a production factor that creates economic growth is also widespread and the subject of many studies.

It was developed and included in the highly acknowledged concepts of cultural capital (Throsby 2001) and social capital (Putman 1993; Portas 1998). In these, social capital is defined as the norms and networks that enable people to act collectively. Furthermore, the perception of culture as production has been widely applied in Germany; see, for instance, the Munich studies that make use of the input-output analysis. The perception of culture as a production factor has also been the core element in the development of *instrumental* experience economy and related concepts dealing with culture as an instrument to create economic growth. Therefore, this chapter takes its departure in culture being a production factor and a generator of regional development.

It must also be noted that culture as such is a concept that can be defined and perceived in a narrow sense (fine art) or it can be perceived in a broader sense including almost everything in daily life. In this chapter the broad concept is applied.

Short presentation of the theories of the calculation

This chapter shortly presents the theoretical approaches applied in Denmark and also the main ways of calculating the impact of culture as a production factor in a broad sense. Furthermore, the chapter presents two different successful cases of culture being the driver of an economic transformation of a society.

The theories presented solely deal with the instrumental perspectives. The most well-known theories are: (1) cultural mapping and planning (Colin Mercer); (2) the 3Ts (Richard Florida); (3) experience economy as developed by Pine and Gilmore; and (4) creative industries (Richard Caves).

Colin Mercer

Colin Mercer is the main exponent for *cultural mapping* and *planning*. The ideas of cultural mapping and planning originated in Australia, Canada, Columbia and the UK. In order to create visibility and to focus on cultural assets the method of cultural mapping and planning was elaborated and one of the main contributors has been Colin Mercer (2002). Normally, cultural resources include and often start from traditional art, but they also include a necessary conceptual broadening of the meaning of culture. These resources are normally not counted or registered as resources and therefore cultural mapping is needed. The calculation includes counting the number of museums, festivals, natural attractions, etc. When the counting is finished a strategy is created in order to make a cultural planning and policy. The process of cultural mapping and planning requires consultation and negotiation with local government officials, librarians, architects, planners in the community organizations and local people.

In short, cultural mapping is an important instrument to investigate the size and form of cultural assets available in a society. Based on the cultural mapping and the cultural planning a policy can be developed and it will often take its departure from a point of view where culture is seen as a generator of economic growth.

It is one of the most applied methods in municipalities when culture as a generator of economic growth is on the agenda. For instance, the method is used in the Danish cities Frederikshavn, Vejle, Elsinore (Kulturhavn Kronborg 2012) and Herning (Herning Messehaller 2012).

Richard Florida

Richard Florida has formulated a theory for instruments to promote both economic and regional development. In his book *The Rise of the Creative Class* (2002) he developed a theory based on three decisive factors, the so-called 3Ts – Technology, Talent and Tolerance. If a corporation/city/region has all the 3Ts it will be possible to attract creative labour in order to innovate and create economic growth. The basic idea is that when the creative labour is attracted the capital will follow and innovative corporations will be established. To attract creative labour it is necessary to have a diversified society, cultural offerings, from sports activities to theatres, with both active and passive participation, a high level of quality in schools and universities and a government/governance system that promotes and supports an infrastructure that is attractive for the creative people.

The decision-makers must invest in attracting open-minded people with higher education and creative competencies and a society that favours such human capital development. At the macro level it demands an economic policy that invests in culture, schools, universities, sports, a green environment, hospitals, etc. Thus, the macro environment can be seen as a production where the human resources are the decisive factors for achieving economic growth.

The model has been applied successfully in Horsens. However, no other positive correlation to economic growth has been identified in applied studies of areas where the 3Ts have been implemented in Demark, such as Lolland.

Pine and Gilmore

Pine and Gilmore published the book *The Experience Economy* (1999). They analyse the development in society and argue that commodities and services are no longer enough to satisfy the consumer. Corporations must create experiences for their consumers if they wish to achieve success in a global world with increasing competition. The corporation can set a frame for the experience, but it is the consumer that creates the experience individually as a reaction to the frames. The ultimate state of an experience is achieved when a transformation of the consumer's perception has taken place by the use of the offerings of experiences.

Pine and Gilmore's main model is the model identifying what constitutes an experience, the 4E model. The 4Es include: entertainment, education, escapism, aestheticism as well as *passive* and *active* participation and *absorption* and *immersion*.

This model has been an essential for the way the city of Horsens has included experiences in their economic development policy.

Richard Caves

In *Creative Industries* (2000) the contrasts between art and commerce are studied. The outcome is a characteristic of the creative industries and their role and impact in the market economy. It is found that creative industries, which include music, fashion, design, books, games, films, etc. (the 14 industries) are drivers of economic growth and new trends. This in turn, is used as an argument for allocating public grants to these industries. This idea is also found in Danish economic policy and integrated in the economic growth based on culture as seen in Skagen and other Danish cities going for economic development based on culture.

Decision-making on cultural projects

The economic impact of culture and experiences is difficult to measure, due to the immaterial nature of culture and services in general. It is why most decision-making on cultural projects in Denmark up until now has been based on a political evaluation without any economic impact calculations. However, the decision-making is undergoing a change and different methods of analysis are being applied that aid in measuring the economic impact.

The most applicable methods to use are the cost-benefit analysis and the input/output analysis as they intend to include all aspects of the economic impact.

A cost-benefit analysis is an investment analysis that includes costs and the value of the production (benefits) of the investment. The method can be used to both forecast and determine future gains of an investment, but also to measure the impact of a previous investment.

The question a cost-benefit analysis seeks to answer is whether the net present value (NPV) of the investment is positive. In order to answer this, all the costs and benefits have to be identified, including both public and private monetary and non-monetary costs and benefits, such as externalities, including derived indirect costs and benefits.

As of now Skagen has introduced this type of calculation for the first time. It has been done in connection with a project on the enlargement of the harbour, where the derived impacts have been calculated. Gemba Seafood Consulting A/S and Rambøll Management have made the calculations with support from the European Fund for Regional Development. Based on the investment of 275 million DKK, the outcome is calculated to create an annual extra income of 280 million DKK and an increase in the number of jobs by 280 full-time positions. The calculations are based on indirect income creation, being 0.7 times the direct income created. The number of jobs is calculated as one full employment job per million DKK in income created. The initial phasing period is estimated to be five years (GEMBA 2011; Rambøll 2011).

Input-output analysis measures the input needed to achieve output or what output can be achieved by the use of different inputs in the production function. An input-output analysis is often a part of the national account and can thereby measure the impact on income (gross domestic product) and employment. The method makes use of income multipliers and technical coefficients. This method is widely applied in Germany, however, it has only been applied to a minor extent in Denmark, where it has been used to measure the economic impact of theatres (Lyck 2010).

To conclude, a cost-benefit analysis is an investment analysis, while an input-output analysis is an analysis based on a production function. They can supplement each other in the decision-making process and also in evaluating the economic impact of the decisions made. They are presented here because there is a trend in Denmark and an interest in proving that culture has an economic impact on society. Calculations based on an economic analysis seem to be needed to convince politicians to financially support culture, due to the increased focus on the willingness to pay and economic reasoning as the primary influences for public decision-making.

Regional development

Denmark got a regional reform from January 2007 (Indenrigs- og Sundhedministeriet 2004 and Indenrigs- og Sundhedministeriet 2005). The prior fourteen counties were reduced to five regions, as seen in Figure 5.1. The cases presented in the following section are Skagen and Horsens, both situated in Jutland.

The two cases presented are success stories with more than a hundred years between them. They are intended as learning cases presenting different perspectives of success stories, where culture and events transformed the respective society, i.e. the culture and events were applied as production factors of input in order to create regional economic development.

Skagen is situated in the region of Northern Denmark (North Jutland). In Figure 5.1 Skagen is the municipality far up north. Skagen takes its name from the region, which projects into the waters between the North Sea and the straits of Denmark. Skagen is considered the boundary between the Skagerrak (named after Skagen) and the Kattegat. Furthermore, from January of 1983 the number of municipalities in Denmark was reduced from 298 to 98, resulting in the municipality Skagen becoming a part of the municipality named Frederikshavn.

Horsens is situated in the Mid Jutland region of Denmark. In the map in Figure 5.1 you can find Horsens close to Vejle. Horsens continued to be a municipality after the municipality reform. The population of the north region of Denmark is 0.58 million and the population size of the Mid Jutland region is 1.268 million.

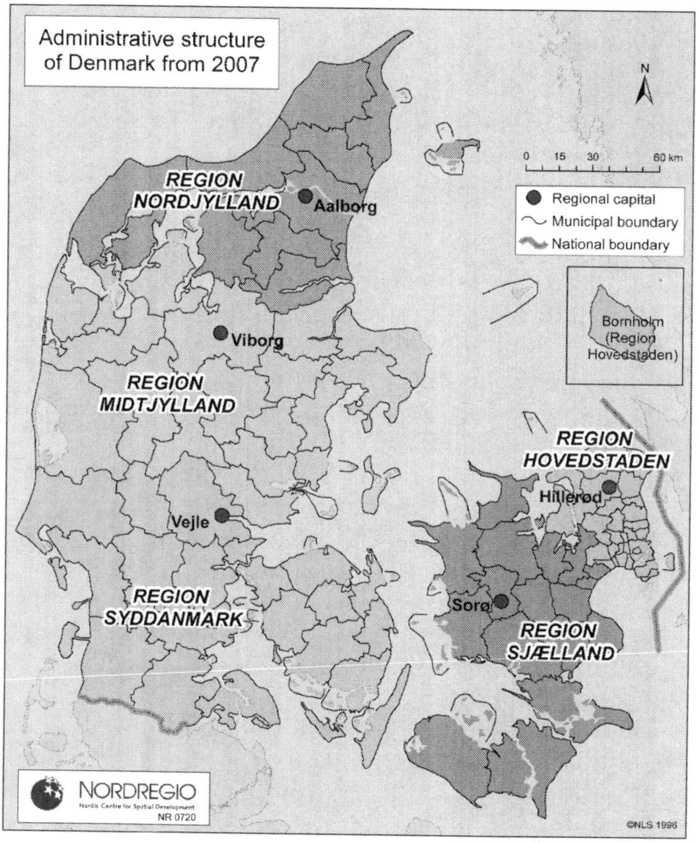

Figure 5.1 The five Danish Regions since January 2007.
Source: Nordregio.

The total population of Denmark is 5.5 million, and the north region of Denmark, Region North Jutland is the smallest of the Danish regions.

Since the reform of the municipalities, the Mid Jutland region of Denmark has spent a bigger proportion of their budget on culture and tourism than previously and more than the average spending of regions in Denmark, due to the inspiration of the experiences from Horsens. The largest municipality in Denmark, Ringkøbing-Skjern municipality in the region Mid Jutland increased the investment in culture and tourism from the index number of 100 in 2007 to index 115 in 2009 and to 117 in 2011 (Lyck 2012).

The municipality Frederikshavn, that now includes Skagen, has also tried to make use of the experiences from Skagen, by investing in experience economy and tourism. Furthermore, most of the municipalities in the northern region of Denmark have changed their spending pattern and devoted more money to tourism and culture than before the reform. It is currently still too early to acknowledge the economic impact of those investments.

Skagen

Skagen is a small city with 8,500 inhabitants. It is a part of the municipality Frederikshavn and is situated in the region of Northern Jutland. Its history goes back to the early Middle Ages when fishing was its primary industry.

In 1413 Skagen earned the right to become an official city. By the sixteenth century, it was a major settlement for its location, with approximately 2,000 farmers making their living there. It was an unusual city; it had no streets or square, but rather consisted of only a few scattered buildings.

At the end of the sixteenth century, Skagen was violently demolished by storms and floods, and by the seventeenth century the fishing industry was declining. The city had no hinterland trade and therefore had to settle for fishing for personal consumption only. However, Skagen's isolated location was the reason for its transformation into one of the four artist colonies that favoured impressionism (the others being Bornholm, Funen and Odsherred).

The painters were especially attracted by the light, the colours and the fishermen's lives. Their paintings became popular and famous and this attracted more artists to visit and to settle down in Skagen in the late 1870s. Among the most famous are Anna Ancher, Holger Drachmann, Laurits Tuxen, Michael Ancher, Oscar Björck, Marie Krøyer and P.S. Krøyer (Skagensmalerne 2012; Gyldendal 2012b). Anna Ancher (married to Michael Ancher) was the only one of Skagen's painters that was born in Skagen. The main theme of her paintings was the local population.

Michael Ancher was born in Bornholm and was educated at the art academy in Copenhagen. He made big compositions of the fisherman and their harsh lives. Among his paintings is the very well-known painting *Vil han klare pynten?* (*Will he round the point?*) from 1879. Marie Krøyer was born in Frederiksberg and was married to P.S. Krøyer. She was very interested in design and in the atmospheres of rooms. After divorcing P.S. Krøyer, she married a Swedish composer Hugo Alfvén and moved to Sweden. P.S. Krøyer was born in Norway but grew up in Denmark where he was educated at the art academy in Copenhagen. Furthermore, he went to Paris in order to further educate himself in the art of painting. He was well known for his portraits, which were sold at high prices. Today he is mostly known for his paintings of people walking on the beach especially his painting *Sommeraften på Skagens Sønderstrand* (*Summer evening at Skagen's Sønderbeach*). This painting is one of the most copied paintings in Denmark, hanging on the walls of many Danish homes. Holger Drachmann was born in Copenhagen and started his career as a marine painter. Later he started writing too. A very famous example of his writing is a midsummer song that is still sung on Midsummer's Eve in Denmark. The group of painters also included Laurits Tuxen, Viggo Johansen, Christian Krohg and Oscar Björck (Skagen Guide 2010).

Infrastructure was developed in Skagen and it began to resemble a city with buildings along the newly constructed streets giving rise to shopping and trade. After the construction of new hotels, Skagen became a popular meeting place and tourism began to emerge. It was a transformation from a city founded on fishing to a service based city with tourism as the main industry. The transformation was entirely caused by the artists and the culture of the city.

Both summer houses and hotels emerged as part of the tourist accommodation development and it became fashionable to spend the summer holiday in Skagen. The tourists consisted of the wealthy upper-class which gave rise to many galleries in Skagen.

Today, Skagen is still, in relation to the size of the population, one of the places with the most galleries in Denmark. Furthermore, sculptures have been placed around the city in order to strengthen the visibility and closeness of art to the city. As the tourism primarily consists of the wealthy upper-class Skagen has also been closely connected to sailing. Sailing enthusiasts commonly sail between Norway, Sweden and Denmark, and in that connection spend some days in Skagen. Longer tourist stays in Skagen mainly consist of trips to summer homes, which is a popular way to spend the holiday, especially for people from Denmark and Norway. Shorter tourist stays are also popular, especially for Danes and international sailors.

The development has transformed the city of Skagen to a quality brand that can function as a platform for new productions. This can be seen in the fact that design now plays an important role for Skagen's economy. The city of Skagen is a recognized brand and a unique selling point, utilized by Skagen Design. Skagen Design's logo symbolizes the meeting of Skagerrak and the Kattegat Seas that surround Skagen. Skagen Design are mostly known for their watches (with retail prices around 150 USD), which are very successful particularly in the US market. The idea behind Skagen Design goes back to 1990, where the watches were originally thought to be used as company presents, bearing a logo with the name of the company (Skagen Design 2006). The annual turnover has increased to close to 100 million USD.

Skagen Design serves as a good example of how further development of an art-based economy can take place when art is seen as a production factor in a dynamic perspective. The development in Skagen has been closely connected to the building of a dynamic cluster around the basic cultural change.

The large economic impact of tourism has also affected the population of Skagen. Skagen experienced the greatest population growth between about 1930 to the mid-1960s, when the population rose from 4,000 to 11,500, primarily in relation to the increased tourism.

However, even though the tourism growth continued, after 1970 and through the mid-1980s the population in Skagen began to decrease drastically and today it has approximately 10,000 inhabitants. The main reasons for the smaller number of inhabitants are the higher real estate prices in Skagen compared to fixed property outside of Skagen as well as the high cost of daily consumer goods. Therefore, a majority of the people employed in Skagen live outside of Skagen in order to avoid the high cost of living there.

Skagen's development is an example of a transformation of a city generated by culture and art. Today, it is a holiday destination especially for wealthier people. It has a high quality brand and image. Fish is served in the many restaurants throughout Skagen, but the primary source of income is the service offered to the tourists. The complex has been further developed with productions based on Skagen as a quality brand.

Recently, Skagen has gone back to its cultural roots by promoting the unique light found there as well as heritage culture. It has been the basis for a new tourism strategy called 'The Top of Denmark', supported by a branding campaign called the 'The Land of Light'. Efforts have also been undertaken to promote Skagen as a year-round tourism destination (opposed to a summer holiday destination).

In summary, Skagen is blessed with an outstanding and unique cultural heritage as well as a distinctive nature environment. On this foundation for the last 100 years Skagen has managed to maintain and expand its position as one of Denmark's leading and most attractive tourist destinations. It was mainly due to its nature and cultural heritage that the artist colony in the late nineteenth century was created, and Skagen still uses this heritage to attract potential tourists and new citizens. The former artists' colony in Skagen was the primary cause of the regional development that took place and it had a huge impact on Skagen's image as an elite tourist destination. For more than a century Skagen has benefited from the development of arts and culture, which has transformed the society into a service-based economy. Furthermore, the clustering around the original art heritage has meant a dynamic development, which has established a basis for creating income in relation to this transformation; the theories presented in this chapter, namely Pine and Gilmore's ideas of the development in production of culture, can be applied.

Even though the development has been based on the uniqueness, quality and interest created by the public through the motives of the painters, the promotion of an alternative lifestyle and authenticity of the sea and nature, instead of through a formulated strategic model as suggested by Pine and Gilmore, the use of these aspects as a tool for developing the economy through culture is still highly applicable.

Horsens

Horsens is a city in Mid Jutland, with 53,800 inhabitants (as of 2011), making it Denmark's eighth largest city. Since the end of the eighteenth century, the city has evolved into an industrial city based on manufacturing, including an iron foundry. In 1968 a train station was built in Horsens, which attracted several large manufacturing companies.

From the 1850s to 2006 Horsens faced a large problem in attracting inhabitants and creating economic growth. During this time the Danish state prison was situated in Horsens and was seen as the main image of the place. The connection to the state prison damaged the image of Horsens and people did not want to live there. In the 1990s it became clear to the council of the municipality that something had to change. Focus was put on developing the city from a traditional manufacturing economy to a service economy, with the aim of promoting Horsens as a good place to live (Gyldendal 2012a).

This transformation started in 1992 as the city celebrated its 550-year anniversary. The main event was a medieval market that took place in the city centre for two full days. The use of the festival as an instrument created both a new cohesion among the inhabitants of Horsens, as well as increased tourism with visitors from outside Horsens participating in the event. The use of a medieval festival was an economic instrument developed on the basis of Pine and Gilmore's theories. It included entertainment, escapism and education as well as active and passive participation.

In 1993 Horsens hosted Europeaden, an international cultural festival with 6,000 performers from 25 countries. Once again, it was seen that the inhabitants of Horsens were willing to engage and commit to cultural events in the city. The event was well accomplished and resulted in positive feedback from the participants.

In other words, during the 1990s many initiatives took place in Horsens, with a high level of ambition, both nationally and internationally, the authorities of the municipality tried to use events as a catalyst to promote the city, however, it was still hard for Horsens to achieve a new city image.

In 1995, the Lord Mayor held – as part of municipal planning and review of the city's business policy – a series of meetings, including approximately 150 leaders from all sectors of the city's business community, trade unions and public institutions. The purpose of these meetings was to get ideas and concrete proposals for developing the city into an experience-based economy. The outcome of the meetings was a list of more than 100 proposals for initiatives that the City Council could undertake.

It was found to be important to create a more attractive image for the city. In 1996, the business managers and tourism managers together with two professional marketers made a plan for improving the image of Horsens. The main objective of the project was to promote the city as attractive to people who can positively contribute to the economy.

In relation to this a survey was conducted, which clearly showed that the image of the city was primarily related to the state prison. It was an investigation in line with Colin Mercer's ideas (Mercer 2009).

Based on the development plan and the completed image survey Horsens municipality teamed up with a communication agency. The agency proposed three different branding strategies: Bay City Horsens, Horsens the Experience City and Future City Horsens. The strategy with Horsens as an experience city was chosen.

Before this strategic change, nobody had foreseen that Horsens would become a famous experience city, especially in the field of music. However, high class music events became the instrument to map Horsens and to give Horsens a new image. In 1999, the Director of Horsens New Theatre, Frank Panduro, invited twelve private business people, interested in urban development, the theatre, and in Horsens municipality, to become a part of what would later be called 'Horsens and Friends'. All participants contributed financially to the change with 1 million DKK for the implementation of a music experience economy in Horsens.

Bob Dylan was the first to perform at the theatre. He was later followed by Joe Cocker. It became the start of attracting many world famous artists such as Tom Jones, Robbie Williams, Bryan Adams, David Bowie, Elton John, Paul McCartney, the Rolling Stones, Madonna, Dolly Parton, U2, AC/DC, Bon Jovi, etc. In just a few years Horsens had become famous as a provincial town with great concerts, which generated both a lot of publicity, but also helped to change the image of city.

In 2002, *Jyllandsposten*, the biggest Danish newspaper, appointed Horsens as the city of the year based on the transformation that had taken place.

Much of the development can be attributed to 'Horsens and Friends' and Horsens Municipality, which through persistent work have managed to make Horsens one of the leading cultural cities in Denmark. Nowadays, 'Horsens and Friends' is a sponsor club with the sole purpose of organizing cultural events that benefit both current and future citizens of Horsens Municipality. 'Horsens and Friends' consists of eighty companies and Horsens Municipality that together contribute nearly 5 million USD annually to cultural life in Horsens.

The role of the state prison in Horsens has also changed. A project called 'World of Crime' has been undertaken, which involves changing the now empty state prison into an experience. The plan is to convert the historic state prison into an international tourist attraction. The city once famous for its prison will now be famous for a cultural attraction – the prison itself.

A really interesting question in the case of Horsens is how it was able to attract all the famous artists from abroad. Here the director Leif Panduro played a decisive role. He found out that the famous artists needed a small intimate place to perform in order to achieve a new and denser relationship with their fans. In this way, they could create a new kind of experience based on performing in a rather small city, where they were the main attraction giving the audience an extremely unique experience. In other words, it was an example of great entrepreneurship.

As a result of the development, Horsens attracts many new citizens to the city due to the many high quality cultural offers and events taking place. The development is in line with Richard Florida's ideas that attractive cultural offers attract the creative class.

Horsens has also managed to develop the cultural basis for production, by creating a design industry. As a result, the producer of *Boligmagazinet* (*The Housing Magazine*) honoured it as the best in Denmark in 2011. Furthermore, it has also given rise to the creation of sixty jobs (Horsens Folkeblad 2011a). Another example is a new series of toolboxes designed in Horsens that was the international design winner of the IF Product Design Award 2012 in the category of 'Industry and Handcraft' (Horsens Folkeblad 2011b). Also a new sporty electric car design has its roots in Horsens. The electric car is called 'ECOmove Essence'. It is a typical Scandinavian design built on simplicity and flexibility. Furthermore, it is constructed of light material that makes the weight of the car extremely low. In the past, Horsens had a tradition for producing furniture. This production has been taken up again but today with a stronger emphasis on design. Furthermore, a new design education has been created, constituting a cooperation between Horsens High School and Horsens Art Museum. It is a four-year high school education where the students alongside the normal high school courses are taught in an art design major (Broz 2012). Aesthetics and visual orientation are the main elements of the new education.

To summarize, through hard determined work, Horsens has over many years transformed the image of the city. Culture and cultural events were the main drivers of the development. Cohesion among the citizens including engaged networks have been important in order to erase the negative social heritage. At the same time the change from a manufacturing economy to a service and cultural economy has transformed the way of living. The development of clusters and activities based on culture and design have created new products and new jobs. This development of clusters is continued with the introduction of a design education.

Horsens has become a role model for economic development in other cities too. However, the original entrepreneur Leif Panduro sees no good examples of direct imitation of the Horsens model. He argues that other cities should find their own uniqueness to develop, like Horsens has done with music and events. His statement is important in the sense that he stresses the need for dynamic developments and not for direct imitation. From an economic point of view, it is the same as prioritizing strategies for 'Blue Ocean' that are based on innovation and uniqueness and not to get stuck in the 'Red Ocean', where competition among the same products takes place and makes competition too concentrated on wages and not on new markets.

Comparison of the two cases

The biggest difference between the two cases is that the development in Skagen was not based on a conscious strategy, while the opposite was the case in Horsens.

The case of Skagen is the story of a transformation made by artists that settled down in Skagen and attracted other artists, thus creating a new start for tourism in Denmark. The transformation was based on high quality art and paintings that attracted people due to its aesthetics and escapism. The paintings gave people a dream, a sort of passive participation, but at the same time they created a curiosity to go to Skagen to experience the nature, the light and the local way of living.

The people who came to Skagen were the creative class of their time. They had a huge impact on the development of Skagen and on the economic growth. The approach in Horsens to culture and experiences has been based on a conscious strategy to change a bad image and a negative population growth through the use of an active event-based strategy relying on experience economy. Horsens has invested in culture, experiences and in branding as well as instruments to create a new image. The strategy has included several steps and has been dependent on entrepreneurship, the municipality council and private business having an understanding of both the need for transformation as well as an understanding of the transformation required.

The biggest similarity between the two cases is that development is seen as a dynamic process that needs to be cared for by adding new components in order to build clusters, so that they can rely on 'Blue Ocean' strategies.

It is interesting to notice that there is a time span of more than a hundred years between the two cases of transformation. It is also interesting to see that both the unconscious and the conscious development can generate transformation and economic growth based on culture. It demonstrates that a culture-based transformation can take place both as an unplanned and as a planned development. Both cases also illustrate that it is important to have ongoing activities that support and give new life to transformation. In other words, it is a dynamic process; teaching people that ongoing changes are needed in order to continue having a successful development.

Conclusion

In the introduction the question was raised as to whether culture should be considered as an expenditure in the form of being part of consumption in a society or if culture should be considered as a production factor that can be used for the creation of economic growth. This question cannot be answered in general, but this chapter demonstrates that it is possible to find success stories based on the perception of culture being a production factor. It is also shown that the success stories have a tendency to become an inspiration for other cities to strive for development based on culture. It is safe to say that there is a wish to develop strategies that are less vulnerable to price competition, by basing strategies on 'Blue Ocean' rather than 'Red Ocean' approaches.

It is interesting to look further into the two cases, where the development of Skagen started more than a hundred years ago, compared to Horsens, which started in the 1990s. Even though these stories stretch over such a different time period, it is in both cases possible to identify the reasons for success. It is demonstrated that good results can be achieved both by having an unconscious as well as a conscious strategy. The perception today is often that an unconscious strategy demands a lot of time and cultivation of cultural competencies during a long time period, before they are strong enough to initiate a positive transformation. The lack of patience is often seen as the reason for applying a more conscious strategic approach as they generally create faster results as is seen in the case of Horsens. Conscious strategic approaches will always be target-oriented, which in turn require both strategic knowledge and factors such as entrepreneurship and cohesion in order to be successful.

It is important to notice that the development of dynamic clusters is a decisive factor for achieving positive results, as is clearly demonstrated in both the case of Skagen and Horsens.

References

Broz, J. (2012) *Kreativt Studie*, Horsens: Horsens Kommune.

Caves, R.E. (2000) *Creative Industries*, Boston: Harvard University Press.

Florida, R. (2002) *The Rise of the Creative Class – and How it's Transforming Work, Leisure, Community and Everyday Life*, New York: Basic Books.

Gemba Seafood Consulting (2011) *Hovedrapport – feasibility af vækst og innovationspotentialerne ved de maritime- og havnerelaterede erhverv i Skagen*, Skagen: Skagen Havn.

Gyldendal (2012a) *Skagen*. Available at: www.denstoredanske.dk/Danmarks_geografi_og_historie/Danmarks_geografi/Jylland/Jylland_-_byer/Skagen (accessed 2 May 2012).

——— (2012b) *Horsens Kommune*. Available at: www.denstoredanske.dk/Danmarks_geografi_og_historie/Danmarks_geografi/Danmarks_kommuner/Horsens_Kommune (accessed 2 May 2012).

Herning Messehaller (2012). Available at: www.mch.dk/MCH/MCH/Om-MCH.aspx (accessed 2 May 2012).

Horsens Folkeblad (2011a) *Horsens-design kåret til landets bedste*, Horsens: Horsens Folkeblad.

——— (2011b) *Horsens-design beløpnnet med international designpris*, Horsens: Horsens Folkeblad.

Kulturhavn Kronborg (2012). Available at: www.helsingor-havne.helsingor.dk/helsing%C3%B8r%20havn.aspx (accessed 2 May 2012).

Lyck, L. (2010) *Experience Economy as an Instrument to Create Economic Profitability*, Guest Lecture at Örebro University.

——— (2012) *Kultur- og oplevelsesøkonomi på landet*, Frederiksberg: Frederiksberg Bogtrykkeri.

Mercer, C. (2002) *Towards Cultural Citizenship. Tools for Cultural Policy and Development*, Hedemora: The Bank of Sweden Tercentenary Foundation & Gidlunds Förlag.

——— (2009) *Convergence, Creative Industries and Civil Society*, Linköping University Electronic Press.

Pine, J. and Gilmore, J. (1999) *The Experience Economy*, Boston: Harvard School Press.

Portas, A. (1998) 'Social Capital: Its Origins and Applications in Modern Sociology', *Annual Review of Sociology*, 24: 1–24.

Putman, R. (1993) 'The Prosperous Community: Social Capital and Public Life', *Public Island Press*, 13(4): 35–42.

Rambøll Management (2011) *Notat: vækst Skagen. Feasibility studie*, Skagen: Skagen Havn.

Region Nordjylland (2012) *Kommunerne i Region Nordjylland*. Available at: www.rn.dk/Regionen/FaktaOmNordjylland/NordjyskeKommuner.htm (accessed 9 July 2012).

Skagen Design (2006) *Becoming an International Player in Designed Watches*, Extra case study del II, Skagen.

Skagen Guide (2010) *Skagen: Guide til kunsteriske oplevelser i Skagen*, Skagen: Skagen Turistforening.

Skagensmalerne (2012). Available at: www.skagensmalerne.dk (accessed 2 May 2012).

Throsby, D. (2001) *Economics and Culture*, Cambridge: Cambridge University Press.

Tourist Information (2007) *Map of Danish Regions*. Available at: www.touristinformation.dk/media/blandet/Dk_adm_regions_2007.png (accessed 9 July 2012).

6 The Roskilde Festival and its importance for regional industrial and cultural development

Jon Sundbo

Introduction

The Roskilde Festival

Since 1972, Roskilde rock festival has taken place annually in the Danish town of Roskilde 30 km from Copenhagen. It is by far the largest Danish music festival and is internationally well known. It involves a professional organisation and 34,000 volunteers. This chapter analyses the importance of the festival for the town of Roskilde and its surrounding environment, particularly its importance for industrial development, which is quite extraordinary for a cultural festival. The municipality of Roskilde has created a business development strategy based on the festival and on the experience and culture industries. This has included the establishment of a large district, called Musicon, which is a culture business incubator.

The analysis of the festival's impact on economic and social life in the region

On the surface, the festival is a cultural event, however it is more than that. It is also a social event and the business organisation of the festival continues to work between the festival's, creating both cultural and business development. Here, both the festival as an event and the festival organisation are analysed. The latter receives the most attention as it is primarily that which has an impact on the regional development. Thus, while this chapter is about culture's impact on regional development, it is even more about the impact of the cultural institution that the Roskilde Festival is. 'Culture' here has two different meanings: the artistic culture (the music) and anthropological culture (the social life of the festival).

The concept of region employed in the analysis is complex. At one level, we investigate the festival's influence on the Roskilde region, which by and large means Roskilde municipality. Roskilde may be characterised as an integrated part of the greater Copenhagen region – even though it is administratively part of another region, the greater Zealand region. Many people living in Roskilde work in the Copenhagen area and vice versa. Roskilde is placed within the greater

Copenhagen traffic structure. At the same time, Roskilde municipality is a region with its own identity. It has been a Danish market town for over a thousand years. The festival organisation has, at present, close relations to the municipality and the industrial development of the municipality has been inspired by the festival and involves the festival organisation.

By contrast, the large majority of the festival guests come from other regions, primarily the Copenhagen region, and abroad. The cultural and social impact of the festival is thus not restricted to the Roskilde region. The analysis presented here focuses on the social and, particularly, the economic impact of the festival and the festival organisation on the Roskilde region, but the influence by and of other regions plays a supplementary role in understanding the importance of the festival for the Roskilde region. The Roskilde Festival and its importance to the industrial development of the Roskilde region have been analysed earlier (2002–03) by the author of this chapter (Sundbo 2004). At the time, the region was in the process of renewing its industrial development. Thus the analysis presented here is a follow-up on earlier research and asks what has happened since 2003.

Issues concerning the analysis

The festival can be divided into three types of activity. These are different aspects of the contemporary rock festival and of the festival organisation's activities:

(1) music (culture);
(2) social gathering;
(3) business innovation.

Here, the cultural (musical) and the social aspects will be analysed as one category since they are very closely connected. While the cultural and social event is most important for the guests, we find business innovation to be the most important feature for our purpose. We concentrate on two questions:

- What influence do the festival and the festival organisation have on regional industrial development in the Roskilde region?
- To what degree, and how, is the festival integrated with the social and cultural life of the Roskilde region?

Theoretical framework

The following discussion of the relevant theory provides a general framework for understanding the importance of the Roskilde Festival to the local community. Four possibilities are discussed, namely culture theory, entrepreneurship theory, cluster analysis and the sociological community perspective. The analysis which follows is empirical and inductive. It provides an understanding of the social and economic impact of the Roskilde Festival which is not aimed at testing a general theory. It is thus an empirical case study (Flyvbjerg 2004). The theoretical framework will therefore be eclectic and selected to support the empirical understanding.

One might try to explain Roskilde Festival's importance to the region as a purely cultural phenomenon: the idea that the festival represents cultural creativity, which in turn creates economic development in the region (cf. Cooke and Lazeretti 2008). However, such an elitist culture theory does not seem to be applicable and fruitful for explaining the Roskilde Festival's impact as it is only one aspect of the festival's importance to regional development. Thus, we need to introduce other theories to provide an adequate analysis. In understanding the economic (or industrial) and the social importance of the festival one might assume that economic and social aspects are related in a region. In entrepreneurship theory (e. g. Hindle and Klyver 2011), these two aspects are sometimes united as the entrepreneurs' social networks are seen as part of the basis for their business activities. Entrepreneurship theory also includes the concept of community entrepreneurship (Johannisson 1987) defined as individuals' attempts to socially create entrepreneurship and entrepreneurial networks in local communities and thereby economic development. However, the Roskilde Festival organisation has passed the entrepreneurial stage. It is a well-established organisation with protracted relations to the local community and society more generally and can thus not be understood in terms of entrepreneurship theories.

In explaining the economic impact of the festival, I will therefore draw on the theoretical tradition of geographic cluster analyses (cf. Asheim 1996; Malmberg and Maskell 2002; Fornahl *et al.* 2010). It seems the most suitable theory as the tradition is based on studies of industrial districts where conglomerates of industries are studied (Piore and Sabel 1984). The main point of the theory – as Porter (1990) has demonstrated – is that the conglomerate has a kind of value chain and thus innovation and development in one link of the chain may have effects for the whole chain. Even related firms and institutions such as research institutes and technology suppliers can be part of the conglomerate (which is often called a cluster). This has been much emphasised in regional, industrial policy (Steiner 1998) because by identifying a cluster it is possible to identify actors that can influence the creation of economic development and growth. The value chain approach shows that development can be created through a cluster due to the influence of one actor which causes a chain reaction. It is easy to see how this could be a political instrument. Cluster theory has been criticised for its fuzziness: conglomerates are loose, chain reactions are uncertain, the clusters are not regionally limited and are, maybe, not coherent agglomerations (Asheim *et al.* 2006). Whether the critics of the total cluster theory are right or not, is not crucial for this analysis because the cluster theory can supply us with some concepts and partial explanations that are useful.

The social and cultural aspects of the festival could be understood from a sociological community perspective (e.g. Park 1952; Lynd and Lynd 1956; Frankenberg 1966; Bruhn 2005; Macgregor 2010; Green and Goetting 2010). This anthropological perspective attempts to understand the total life of a community – a smaller area than a region. However, focusing on a community would be too narrow for understanding the social involvement and impact of the Roskilde Festival as these go wider than the town of Roskilde. The volunteers and the guests come from the whole country, primarily the Copenhagen area, and from abroad. While here the focus is limited to the festival's importance to Roskilde, the sociological community approach is only of some help because, lasting just a week, the festival event is not an integrated part of the community's life. However, the festival organisation is permanent and is integrated into the community life, primarily its cultural life. Some aspects from the sociological community study tradition can thus be used in the analysis, but it will be a partial rather than a general community analysis. We will primarily look at the impact of the festival on the cultural life of Roskilde. Some concepts and theoretical perspectives from the sociological community theory tradition can thus be used, particularly that part of the tradition which studies cultural life in communities (Cooke and Lazeretti 2008).

We thus will base the analysis on theoretical elements from cluster theory and sociological community analyses.

Method and empirical basis

Methodological approach

The analysis belongs to the tradition of anthropological and sociological case studies (Russel 1998; Flyvbjerg 2004). It might also be considered hermeneutic ('verstehen' in the Max Weber sense, Weber 1958) or, to use a contemporary notion, constructivistic (Burr 1995). The approach of the chapter is not to deny that empirical facts exist, rather the position is that they may be difficult to observe and a total understanding of the Roskilde Festival's importance to the Roskilde region requires some interpretation by the researcher. The empirical data and observations are the basis for the analysis. The data and observations are interpreted by the researcher (myself). Even though some facts are given, the interpretation cannot avoid some subjectivity. The researcher decides which empirical facts to select and combine. The researcher must try to be as objective and neutral as possible, but another researcher might select and combine other empirical facts to present another interpretation. Even though this – often necessary – approach may imply some subjectivity in the interpretation (which characterises the anthropological, ethnographical and parts of the sociological tradition), it often has the advantage of presenting a more total, and innovative, understanding of the phenomenon.

Empirical material

In the following paragraphs I will present the empirical material that has been the basis for the analysis. The interpretation of the material will be presented in the coming analytical sections.

The Roskilde Festival was observed (by the author) over a period of nine years from 2002 to 2011. This included participating in regional development projects in which the Roskilde Festival has been a partner and in projects that should develop innovations for the festival; members of the festival organisation have also been lecturers at the author's university, Roskilde University, and have, in doing so, provided empirical information. Other researchers at Roskilde University have also participated in collaborative projects with the festival. This is not surprising as Roskilde University is situated in Roskilde and has close relationships to the surrounding region. This has been a participant observation of the festival organisation.

The empirical material includes:

- observation in meetings, project activities, etc. with the festival organisation and regional networks, associations and projects 2002–11;
- interviews with research colleagues (two interviews);
- observation of the festival activities by participation some years in the period 2002–11;
- interviews with representatives from the festival organisation in 2002–03 and in 2011 (six in 2002–03 and three in 2011);
- interviews with representatives from the Roskilde region (retailers, representatives for the municipality administration, trade associations, etc.);
- information from lectures by festival organisation representatives;
- the festival web page (http://roskilde-festival.dk);
- documentary material:
  - a internal documents from the festival organisation;
  - b books about the festival (subjective descriptions by festival guests and journalists (Jensen 2003; Christensen 2008; Rydahl and Søegaard 2008));
  - c newspaper articles;
  - d analyses of festivals (e.g. Rambøll 2011).

The Roskilde Festival and its history

The festival, its music and guests

The festival started in 1972 as a result of an initiative taken by a middle manager in Roskilde municipal tax administration. He was active in an old association called the Roskilde Fund, and saw the potential of attracting people to Roskilde via a rock festival. He engaged several local associations – from scouts to unions and humanitarian organisations – in order to organise the festival. The first was organised by two high school students from Roskilde and a person from Copenhagen at the cattle show area on the outskirts of Roskilde town. This was a large grass area which had existed for many years. The festival became a success and the Roskilde Fund decided to continue arranging festivals, which since then have been organised annually around 1 July at the cattle show area.

During the entire period (1972 to date), the festival has been a mixture of rock and popular music. The number of music scenes has grown from one in 1972 to seven today. The strategy for the music has always been to present upcoming bands from both Denmark and other countries mixed with a few well-known international names. In this way, the festival helps upcoming bands and gives the guests an experience of being among the first to see bands which rise to fame later. The Danish and international press attention to the festival and its music is enormous. In 2009 the Roskilde Festival was mentioned in 10,000 newspaper articles plus many TV broadcasts throughout the world. The critics discuss the music repertoire every year and very often the festival is criticised for its choice of music; it is accused of not having enough well-known bands. According to the festival organisation representatives this has always been so and the guests are satisfied with the possibility of discovering new, interesting bands themselves.

By 2011, the festival had grown to the extent that 78,500 people attended, there were 25,000 volunteers, and many guests visited the festival for a short period (e.g. researchers, representatives of the municipality and the greater Zealand region, firm managers and suppliers). On the last day of the festival, there was free admission for those over 50, which attracted many. In total about 140,000 people visited the festival for shorter or longer periods, a figure which compares to a small city. In 2009, 7 per cent of the Danish guests came from the greater Roskilde region (Eastern Zealand), 49 per cent from the greater Copenhagen region; the rest came from other parts of Denmark (Rambøll 2011). The festival lasts four days with music, however, most people come some days before – some a week before. They stay in tents and the festival area includes large tent districts. The paying guests are mainly young people. However, even older people participate in part of the festival period. In all, 47.5 per cent of the Danish population has visited the Roskilde Festival (Rambøll 2011).

The music has always been the core of the festival. People come to listen to the music and experience it together with others. However, for the guests at the festival, the social gathering has always also been a crucial element – the festival was born out of the collective oriented hippie generation of the 1960s. The social culture at the festival is an important motive for many people to come. In a survey of the guests of the 2009 festival the following reasons were given for attendance (Rambøll 2011):

	% answering
The festival's selection of music	62
Social gathering with friends	56
It is fun	46
It is cosy	33
It is a tradition	16

Thus the social motives for visiting the festival are as important as the music.

Many activities in addition to the music have developed over the years. Examples are restaurants, shops, amusement areas (in 2011, for example, a 35 m high chair lift), experimental stalls and stalls where people can do physical exercises. Now there is a police station, several medical centres, and a very large press centre. Side activities are numerous and are an important part of the festival. The festival area functions as a small city with all facilities present. An important part of the arrangement of the festival is logistics – organising sanitary installations, security, food provision and traffic to the festival has become crucial to carrying out the festival and has been taken care of by the festival organisation.

The festival organisation

In this analysis we distinguish between the festival event and the festival organisation. Some aspects of the analysis are related to the annual event. The organisation is one of event management (Berridge 2007; Getz 2007). However, a permanent organisation has developed so that 52 employees and many volunteers are active all year round. In addition, many people are employed part-time. The organisation has a managing director, who is a business economist and several other managers. The festival organisation has increasingly acquired functions that are not related to the annual rock festival event.

This organisation prepares and arranges the festival events, but it also carries out other activities. The festival organisation is situated in Roskilde.

The organisation presently includes:

The Roskilde Fund			*The association Roskilde Festival*
Business fund that pays taxes and can accumulate capital Carries out business activities outside the festival event			Organises the festival event Volunteers can be members
Roskilde event and consultant	*Roskilde culture service*	*Roskilde equipment rental*	
Organises events	Administers the festival event	Rents event equipment	

Most of the people in the organization have administrative, practical and logistic tasks. A development department led by a development manager takes care of the innovation of the side activities at the festival and the activities outside the festival. Music plays a surprisingly minor role in the organisation. The selection of and contracting with bands is taken care of by one full-time employee with a few assistants of which some are volunteers. The culture of the festival organisation is only to some degree characterised by music and culture, the practical and logistic issues seem to be more important to everyday culture (as can be seen from interviews).

The volunteers

The Roskilde Festival is a special organisation because many volunteers participate; 34,000 volunteers are members of the Roskilde Festival Association. Everybody who delivers 50 hours unpaid work per year as a volunteer can be a member of the association. Once they are members, they have to undertake 24 hours unpaid work a year. The volunteers come from all parts of Denmark and abroad, most of them from the greater Copenhagen region, but many also from the Roskilde region. They vary in terms of age, sex, occupation and other interests. Most of them have been guests at the festival earlier, but many are 'part-time' volunteers, for example members of associations in Roskilde that organise activities at the festival event in return for getting a part of the festival surplus.

The association follows the general rules for associations. The highest authority is the annual general assembly that elects the board, which has been the highest authority of the total corporation on a day-to-day basis. The board employs a managing director and employees. This structure has recently been changed, thus the festival organisation has now been separated from the more business-oriented parts of the festival.

Development strategy

The Roskilde Fund, which now is the professional business part of the festival corporation, has a development strategy for developing new activities, both those relating to music, such as arranging *ad hoc* concerts, as well as service such as organising all types of events, for example sports events and exhibitions. The basis for this strategy is that the festival organisation has certain competencies. Concerning music, they know about rock and other popular music and have a large international network. Service competencies have been the basis of most of the extra activities that have been sold on the market (not the music). The organisation has competencies concerning how to organise events such as concerts – logistic ones such as providing sufficient toilets, meals, how to get people into and out of the event area, security, and selling tickets, etc. This ability can be transferred even to areas where the Roskilde Festival organisation has no core competence, for example golf courses, other large sports events or operas.

The festival organisation wants to have all their business activities under the same roof, even if they are organised into independent firms. The purpose is to produce a development and innovation synergy where ideas from one firm or section can be developed in others.

They are developing an IT-network strategy. Tickets can be booked via the internet, and members of the audience can chat with each other at the festival websites all year around. However, they want to present more music-related activities throughout the year and have developed a system where people can download concerts and other events from the Roskilde festival and other music events.

The festival organisation has also recently established a strategy emphasising innovation and engaging in the regional industrial and cultural development. The festival organisation presently participates in local networks, committees and projects.

The humanitarian aspects of the festival

Humanitarian engagement has been part of the festival's ideology from the early days. This ideology was also connected with formal legal issues. Because of tax rules, the festival is not allowed to accumulate a profit and each year's surplus must be spent by the same year if the festival is to avoid paying income tax and VAT. The surplus from each year's festival is therefore donated to humanitarian organisations in Denmark and voluntary associations in Roskilde. While being in accordance with the festival's ideology, it also creates financial problems because the festival has no capital to invest in the next year's festival. It needs to get a loan every year to organise the festival.

The festival also collaborates with Roskilde municipality to employ long-term unemployed people that have difficulties entering the normal labour market. These humanitarian aspects have become a part of the festival's brand and have been emphasised recently by business communities as Corporate Social Responsibility has become a hot business issue (Horrigan 2010).

The festival's importance for the industrial development of Roskilde

The festival is important for the Roskilde region – and to the Copenhagen region and Denmark – in different ways. In this section the festival's different impacts will be described and discussed. The analysis will primarily focus on the impact on the Roskilde region, but the impact on the Copenhagen region and national economy and business life will also be discussed. First, the direct economic impact of the festival on the Roskilde region will be discussed, then its importance to the industrial development of the region, and finally we will turn our attention to the festival as an innovation laboratory.

The direct economic impact of the Roskilde festival

The full economic impact of the festival is difficult to measure. The festival organisation and researchers from Roskilde University have attempted to measure it in terms of the direct economic effects (direct turnover that the festival organisation and the guests create in the Roskilde region) and its multiplier effects. This attempt was abandoned because the data for the direct turnover from the festival guests were uncertain and the multiplier calculations even more uncertain.

However, the festival organisers themselves made an analysis in 2008 of the direct economic turnover created by the festival organisation and the guests. The effect of this turnover does not only benefit the Roskilde region since, for example, much turnover from the festival goes to firms or organisations coming from other regions (typically Copenhagen). Even though this measurement might be problematic, it gives some impression of the festival's economic impact.

Estimates suggest:[1]

- in 2008 the festival generated a direct turnover of 384 million DKK;[2]
- it generated 113 million DKK in foreign currency (export and import);
- the guests used 3 to 400 million DKK extra via purchase at the festival and in the Roskilde municipality; an analysis (Rambøll 2011) has calculated that 17 per cent of these purchases were made within the Roskilde region;
- the festival generated six tourist overnight stays per guest;
- the festival generated in 2008 one-third of the annual tourism turnover in Roskilde;
- each festival guest spends on average 4,700 DKK (which is quite a lot; it compares to an average spending of 1,175 DKK per day if one takes the four festival days as a basis – or a minimum of 671 DKK if one assumed that each guest stayed a week);
- turnover is generated as follows:

  a 52 per cent is consumption of food and drink at the festival area during the festival;
  b 29 per cent is the entrance fee;
  c 11 per cent is purchases made in the Roskilde and Copenhagen regions during the festival;
  d 8 per cent is goods that the festival guests bring with them from home.

An analysis of the Danish music festival's cultural and economic importance (Rambøll 2011) also provides data about the Roskilde Festival from 2009. This analysis includes a calculation of the impact of the festival on the local economy:

- the festival organisation bought goods and services amounting to 54 million DKK in the local community (the Roskilde region);
- the festival created an economic effect in the local community of 203 million DKK outside the festival activities (among others via festival guests' purchases or tourist activities in the town);
- the festival created 93 local jobs outside the festival and the festival organisation – primarily in retail, but also in hotels and restaurants and in knowledge services (lawyers, accountants, communication firms, etc.).

These facts stress that the Roskilde Festival is important to the regional economy. A total turnover of about 7 to 750 million DKK is a substantial amount. As a firm, the Roskilde Festival is, in Danish terms, medium sized. Much of the turnover benefits firms in the Roskilde region – retail, crafts, tourism – even though there is no exact measurement of how much this is. The fact that one-third of the region's tourism turnover is generated by the festival shows how important it is to the region's economic life. Of course this is limited by the fact that the festival tourism only lasts about a week every year. However, the festival organisation is active permanently and generates economic activities in the Roskilde region, for example employment in the organisation and the purchase of local goods and services.

The local retailers have not always had a positive attitude towards the festival (as interviews with representatives of the festival organisation and local business people show). The festival was long considered a cultural and social stranger in the relatively provincial retail business life of Roskilde town. However, in recent years, the attitude has changed and the retail business now considers the festival a positive event that generates turnover and income for them. The problem is now often seen as one of the town not getting enough benefit out of the festival. It has, for example, been suggested that Roskilde does not brand itself enough in the festival period. Improved branding might create more tourism outside the festival period (this is mentioned in interviews and meetings). The retailers saw the possibility and changed their attitude towards the festival – they established branches in the festival area. This increased their turnover 'just like having four extra Christmas sales days' (Rambøll 2011).

Assessments have also calculated that the festival had a branding value of 45 million DKK for Roskilde town in 2009 because of publicity in Danish and international press (Rambøll 2011); 50 per cent of respondents in a representative survey of Danes say that they connect Roskilde with culture and music, which is the largest share of culture in any town reputation (Rambøll 2011); 3,000 Danish and international members of the press were present at the 2011 festival (which made it the largest media event in Denmark). This is by far the largest branding effect for the surrounding region of any Danish music festival. In particular the international press publicity is in a class of its own.

Humanitarian organisations also benefit from the festival. Not all of these humanitarian organisations are situated in Roskilde, but many are. These donations create local economic activities: the humanitarian organisations buy services and goods locally to carry out their activities. The donations vary with the surplus, but have since 1971 totalled more than 135 million DKK. Associations in Roskilde have received about 21 million DKK. Voluntary associations from all over Denmark have, since 1971, earned more than 150 million DKK via their activities and shops at the festival (http://roskilde-festival.dk).

The festival's importance for regional industrial development

Roskilde Festival has been the inspiration and basis for the Roskilde region's industrial development since 2002. This industrial development has been politically created, based on cluster theory (Asheim 1996; Malmberg and Maskell 2002; Fornahl *et al.* 2010). Around 2002 actors in the community and the city council discussed the future industrial development of the region. They concluded that the only international branding of Roskilde was the festival and developed a strategy based on the festival, namely industrial development based on rock music and other cultural fields (Sundbo 2004). This strategy was confirmed by the town council. The idea was to develop a cultural industrial cluster, which not only would include culture and music production, but the whole value chain (cf. Porter 1990), which includes, for example, production of sound and lighting equipment, knowledge services (e.g. about the organisation of large events), manual services (such as hiring out equipment for concerts and other large events). This cluster strategy was called Musicon Valley. A project was established, a regional network of local stakeholders (firms, associations, the municipality, the university and other education and research institutions) was developed and the municipality created an active industrial policy to develop the cluster. The hope was to attract and develop large firms. The Roskilde Festival organisation was a major partner and player in all these initiatives.

Observation based on meetings and interviews with municipality civil servants showed that cluster theory provided the inspiration for this development strategy, probably because the strategy was formally formulated by civil servants of the municipality who had learnt about clusters at university. It is possible that the cluster idea was not sustainable. After some years with much activity in the project and the network, not much industrial development based on the festival and culture had really happened. The development of culture industry in the town was limited, no related manufacturing firms had moved to Roskilde or developed in the town, and other economic activities connected to the music/culture value chain (e.g. services or tourism) had only developed to a limited degree. The optimism had turned into weariness and there was some uncertainty about the strategy.

A third phase started around 2007 when the municipality actively revitalised the strategy. They made a development plan based on a large area called Musicon (a former concrete factory). Cultural and related industries were to be developed in this area. The industry would be mixed with living-quarters and creative and tourism activities such as a rock museum, small music arenas and other cultural activities, thus changing the cluster strategy. Instead of aiming to attract large firms, particularly manufacturing ones, the municipality aims at developing and attracting new, small firms, which may very well be within the whole culture value chain. The scope has also been broadened to more than music and culture industries, it covers the whole area of the experience economy (Pine and Gilmore 1999; Sundbo and Darmer 2008). This means that related industries from the culture industry value chain are still included in the planned growth area. Also experience products can be used in manufacturing or services (e.g. communication and PR, design and creative management consultancy) are part of the strategic scope. This broadening from the core area of culture to the experience economy developed as a focus as early as the first phase 2002–7, however in the current phase it has become a clear strategic focus.

Musicon is considered to be an entrepreneurial incubator (Campbell and Allen 1987; Allen and McCluskey 1990). An industrial change agent from the greater Zealand region (Væksthus [Green house] Zealand) has established an incubator house particularly directed towards experience and industries in the area. Several small experience firms (such as booking agencies, event organisers, IT-software developers) have been established in the incubator house.

The Roskilde Festival organisation is still a major partner in this third phase. The development of the strategic cluster scope from a narrow music and culture focus to a broader experience focus is in accordance with the development of the festival's strategic development.

This contemporary third phase may not aim as high as the first phase, but it is probably more realistic. The first phase established a network of important local stakeholders that still is an important development factor. The municipality really aims at fulfilling the strategy and investing in industrial cluster development. The prospects for the industrial development may be assessed more optimistically now and the Roskilde Festival still has a major role to play – not just because the festival is a brand, but also because the festival organisation has some business development competencies to offer.

The festival as an innovation laboratory

Even cultural events such as music festivals are hit by the product life cycle (Vernon 1966). Many new rock and other types of music festivals have been established in many countries within the last decade. The competition has increased nationally and internationally and the market is possibly coming closer to the mature stage. The number of guests at each festival has stagnated and many music festivals have got economic problems. Several Swedish festivals, among those the well-known Hultsfred festival, have gone bankrupt. Even though the Roskilde Festival is one of the world's largest festivals with a big brand, this festival has felt the market maturing. In 2008 and 2009 when the international financial crisis emerged, the Roskilde Festival had problems in selling all the tickets. The festival organisation had to carry out a budget reduction and save costs. Many volunteers participated in that process. The festival has in 2010 and 2011 overcome the crisis, partly due to the cost reductions implemented in the years before.

This recent development demonstrates the fact that the Roskilde Festival is also a business as well as a cultural event. It is dependent on market demand, cost focus and proper economic behaviour. This fact has long been a basis for the festival organisation's self-understanding (as can be seen from the organisation plan that was presented earlier). The festival organisation sees itself as a business organisation that must act strategically in relation to the market and must be innovative and develop the business. The festival organisation is of course based on the combination of rock music and social gathering, but the business development is not within rock music. The festival organisation exists between the annual festivals and attempts to create activities throughout the year. The business development has two lines. One is the development of services that the festival organisation can sell on the market (the festival organisation thus sees itself as part of the experience economy, Pine and Gilmore 1999). The other is to develop the festival event as an innovation laboratory where researchers and firms can develop and test new products, services and ideas.

The festival organisation attempts to develop permanent service businesses in addition to the annual festival event; they have established several companies for this purpose. The organisation has competencies in different areas that can be the basis for the sale of services. The organisation attempts to be innovative in utilising these competencies. The permanent business activities are not particularly focused on music or cultural activities; some of them are, but most of them are manual or knowledge services (Delaunay and Gadrey 1992; Illeris 1996). The festival organisation and the subsidiary companies currently develop business areas and activities including:

- organisation of events and exhibitions (e.g. culture, sport, promotion);
- security services including hiring out equipment;
- games (e.g. computer games);
- organising concerts;
- travel agency (particularly travelling to music events);
- food;
- lectures and courses;
- TV channel;
- rock museum;
- management courses (team building);
- innovation laboratory: development of products and equipment;
- education: establishing a high school emphasising event management and services;
- sales of branded goods (e.g. clothing).

These business activities contribute to the industrial development of the Roskilde region because the festival organisation carries out the activities in Roskilde and uses firms from Roskilde as suppliers and business partners. The innovation activities may also spread in the region via the Musicon area in which the festival organisation is an active partner.

Another innovative business development concerns developing the festival event as an innovation laboratory for actors from outside. Over the years, different groups have developed activities at the festival, examples include a computer game where guests can select music by stepping on floor plates developed by IT researchers, and special food. These activities are very important for providing a total experience for the guests. The activities have rarely anything to do with music, but are parts of the social festival culture. Firms, researchers and other organisations also have used the festival as a testing ground for innovative ideas and a place to develop new ideas, services or products. Social researchers have, for example, created an innovation laboratory where guests are involved in developing social innovation for developing countries. Energy researchers have created small bio-energy factories to demonstrate and test how these can be developed into small units that can, for example, be used to power a festival or households. The retail firms from Roskilde attempt to be innovative in their shop concepts. International fashion firms come to the festival to observe how the young people dress in order to develop the next year's trends. Thus, the festival has developed into a large innovation laboratory for firms, associations, researchers and many creative groups. This development has been emphasised by the festival organisation, which encourages groups to develop creative activities. These groups can be volunteers, the festival organisation itself, researchers, the retail (or other) firms from Roskilde or firms from elsewhere. The festival organisation also launches specific development strategies for the festival, for example focusing on food. In 2010 over 100 restaurants existed within the festival area. The festival organisation has decided to develop healthy, organic and good-tasting fast food. A Danish gourmet entrepreneur has been a consultant for the festival and the festival participates in several innovative food projects with researchers and the greater Zealand region. The festival wants to participate in development of a general societal food innovation process. Healthy, gastronomic fast food should be developed in society at large and this could start with young people learning to appreciate that at the Roskilde Festival.

The innovation laboratory part of the festival does not particularly benefit the Roskilde region unless firms and groups from the region utilise this possibility. The stakeholders from Roskilde (including the municipality administration) are not yet fully aware of the large number of possibilities available (as interviews with local business and administrative people and representatives from the festival organisation show). However, the collaboration between the festival, local entrepreneurs, researchers and the municipality in the Musicon area is a basis for utilising this possibility better in the future.

These business developments are only partly in accordance with the cluster theory that has been the basis for the regional industrial development plan. The festival organisation's own business development may be characterised as part of a cultural cluster if we take this cluster in a wide sense to include logistics, services and so forth. However, since, for example, the festival organisation may provide services to a sports event or even a commercial promotion event, the concept of culture becomes very broad. It may be more correct to characterise the festival organisation as being part of the experience economy (Sundbo and Bærenholdt 2007; Sundbo and Darmer 2008). In this case, the experience economy may, originally, have been based on cultural activities, but it now crosses the traditional sectors. The development of the festival as an innovation laboratory does not particularly support the regional strategy of developing a culture industrial cluster because firms outside the culture or creative industries (such as food producers or energy firms) use the festival as an innovation laboratory. One may argue that the aspect of innovation laboratory still defines the festival and its organisation as being within the experience economy since all testing, even of material goods, is combined with an experience for the festival guests. The notion of the experience economy is, however, broader than the cluster idea in Porter's (1990) sense. Further, the festival is characterised more by 'free' entrepreneurship and innovation that is not bound to culture than both the cluster theory and the regional development strategy suggest.

The festival's importance to social and cultural life in Roskilde

The festival's integration into the social life of the region

The festival is integrated with the region's social life in many complex ways. Sociological community theory suggests that towns or smaller regions are socially integrated (Bruhn 2005; Macgregor 2010). Conflicts, class divisions, crime and other negative phenomena exist, but the community is a unit within which the total social life – positive as well as negative – is carried out. Roskilde is a 'Middletown' (Lynd and Lynd 1956); the town has a coherent social system with a local trade and small-industry middle class, associations where people have primary relations (i.e. they know each other personally) and intertwined social networks. This community system has, as with all other communities, some aspects of conservatism (Macgregor 2010) and scepticism towards changes, particularly coming from outsiders.

The Roskilde Middletown community's relation to the festival was, from the beginning, characterised by antagonism and negative attitudes (as said in interviews with interviewees from different groups). The social festival culture was strange to the community, and the music was also unfamiliar in the beginning. Even though people from Roskilde municipality were the originators of the festival idea, the festival was seen by the traditional citizens of Roskilde as something that was not integrated in the town, but organised by young people from Copenhagen. In the beginning, the festival had no cooperation with Roskilde municipality. This relation has slowly changed over the years. Rock music became more mainstream, even for the local community, and many of the employees live there. Many inhabitants from Roskilde became volunteers at the festival and the festival has donated large amounts of money to local voluntary associations. The citizens of Roskilde have become used to the annual festival event, although most of them do not see or hear anything; the festival guests remained at the cattle show area outside the town and did not come to the town centre. The social relations between the town and the festival became much better after 2000 when the Musicon Valley, and later the Musicon started. These projects, where the festival was emphasised as Roskilde's largest international brand and the town's industrial development was connected to the festival, made the official Roskilde change its attitude. The city council, trade associations and so forth began to see the festival as socially acceptable and the festival organisation even as a leading partner in the town's economic and industrial development. As mentioned earlier, shops from Roskilde started establishing outlets at the festival and the managers of the festival organisation are contemporarily invited to participate in many local committees and associations. The attitude of many citizens and local organisations has changed, thus now a common attitude is that the town does not benefit enough from the festival and the festival organisation. The community has changed its attitude to the festival almost from being completely negative to completely positive, however, the festival as such has not influenced the social life and structure of the town very much. Its contribution to the Roskilde region has primarily been economic and it has influenced industrial development.

There is another aspect of social life in Roskilde. Postmodernity that dissolves the locked local oriented structure of traditional communities (Giddens 1991) has emerged and Roskilde is part of the greater Copenhagen region. Many academics live in Roskilde, but work elsewhere in the Copenhagen region. Many people living in Roskilde do not feel any particular relation to the old Middletown Roskilde community. They are part of a national or international postmodern society. To many of these people, the Roskilde Festival is the symbol of the 1960s and 1970s when many postmodern norms and behavioural patterns emerged. The festival as a symbol and often as a practical reality is an important part of the constitution of their social life and of their leisure and experience life as well. Many of them work as volunteers or visit the festival every year. The festival does not have important social value for postmodern people from Roskilde alone, but also for people from all over Denmark as well as for those from abroad. In 2010, 98 per cent of all Danes had heard about the Roskilde Festival and 47 per cent had visited the festival (Rambøll 2011). The volunteers are often middle-aged people that have gained a high social status.

The Roskilde Festival has a special symbolic social value, even among music festivals and even internationally, because it was one of the first rock festivals in Europe (and the world), it is one of the largest and because the festival organisation wisely has cultivated and strengthened this brand.

However, relatively many postmodern people from Roskilde participate in the festival activities because of the geographical proximity.

The festival's cultural impact

The Roskilde Festival has had a general impact on cultural life in Denmark and internationally if we look at rock and popular music. The festival's brand contributes generally to promoting rock music and the festival's particular strategy of presenting upcoming bands contributes to promoting musical entrepreneurship by helping these bands to get a large audience and international press exposure. The festival thus functions as a cultural incubator and as a lighthouse that maintains rock music's cultural status and popularity.

To the Roskilde region, the festival has not had any particular effect in terms of music. Roskilde is not a particular breeding ground for rhythmic or rock music. This might be explained by the negative attitude from the town towards the festival in the first period; however, the festival has never been based on a special rock music life that existed in Roskilde. In the first years of the festival's existence there were no concerts or music arrangements outside the festival week and the connections between the festival organisation and rock music communities were to Copenhagen and abroad. Since about the year 2000, when the local attitude changed, the festival organisation has influenced culture and musical life in Roskilde outside the festival period. The festival organisation runs a municipal music house (called 'Gimle') and is deeply involved in the development of new local cultural institutions such as a rock museum. The regional aim to enhance industrial development based on the experience economy and culture is based at the festival. This aim will have no basis and authenticity if there is not a cultural life in Roskilde. The festival organisation needs to have a central position, both in industrial development and cultural life. However, the important factor is that it is the festival organisation with its competencies, not the festival event, which is a background for the local cultural activities and which can play a role for the cultural life of the region outside of the annual festival events.

Conclusion

The importance of the Roskilde Festival to the Roskilde region is not so much about music and culture, but more about business and industrial development, particularly service business and the experience economy. The festival has developed from a social and musical event to something that is also about business, innovation and regional development. This has happened as the professional festival organisation has grown and expanded its activities, which are increasingly carried out between the festival periods.

Despite the social resistance from Roskilde community in the first period of the festival's existence, the festival – particularly the festival organisation – has currently gained a key role in the region's industrial development. The social relationship to the community has improved and the festival organisation begins to play a role in the cultural activities in Roskilde.

In the future, the festival may play an even more important role in the industrial development of the Roskilde region – if the festival does not choose to develop into an innovation laboratory for firms and organisations from outside Roskilde. The festival organisation is very efficient in participating in local industrial and cultural networks, for example with universities (where there is a particularly close cooperation with Roskilde University) and is now considered by the community to be a major player in industrial, cultural and tourism development.

Further, the festival is now also considered an acceptable network partner for many large Danish and international companies that see the festival as a place where innovations relating to future markets can be developed and tested. Interest in an innovative development of the festival and the festival organisation thus comes from several actors outside the Roskilde region.

Notes

1 Source: Documents from the Roskilde Festival Fund.
2 A Danish Krone equals about €0.135.

References

Allen, D. and McCluskey, R. (1990) 'Structure, Policy, Services and Performance in the Business Incubator Industry', *Entrepreneurship: Theory and Practice*, 15(2): 61–77.

Asheim, B. (1996) 'Industrial Districts as "Learning Regions": a Condition for Prosperity', *European Planning Studies*, 4(4): 379–400.

Asheim, B., Cooke, P. and Martin, R. (eds) (2006) *Clusters and Regional Development*, New York: Routledge.

Berridge, G. (2007) *Events Design and Experience*, Amsterdam: Butterworth-Heinemann.

Bruhn, J. (2005) *The Sociology of Community Connections*, New York: Kluwer.

Burr, V. (1995) *An Introduction to Social Constructivism*, London: Routledge.

Campbell, C. and Allen, D. (1987) 'The Small Business Incubator Industry; Micro-Level Economic Development', *Economic Development Quarterly*, 1(2): 178–191.

Christensen, B. (2008) *Roskilde Festival – Keep on Rocking*, Copenhagen: Danmarks Radio.

Cooke, P. and Lazeretti, L. (eds) (2008) *Creative Cities, Cultural Clusters and Local Economic Development*, Cheltenham: Edward Elgar.

Delaunay, J.-C. and Gadrey, J. (1992) *Service in Economic Thought*, Boston: Kluwer.

Flyvbjerg, B. (2004) 'Five Misunderstandings About Case-study Research', *Sociologisk Tidsskrift*, 12(2): 117–142.

Fornahl, D., Henn, S. and Menzel, H-P. (eds) (2010) *Emerging Clusters*, Cheltenham: Edward Elgar.

Frankenberg, R. (1966) *Communities in Britain*, Harmondsworth: Penguin Books.

Getz, D. (2007) *Event Studies*, Amsterdam: Elsevier.

Giddens, A. (1991) *Modernity and Self-Identity*, Cambridge: Polity Press.

Green, G.P. and Goetting, A. (eds) (2010) *Mobilizing Communities: Asset Building as a Community Strategy*, Philadelphia: Temple University Press.

Hindle, K. and Klyver, K. (eds) (2011) *Handbook of Research in New Venture Creation*, Cheltenham: Edward Elgar.

Horrigan, B. (2010) *Corporate Social Responsibility in the 21st Century*, Cheltenham: Edward Elgar.

Illeris, S. (1996) *The Service Economy*, Chichester: Wiley.

Jensen, E. (2003) *På Roskilde* [*At Roskilde*], Copenhagen: Politikens Forlag.

Johannisson, B. (1987) 'Beyond Process and Structure: Social Exchange Networks', *International Studies of Management and Organization*, 17(1): 3–23.

Lynd, R. and Lynd, H. (1956) *Middletown. A Study in American Culture*, New York: Harvest Books.

Macgregor, L.C. (2010), *Habits of the Heartland: Small-town Life in Modern America*, Ithaca: Cornell University Press.

Malmberg, A. and Maskell, P. (2002) 'The Elusive Concept of Localization Economies: Towards a Knowledge Based Theory of Spatial Clustering', *Environment and Planning*, 34(3): 429–450.

Park, R. (1952) *Human Communities*, New York: Free Press.

Pine, B.J. and Gilmore, J.H. (1999) *The Experience Economy – Work is Theatre & Every Business a Stage*, Boston, MA: Harvard Business School Press.

Piore, M.J. and Sabel, C. (1984) *The Second Industrial Divide*, New York: Basic Books.

Porter, M. (1990) *The Competitive Advantage of Nations*, London: Macmillan.

Rambøll (2011) *De danske musikfestivaler. Den kulturelle og økonomiske betydning* [*The Danish Music Festivals. The Cultural and Economic Importance*], Copenhagen: Rambøll.

Russel, B. (1998) *Handbook of Methods in Cultural Anthropology*, Walnut Creek California: AltaMira Press.

Rydahl, K. and Søegaard, K. (2008) *Roskilde Stories*, Copenhagen: Radius.

Steiner, M. (ed.) (1998) *Clusters and Regional Specialisation*, London: Pion.
Sundbo, J. (2004) 'The Management of Rock Festivals as a Basis for Business Dynamics: an Example of the Growing Experience Economy', *International Journal of Entrepreneurship and Innovation Management*, 4(6): 587–612.
Sundbo, J. and Bærenholdt, J.O. (eds) (2007) *Oplevelsesøkonomi. Produktion, forbrug, kultur* [*Experience Economy. Production, Consumption, Culture*], Copenhagen: Samfundslitteratur.
Sundbo, J. and Darmer, P. (eds) (2008) *Creating Experiences in the Experience Economy*, Cheltenham: Edward Elgar.
Vernon, R. (1966) 'International Investment and International Trade in the Product Cycle', *Quarterly Journal of Economics*, 80(2): 190–207.
Weber, M. (1958) *From Max Weber*, Translated, edited and with introduction by H.H. Gerth and C. Wright Mills, New York: Galaxy Books.
Web page available at: http://roskilde-festival.dk.

7 Translating global ideas into local practices

Creative Tampere Programme

Niina Koivunen

Necessity is the best motivator

Tampere has like many of its European counterparts experienced a painful decline of its textile and mechanical engineering industries and a slow transformation into an international hub of ICT and creative industries. In Finland this transformation was particularly drastic since the country relied heavily on foreign trade with the Soviet Union – a special kind of bilateral trade that was not easily transferable to other market areas – that took a dramatic downward turn and in fact came to a complete halt with the collapse of the Soviet Union. The coinciding and rather uncontrollable deregulation of the banking sector added to the misery of Finnish companies and entrepreneurs, leading to many difficulties, such as bankruptcies, reorganizations, record high unemployment rates and other human suffering.

So there was Tampere, a city founded in 1779 with some 200,000 inhabitants, with its red brick factory buildings right in the centre of the city along the rapids becoming increasingly empty when one textile factory after another closed its doors. Necessity is often the best motivator or a source of creativity – that was the case in Tampere too. The city needed to find work for its people, new businesses to provide these jobs and new uses for all of this empty factory space in the middle of the city – urban fallow. The transition period took over ten years and consequently in the beginning of the twenty-first century the situation was rather different. Fortunately the phenomenal emergence and development of the ICT sector, with Nokia leading the way, came to the rescue in the mid-1990s. Simultaneously, urban development progressed and the factory buildings were transformed into movie theatres, museums, restaurants, shops, and office space. Coffee shops and restaurants were placed in the old cotton mills, museums and galleries found new homes where blast furnaces used to produce cannons and turbines. The once famous company Tampella lent its name to a new part of the city that was built based on an architecture competition. The old and the new continue to live next to one another. The urban landscape created by these red brick factories along the rapids – one of the first sites of industrialization in Finland – is now a cherished trademark of the city. The landscape is also a candidate for UNESCO's World Heritage List.

This is the site and the surroundings of the Creative Tampere Programme, a developmental programme initiated and financed by the city government between 2006 and 2011 with the aim of strengthening the creative industries, innovations and attractiveness of the city. This chapter seeks to highlight the main purposes and outcomes of this programme and provide inspiring examples of projects, initiatives and ideas created within the programme.

Some facts about Tampere

Tampere region is the second largest economic region in Finland with a population of 490,000. The region comprises 22 municipalities. 210,000 people live in the city of Tampere itself. Tampere is located 176 km north of the capital Helsinki. It is a popular congress city and a favourite holiday location for families, culture enthusiasts and business tourists. The city has been voted the most attractive city in the country several years in a row which has further strengthened its growth and the positive flow of people into the city (Tampere Business Region 2012).

The quality of life in Tampere signifies that you can live and work in a safe, unspoiled and friendly environment with excellent infrastructure. One can enjoy a wide range of cultural and sports events, the beautiful city located between two large lakes, and the surrounding countryside with forests and pure nature. The city is lively and active, but not too crowded. It is also an international city in which English is widely spoken. It hosts a lively student life and an easy-going atmosphere.

Tampere is known for education, research and technology. There are two universities, an open university and a university of applied sciences. The University of Tampere has 12,500 degree students and 700 postgraduates; the Tampere University of Technology has almost 9,000 students and 1,600 postgraduates. The Tampere University of Applied Sciences is the second largest in Finland with 10,000 students.

Up to 15 per cent of Finland's national R&D budget is spent in the Tampere region. The GDP of the region was €14,330 million in 2006 according to the Tampere Chamber of Commerce (2012). The region has strong and focused business activities and research expertise in the following seven fields: biotechnology, digibusiness, energy technology, health technology, intelligent machines, nanotechnology and ubiquitous computing. The Tampere region is also still an industrial region. Machine construction and automation, mechanical engineering, electrical engineering and electronics as well as the wood pulp and paper industry are among the highly active industries in the region (Tampere Business Region 2012).

The Invest in Tampere website (Tredea 2012) provides intriguing information about the high-tech innovations created in Tampere. They include a NMT phone call in 1974 (an early mobile phone), a biodegradable implant (1984), electromechanical film (1985), a GSM phone call (1991), a walking forest machine (a robotic lumberjack 1995), game and image phones (2001), a fog screen in 2003 onto which images can be projected and an antibiotic-releasing biodegradable implant (2009). In this innovative environment the Creative Tampere Programme had nurturing conditions and a solid foundation.

Solid foundations: experience, arts and education

No matter how desirable it may be, creativity is notoriously hard to pin down. Some connect creativity strictly to the fields of arts and culture; others prefer the notion of 'everyday creativity'. Researchers have approached the topic by investigating leadership and change processes of economical life as manifestations of contemporary creativity (Koivunen and Rehn 2009), creativity and innovation (Amabile *et al.* 2004; Mumford and Licuanan 2004; Rickards and Moger 2006; Wilenius 2004), appreciation of the aesthetic judgement (Guillet de Monthoux *et al.* 2007) or flow experiences (Csikszentmihalyi 1990). Other researchers have investigated the special characteristics of business in the field of art and culture (Guillet de Monthoux 2004; Hjorth and Kostera 2006; Lampel *et al.* 2006). Since the discussion on creative economy and creative industry gained legroom in the speeches of politicians, urban developers and consultants, the shift has been increasingly from a limited space of art and culture towards a much broader use of the notion of creativity: creativity is something for everybody. Here many researchers (Galloway and Dunlop 2007: 18; Jeffcutt and Pratt 2002: 227) refer to the UK government's decision to brand former cultural industries as creative industries as a turning point, thus signalling a contemporary policy focus on a sector that is engaged in producing novel cultural products of any kind. The creative industries are now defined in the following terms: 'those activities which have their origin in individual creativity, skill and talent and which have a potential for wealth and job creation through the generation and exploitation of intellectual property' (Jeffcutt and Pratt 2002: 227). Other European countries soon followed suit.

Since ideas travel (Czarniawska and Joerges 1996) fast in today's global world, the Scandinavian countries and Finland also wished to explore the potential of the newly defined creative industries. The Creative Tampere Programme did not, however, start from scratch nor was the city a *tabula rasa* in areas of culture and creative activities. On the contrary, the programme followed somewhat smoothly in the series of other development programmes initiated by the city. In other words, developmental programmes were an institutionalized practice in the Tampere area. This in my view is one of the reasons for the success of the programme. Another success factor is the versatile supply of arts and culture in the city: a symphony orchestra, a conference hall, many museums, two large institutional theatres and many smaller theatres, as well as a large number of annual culture festivals and rock events. These institutions employ many artists and professional managers in the arts field, all belonging to the core population of the creative industries. Finally, Tampere has two large universities, one of the largest polytechnics in the country and several other educational institutes. The people educated by these institutions have a high level of education, command of many languages, often have international experience and importantly enough, have had to learn to work in a project format and to network in order to seek external finance. I will discuss these factors in more detail in the following.

Local experience in development programmes

The city of Tampere has facilitated the growth of knowledge-intensive businesses and innovations through knowledge centres and development programmes – a unique way to boost its economy. The principle has been to support emerging business areas with a development programme created in cooperation with the key actors which is then partly financed by the city. These municipal-level business development programmes are a unique approach that have been invented locally. According to Paananen (interview 2011), they are an exceptional way of operating in Finland. First of all, these programmes are relatively lengthy, ranging from five to seven years. The city has strongly committed to these programmes; both by financing them and by having politicians support them by working on the advisory boards. The financial investments of the city have been substantial. The programmes and their themes are included in city strategies, for instance the strategies of city development and business development. Another unusual feature of these business development programmes has been their continuity: the processes created by one programme have remained in operation after the programme itself has concluded. The networking and collaboration with several local actors, such as companies, civil servants and universities, has been strong. Many kinds of business development programmes exist in other cities as well, also in the creative sector, but they lack the systematic and long-term approach developed in Tampere. The city seems to have created a good recipe for business development.

Examples of such programmes are, for example, the eTampere (2001–2005) and the recently introduced BioneXt. The objectives of the eTampere were to make Tampere a global leader in research, development and the application of issues related to the knowledge society. The programme was collaborative in nature and combined the input of educational and research institutes, businesses and communities. The programme focused on three themes: network services to ease citizens' daily life, strengthening the foundation of research and education expertise and creation of new innovative businesses. The programme was massively financed with €132 million – a reflection of the general atmosphere and high hopes for technology during the IT bubble. The city invested some €11 million in the programme. The programme did not meet the target in terms of creating new businesses but was very successful in creating networks and supporting collaboration between research and business organizations. In other words, this technologically oriented programme managed to enhance social networks and the ability to work with experts from different backgrounds. This social capital would turn out to be increasingly important in the future.

The Creative Tampere Programme was in many ways a follower of eTampere, although it received a dramatically smaller financial investment: €7.2 million, only 5.4 per cent of the sum given to its predecessor. However, the expectations were not smaller, on the contrary, the Creative Tampere Programme was almost expected to fulfil the unmet targets of eTampere – particularly important was the generation of new businesses. Despite the considerable discrepancy in financial inputs – that is indeed very illustrative of the common attitude towards creative industries – it has to be emphasized that the Tampere Programme was the only municipality-level programme in Finland to invest in the creative sector. Despite the modest financial incentive, there was political goodwill and faith in the creative sector to launch this programme.

The city government has found development programmes to be a good way to enhance business activities and areal development. 'Developmental programmes are like midwives', says Kari Kankaala, the Director of City Development of Tampere, 'no child is left unborn because of them and no child is born because of them, but still development programmes as well as midwives are very useful in crucial moments' (Kankaala 2010). There are intentions to continue the practice of development programmes and a new innovation-related programme is going to be launched in the near future.

The importance of core art fields

The Economy of Culture in Europe report (2006) defined the cultural and creative sector as consisting of four subfields: the core art fields, cultural industries, creative industries and activities and related industries. My reading of the report and revisualization of the table suggest that flourishing and versatile core art fields are absolutely necessary for the existence and development of cultural and creative industries. The fine arts, such as theatre, ballet, symphony orchestra, literature and the visual arts are usually publicly supported in Europe since they are considered necessary for the well-being of the citizens. The fine arts, however, also have an important role in providing inspiration, invigoration and ideas to the people working in the creative sector. In addition to the intrinsic value of the fine arts, they also have instrumental value for the creative sector. If a city or an area wishes to develop the creative industries in the area, it is vital to first support and secures the local art institutions (Figure 7.1).

Universities and other educational institutions

Universities educate people with a high level of expertise who can then work in the creative sector. There is a university with social sciences, humanities, medical science and business studies and a university of technology that offers degrees in various subfields of engineering. In addition, the largest polytechnic in the country resides in Tampere and offers studies in art and communication and tourism, among other things. There is also a music institute and a conservatory for music studies. All of these educational institutions produce knowledge and knowledgeable people for the industry and start-up businesses. Academic and

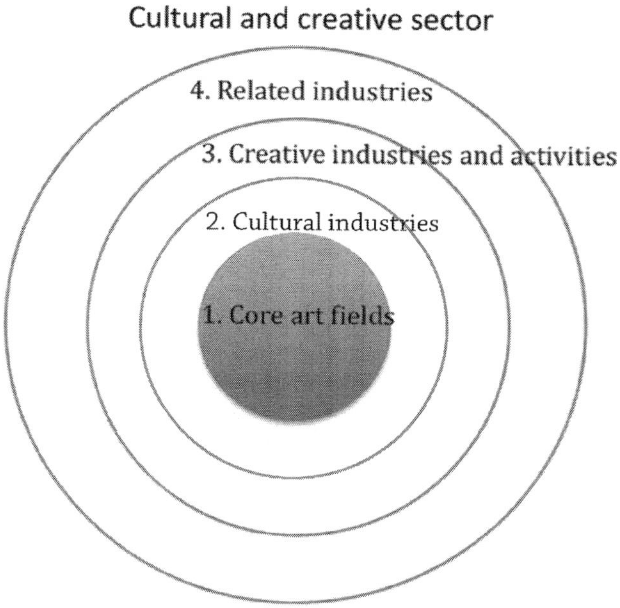

Figure 7.1 Cultural and creative sector (Economy of Culture in Europe 2006).

applied research also provides important results for the local organizations. Furthermore, universities provide international connections, both to and from abroad.

Translation from global ideas into local practices

The travelling of ideas is an intriguing phenomenon. Why does it seem that many organizations introduce similar changes at about the same time? How is it possible that countries and regions around the world are keen to introduce development programmes to initiate innovation and creativity? Since Richard Florida (2002), John Howkins (2002) and others introduced the concept of the creative economy and brought it to the attention of mass audiences, its popularity has spread at an amazing speed. On 27 January 2006, in the beginning of the Creative Tampere Programme, googling 'creative economy' produced the rather substantial number of 54,700,000 hits. These search results reveal that countries, communities and corporations around the world are counting on the prospects of a creative economy to lift themselves out of post-industrial depression and to revitalize their crumbling economies. Both public and private organizations are initiating development programmes to tap into the potential of art, culture, and other creative sectors in order to boost business life and the urban condition. Towards the end of the programme, on 27 September 2011, Google finds 97,200,000 web pages which in one way or another deal with matters related to creative economy. The idea of creative economy certainly has travelled to each and every part of the globe.

What are the processes that enable such spreading of ideas simultaneously? Czarniawska and Joerges (1996: 13–48) use the notions of localized time/space and globalized time/space – also called translocal – to explain travel of ideas. Translocal is a process that links the interconnecting localized time/spaces (ibid.: 22). Global and local are not defined as a dichotomy, but a continuum. In other words, global is not above or beyond local, it is a hugely extended network of localities. When ideas travel, they first become quasi-objects, transgress the barriers of local time, enter translocal paths, become 'disembedded', land in various localities, become 're-embedded', materialized into actions and when successful, become institutionalized.

Czarniawska and Joerges further explain this spreading of ideas by the notion of translation, originally suggested by Latour (1986). In contrast to the traditional belief in the diffusion of ideas, translation is perhaps a more illustrative means to describe this fascinating process. In Latour's words about translation: 'the spread in time and space of anything – claims, orders, artefacts, goods – is in the hands of people: each of these people may act in many different ways, letting the token drop, or modifying it, or deflecting it, or betraying it, or adding to it, or appropriating it' (Latour 1986, cited in Czarniawska and Joerges 1996: 23). In other words, ideas spread through people who carry them further and modify, adjust and reshape them on the way. Although the idea is a quasi-object here, it can be read in differing ways.

The travelling also needs energy: it is thus the people who energize an idea whenever they translate it for their own or someone else's purposes. If only a few people give energy to an idea by translating it, it may not travel very far from its original local context. And when many people energize an idea by translating it into other local contexts, the idea will continue its travels. Watching ideas travel we 'observe a process or translation – not one of reception, rejection, resistance or acceptance' (Latour 1992, cited in Czarniawska and Joerges 1996: 23). Latour emphasized that translation far surpasses the linguistic interpretation of the word: 'it means displacement, drift, invention, mediation, creation of a new link that did not exist before and modifies in part the two agents' (Latour 1993, cited in Czarniawska and Joerges 1996: 24). Although translation sounds like a micro-process, something that happens between two people only, today ideas travel extremely fast. New technologies and mass media enable travelling to take place at the speed of light.

'Such ideas are powerful whose time has come' (Czarniawska and Joerges 1996: 44–45). As more and more people are willing to translate the idea for their own use, it can be materialized into a collective action. In order to become public knowledge, the idea must become objectified, made into a quasi-object, only then can it travel between local places. This process can be supported by willing actors, and usually a strategically important group of people has to 'discover' the idea as something completely new. The idea is then enacted: other people are persuaded to join in, decisions are formally made, programmes are introduced, committees founded and prototypes built. In order to solidify and legitimize the idea, signals are sent to a wider community: selling, marketing and justifying the idea – energizing it. An idea, locally translated into action, is reified into a quasi-object that can travel: a book, a picture, a design, for purposes of non-local communication. In the case of the Creative Tampere Programme, one quasi-object was an open announcement for projects and ideas within the frame for the intended programme.

Programmed creativity

If the field of art and business has traditionally dealt with the interplay between these two fields (Koivunen 2009), the Creative Tampere Programme brought in a third player to the game: the public sector. As Ruokolainen (2008: 76) describes it: the programme was located in between very different worlds. The logic of economy is strongly present, but one has to understand the principles of arts and culture as well, and make this work in the context of the public sector. Although organized in a programmatic fashion, the programme was closely connected to the procedures of municipal decision-making and other practices. The programme ran for six years, between 2006 and 2011. It had a very light governing organization, consisting of a programme director, a coordinator and a project secretary (Luova Tampere 2011). The programme was perceived as very active, flexible, agile, easy to approach and very cooperative (Ruokolainen 2008: 77).

The programme was created and built in 2004–2005 partially to continue the eTampere Programme and to address the then fashionable public discussion on the emergence of the creative economy and potential of the creative industries. The launching of the programme was certainly affected by Florida's ideas (2002) on the creative class and the creative economy but the city planners did make their own interpretation of these ideas to match the local needs. In other words, the globally known concept was translated to fit the local context or disembedded from the original context and re-embedded to the new local context (Czarniawska and Joerges 1996: 26). Ruokolainen (2008: 65–71) describes how the programme was created in a very emerging fashion. The planning started after a preliminary analysis and proceeded to a city government decision to launch a strategic development programme and to nominate a project group to plan this programme. This planning group, with the help of four advisory boards, continued to work on the project plan. The plan turned out to be a combination of very pragmatic ideas and somewhat wild ideas about creativity, clearly dovetailing Florida's suggestions. The preparation period was followed by an open announcement for projects and ideas from local actors in the creative field, which were then processed to select the ones that would receive financing. It was through this announcement that the programme received its final shape. In other words, the city provided a basic structure that was then supplemented and moulded by the substance from actors in the creative sector. The flexible format was one of the learning outcomes of previous programmes that had been criticized for being overly bureaucratic and rigid.

In the programme statement three central targets were written down: to create new service innovations, to build creative structures and to strengthen the creative industries. The topic area service innovations was aimed at producing user-based new technology services to citizens and organizations. One example of this was the Wireless Tampere project that strived for a shared wireless network community. Creative structures worked toward building such facilities and structures in the city that enable creativity, innovation and entrepreneurship to bloom. Examples of this were Urban Fallows, a subproject that sought to turn unused factory, office or other space into productive space for new businesses or other creative activities. The Centre for Creative Industries, an ambitious project to transform one old sock factory into office space with a plan to build new buildings too, is an ongoing process to construct a shared space for many actors in the creative sector. 'Creative industries' was the largest topic area of the three and has also received most applications for project funding. The broad objective of this theme was to develop the creative sector into becoming an independent and strong field of industry. To enhance these targets, the theme sought to advance the knowledge of business activities and branding, entrepreneurship and networking as well as internationalization and exporting, among others (Ruokolainen 2008: 63–65; Luova Tampere 2011).

In 2008, after the experiences of the first two years, the programme strategy was updated and some of the targets reformulated. The topic area 'service innovations' was replaced by 'innovations and entrepreneurship'. 'Creative structures' became 'attractive city' that includes the former target and adds event production under this theme (Viljamaa and Lahtinen 2010: 24). These changes took place rather organically to meet factual demand for these kinds of topic areas and to emphasize areas that had been running successfully already. No greater drama was thus involved in this slight refocusing of the programme, which reveals a fluent processual approach to programme management.

Ruokolainen (2008: 74) claims that the programme managed to create its own space, a novel market niche, in regional development. It does not compete with the institutionalized sector of arts and culture nor collide with existing business areas. It truly develops new openings for cultural businesses that can be considered a good accomplishment. The programme has managed to reach such cultural actors who have benefited from financial and other support and who have taken their chances to start business activity. Ruokolainen divided the actors of the cultural field into four categories: the established actors, entrepreneurially oriented actors, emerging avant-garde and scholarship candidates. The established actors already have an organization and they usually want to develop their business activities. The entrepreneurially oriented actors have usually started their operation recently or moved from an association to a business organization. The scholarship candidates represent persons whose projects most often fall into the area of publicly supported arts – they tend to resist any signs of commercialization. The most interesting group appears to be the emerging avant-garde who for the most part are responsible for creating entirely new substances.

This most exciting group is also the most elusive one whose ideas are sometimes impossible to implement.

In the next section, some of the success stories of the Creative Tampere Programme are briefly presented and described.

Successful case examples

Visiting the office of the company that coordinates and runs the programme is illuminating and full of symbolic meaning. A worn out iron staircase leads to the fifth floor of this old factory building. I am intrigued by the fact that the staircase is from another textile mill in Manchester, UK that was transported to Tampere, the 'Manchester of Finland'. The building itself is the old factory building of the textile production company Finlayson, dating from the 1830s. The mill became the vanguard of Finnish industrialization. According to Creative Tampere Story (page 3), 'with knowhow from the British Isles, workers from the Finnish countryside and the very latest European and North American industrial and social innovations, the mill is technologically advanced even in global terms'. International cooperation is by no means the invention of the 1990s – international trade and business bloomed as early as some 150 years earlier even in the remote northern corners of Europe. Moreover, the symbolism only increases by the fact that in these mills the first electric lights in Northern Europe were lit in 1881. This took place as a product of another international collaboration: the son of the director of the cotton mill worked as a trainee at Thomas Alva Edison's factory in New York and brought along this revolutionary lighting solution. Ideas did travel in the nineteenth century too; knowledge did transfer between countries and continents.

The Creative Tampere Programme organization was very light, consisting of a director, a coordinator and a project secretary, whose office space is located in one corner of HUB – a international community building organization that offers work space for distant workers, entrepreneurs and contract workers for a very reasonable fee (Hub Tampere 2011). The interior design of the space is colourful, creative and cosy. The colours consist of bright yellows and greens, creating a energetic impression. There is a shared kitchen and other shared activities are encouraged and actively arranged by the HUB hosts. There are piles of soft felted slippers close to the entrance, encouraging people to make themselves comfortable and to demonstrate the relaxed atmosphere. The programme director Lasse Paananen kindly shows me around the space and then chooses a comfortable little cubicle in which we can have the interview in quiet.

He is proud to tell me that the programme's project portfolio is worth more than €30 million. More than 1,000 companies have participated in one way or another, over 200 new companies have been established and over 120 projects have also been financed by the programme. Next a short description of some of the successful case examples is given.

LUKE is the creative economy development programme that has been one of the success stories of the programme. It has provided coaching through the programme that led to the foundation of more than 700 creative companies and 16 cooperatives. LUKE gives guidance and support about general business skills, networking and contact building. The greatest challenges a new entrepreneur in the cultural field usually meets are sales and marketing skills, product conceptualization and branding. In the beginning of the programme, some 70 people with a business idea contacted LUKE, the next year the number was 150 and now over 300 budding entrepreneurs receive advice in business skills. The creative field initiatives account for 10 per cent of the total number of entrepreneurial candidates (Luova Tampere 2011).

New Factory is a community that is open to all actors and lines of business and that creates a significant amount of new business, open job positions and growth company know-how. New Factory is an enabler that offers potential entrepreneurs, companies, universities, the public sector and citizens tools and channels for creating innovations. With the help of Factory machinery (tried and tested innovation apparatuses), the students and R&D professionals can unite their know-how with that of others and take their idea quickly into production. The operations of the Factory comprise practical, open and collaborative work. No stiff bureaucracy is involved, the tentative ideas can quickly be processed into prototypes and products. Plenty of companies, universities, professionals and international partners take part in the Factory programme. The New Factory incorporates four 'Engine Rooms': Demola, Protomo, Suuntaamo and StartupStairs. In Demola, students develop product and service concepts together with companies and create new solutions to authentic problems. The incorporeal rights of the innovations and development work remain with the student team that has created them, and a company may then redeem a right to use them though a purchase of a licence. Protomo is an innovation apparatus that generates new combinations of knowledge and creates new companies and job positions for experts. Protomo is an innovation environment that offers free of charge facilities, community support and expert advice for developing new products and services and launching them to market. Suuntaamo is an active community open to all through which you can contribute to the development and functionality of our living environment and gain access to the creation of new products and services. StartupStairs offers coaching and support for start-up companies with growth potential (Uusi tehdas 2011).

Iron Sky is a science fiction comedy film produced by two Finnish film companies and co-produced by a German and an Australian film company. The trailer of the film and a large number of computer-animated special effects were produced in Tampere. The particular feature of this production is the crowd sourcing of ideas and funding from movie enthusiasts and fans. The full-length film has by Finnish standards a large budget of €7.5 million and follows the famous internet movie *Star Wreck* (Star Wreck 2011) by the same producing team that made fun of legendary science fiction films. By investing in the film platform the Creative Tampere Programme wishes to help generate more film work, such as postproduction (Iron Sky 2011).

LAK – Centre for Creative Industries. The culmination of the Creative Tampere Programme – and also something tangible for the future – would be a centre dedicated to creative industries. The programme and the city have initiated a study of such a centre to be built in one of the old factory buildings – a former sock factory – situated some 2 km from the city centre. The study was finalized in 2008; it included a refurbishing of the old factory space and complete new buildings. Unfortunately the neighbouring houses filed an official complaint that took some three years to process through the court system. In April 2011 the complaints were rejected and the planning could proceed. The elapse of time had, however, changed some of the plans but the centre will be built on a smaller scale. The centre will be a place where actors of different backgrounds and size can meet and interact. This is a familiar idea also presented in research literature where the aim is to create 'mixed practice zones' which help people from different backgrounds to mingle (Koivunen 2009). The aim of this is naturally to develop new business activities. The plan is to have different actors, such as artists and ICT professionals, to have different fields from environmental technologies to TV production, and to have everything from artists' studios, band rehearsal spaces, art galleries and shops to advertising and architecture agencies all under one roof where the different actors can provide inspiration and ideas for one another.

Finlandia Comic Award is given annually to the best Finnish comics during the Bubbles over Tampere Festival. The Creative Tampere Programme has financed the award since it was established in 2007. The award and festival aim at advancing and developing comics and raising the awareness of this art field. The festival also targets the creation of internationally recognized comics in Tampere (Tampere Kuplii 2011).

Palatsi Music Theatre or Palace Music Theatre is a privately owned theatre that introduced the 'dinner and a show' concept to the Finnish customers. In addition to the musical show, the customers can enjoy a three-course meal with their theatre experience. The owners are theatre professionals who had a dream of founding a theatre that would specialize in producing musicals and music theatre. This was a very ambitious plan, particularly from a financial perspective, since most institutional theatres in Finland receive large public subsidies. Competing with the publicly supported theatres was going to be tough. The entrepreneurs had a clear artistic vision and received guidance and support in creating a business plan from the business coaches of the Creative Tampere Programme. The programme invested €15,000 in the theatre, and very soon the Palace Music Theatre became a profitable enterprise that continues to operate and draw full audiences.

Aito Media is a content and production company that wants to produce both entertaining and clever television programmes. Aito means genuine in the Finnish language. The company has produced factual entertainment, talk show series and documentaries for Finnish television. The special connection to the Creative Tampere Programme is, however, through development of the so-called 'format factory', a specialization in producing formats that can be redeveloped and sold abroad. The company has exclusive rights to co-develop and represent the Finnish

Broadcasting Company's formats. It specializes in factual entertainment, family and relationships and life changing experiences. The formats, according to the website, 'have a fresh twist, an efficient production engine – and a mission to handle tough issues in an entertaining way' (Aito Media 2011). This company has managed to find a niche market area in the creative sector where its expertise can be developed and expanded further even to international markets.

Kulttuurivartti or Culture Quarter is a company that provides small cultural events to senior citizens. The company operates in the interface between the private and public sectors to produce services that partially belong to the responsibilities of the public sector, like the health and nurture organizations that often lack this kind of professional knowledge. The senior citizens' homes, for example, were in need of cultural activities, but the nurses and other personnel could understandably not provide a very versatile supply of these. This company was founded to provide such cultural activities and bring them to senior citizens, who often could no longer attend regular cultural events. The sessions usually last one hour and include music, poetry, literature, singing, theatre, dance, lectures or handicraft work. Annually the company produces almost 500 cultural sessions attended by 10,000 participants. These cultural sessions are greatly appreciated by senior citizens as well as the personnel of these care organizations and they provide work opportunities for many local artists and other professionals in the cultural field.

Outcomes of the programme

The Creative Tampere Programme has resulted in many positive outcomes that are very beneficial to the local economy, the community of artists and other professionals in the cultural sector. It has produced greater visibility for creative industries and increased their importance in the city. According to the end report of the programme, the following six outcomes are the most influential (Viljamaa *et al.* 2012).

The activation of new potential actors for business development

The number of new enterprises in the cultural and creative sector has increased substantially during the programme. During this five-year programme, over 700 new companies have been established in the creative sector. In 2007–2008 the growth rate of new companies in the creative sector was 8 per cent – compared to the 4 per cent growth in other industries. That is a significant difference. The value added by the programme lies particularly in this ability to activate new groups of actors. The programme has reached out to such people who had not ever before considered themselves to be potential entrepreneurs in this field – no small accomplishment. The programme has also advanced the development and establishment of clusters in the creative sector (Viljamaa and Lahtinen 2010). For example, the audiovisual cluster has developed significantly and is currently the most important cluster of the creative sector in the Tampere region.

Education for creative industries

The programme has organized various kinds of business skills education in many educational institutions. Over 1,000 students and 200 teachers have received instruction in these topics at bachelor, masters and adult education levels.

Business advice services for creative industries

One of the most significant outcomes of the programme has been the development of tailor-made business advice activities for the potential entrepreneur in the creative field. In addition to the general kind of business advice, special guidance has been provided in internationalization processes and in sales and marketing efforts.

Professionalization of actors

The programme has during its five-year existence considerably increased and broadened the level of expertise of the actors in the cultural field. In particular, the professional artists and business people have learned from one another. Although there are still often these two tribes, artists and managers, increasingly one meets people who have a foot in both areas. They can be called hybrids (Koivunen 2009), professional mediators between these two worlds. In the field of art they are often called art managers or artistic directors, in the field of cultural industries they work as managers, agents, producers or promoters. Their educational background is often in some art form, but instead of becoming a professional artist they have decided to seek additional education in management or administration. Many also have extensive experience in the amateur or non-profit field, for instance they have been active in organizing cultural festivals or events.

Changing attitudes to business opportunities in creative industries

According to the final evaluation report of the programme, the programme has had a very good image among the key stakeholders. In the beginning, some actors in the artistic field voiced their doubts about the programme, but these concerns melted away as the programme proceeded and the interaction between various actors took place. Also the civil servants have become more knowledgeable about the potential of the creative sector and now perceive the creative sector as belonging to business fields, rather than just a sector that receives public funding. These attitude changes are quite remarkable, since the traditional view holds art and business as two things quite separate.

Networking

One of the major outcomes of this endeavour is the possibility to develop networking. The people interviewed for the end report considered the international networks hugely beneficial and an important achievement. Tampere was selected to be part of the European Creative Industries Alliance that prepares recommendations for the European Union about the future of creative industries. Here Tampere is in very good company, since other participating cities are Amsterdam, Berlin, Barcelona, Milan and Nantes.

To conclude

Czarniawska and Joerges (1996: 34–44) explain how ideas are translated into objects, actions, institutions, and again into ideas, although different from their original form, through processes of translation. This travelling needs energy; a few people cannot ensure a successful translation of an idea, but rather many people are needed to energize an idea when translating it for their own or someone else's purposes. In addition to a large number of willing translators, timing is crucial. Such ideas, whose time has come, are powerful (ibid.: 44–45). Furthermore, this process also needs a strategically influential group of people to discover the idea and support it. All of these crucial elements were present in the Creative Tampere Programme. There were enough people to translate the global ideas about creativity and the potential of creative economy into local ideas which were then developed and processed further. The strategically important financial and political support of the city of Tampere was there as well.

The programme managed to create a lot of energy and action in the creative field. Many projects and processes were initiated and energized. The community of artists and business people have increasingly found each other and learned from this interaction. Altogether 700 new companies were founded during the programme, and many existing actors have gained more professional knowledge about their trade.

Ideas that brought to life the Creative Tampere Programme continue to travel to other European local contexts through the European Creative Industries Alliance, a consortium between several European cities to create and share innovation tools and other best practices. Tampere was invited to join this alliance as the only city in Finland to share their experience and success stories. Although the programme officially finished at the end of 2011, the projects, new businesses and ideas will continue to live and grow into new ideas, objects, actions and institutions. Tampere will host the Creative World Forum in 2013, an honour that is clearly a product of the programme. There will also be a follow-up programme called 'Open Tampere' that will continue some of the work of its predecessor. The translations carry on.

References

Aito Media (2011) Available at: www.aitomedia.fi (accessed 20 September 2011).

Amabile, T.M., Schatzel, E.A., Moneta, G.B. and Kramer, S.J. (2004) 'Leader Behaviors and the Work Environment for Creativity: Perceived Leader Support', *The Leadership Quarterly*, 15(1): 5–32.

Creative Tampere Story. A printed booklet.
Csikszentmihalyi, M. (1990) *Flow: The Psychology of Optimal Experience*, New York: Harper and Row.
Czarniawska, B. and Joerges, B. (1996) 'Travels of Ideas', in B. Czarniawska and G. Sevón (eds), *Translating Organizational Change*, Berlin: de Gruyter, 13–47.
Florida, R. (2002) *The Rise of the Creative Class – and How it's Transforming Work, Leisure, Community and Everyday Life*, New York: Basic Books.
Galloway, S. and Dunlop, S. (2007) 'A Critique of Definitions of the Cultural and Creative Industries in Public Policy', *International Journal of Cultural Policy*, 13(1): 17–31.
Guillet de Monthoux, P. (2004) *The Art Firm. Aesthetic Management and Metaphysical Marketing*, Stanford: Stanford University Press.
Guillet de Monthoux, P., Gustafsson, C. and Sjöstrand, S.-E. (eds) (2007) *Aesthetic Leadership: Managing Fields of Flow in Art and Business*, Houndmills: Palgrave Macmillan.
Hjorth, D. and Kostera, M. (eds) (2007) *Entrepreneurship & The Experience Economy*, Copenhagen: Copenhagen Business School Press.
Howkins, J. (2002) *The Creative Economy: How People Make Money From Ideas*, London: Penguin Books.
Hub Tampere (2011) Available at: http://hubtampere.wordpress.com (accessed 21 September 2011).
Iron Sky (2011) Available at: www.ironsky.net (accessed 4 July 2011).
Jeffcutt, P. and Pratt, A. (2002) 'Editorial: Managing Creativity in the Cultural Industries', *Creativity and Innovation Management*, 11(4): 225–233.
Kankaala, K. (2010) Luovuuden vuoro, *Creative Tampere Information Magazine*, 2/2010. Available at: http://luovatampere.smartpage.fi/fi/tiedotuslehti_210 (accessed 20 June 2011).
Koivunen, N. (2009) 'On Creativity, Art and Economy', in N. Koivunen and A. Rehn (eds), *Creativity and the Contemporary Economy*, Copenhagen: Copenhagen Business School Press, 13–32.
Koivunen, N. and Rehn, A. (eds) (2009) *Creativity and the Contemporary Economy*, Copenhagen: Copenhagen Business School Press.
Lampel, J., Shamsie, J. and Lant, T.K. (eds) (2006) *The Business of Culture. Strategic Perspectives on Entertainment and Media*, New Jersey: Lawrence Erlbaum Associates.
Latour, B. (1986) 'The Powers of Association', in J. Law (ed.), *Power, Action and Belief*, London: Routledge and Kegan Paul, 264–280.
——— (1992) 'Technology is Society Made Durable', in J. Law (ed.), *A Sociology of Monsters: Essays on Power, Technology and Domination*, London: Routledge, 272–292.
——— (1993) *Messenger Talks*, Lund: The Institute of Economic Research Working Paper, No. 9.
Luova Tampere (2011) Available at: www.luovatampere.fi (accessed 3 May 2011).
Mumford, M.D. and Licuanan, B. (2004) 'Leading for Innovation: Conclusions, Issues, and Directions', *The Leadership Quarterly*, 15(1): 163–171.
Rickards, T. and Moger, S. (2006) 'Creative Leaders: A Decade of Contributions from Creativity and Innovation Management Journal', *Creativity and Innovation Management*, 15(1): 4–18.
Ruokolainen, O. (2008) *Kulttuuri ja aluekehittäminen. Luova Tampere –ohjelma uusien mahdollisuuksien avaajana* [*Culture and Regional Development. Creative Tampere Programme Opens New Possibilities*], Sente 28/2008, University of Tampere. Available at: http://tutkielmat.uta.fi/pdf/gradu03380.pdf (accessed 26 January 2009).
Star Wreck (2011) Available at: www.starwreck.com (accessed 4 July 2011).
Tampere Business Region (2012) Available at: www.tbregion.fi (accessed 20 July 2012).

Tampere Chamber of Commerce (2012) Available at: www.tampere.chamber.fi/en (accessed 20 June 2012).

Tampere Kuplii (2011) Available at: http://2011.tamperekuplii.fi (accessed 4 July 2011).

The Economy of Culture in Europe (2006) Available at: http://ec.europa.eu/culture/key-documents/doc873_en.htm (accessed 20 June 2011).

Tredea (2012) Available at: www.investtampere.fi/tampere-facts/economy (accessed 20 June 2012).

Uusi tehdas (2011) Available at: www.uusitehdas.fi (accessed 4 July 2011).

Viljamaa, K. and Lahtinen, H. (2010) *Luova Tampere –ohjelma. Väliarviointi* [*Creative Tampere Programme. Intermediary Evaluation Report*], Advansis Oy. Available at: www.luovatampere.fi (accessed 20 June 2011).

Viljamaa, K., Lahtinen, H. and Valkonen, T. (2012) *Luova Tampere –ohjelman loppuraportti* [*The Final Evaluation of the Creative Tampere Programme*], Ramboll Oy. Available at: www.luovatampere.fi/arkisto (accessed 21 May 2012).

Wilenius, M. (2004) *Luovaan talouteen. Kulttuuriosaaminen tulevaisuuden voimavarana* [*Toward Creative Economy. Cultural Knowledge as Future Resource*], Helsinki: Edita.

8 Great expectations

Turku as the European Capital of Culture 2011

Alf Rehn, Nina Kivinen, Astrid Huopalainen, Jutta Tailas and Mika Mård

Introduction

> Turku 2011 is more than one year. It is a process through which Turku emerges as a pioneer and a creative centre of the Baltic Sea region cooperation, a city that produces and mediates arts and science.
>
> (Helander *et al.* 2007: 8)

> As Capital of Culture, Turku makes the year 2011 unforgettable for all Europe. Turku 2011 provides experiences and encounters that cross borders, renew everyday life and live on.
>
> (Helander *et al.* 2007: 8)

Today creativity and culture are often invoked as signifying an almost limitless potential for economic and social renewal in cities and regions (Florida 2002). In contemporary city administration, this 'power of culture' is often seen as a key driver of economic development, and has hence in recent years received a great deal of academic and political attention. Cultural initiatives have changed from being a rather marginal matter in the world of city development to being cast as central to the development of a city or a region. The impact of such initiatives has also been illustrated in a number of works (Lindeborg and Lindqvist 2010; Landry and Bianchini 1995; Landry 2008).

We will argue that this has cast the issue of creativity and regions in a distinctively ideological light, where culture is seen as a catalyst of creativity and regions are expected to flourish by embracing issues of creativity and culture – *by necessity*. In the current discourse surrounding regional development, the notion that culture can have a positive impact on a region or a city is often turned into a promise: cultural initiatives *will* have a positive impact. Rather than being an alternative approach to value production in the contemporary city, creativity and culture are in this manner positioned as central and even necessary aspects of the modern city economy, and thus linked to notions of economic power. In fact, it might be argued that the discourse regarding the creative city is establishing itself as a new kind of hegemonic practice, something that also raises the expectations placed on the power of culture as a transformative force. Partly, this will act as an affirmation of the discourse itself, but it will also affect the ways in which cultural initiatives raise expectations in the cityscape.

This chapter will hence discuss what forms these expectations may take, and how a city attempts to manage the expectations. This is done in the context of the city of Turku, in Southwestern Finland, which in 2011 was the European Capital of Culture (ECC). Turku is Finland's oldest city and the first capital in the country, hence home to a rich historical and cultural heritage, with 178,000 inhabitants in 2011. Being an ECC represents a full year of major investments in culture, and is hence often seen as a stepping-stone for developing Turku into a future 'creative city'. We will show the different forms in which the expectations on the ECC-year shape participants' sense-making, and further the complex issues involved in managing contemporary expectations on the power of culture. Rather than treating culture as a moral good a priori, we will see it as part of a complex negotiation, where forms of power and idealized imagery of the transformative capacities of culture intermingle to create a multifaceted tapestry of hopes, dreams and sometimes harsh realities.

Studying a capital of culture

So, in 2011 the city of Turku, Finland acted as the European Capital of Culture (ECC), together with the city of Tallinn in Estonia. These two cities together form a vital part of the Baltic Sea region, hence the joint ECC-year was expected to deepen the collaboration between the cities and benefit the whole region. Due to the short time period passed after the year when writing this, the outcome of this collaboration remains unseen, and hence we focus in this chapter on the Turku region. While Turku/Åbo obviously had a rich cultural scene before the ECC-year, we've opted not to illustrate this in any greater detail, although it has to be acknowledged that the expectations based on the year included both ideas of support for existing cultural actors, support for those who did not belong to the established cultural field, as well as notions of creating a whole new cultural identity for the city. As describing the entire cultural scene of the region pre-2011 would take at least an additional chapter, we've opted for a 'year zero'-approach in our analysis. The concept of the ECC was created through a decision made by the Council of the European Union in June 1985, on the basis of an initiative put forth in 1983 by the Greek Minister of Culture, Melina Mercouri. Since 1985, over 30 cities have served as cultural capitals or cities, and according to the European Commission (2010a) the intention and main idea of the ECC events is as follows: 'to highlight the richness and diversity of European cultures and the features they share, promote greater mutual acquaintance between European citizens, foster a feeling of European citizenship'.

The research reported in this chapter is part of an ongoing study conducted by the research group for the creative economy at Åbo Akademi University, a study conducted in close collaboration with the projects that first applied for, later won, and then ran the programme that formed the activity of Turku as the ECC in 2011.

The programme of the ECC-year included, in addition to the cultural activities, a research initiative and a series of projects focusing on well-being. We applied for and were invited to be part of the official research initiative of the programme, and the research project is also partially funded by the Foundation for Turku2011 Capital of Culture. This collaboration gave us exceptionally good access to the working of the ECC-project both before and during the year 2011. In addition to good access, we were able to interact directly with those producing the cultural programme, those left outside it, and the political leadership of the city, while maintaining our independence as researchers.

This research project is a longitudinal study of the events before, during and after the cultural capital year of 2011, running from 2009 to 2012. Three different, yet complementary approaches have been adopted for the gathering of empirical data of the Turku2011 events. All three approaches focus on gathering data that describe the different discourses surrounding Turku2011 (see, for example, Czarniawska 1997; Alvesson and Sköldberg 2009; Kostera 2006; Oberhuber and Krzyzanowski 2008). First, formal interviews were conducted with organizers of 25 projects that were part of the official programme for Turku2011. These interviews have primarily focused on the planning and preparations for Turku2011 and they have mainly taken place during 2009 and 2010. We have also conducted extensive archival studies of documents produced in and around the Turku2011 project as well as media coverage thereof.

Second, numerous informal discussions have been held with members of the Turku2011 staff, city of Turku officials and other individuals closely connected to the political effort of Turku2011. These discussions began in 2009 and are still ongoing. The role taken on by the research group here closely resembles that of a participant observer.

Third, the research group has taken on an ethnographical approach, aiming to live and experience the year 2011 by taking part in both official and unofficial events in and around the city of Turku during the actual cultural capital year. Through a lived experience of the cultural capital year, we have aimed to share this year with the inhabitants of the city as well as with visitors to the city. We have attended approximately 60 different events, seminars, workshops, exhibitions, concerts and the like relating to Turku2011.

The everyday experience of living in the city has given rise to even greater numbers of observations and insights. Half of the members of the research group live in the city and have experienced the changing cityspaces, while the other half of the research group have travelled back and forth, therefore providing a different view of the year already within the group itself. This lived experience and the unplanned encounters with the city, its inhabitants and visitors have also given important opportunities for discussions with 'the man on the street'.

Taken together, the research project reported here has thus gathered a rich data set regarding the activities of the Turku2011 year, combining interviews, observations, notes, documents, as well as photographs and media outputs. In the following, we will highlight some of the key elements at play in this event.

The theme, the logo, the foundation and the programme

The theme and the logo – Turku on Fire

The theme and corresponding slogan of the year was *Turku on Fire*. In addition to the fact that the city of Turku has literally been on fire several times over the centuries, it is stated that the slogan alludes to the enthusiasm, determination and desire that has risen from preparing arrangements for the Capital of Culture: 'Turku has been on fire dozens of times over the centuries. Now we burn again – with excitement and desire to make Turku an unforgettable experience for everyone', as it is stated on the Turku2011 web page (Turku2011). The fire theme was strongly present throughout the year and could be seen represented in things such as exhibitions (e.g. *Fire! Fire!*), theatre (*Fire away!-festival*), dance (e.g. the dance performance *Great Fire of Turku*) and music (the concert *Fire and Death in the Castle*). It was also a carrying theme at the opening ceremony in January 2011. The logo of the year was formed as a flame, mostly in yellow-orange, with the text Turku2011 inside of it. The main colour of the year, a deep orange, was also inspired by fire.

The ECC-year stated that the programme was guided by the following themes: sustainability, creative economy, well-being and new ways of using culture. Progress in and awareness of these on a city-level were stated as main goals for the Turku2011 year, as well as for the future.

Organizing the ECC

The first step that the city of Turku did to establish itself as a cultural city was to commission an organization that was responsible for managing the ECC-year, and ensure long-term effects after 2011. The Turku2011 Foundation, as the organization was named, worked independently from the city council, but it was managed by a board and a delegation. The board consisted mostly of members from the political and the cultural sector, while the delegation was represented by 15 members with a background in culture, 10 in research and education, 6 in politics and 14 in other areas (most with a background in business). It is worth mentioning that the Foundation was divided into different teams that actualized the Capital of Culture year: the Turku2011 programme team, production support, research, communications and administration.

The programme – 'Wow. 365 days of culture'

The Turku2011 programme was the crucial, most important and visible part of the ECC Turku2011 year. During 2011, it was said that something is happening in the city of Turku every single day. The Turku2011 Programme, '*a convergence of creative points of view, within different domains and people*' (Turku2011 Programme) was the core of the Capital of Culture year. The official

Turku2011 Programme consisted of approximately 150 projects and individual events of various sizes, based on a wide definition of culture as stated in the original bidding document. The overall programme content offered a range of events and performances from 'low' to 'high' culture, from science to art and from small activities to major public urban city events. The programme was furthermore said to offer '*surprising encounters in our everyday lives, culinary experiences, exercise and well-being*' (Turku2011 Programme) with the aim of creating long-term impacts, new cooperative projects and future networks in the city.

Three out of four projects in the programme were selected from the open call in 2006, whereas one out of four projects had been commissioned directly by the Foundation. The programme content was divided into the following five individual themes: 2011 Transformations, 2011 Take offs, 2011 Archipelago explorations, 2011 Personally and 2011 Memories and truths. The theme '2011 Transformations' included projects bringing culture to everyday life whereas '2011 Takeoffs' was about emphasizing key cultural aspects of Turku. The theme '2011 Archipelago explorations' included projects relating to the archipelago, the River Aura and the Baltic Sea region, such as, for example, Contemporary Art Archipelago (CAA) which was an international contemporary art exhibition held in the archipelago of Turku. '2011 Personally' had to do with projects examining issues related to personal identity, the self and the mind. '2011 Memories and truths' linked projects that engaged with the history of the city and variations thereof. Taken together, the themes and thus the programme as a whole, attempted to be something for everyone, engaging both the city inhabitants and prospective tourists in the ECC-year.

The theme, the logo and the programme tried to create an engaging entity of the ECC, while the Foundation attempted to coordinate this engagement. Examining this, we might say that the Foundation established the manner in which creativity can be invoked in the city, with the underlying assumption that the aim should be to engage as many as possible into the notion of the ECC-year as a transformative project. By invoking fire and its powers of destruction and renewal, the ECC-year attempts to 'own' all change in the city, while at the same time symbolically connecting itself to elemental forces. The theme, again, was written in a way, which tried to encompass all potential – transformative movements, personal change, memories. At play here is dialectic of change and totality, where the year was connected to both destructive transformation and personal well-being, both radical novelty and the history of the city. Culture becomes something that can be told in a number of varying ways, and also something that is positioned as both exclusive and inclusive – something everyone can partake in, as long as one accepts the underlying premise that the cultural and creative city must invoke. The key repeated issues – fire, transformation, the word 'culture' as something that needs to be set apart – then become the rhetorical instruments through which this is done.

The spectre of expectation management

Landry and Bianchini argue in their widely cited book, *The Creative City*, that one way to become a creative city is to use catalyst events:

> Catalyst events and organisations can create opportunities for people with different perspectives to come together and share ideas. A US-inspired organisation, Common Purpose, has a year-long programme in a number of European cities, bringing together operational managers from diverse sectors, such as health, education, the arts, the media, local government, business and charities. The objective is to create mutual understanding of the city's problems and possibilities and in this way, to develop a leadership group able to address issues comprehensively ... Public spaces can also act as catalysts by attracting different types of people and encouraging interaction.
>
> (Landry and Bianchini 1995: 28)

What could be a better catalyst for becoming a creative and innovative city than celebrating culture for a whole year? According to the European Commission (2010b), being chosen as European Capital of Culture is a privilege and a great honour for the city in question. In addition, studies (e.g. the Palmer-research has studied the capitals and cities of culture between 1995 and 2004) suggest that the cities that have acted as Culture Capitals and Cultural Cities have received a boost in their cultural diversity and contributed to positive changes in the city. Examples of benefits include a boost to local culture and the creation of new spaces for cultural use (Palmer 2004).

It is thus not surprising that when the city of Turku was awarded the right to be the joint ECC in 2011, this created a set of expectations around this 'catalyst event', a set that included both internal and external expectations regarding a plethora of things. Thus the case of Turku in 2011, in conjunction with the claimed effects that an ECC is supposed to have on a region, is an ideal setting for analysing the nature of the expectations placed on the power of culture. Will the expectations for culture's effect on the city's future be exaggerated or restrained? How are these expectations related to the recent boom in analysing culture's role in regional economies, managed within the scope of the project, and how will these affect the effects that Turku might receive through this specific mega-event? Might the ECC even create a conflict in the city, as Mommaas (2004) suggests, between the strong emphasis on culture's role in renewing the city and other multi-toned interests:

> Amongst other things based on ideologies of 'enterprise culture', the quest for urban imagery and positioning strategies, the changing spatial fabric of cities and a search for economic and cultural revitalisation, for the past 5–10 years, the formation of cultural clusters has turned into something of an urban cultural development hype. However, what at first glance appears as a common model, often accompanied by boldly expressed slogans concerning

> the new role of culture and creativity in the physical and economic revitalisation of cities, in more detail unfolds as an ambivalent and conflict-ridden mixture of cultural, economic, social and spatial interests and sentiments.
>
> (Mommaas 2004: 507)

The role of expectations is important here, as is the management of these expectations, not only due to the possibility of fulfilling these expectations (or not), but because the expectations actually work as a more complex network of emotions, projected ideas and envisioned futures. Rather than seeing expectations as objective statements about how one believes things will turn out, we here work from a perspective where expectations function as a kind of *bricolage*. The various actors around the project, be they insiders or outsiders, obviously didn't have one, clearly delineated expectation. Rather, we might say that the expectations established regarding the ECC-project were constructed from a wide range of different materials, such as:

- academic claims regarding the importance of cultural events for a region;
- institutionally legitimized discourse around ECC-projects;
- cultural policy discourse more generally;
- media portrayals of specific cultural events;
- political statements regarding the future of the region;
- notions regarding the importance of culture made by cultural agents themselves;
- and so on ...

In other words, the expectations on the ECC-project were at least in part built up of 'pre-fabricated' elements, i.e. re-purposed prevailing notions of the cultural and creative economy and its importance. This institutional discourse then met the often more prosaic expectations of the actors taking part (or being shut out of) the materialized project, not to mention those actors who stood outside the project proper and attempted to make sense of the at times conflicting claims made regarding the impact such a project can have. We will in the following show how these different expectations and the management of the same affected the establishment of the ECC-year in Turku.

The expectations of the organizers (and the EU)

Before we address the issue of what the various actors in Turku expected of the project, it might be valuable to note what the EU, as an awarding institution and a funder, expects of the ECCs:

> Cities wishing to become European capital of culture have to prepare a cultural programme that meets rather specific criteria: it must reflect the European character of the event and involve the participation of the people

> who live there. The EU wants to see the forthcoming cultural capitals do yet more to encourage the long-term impact on the cultural development of the cities and their environs.
>
> (European Commission 2010b)

In other words, the expectation on the city of Turku, and in practice in this case the Foundation set up to run the project, was to establish a programme that not only reflected a 'European character' and involved the inhabitants of the city, it was to have an impact reaching beyond the programme itself, and beyond the year itself. In fact, beyond the limits of the city itself. This is of course well in line with the *general* expectations of what large-scale cultural events are capable of doing, but it is important to note that the ECC-projects through the establishment of such expectations are already placed in a situation where long-term effects and general participation (and thus, implicitly, acceptance) is made a prerequisite of these events. The ECC could thus not *choose* its effects, they were in effect already assumed.

With such expectations forming the very backdrop of even applying for the status of ECC, it is not surprising that the committee (later Foundation) that made Turku's application and defined its character were keen to set the aims high.

> Turku 2011 is more than one year. It is a process through which Turku emerges as a pioneer and a creative centre of the Baltic Sea region cooperation, a city that produces and mediates arts and science.
>
> (Helander *et al.* 2007: 8)

The cities of Turku and Tallinn, called 'twins of the Baltic Sea' (ibid.: 22), are according to the bidding document planning to cooperate closely. The quote below illustrates how the cultural capital title is not only important for the city of Turku, but for the whole country and the Baltic Sea region:

> The Capital of Culture is a project for the whole of Finland and will showcase Finnish expertise and welfare society. The year 2011 will turn the eyes to the Baltic Sea region, because the other Capital of Culture for the year is Tallinn. Turku and Tallinn will implement the Capital of Culture year in close co-operation.
>
> (Helander *et al.* 2007: 22)

There is no doubt that the Foundation had very ambitious expectations for the ECC-year, including but not limited to Turku becoming a creative centre in the greater region, revitalizing the city, increasing cultural awareness and even promoting the health and well-being of the city's inhabitants. However, many of these expectations were expressed in vague and hard-to-measure terms, something that many of the project's critics pointed out. How, for instance, do you measure whether a year has been 'unforgettable' or if a city is a 'pioneer'?

The decision – which may not have been a particularly conscious one – to portray the expectations through a discourse that was at the same time both vague and grandiose made expectations management something of an issue for the Foundation. Obviously, this discourse made it easy for the supporters of the ECC-year to state that things are going well, as it obviously had provided 'experiences and encounters'. However, it also made it disconcertingly easy for critics to ask where the 'renewal' has taken place and whether the city of Turku is much closer to being a creative hub for the Baltic region.

As something of a side-note, it should also be pointed out that the Turku2011-project had the misfortune to occur during a period of widespread economic crisis, a global slump of a magnitude that a single cultural event cannot really compete with. This too had a complex relationship with the expectations on the ECC-year. On the one hand, the global recession provided an 'easy out' for the Foundation. When queried about the final number of foreign tourists that would visit that year – which were unlikely to be quite as impressive as the more optimistic projections would have it – representatives at the Foundation could blame a more general trend in consumer behaviour. In such a way, it became possible to start referring to the effects of the year in 'What if?'-terms, i.e. to state that sales in, for instance, the city's restaurants would have been hit even harder if the event had not taken place. Such claims are very difficult to prove, but their benefit was that they were equally difficult to disprove. However, the economic slump did also position the ECC-year in a somewhat harsher light. In a situation where stakeholders are actively looking for both positive signals and someone to blame, the Turku2011 Foundation became an easy target. Even though no one could reasonably have demanded that the event would turn a recession around, the perceived effects or non-effects of the year became part of the greater discourse around the role of the cultural economy – including disparaging comments regarding whether the money should have been invested in something more tangible.

The expectations of the official projects

As noted above, the official Turku2011 programme consisted of approximately 150 projects and individual events of various sizes. The initial plans for most projects were made several years ahead of the year 2011. The choice to have an open bid for projects created in itself expectations of in particular the inclusion of the grassroots and civil society. However, the prolonged decision-making process on whether or not a project was selected as part of the official programme, created much concern and unrest among the bidders as they saw their time schedules crumble, and the high expectations started to fade out. This uncertainty turned the heat on the Turku2011 Foundation and questions regarding their expertise and their agenda were raised.

Most projects received their approval by 2009, which gave the research project the opportunity to follow them in their preparations for the year 2011. Since these projects constructed the core of the programme, the expectations among people actualizing the ECC-year were varied and often quite colourful. In the following we have included comments from the realizers of the individual projects in the programme.

> I just hope that it (ECC Turku 2011) would be more visible and would wake up the whole of Finland and would get the decision-makers of Turku to commit and as far as I've understood they still haven't realized what a great thing it is.
>
> I would hope, that it as a matter of fact becomes a pleasant feeling in the whole town and that people think that, 'how fun!' and 'good!'

Many of the people interviewed from the projects talked about the neglected cultural policy in the city of Turku and saw the capital of culture year as an opportunity to raise awareness among politicians, local businesses as well as among citizens. As culture in Finland is financed primarily through public funds, an understanding and a long-term commitment to culture was clearly expressed by the projects.

> ... of course it [the ECC-year] brings Turku more fame and visibility and tourists and so on ... And surely it is visible like after the ECC-year ... Or stays in a way ... even in a commercial way when thinking about it ...
>
> Well ... I hope, I'm a little afraid though, if it (ECC Turku 2011) will receive the visibility it deserves.

A recurring narrative among the projects was the indication of a lack of faith in citizens' current notion of culture, that the ECC would miraculously inject a positive and redefined notion of culture in the city, and that the cultural sector would see an upswing in attention and people's understanding of its importance.

> I can't say. I hope for many things. I hope for those settlements and inspiration.
>
> ... we can hope that the culture gets an extra ... I mean ... boost ...
>
> I just hope that it gets the honour, space and attention that it deserves

It is noteworthy that the individual people we have interviewed represent diverse cultural actors, including cultural institutions, not-for-profit organizations and free artists. Almost regardless of their background, they adopted the rhetoric of the ECC. One can only speculate if this is also one of the reasons that these projects were successful in the open bid for the official programme. This same rhetoric, highlighting cultural diversity and its innovative force, is used in the European Commission to explain the ECC's main function. A similar rhetoric, between the 'meta-level' European Commission and the grass root level is either a sign of a successful implementation of the main ideology of the ECC or a sign of a power structure where higher levels of institutions define and restrict the discourse of the ECC a certain way.

> The meaning isn't just to organize one year of festivals ... but everything that we do must have long-term impacts so when that year's over we won't stand on an empty ground, but strengthen the field of culture and production and, and then explicitly create new innovative forms of action here and then get the corporate world and field of culture to meet, to bring these together or try to bring them closer so that we could get more of these product-like cultural industries even here, through that.
>
> But when already thinking of how many programmes and events 150 programs will produce, so ... it is like ... thousands, can I say thousands, but ... Anyway, a lot related to the normal cultural life of Turku ... So quite a ... hustle going on. I haven't personally been to a cultural capital ... capital like during the particular year, on the spot, but ... One would think and hope that there would like be ... lots of surprises.

A shared concern among the projects was the long-term impact of the ECC-year. Profound changes in the cultural structures were often called for, although the interviewees found it difficult to specify what exactly needed changing. The ECC would be a missed opportunity if it turned out to be a year of spectacles, which would only attract the elite and would not change the structures of cultural spaces and opportunities.

> One would hope that ... that something in the structure, not among the doers, would change permanently, and the meaning of it would be realized.
>
> ... that a good cultural cooperation would remain inside the city ... that we would learn like a new way of approaching, just that, that ... [pause] That the citizen would probably be served in a better and more diverse way ...

The expectations were thus well in line with the expectations of the greater institutions realizing the event, and included similarly vague yet hopeful notions of renewal and change. At the same time, the expectations on this level also contained distinct hopes for redrawing lines of power, so that a sector that perceives itself as having limited power (i.e. the cultural sector) positioned the ECC-year as a kind of saviour. As a mega-event, Turku2011 was expected to bolster the position of the 'culturals', particularly in their relationship to city officials and politicians. Whereas the notions of renewal and renaissance that the arranging institutions alluded to can be understood as very general, the renewal expected here was much more specific and material – cultural actors expecting a permanent and measurable change of their circumstances for the better.

Expectations in media

Media functions as one of the most influential arenas when it comes to forming, expressing and ventilating expectations on what a cultural initiative like the ECC will bring to Turku. Media can be and has been used as a platform for journalists, politicians, citizens (both insiders and outsiders), and organizers to discuss, criticize and recognize different forms of expectations of the ECC 2011 event. Turku as an ECC in 2011 attracted, and was expected to attract, a lot of attention in different media throughout the year. It was expected that over 1,000 journalists would visit Turku during 2011. For instance, the opening ceremony (15 January 2011, *This side, the other side*), which was the first step in establishing Turku as an ECC in 2011, attracted about 300 journalists, of which 100 came from abroad. Furthermore, MTV3, the biggest commercial television channel in Finland, broadcast this event live nationwide. During January 2011, the ECC 2011 was mentioned 332 times in the biggest newspapers in Finland. The ECC 2011 even received attention from large international newspapers, such as *The New York Times*, *The Guardian*, *The Independent* and *Die Zeit* (Lilja 2011). This media attention contained many different views and expectations on both the ECC as an event, and on the ECC's effect on the city of Turku. Media have a crucial role in representing, and forming the general opinion on the creative and cultural side of a city. Without the discussion in media, the expected effects of an event like the ECC can easily dissolve, due to the fact that it is mostly through media that citizens build a notion of which cultural initiatives are made in their city.

Media forms opinions, functions as a gatekeeper and channels crucial information about different events. We have collected articles concerning the ECC between August 2009 and February 2011 from in particular four newspapers in Finland (*Hufvudstadsbladet*, *Åbo Underrättelser*, *Turun Sanomat*, *Helsingin Sanomat*). During this time period expectations are highlighted, not reactions to experiences. Through a closer analysis of the ECC-related articles in these newspapers, we have mapped the voices of expectations on the impact of culture that Turku is expected to have due to hosting the ECC in 2011. We could identify especially three clear voices that came through this media analysis: imaginative expectations, restricted expectations and critical expectations.

Imaginative expectations

The most optimistic expectations in the media focused mostly on culture's influence on the general well-being, and how the ECC would inject new life into the city. These voices also expected Turku2011 to broaden people's views and interests of/in culture. The financial benefits of such a major investment in culture were also clearly emphasized. The most optimistic of these discourses even talked about a fundamental change in the identity of Turku and a major uplift in the image of Turku, both nationally and abroad. The ECC was in these discourses expected to raise a lot of interest in culture and its importance in developing

Turku as an attractive contemporary city. The discourse also assumed that the ECC-year would have an impact on the ideological view on culture, i.e. that it would help implement a positive notion on the power of culture, a notion where culture *is* a catalyst of creativity in cities and that a city *will* flourish by embracing cultural initiatives.

Restricted expectations

More modest voices of expectations on the power of culture could be seen as struggling between the awareness of culture's strategic role in Turku, and the questioning of the large financial investment. The discourse of modest expectations believed in the role of culture as a tool in creating a new cultural and creative city, but at the same time maintained restricted expectations on what role the ECC will have on Turku's future development. The ECC-year as a single event, although a year long, was not seen as enough to change Turku's image to become a given cultural city, but it was seen as a good starting point. Thus these voices mostly saw the ECC as a good thing and expected to see some unknown measure of power emanating out of this cultural initiative, but raised criticism whether cultural initiatives would decline dramatically after 2011 – in other words, that the ECC would be used by politicians as an excuse to not make further investments in culture. This was a defining feature among the modest expectations; that cultural investments *will* generate positive impacts on Turku, but questioned whether the city would be able to fully utilize these effects, or let the power generated by the event eventually peter out.

Critical expectations

Probably due to media's interest in colourful discussions, the critical expectations against the ECC received a large share of visibility in the media, and especially criticism against voices of imaginative expectations. Most of this criticism was directed especially against the organizers of the ECC, the big price tag of the event, and the Foundation's investments in cultural actors from outside Turku. The critique came from many different directions, both from culturally involved and 'the man on the street'. Due to the organizers investments in cultural actors from outside the city, these voices argued that long-term effects for the city of Turku are not to be expected. 'The man on the street' mostly criticized what according to them was a big price tag for a year of culture, arguing that the power (effects) of such big cultural initiatives cannot be expected to cover its costs. Through the underlying theme for the year, 'culture does good', the organizers invoked cultural initiatives' long-term effects; that culture *will* be a catalyst for a more creative and prosperous city. This assumption is, according to the critical voices, taken too much for granted. The counter-discourse thus becomes one where individuals – both journalists and people commenting on op-ed pages and through the comment functions on the newspapers' websites – claimed that there is no given reason why the ECC would affect Turku after 2011, and that the high expectations were unfounded.

The expectations in the media were in this manner not a unified whole, but rather a case of contested and contesting discourses. An interested individual could in the media pick and choose the expectations or non-expectations they felt most valid, and find support for them. What the media discussion regarding Turku2011 shows is that the expectations on a large-scale cultural event are far from clear and given, but a contested field. If we compare this with the much more streamlined set of expectations set forth by most of the literature on cultural events as catalysts and the institutions that have a vested interest in the same, we can see this as a game of competing discourses. The expectations set will have clear political and economic repercussions, and the by now traditional way of presenting expectations on cultural events in extremely positive terms may in fact strengthen this tendency of strong counter-discourses.

Discussion

This diversity in expectations on the power of culture can be partly understood in the same vein as the problematics Palmer, Richards and Dodd (2011) point out (note that they prefer the abbreviation ECOC):

> The coming of age of the ECOC after 25 years brings new responsibilities, as cities now have to deal with a wider range of issues, including more diverse communities, reconciling the needs of past, present, future, transforming daily life, responding to current global challenges, still ensuring the promotion of imagination and beauty, fostering integration. In organizing the contemporary ECOC, there is a need to design new forms of civic engagement as tools for change.
>
> (Palmer *et al.* 2011: 11)

Cities are more diverse, involving many different communities that want to highlight their own forms and notions of culture. This, put together with the fact that the European Commission echoes and underlines that the main idea of the ECC is to highlight the diversity in European cultures, can partly also explain the diversity of expectations on the power of an event like the ECC. Due to the echoing of the ECC's function to highlight cultural diversity, the expectations naturally vary a lot for what culture will bring to a city during such a year. Underlining cultural diversity brings some inevitable issues that have been highlighted by Lähdesmäki and also seen in the case of Turku:

> Cultural diversity, as well as multiculturalism, is profoundly political concepts and their definitions and representations involve inevitably the power structures and production of cultural and political hierarchies. In the discourse of cultural diversity some groups or cultures seem to be more important than others: only some cultures and groups are promoted in the

> discourse. Moreover, the discourse itself is often produced from the power position of some majority group or culture. In the application books and promotion material, the discourse of cultural diversity is often outlined narrowly, mainly in reference to nationality, ethnicity or religion, not emphasizing, for example, as much social class, sub-cultures or sexual identity.
>
> (Lähdesmäki 2010: 39)

We argue that organizing and embracing an event that bears the name *European Capital of Culture* is, whether one wants it or not, an establishment and definition of the concept of culture in itself, even if its diversity is underlined. In the process of organizing the ECC 2011, the organizers have selected programmes, events and projects that construct the official cultural programme during the year, and hence through this process given *one* definition of culture. Due to the fact that everyone has his/her own notion of what a 'year of culture' means, organizing a major event 'in the name of culture', signals *one* kind of definition that may not suit other people's own definitions, hence we can see a broad diversity in opinions and expectations concerning the power of the ECC.

We could clearly see that the city's definition of culture, brought to light through Turku2011, did not please everyone and even resulted in a resistance movement, which criticized the organizers, 'definition' of culture. One specific facet of this resistance movement, 'the European Capital of Sub-Culture', criticized the fact that culture, according to their own definition, must be independent, non-commercial and open to all. Even if the organizers promoted the ECC as a year of culture for everyone, the organizers' monopoly position in organizing the ECC year was seen as an advantage in showing what Turku defines as culture. This raised many opinions and attitudes regarding the selection of projects that formed the programme of the year, as many did not agree with the organizers' definition of culture.

Managing the diversity of opinions, expectations and attitudes is in line with the conclusion that Palmer, Richards and Dodd (2011: 11) draw: 'In organizing the contemporary ECC, there is a need to design new forms of civic engagement as tools for change.' A platform for civic engagement would enable citizens to ventilate and express expectations that have arisen due to a major cultural initiative, in other cases op-ed pages and comment functions on the newspapers' websites will be used as opinion-sharing spots. In Turku we could even see another thing happen, people started using the concept of the ECC to express feelings and attitudes about other aspects related to the city, not necessarily issues related to the ECC:

> A YouTube posting made by the students of the Arts Academy at Turku University of Applied Sciences, and used to promote the candidacy of Turku has been littered with postings about fascist assaults in the capital of culture.
>
> (Palmer *et al.* 2011: 18)

In other words, when it comes to arranging large-scale cultural events, it is not enough to merely establish grand expectations, one also needs to understand and manage the multiplicity of the same.

Conclusion

In this chapter we have tried to analyse and understand what kind of expectations surface when, through organizing a European Capital of Culture, a city markets itself as cultural, when it for a year carries the 'flag of culture', and claims to use the power of culture to become a creative city. The concept of the ECC is not limited to showcasing established cultural capitals, but it is a platform that enables chosen cities to *become* a cultural capital, much like Turku tried to become a *pioneer* and *creative centre* (Helander *et al.* 2007: 8) through this event. This indicates an ideological notion of a great deal of expectations on the power of this title, and such cultural initiatives – on various levels. We have tried to highlight these, and the complex problems that emerge as they meet and intermingle.

As the grand expectations of the organizing institutions and the at times grandiose expectations we can find in the literature on cultural events meet the more practical concerns of those who try to eke out a living in the cultural sector, or even try to eke out a living at all, there are sure to be some clashes. We have not in this text even attempted to fully follow all the circuits of feedback and criticism that have emerged out of the meetings of different expectations, but rather attempted to highlight the importance of understanding and managing the same. Expectations management *is* a vital factor in determining a project's success or failure, especially when it comes to an event like the ECC, where citizens' decisions (whether it was a success or failure with regard to their expectations) play a huge role in determining the success or failure of the event.

Currently, in the debate regarding the importance of the cultural sector and cultural events on the development of a city or region, such matters have often been bypassed. This might in part be due to an ideological bias among those who write about such matters – selection bias tends to make one less likely to pay attention to dissenting voices and expectations – but also due to the fact that actors in this field have found it difficult to get their voices heard, and in such a situation one is less likely to highlight problems and question marks. We would, however, contend that this is something that becomes increasingly important as cultural initiatives become more popular. Without a level-headed understanding of how expectations are created and managed, we run the risk of making grander and grander promises regarding the power of culture, and thus invite an almost inevitable backlash.

We obviously do not know what would have happened if, for example, the Foundation behind Turku2011 would have presented their expectations in a different manner, or whether it would have been politically feasible for the European Commission to present the ECC-programme as anything but a revolutionary force. However, we do contend that an improved understanding of these kinds of events will require more studies not just of the effects and power of cultural events, but the effect and power of the expectations surrounding them.

References

Alvesson, M. and Sköldberg, K. (2009) *Reflexive Methodology. New Vistas for Qualitative Research*, 2nd edn, London: Sage Publications.

Czarniawska, B. (1997) *Narrating the Organization. Dramas of Institutional Identity*, Chicago: University of Chicago Press.

European Commission (2010a) *About the European Capitals of Culture*. Available at: http://ec.europa.eu/culture/our-programmes-and-actions/doc433_en.htm (accessed 20 May 2011).

——— (2010b) *European Capital of Culture*. Available at: http://ec.europa.eu/culture/our-programmes-and-actions/doc413_en.htm (accessed 20 May 2011).

Florida, R. (2002) *The Rise of the Creative Class – and How it's Transforming Work, Leisure, Community and Everyday Life*, New York: Basic Books.

Helander, N., Innilä, S. and Talve, J. (2007) *Turku on Fire: The Application of the City of Turku for the European Capital of Culture 2011*, The City of Turku.

Kostera, M. (2006) *Organisational Ethnography. Methods and Inspirations*, Lund: Studentlitteratur.

Lähdesmäki, T. (2010) 'European Capitals of Culture as Cultural Meeting Places – Strategies of Representing Cultural Diversity', *Nordisk kulturpolitisk tidskrift [The Nordic journal of cultural policy]*, 1(13): 27–43.

Landry, C. (2008) *The Creative City: A Toolkit for Urban Innovators*, London: Earthscan Publications.

Landry, C. and Bianchini, F. (1995) *The Creative City*, London: Demos Publishers.

Lilja, K. (2011) 'Kulttuuripääkaupunki kiinnostaa matkakohteena', *Turun Sanomat*, 6 February 2011: 18.

Lindeborg, L. and Lindkvist, L. (eds) (2010) *Kulturens kraft för regional utveckling*, Stockholm: SNS Förlag.

Mommaas, H. (2004) 'Cultural Clusters and the Post-industrial City: Towards the Remapping of Urban Cultural Policy', *Urban Studies*, 41(3): 507–532.

Oberhuber, F. and Krzyzanowski, M. (2008) 'Discourse Analysis and Ethnography', in R. Wodak and M. Krzyzanowski (eds), *Qualitative Discourse Analysis in the Social Sciences*, Basingstoke: Palgrave.

Palmer, R. (2004) *European Cities and Capitals of Culture. Study Prepared for the European Commission, PART 1*, Brussels: Palmer-Rae Associates.

Palmer, R., Richards, G. and Dodd, D. (2011) *European Cultural Capital 3 Report*, Arnhem: ATLAS (Association for Tourism and Leisure Education).

Turku2011 (2011) Available at: www.turku2011.fi (accessed 24 September 2011).

9 The essential power of culture

Museums and the Archipelago Trail in the Southwest Finland Archipelago

Katriina Siivonen

Why culture affects tensions?

The economic value of various symbols in culture will increase as a result of the process of the globalization of our time, as many researchers have noticed. Accordingly, culture and cultural heritage as symbols of localities are considered resources in cultural and regional politics in the European Union. The aim of using them as instruments is to develop local economic activities and well-being (see, for example, Wilenius 2004: 22–29; Shore 2000: 42–54). Both earlier industrialization and the globalization of our own time have brought significant structural and cultural changes to the Southwest Finland Archipelago (Andersson 1998; Vainio 1981). Thus, there is a need for local development in the area. In practice this need is realized, for instance, in the development projects where local culture is instrumentally used in different ways in the Archipelago area.

In this chapter I will analyse two examples of regional development projects in the Southwest Finland Archipelago. These were implemented shortly after Finland became a member of the European Union in 1995. My qualitative analysis is based on my own ethnographic fieldwork in the Archipelago.

In the first of the examples, two museum projects called *Puhti*[1] and Discover Museums in Åboland (*Upptäck museer i Åboland*[2]), the clear intention was to use local culture and cultural history as instruments in the development of the Archipelago region. In the other example, the Archipelago Trail (*Saariston Rengastie/Skärgårdens ringväg*[3]), local culture was not used as a tool in the project.

The mutually cooperating museum projects were successful projects in many ways, but they were also confronted with clear socio-cultural tensions in their activities. The Archipelago Trail was considered to be very successful and functional and no tensions were connected to it. Why were tensions visible in those projects where culture was instrumentally used, and not in the project where this was not the case? Why didn't local culture as a resource ensure socio-cultural well-being in the region?

Bilingual archipelago area in the Southwest Finland

The Region of Southwest Finland has a wide and idyllic archipelago (see Figure 9.1). According to geographical investigations, it covers 10,000 km^2 of water and includes over 22,000 islands. There are, on the one hand, large and fertile islands in the inner archipelago, suitable for farming. Yet on the other hand 75 per cent of the islands, mostly situated in the outer archipelago, have less than one hectare of surface area, and many are also very barren (Granö *et al.* 1999: 33, 38). The area is divided into eight municipalities.[4] Some of these municipalities are partly on the mainland, so that only some of the populations are islanders. The population of the islands is in all *c.* 17,000 (*Suomen tilastollinen vuosikirja* 2005: 92–94; Sisäasiainministeriö 2007: 56–57). According to the statistics the majority of people living in two neighbouring municipalities[5] of all of these Archipelago municipalities have Swedish as their mother tongue. Thus the relation between Finnish and Swedish in these municipalities is the opposite of that of Finland as a whole, wherein the proportion of the Swedish-speaking population is 5.5 per cent. The amount of Swedish-speaking population in the other archipelago municipalities in Southwest Finland is less than 2 per cent (*Suomen tilastollinen vuosikirja* 2005: 92–94).

According to constitution and a special language law in Finland there are two official languages, Finnish and Swedish (Kielilaki 1922/2003; Suomen perustuslaki 1999).[6] As the research of history and languages confirms, the position of these languages in Finland has longstanding roots. Both of these languages and their preliminary stages were already in use in prehistoric time in the territory of what is now Finland. The border between the area of Uralic languages and the area of Indo-European languages goes through Finland. Languages belonging to these two language groups are totally different, and they have had an impact on each other (see e.g. Meinander 2011: 12–13; Carpelan 2002a, Carpelan 2002b). On the border of these two languages there are and have been individuals who speak both of them and who possibly have changed the main language they use to the other language in the course of their life. There is and has been a mixed population of people belonging to both language groups, and bilingual people.

This is the case also with the culture. As ethnologists and anthropologists have noticed, culture consists of both the material and non-material elements, which are transferred, as traditions always are, from one human being to another. Simultaneously traditions always change. Transfer and change of traditions also happens when there is interaction between people who speak different languages. Boundlessness, individual heterogeneity and change are thus inevitable basic qualities of culture. Culture, therefore, is and has always been in this sense primarily one global, dynamic process (Siivonen 2008: 49–72; see also e.g. Bringéus 1981: 122–130; Hannerz 1992; Gerholm and Gerholm 1989). It is possible that in the basically boundless, heterogeneous and global culture, relatively homogenous and separate units will arise. But it is, however, not possible to draw clear boundaries for these separate cultures, it is not possible in

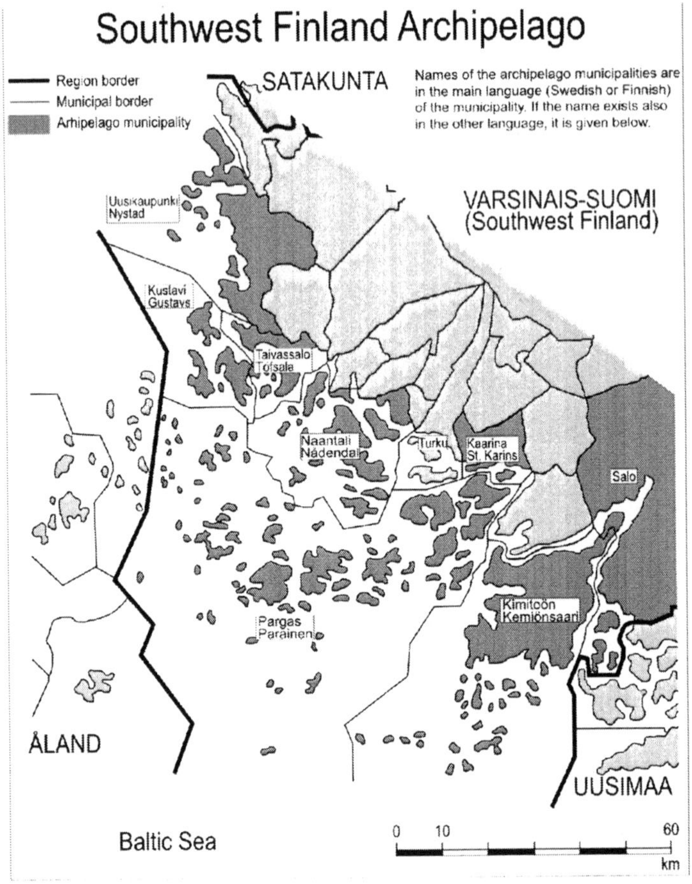

Figure 9.1 Southwest Finland Archipelago.

place, time or in social structures. And it is not possible to found real homogenous cultural units. People can also belong to several such cultural homogeneous clusters at the same time. They can associate with them or estrange themselves from them. In this way the crowd of people that belongs to these clusters is also in continuous motion. The common denominators in the relatively homogeneous clusters can be a place, language or religion, but it can also be, if we take examples from current time, an organization, the internet and other media, ethnicity, nationality, an ideology or, for example, some interest shared in common. It can also be some combination of these different elements (Siivonen 2008: 54–72; see also e.g. Croucher 2004: 185–196).

Like Roger M. Keesing points out, in this connection it is, first, important to seek definitions of culture without a priori ideas about certain cultures. Second, the important models for analysis in cultural research are those which help in recognizing homogenizing, essentializing and static phenomena in the basically global, dynamic and boundless cultural process (Keesing 1994: 309–310). In this respect the different institutions related to economic, religious and ideological powers are the central objects for study.

According to Henrik Meinander, in the second half of the first millennium this kind of homogenizing and symbolic cultural power was especially the Catholic Church, which was at that time spreading its influence to the area of what is now Sweden and Finland. The emerging kingdom of Sweden had the same kind of influence. It spread its power during the following centuries to the territory of the Baltic Sea area, sometimes to a wider, sometimes to a smaller area (Meinander 2011: 18–19 and *passim*). The Southwest Finland Archipelago together with the Åland Islands and the Stockholm Archipelago had a central position between two important medieval cities in this kingdom, Turku in present day Finland and Stockholm in present day Sweden. At the end of the first millennium Novgorod and the Orthodox Church also spread their influence from the east to the area of current Finland (Meinander 2011: 19). As Meinander points out, languages didn't have any symbolic meaning as a denominator of a nation at that time. The Swedish language was rooted in Sweden, which included a part of present day Finland, as the language of royal power and persons of rank, even though Finnish, Latin, Danish, German and French languages were also used during the following centuries. Through the reformation in the sixteenth century the Lutheran Church was established in Sweden and Finland. Its aim was to use vernacular languages in religious activities. In this context both Finnish and Swedish languages were in use in the current area of Finland. In the administration of the crown Swedish was still the dominating language (Meinander 2011: 21, 41–42).

According to historians, the power interests of, first, Sweden and Novgorod, then Sweden and Russia, moved the border between them on several occasions during the centuries, sometimes eastwards, sometimes westwards. The borderline went through different lines in the area of what is now Finland. In the peace negotiations in 1809 the whole area of Finland was incorporated into Russia. As a consequence, the connection to the kingdom of Sweden was broken after many hundreds of years, and Finland became an autonomous Grand Duchy of Finland under the Russian Empire. The Lutheran Church, Swedish law, and at the beginning also the Swedish language, as the language of the administration, retained their positions in the Grand Duchy (see e.g. Meinander 2011: 106–107 and *passim*).

According to Meinander, in the beginning, people identified themselves with the religious community and with the emperor as a part of the Russian Empire. In the course of the nineteenth century and under the impact of the European national movement the Finnish language rose to become the written language of administration and culture. The area of Karelia with its cultural attributes became the symbol of Finnish nationalism. When the Finnish language acquired a stronger position, the Swedish speaking minority in Finland was roused in order to strengthen the position of the Swedish language and the Swedish speaking population in Finland. Finland got an independent position as a state in 1917 in the maelstrom of the World War I and Russian revolution. Both the Finnish and

Swedish languages were defined as official languages in the constitution and language law of the new state (Meinander 2011: 125–132, 160–165).

The Swedish-speaking population in Finland lives mainly on the coast and in archipelago, not only in Southwest Finland, but in the whole coastal area. According to Bo Lönnqvist, since the beginning of the twentieth century, the Swedish-speaking Finns have been defined in an institutional way as an ethnic group of their own on the side of the formation of Finnish nationality in the process of nationalism. One part of this formation was the emphasizing of the archipelago area on the whole coast of Finland as one of the symbols of the Swedish-speaking Finns (Lönnqvist 2001: 26–30; see also Meinander 2011: 185). Thus, in a symbolic way the archipelago has been a Swedish-speaking area, although in the Finnish-speaking archipelago municipalities people have been living in the same natural and socio-cultural environment and with the same kind of livelihoods and material surroundings in their everyday life as do those who inhabit the Swedish-speaking areas of the archipelago, that is, even though they speak Finnish (Siivonen 2008: 104, 344). The position of archipelago culture as the symbol of the Swedish-speaking Finns has been created for instance in museums. It is worth noting that the oldest open air museum in all of Finland, Sagalund, is situated in the Swedish-speaking area of the Southwest Finland Archipelago.[7] This museum is one of the local professional museums in the Southwest Finland Archipelago. It was grounded in 1900 (Sagalunds museum 2012).[8] There is also another professional museum on the islands, and it too is situated in the Swedish-speaking area of this Archipelago (Pargas hembygdsmuseum 2012). In addition, there are several museums managed by amateurs both in the Swedish-speaking and the Finnish-speaking area of the Archipelago. All of these museums participated in the museum projects analysed in this article.

A changing world and a changing Archipelago

According to several researchers, the core of global transition in our time is considered to be cultural change. First, as an essential point the transition from the intentional uniformity of the industrial age to the creative individuality and cultural heterogeneity of the present day and in the future, can be seen. This is not only visible in everyday life, but also in other changes, such as in the economic and administrative activities and structures. Second, an essential element in the global transition is seen to be the dematerialization of the economy and society. Increasingly, part of production and consumption will become intangible items, and the material part of the economic value of products will decrease proportionally. This will increase the economic value of various symbols in culture. Third, cultural change consists of networks which connect local and global elements to each other and thus, to more and more multidimensional and dynamic social structures (Castells 1996, Castells 1998: 336–360; Wilenius 2004: 22–29; see also Florida 2004: 1–17, 267–269).

The global economic and structural changes also affect changes in distant rural areas, like in the Southwest Finland Archipelago. The European Union encourages citizens and regional organizations to exploit the features seen as special parts of local culture in development projects in order to achieve further prosperity, vitality and economic gain in the changing world (Shore 2000: 42–54). As, for instance, Antti Hautamäki points out, at the same time according to EU principles these organizations and the areas they represent are subjected to mutual competition, and significant economic support is being offered. In this whole process the idea of the originality of the culture with its essential symbols becomes a tool for fostering development and competition (Hautamäki 1999: 26–27).

According to Kjell Andersson, the living conditions in the Southwest Finland Archipelago have changed in the course of the modernization process. The former sources of livelihood, mainly agriculture, fishing and rural shipping, are no longer as profitable for the inhabitants. There is some industry in the area, which is partly rooted in the seventeenth century (Lukala 1986: 228–232). Nevertheless, primary livelihoods maintained their relatively strong position even during the industrialized era. In the nineteenth century and at the beginning of the twentieth century, fishing was extremely profitable. The situation changed, however, after Finland became independent in 1917 and lost its position in the Russian internal market. The number of people dependent on fishing and agriculture for their livelihood has fallen considerably in the Archipelago. The most extensive branch of industry is currently the services, and tourism is considered promising (Andersson 1997: 26–28, Andersson 1998). During the twentieth century the population fell steadily, especially in the outer Archipelago, where fishing has had a relatively strong position. Nevertheless, since the 1970s, the size of the population has remained quite stable (Vainio 1981: 33; Bergbom and Bergbom 2005: 57–61). Although living conditions have been changing rapidly, many old cultural traits are still practised in some form.

In the Archipelago, the particular local characteristics and the importance of tourism is expected to grow in the wake of globalization on both a national and international level. Valuable exotic symbols of the past are to be found in the Archipelago region which can be commodified, for example, in the global competition of the travel market. In the deeds and memories of the people living in the Archipelago, and to some extent in their means of living, despite the multicultural radical changes, an age-old primary form of livelihood, the seafaring activities practised in the area and the customs related to these continue to be preserved through many features.

In regional development work all development organizations thus develop and exploit, for instance, cultural features that are seen to be specialties of their own region and defined as its cultural heritage. Each area strives to be unique and to create an authentic identity or brand, based on its own culture. These specialties should then further materialize into products and services; different EU-projects and organizations taking the responsibility of cultural heritage and cultural products function as such development organizations, and define their own area as an own culture with help of them. None of these organizations has the whole archipelago in Southwest Finland as working area. Thus they are creating competing definitions of archipelago (Shore 2000: 42–45; Siivonen 2008: 105–108, 219–223).

Culture is not just an instrument in the use of regional development. It is the way we as human beings are, interpret and act in the world together with other human beings. In the context of the cultural analysis of local development work it is, thus, relevant to take different organizations, such as the European Union and the various organizations concerned with regional development and the administration of cultural heritage, like museums, to become part of the culture. I'm analysing the chosen development projects, and through them the regional development work, as a part of culture.

Local culture as everyday life and as a tool for development

In the following I compare regional development with the promotion of the welfare of different ethnic groups using the model that the Norwegian anthropologist Fredrik Barth has developed for analysing ethnicity and ethnopolitics. Barth divides activities and phenomena in ethnic processes into three levels. The micro level consists of the unorganized everyday life of all people. According to Barth, on the micro level people formulate their own local identities and culture, their relationship to their own surroundings, its people and its nature – or their ethnicity – in a constant interaction with other people. This happens through their own contacts both in their local neighbourhood and in international networks, for example, through trade, the media and the internet, or other contacts. On the micro level, then, culture accords with the definition of culture as a global process of interaction between different individuals and individuals and their environments. Culture, images of cultures, tangible and intangible traditions, and belonging to some area or a group of people – cultural identity – are not piles of fixed collective features, but rather, processes that are in a constant state of change in the cultural interaction process. Homogeneous cultural entities with clear borders do not exist on the micro level (Barth 1994: 183–184; see also Hannerz 1992).

According to Barth, local and regional organizations function on the middle level. They are, for instance, those organizations in regional development or related to tourism or cultural heritage. In society, these organizations have the right to use power and define different cultural meanings, and perhaps also to define the rights and duties of citizens, depending on the type of organization. According to Barth, the intention of these organizations is to create a feeling of community and to motivate people to strive towards some goal – be it ethnic or regional (Barth 1994: 183–184). In terms of the regional development, the intention is to create unique slogans, brands and concrete products from local culture on the one hand, and to strengthen cultural identity in the search for cooperation and enterprise, on the other. Tangible and intangible cultural heritage are important tools in this work. People working in different organizations on the middle level need to create homogeneous and stable images of certain regional, local and group-based cultures for their tools. A dynamic and heterogeneous definition of culture as a process is not easily suited to such a tool. Consequently, in the activities on the middle level culture is usually seen opposite to it, which means it is seen as the essential, homogeneous and stable cultural whole of an area or a group of people.

On the micro level the process of culture itself is the constant and essential element of culture on both the individual, local and global spheres. The cultural heritage symbolizing cultures emerges in the interaction between individuals on the micro level and different organizations on the middle level. With the cultural heritage, people working in these organizations create images of homogeneous and stable cultures with clear boundaries. All individual human beings create their own relationship with this cultural heritage, and they are not necessarily bound by the cultures described through them (Barth 1994: 183–184; Beckman 1998).

Therefore, the micro and middle levels are opposites by their very nature. However, they cannot be mechanically separated and they have an impact on each other. Defined in too narrow and inflexible a way on the middle level, culture and identity as cultural heritage is capable of causing tensions or conflicts with the dynamic complexity of everyday life. It is also possible that there arise tensions and conflicts between different middle level organizations and their definitions of cultural boundaries and cultural heritage symbolizing those boundaries.

It is important to note that the tensions and conflicts mentioned above are not dependent on the origin of those people working in these areas. Rather, the determining factor is the nature of the activities of these people. In different organizations on the middle level both those native to the region and others do their work in similar situations and under the same conditions. Consequently, the definition of a local or regional culture is based on the nature of the tasks of those engaged in work in different regional organizations (Barth 1994: 183–184).

According to Barth's model, on the middle level it is impossible to act without integrating on the macro level, too. On the macro level the actors are national and international organizations, and they create a framework for local activities through legislation, administration and the financing of various activities (Barth 1994: 183–184). In the contexts of regional development and cultural heritage these are, for instance, the European Union and the national organizations concerned with regional development and cultural heritage, such as ministries and national museums. They take care of, among other things, the production of cultural heritage and provide the guidelines for regional development work. Also on this level, as on the middle level, culture is usually viewed from the perspective of the definition of culture as consisting of essential, homogeneous and stable cultural wholes.

It is not possible to mechanically divide culture into different, separate levels. In reality they are all intertwined. Even one and the same person can function on all three levels in his or her different roles and tasks in culture and society. All these three levels are parts of the cultural entirety and interact in the local and global context.

Important elements in the everyday life of the Archipelago[9]

There are several different ways in which, first the archipelago and its borders and second the experience of one's own archipelago area, take shape in the habitual everyday life of the Southwest Finland Archipelago. Even in the broadest sense, the archipelago[10] does not include any large islands situated close to the mainland. In all, the archipelago can be defined as a continuum, which in its largest sense covers almost all of the islands in the surrounding sea. The strictest definition would be that the archipelago only includes those islands that can be reached in one's own boat or perhaps by ferry, but not by a bridge. It is also necessary for people to live there throughout the year, people with their familiar roots in the archipelago. They should also be able to survive in the demanding environment of the archipelago. All told, according to these criteria, symbolically, the outer archipelago is, for some people, a more proper archipelago than the inner archipelago. At the same time the archipelago in its largest sense is a proper archipelago for others. These ways of defining the archipelago are similar on both sides of the language border. Inside the continuum of definitions there are several smaller archipelagos. Even one and the same person can define them in varying ways in different situations. Ideas about the archipelago concept continuously change and a new bridge or ferry connections can cause reappraisals of definitions even concerning what the very nature of a proper symbolic archipelago is.

Mostly the definition of one's own archipelago has already been outlined with its familiar areas related to everyday activities, thoroughfares and waterways, while still other areas may remain unfamiliar. Unfamiliar areas could also consist of archipelago districts wherein one's own mother tongue was not used as the majority language. In cases such as these, one's own area was not defined in terms of conscious symbols, but rather as familiar, habitual activities. As with the outer archipelago the language boundary was also mentioned as a symbolic border. In this case it was a border around one's own archipelago area or inside of it. In the latter and most common case one's own archipelago was bilingual and the language border was one of its characteristics.

In the everyday culture of the archipelago, nature is the element which ties people most strongly to their own archipelago area. All of my informants in the Archipelago area consider nature as an important matter in their relationship with their home area, but their descriptions of it vary from individual to individual. What is essential can be the familiar view from the kitchen window. It can also be one's habit of using one's own navigable passages, if these are part of daily life. Not everyone living in the archipelago has their own boat. The experience of one's own landscape can have a concrete form such as the enjoyment of the continuously changing sea and nature – whether this is seen from the kitchen window or from a fishing boat in the early hours of the morning, as the following quotation from one of my interviews shows:[11]

> I: The sea air in particular is to me something about which I cannot imagine anything greater, when spring and the breaking up of the ice comes and... You see, when you get up with the sun and then go to your perch-pike nets, and the birds are singing and it is quite calm and you can be alone and in peace and... That is what is most essential of all. Of course, sometimes the weather is bad, there are winds and everything, but... I don't know, I suppose people who are not interested in fishing...they would never do it, the weather is so bad sometimes, there are weak ice and storms and everything. But, you see, you can actually do it, when you have an interest in doing it. But you must have this interest. I was a very small girl the first time, I went as a four- or five-year-old, so.
>
> (TYKL/SPA/435)[12]

Many of my informants felt they are at one with nature and capable of surviving even in a harsh environment. One example of this is the ability to cross over the ice covered sea in wintertime. It sometimes happens that someone falls through the ice, and is often also able to get out again. Such events are a symbolic reminder of the skills needed in the archipelago areas, where, for instance, communication is more often dependent on the capricious state of nature, than on the mainland. These skills are part of the archipelago identity of the informant with whom I next discuss.

> KS: Aha, so this is a part of insular life?
>
> [...]
>
> I: Yes, it is, this was one experience. First time I fell through the ice with a sledge was in my secondary school days, one Wednesday afternoon, when we went home, we always went home on Wednesdays in wintertime, and it so happened that we fell, the sledges, the neighbor's girl and I. And it was my first time then.
>
> (TYKL/SPA/403)[13]

For many people living in the archipelago important cultural features also include familiar neighbours and regular contact with them. People always meet others when they are going about their daily affairs in the village and they usually exchange some words with them. This is a very simple but very important part of their life. The community supports people when they belong to it. One concrete expression of this is the mutual help given in the neighbourhood, according to need. The next quotation is from an interview and relates to this.

> I: [Y]ou can always get help. I don't have any problems if my car suddenly stops, then I make a phone call and say, oh... can you drive me, I need to go to the bank, or whatever, so there is [help], all is near, and you can get everything done well, no problems, it is of course possible that you will be asked [for help as well], but I think that basically the positive side of a small

> community is that, if you want it yourself, and you trust yourself to do so, as is the case in a small community, you probably feel damn good, but I must admit that in a small community it is also so that they don't tolerate very much, it's sad, but they really don't.
>
> (TYKL/SPA/427)[14]

But, as the same quotation shows, small communities also have negative sides. Intolerance towards new settlers and new ideas are among these. Many of my informants also told me about never-ending quarrels in some Archipelago villages or on some islands. Nevertheless, communities are elementary and important parts of the living environment for many inhabitants of the archipelago. They have a feeling of belonging despite the positive and negative circumstances. The following quotation from an interview tells about this.

> I: [Y]ou just belong together, it is really important, you belong together, you belong to the past and to the people here, in both a positive and negative way, but it is natural, it is obvious, it is a connection, I suppose that this is the most important thing, the connection, there is a strong, and important connection with regard to actions, I think at least, that this is of the essence.
>
> (TYKL/SPA/441)[15]

All in all, identification with the archipelago consists of participating in practices related to nature and the community. These operate partly as tacit knowledge, which is sometimes difficult to grasp and describe in words. In some contexts identification consists of conscious symbols. Symbols of this kind are at the same time the beautiful and violent nature of the archipelago, the shores of the islands which form the boundaries, the freedom to work and define one's own way of life inside these limits, and the skills and knowledge learned on the islands, which take priority over the administrational and literal knowledge defined outside of them. Nowadays, these elements of identities are connected with modern livelihoods and the modern way of life with its various commodities.

Therefore, the core element in archipelago identities is living on one's own island in a sensitive balance with the other people living there, assisted by one's own skills and knowledge and dependent on the conditions of nature. Culture and identities are in constant motion, also in the archipelago. Moreover, a very prevalent element in these identities is the will of the residents of the archipelago to define changes themselves within the shores of the islands. Nature is an acceptable and strong definer of actions and identities unlike the administrational and literal knowledge defined outside of the islands. However, impacts are and have been given and received in many ways both through the local and the global interaction networks.

How culture takes action in the regional development

In the twentieth century, mostly after World War II, Swedish-speaking activities have dominated archipelago politics and local development in the archipelago areas. Thus, language policy has been realized through archipelago politics, which has not been expressed for everyone. The archipelago as a cultural symbol of the Swedish-speaking Finns has been customized in administrative and political practices by means of tacit knowledge with strong continuity and this has guided the activities of the developers of the region, although not resulting in conscious dialogue (Siivonen 2008: 212–215; see also Andersson 1997).

Along with the work of development integrated into the European Union, the Finnish-speaking population in the archipelago had more reason than ever to present their living area as an archipelago in the symbolic sense also, not just in respect of the practical matters of everyday life on islands. With the help of this symbolic presentation it has been possible to acquire more resources for local development than before. As a member of the European Union the source of economic support for the development was the EU on the side of national sources. In practice this happened by exploiting cultural items seen to be the archipelago's own distinctive culture (Siivonen 2008: 215–219).

Nevertheless, at the same time the conventional practices of the administrative and political elite regarding the symbolic Swedish-speaking nature of the archipelago and structures for cooperation have been difficult to change. This has been visible in disputes and the missing cooperation that have occurred every now and then in those activities that concern regional archipelago development. The language issue has not been a topic of discussion in everyday life at the micro level in the archipelago; rather this has occurred on the middle level in different organizations among archipelago developers (Siivonen 2008: 219–223).

One example of the failed cooperation over the language border is the activities of the museum projects *Puhti* and Discover Museums in Åboland (*Upptäck museer iÅboland*).[16] These projects were active simultaneously at the end of 1990s. The purpose of these projects was to mentor local museums in the Archipelago and to create a common marketing for the museums. The goal was to advance cultural tourism in the Archipelago. As mentioned, mostly, the museums in this archipelago area are small museums managed by amateurs, but also professional museums with a long local history exist on Swedish-speaking islands. The initiative for the museum projects was made by the Regional Museum in the town of Turku in Southwest Finland. The aim was to have only one project for the whole Archipelago area in order to strengthen cooperation between different small museums over the language border. The projects were funded by a local LEADER-association called On the Same Boat (*I samma båt – samassa veneessä r.f.*[17]). It was against separate projects. In the area with Finnish as the majority language the idea of a common museum project was supported. But, due to the strong resistance of the common project by the representatives of museums in the Swedish-speaking area, two different projects were established. In this situation these museums were the professional ones, and they were in charge of the project Discover Museums in Åboland with several museums managed by amateurs.

Nevertheless, the museum projects were cooperating in some activities, which was also the condition of the funding of the projects. They produced common marketing material for Archipelago museums, published common publications and organized a common ambulatory exhibition and visits to other museums in the area. The local work with museums was separate in the two projects.

The essential point with the separate museum projects was that it was not possible for museums in the Swedish-speaking area to have a common project with the museums of the Finnish-speaking area without losing the idea of the Archipelago as a phenomenon which is characteristic especially of the Swedish Finns. For them it was not possible to present the Archipelago as something which is also a part of Finnish nationality through the language. Cultural heritage is the central element presented in museums, and it was tightly connected to the Swedish language in museums in the Swedish-speaking area. Among them, it was important to keep language groups separate, even though elements of everyday life with different traditions, from which the cultural heritage emerges, are most similar on the both sides of the language border in the Archipelago.

The project Archipelago Trail[18] was considered to be very successful in creating cooperation between different archipelago areas and over the language border in the Archipelago. A regional development centre in the Archipelago (*Saaristomeren kehittämiskeskus/Skärgårdshavets utvecklingscentral*[19]) carried out the project at the end of the 1990s with several partners. The Archipelago Trail forms a circle around the whole Archipelago area. It goes through both the Swedish- and Finnish-speaking areas, and thus also over the language border. It was necessary to open new thoroughfares between islands in order to create a solid circle for the trail. This served both the local inhabitants and tourists. Because of the project a big group of archipelago entrepreneurs were gathered into cooperation, which familiarized them with each other in a new way. Also archipelago services were developed in a new kind of cooperation through the project and after it.

The services were marketed with a common illustrative map (see Figure 9.2), which was distributed to tourists. The condition for entrepreneurs to have their information on the map was that their own municipalities were participating in the project and shared in the costs of the project. In the beginning, not all of the Finnish-speaking municipalities were convinced of the advantages of the project, but after a while they realized them and participated in the project. The Archipelago Trail was considered to bring with it new opportunities for enterprises, but also more disturbing traffic. Culture was not mentioned explicitly in the project, and it was not used as an instrument in the project.

Avoiding tensions with cultural understanding

Many of those who are engaged in the local development of the Archipelago also live in the area. Thus, in their everyday life they sense, perceive and act as a part

Figure 9.2 Archipelago Trail Service Map.

of its basic interactive cultural process at the micro level. However, in their activities, they also realize the different goals of organizations on the middle level. To some extent the actions of organizations were expressed clearly in different projects of regional development. These often consciously positioned themselves in opposition to the everyday life in the Archipelago with the goal of bringing some changes to it. In these activities, tensions easily arose between the everyday life in the Archipelago and the constructions of the Archipelago used by regional development.

To a degree, actions in local development work emphasized essential traits taken from everyday life identities in the Archipelago. These were, for instance, the value of the former way of life, and the archipelago skills and knowledge that were part of it, like in the museum projects. They had deep meaning for local people, although these local people did not wish to limit the development of the Archipelago only to protect and preserve a past way of life.

However, a strong division of cultural heritage in the Archipelago based on the language border is not in accordance with the reality of everyday life there. As already mentioned, on the micro level the language border was in most cases one characteristic of the own archipelago, not a border around it. Also everyday life in the Archipelago with different livelihoods and tangible and intangible cultural elements is most similar on both sides of the language border. Therefore the use of local cultural heritage as a characteristic of only one language group, which was the case in museums and their activities on the middle level, was in tension with the reality of the everyday life on the micro level.

In some respects, the aims of the development projects were consciously opposed to the local archipelago identities. This was the case, for instance, in projects in which the goal was to create new forms of cooperation in the area. Then, for many people, these activities began to overstep important island boundaries where a will existed to define life forms inside of these boundaries without the impact of the outside authorities. These began also to violate the area in which a difficult social balance of Archipelago communities was being maintained. However, novel practices and relations in cooperation were established, if people working with the development process were aware of these traits of the archipelago culture. This was the case with the project Archipelago Trail.

Culture should be used in the right way in order to avoid socio-cultural tensions. First, culturally sustainable development takes into consideration all cultural processes functioning on the micro, middle, and macro levels. This must be done both in those cultural forms which function as non-verbal habits, and those cultural forms which are clearly expressed as symbols. Second, culturally sustainable development has as a principal the notion that it is also necessary to take into consideration other areas or groups of people when culture is defined according to a group of people or an area seen to be one's own. None of these groups have the right to declare that some cultural traits belong only to them, if other groups display similar traits in their everyday lives. The most important notion is that the best results will be reached in the regional development if the local culture is not only used as an instrument in development work but also as a basic understanding of local and glocal ways of understanding the world and act in the environment and among people. Knowledge and understanding of essential traits in local culture should primarily be a part of the mode of activities of the development work, like in the case of the Archipelago Trail. Then the essential power of culture will be used in development processes.

Notes

1 The name is in Finnish.
2 The name is in Swedish.
3 The name is both in Finnish and Swedish.
4 These are Kaarina, Kimitoön, Kustavi, Pargas, Masku, Naantali, Salo, Taivassalo and Uusikaupunki. At the beginning of 2009 the number of municipalities in the Archipelago decreased from 18 to 9 and at the beginning of 2011 from 9 to 8, because many of them merged to form larger units than before (Penttilä 2012: 5; Valtioneuvoston asetus saaristokunnista 2008; Valtionvarainministeriö 2010). The towns of Kaarina, Naantali and Turku have some islands in their territory which are not included in the Archipelago. In Finland, the Archipelago is governed by a separate law (Laki saariston kehityksen edistämisestä 1981/1993). According to a statute based on this law, certain islands belonging to Kaarina, Naantali and Turku do not belong to the Archipelago (Valtioneuvoston asetus saaristokunnista 2008). This chapter is based on my doctoral dissertation. In it, I used this definition of the Archipelago as a starting point. In my research, I interviewed people living in the Archipelago. According to my interviews, people living there also have their own definitions of the area. In many cases they are, however, in harmony with the definition of the Archipelago in this statute (Siivonen 2008: 219–223).
5 These are Kimitoön and Pargas.
6 Finnish and Swedish languages have been defined as official languages from the beginning of the independency of Finland.
7 The reason for this is not different culture on the two sides of the language border; the reason was the need to emphasize the Swedish-speaking archipelago with the cultural characteristics of archipelago life. This was done, even though the attributes of material culture, presented also in museums, don't have special character according to language border (Ahlbäck 1945).
8 In comparison, the next old open air museum in Finland is the national Seurasaari Open Air Museum in Helsinki, which was establsihed in 1909 (Seurasaaren ulkomuseo 2012).
9 The analysis and examples in this section are based on my doctoral dissertation and the fieldwork material I collected for it (Siivonen 2008).
10 Because here and in certain other cases, I do not necessarily refer to the administrative region of the Archipelago, I have decided to use a small case initial 'a'.
11 'I' in every quotation means Informant.
12 With the code it is possible to find the interview from the Archives of the School of Cultural Research at University of Turku (see References, Research material). The same quotation in Finnish:

> I: Meri-ilmasto nimenomaan se on mul semmonen, et tota ei hianomppa ol, ko tule tämmöne keväaika ja ruppe jäät lähtemä. Sit nouse aamul aikasi ylös ja sää lähret kuhaverkoil, nii linnut laulaa ja o ihan tyven ilma ja saa iha rauhas olla kato. Se on niin kun se aa ja oo siin asias. Tietysti siäl on kurjakin keli, et on tuulet ja kaikki, mut et. Mää tiärä, et varma semmoset kuka ei ol kiinostunu

kalastuksest, ei ikinä menis sitä tekemä, et kyl siäl niin pal kurja keli välil on, et on heikot jäät ja on myrskyt ja kaike näköst. Se vaa jaksa, kato niin ko on kiinostunu siihe. Tai siin täyty olla niin ko kiinostust. Mää olen piänest tytöst lähtien sillon, ko mää ole joskus ollu tommone neljä viisvuotias, nii.

13 The same quotation in Finnish:

KS: Jaaha, niin tämä kuuluu tähän saaristolaisuuteen?

[...]

I: Joo, kyl se kuuluu, tää oli niin kun yks kokemus. Mää oon tota ensimmäisen kerran ollu kelkan kans jäissä yläasteaikan yks keskiviikkoiltapäivä, kun tultiin sitten kotiin, kun talviaikan keskiviikot käytiin, niin oli semmonen tilanne, että naapurin tytön kans mentiin kans jäihin kelkkojen kans tossa. Ja se oli ensmäinen kerta ja.

14 The same quotation in Swedish:

I: [D]u har ju alltid hjälp, jag har ju inga problem om bilen plötsligt stannar så ringer jag och säger, oj... kör du mig, jag skulle till banken, eller vad som helst, så det finns, allting det nära, och man får allting välgjort, inga problem alltså, det kan ju hända att du blir uppställd, men jag tror att över huvudtaget alltså att ett litet samhälles plussida är det att, om du vill det själv, litar på vad du gör, så som man nu gör i ett litet samhälle, så mår man nog förbannat bra, men jag måste nog medge, att i ett litet samhälle det finns sådant också som, den tolererar nog inte allt för mycket, det är olyckligt, det gör den nog inte.

15 The same quotation in Swedish:

I: [M]an hör ju ihop, det är väldigt viktigt, man hör ihop, man är med den förflutna och med människorna här, så på gott och ont, men det är liksom naturligt, det är liksom självklart, det är ett sammanhang, det är väl det som är det allra viktigaste, sammanhanget, det finns ett starkt, och viktigt sammanhang att verka i, det tycker jag i alla fall, är väldigt väsentligt.

16 This case is presented in more detail in Siivonen 2008: 290–293.
17 The name is both in Swedish and Finnish.
18 This case is presented in more detail in Siivonen 2008: 290–291.
19 The name is both in Finnish and Swedish.

References

Research material

Archives of the School of Cultural Research, the Ethnology Archives (TYKL-kokoelma), University of Turku:

Manuscripts, Interviews and fieldwork material for her doctoral thesis, Katriina Siivonen, TYKL/SPA/395–468.

Literature

Ahlbäck, R. (1945) *Kulturgeografiska kartor över Svenskfinland.* Folklivsstudier 1. Skrifter utgivna av Svenska litteratursällskapet i Finland Nr 300, Helsingfors: Svenska litteratursällskapet i Finland.

Andersson, K. (1997) *Den finländska skärgårdspolitikens framväxt och utveckling, Strukturell bakgrund, aktörer och institutioner,* SSKH Meddelanden Nr 44, Helsingfors: Forskningsinstitutet, Svenska social- och kommunalhögskolan vid Helsingfors universitet.

——— (1998) *Näringsutveckling i sydvästra Finlands skärgård, Tolv kommuner i ljuset av offentlig statistik,* Rapporter och diskussionsinlägg 4/98, Helsingfors: Svenska social- och kommunalhögskolan vid Helsingfors universitet.

Barth, F. (1994) *Manifestasjon og prosess*, Oslo: Universitetsforlaget.

Beckman, S. (1998) 'Vad vill staten med kulturarvet?', in A. Alzén and J. Hedrén (eds), *Kulturarvets natur*, Stockholm/Stenhag: Brutus Östlings Bokförlag Symposion.

Bergbom, G. and Bergbom, K. (2005) 'Befolkningsförändringar och ägoförhållanden på utskären i Skärgårdshavet 1954–2004', *Skärgård. Tidskrift utgiven av Skärgårdsinstitutet vid Åbo Akademi* Nr 1/2005: 57–67.

Bringéus, N.-A. (1981) *Människan som kulturvarelse*, Lund: LiberLäromedel.

Carpelan, C. (2002a) 'Esihistorian vuosiluvut, ajoitukset ja kronologia', in R. Grünthal (ed.), *Ennen, muinoin, Miten menneisyyttämme tutkitaan*, Helsinki: Suomalaisen Kirjallisuuden Seura.

Carpelan, C. (2002b) 'Arkeologiset löydöt aikaportaina', in R. Grünthal (ed.), *Ennen, muinoin, Miten menneisyyttämme tutkitaan*, Helsinki: Suomalaisen Kirjallisuuden Seura.

Castells, M. (1996) *The Information Age, Economy, Society and Culture, Volume I The Rise of the Network Society*, Cambridge: Blackwell Publishers.

——— (1998) *The Information Age, Economy, Society and Culture, Volume III End of Millennium*, Cambridge: Blackwell Publishers.

Croucher, S.L. (2004) *Globalization and Belonging, The Politics of Identity in a Changing World*, Lanham & Boulder & New York & Toronto & Oxford: Rowman & Littlefield Publishers, Inc.

Florida, R. (2004) *The Rise of the Creative Class – and How it's Transforming Work, Leisure, Community and Everyday Life*, Paperback Edition, New York: Basic Books.

Gerholm, L. and Gerholm, T. (1989) 'Om inte kultur fanns, så skulle man behöva uppfinna den', *Nord Nytt* 37: 8–16.

Granö, O., Roto, M. and Laurila, L. (1999) *Environment and Land Use in the Shore Zone of the Coast of Finland*, Publicationes Instituti Geographici Universitas Turkuensis N:o 160, Turku: University of Turku.

Hannerz, U. (1992) *Cultural Complexity. Studies in the Social Organization of Meaning*, New York: Columbia University Press.

Hautamäki, V.-P. (1999) 'Aluepolitiikan tavoitteet lainsäädännössä', *Kunnallistieteellinen aikakauskirja* 1/1999: 22–33.

Keesing, R.M. (1994) 'Theories of Culture Revisited', in R. Borofsky (ed.), *Assessing Cultural Anthropology*, New York: McGraw-Hill, Inc.

Kielilaki 1.6.1922/148, 6.6.2003/423.

Laki saariston kehityksen edistämisestä 26.6.1981/494, 10.12.1993/1138.

Lönnqvist, B. (2001) 'Myten om den finlandssvenska familjen', in A.-M. Åström, B. Lönnqvist and Y. Lindqvist (eds), *Gränsfolkets barn, Finlandssvensk marginalitet och självhävdelse i kulturanalytisk perspektiv*, Skrifter utgivna av Svenska litteratursällskapet i Finland nr 633, Folklivsstudier XXI, Helsingfors: Svenska litteratursällskapet i Finland.

Lukala, M. (1986) *Dalsbruk 1686–1986*, Dalsbruk: Ovako.

Meinander, H. (2011) *Suomen historia, Linjat, rakenteet ja käännekohdat.* Revised edn, Helsinki: Werner Söderström Osakeyhtiö.

Pargas hembygdsmuseum (2012) *Pargas hembygdsmuseum*, Pargas: Pargas hembygdsmuseum. Available at: www.pargashembygdsmuseum.fi/swe (accessed 14 August 2012).

Penttilä, T. (2012) *Varsinais-Suomen liiton saaristo-ohjelman päivitys vuosiksi 2012–2014, Uppdatering av Egentliga Finlands skärgårdsprogram för åren 2012–2014*, Turku: Varsinais-Suomen liitto.

Sagalunds museum (2012) *Aktuellt*, Kimitoön: Sagalunds museum. Available at: www.sagalund.fi/pages/svenska/aktuellt.php (accessed 14 August 2012).

Seurasaaren ulkomuseo (2012) *Museon historiaa*, Helsinki: National board of Antiquities. Available at: www.nba.fi/fi/museot/seurasaaren_ulkomuseo/historiaa (accessed 14 August 2012).

Shore, C. (2000) *Building Europe, The Cultural Politics of European Integration*, London and New York: Routledge.

Siivonen, K. (2008) *Saaristoidentiteetit merkkien virtoina, Varsinaissuomalainen arki ja aluekehitystyö globalisaation murroksessa*, Kansatieteellinen arkisto 51, Helsinki: Suomen Muinaismuistoyhdistys.

Sisäasiainministeriö (2007) *Saaristo-ohjelma 2007–2010, Saaret, meri, järvet, joet ja rantavyöhyke aluekehitystekijöinä*, Helsinki: Sisäasiainministeriö, Saaristoasiain neuvottelukunta.

Suomen perustuslaki 11.6.1999/731.

Suomen tilastollinen vuosikirja (2005) 100. vuosikerta (uusi sarja) 2005, Helsinki: Tilastokeskus.

Vainio, J. (1981) *Flyttningsrörelse och avfolkning i syvästra Finlands skärgård (Korpo, Rimito och Merimasku 1950–1974)*, Turun yliopiston maantieteen laitoksen julkaisuja N:o 92, Turku: Turun yliopisto, maantieteen laitos.

Valtioneuvoston asetus saaristokunnista ja muiden kuntien saaristo-osista, joihin sovelletaan saaristokuntaa koskevia säännöksiä 18.9.2008/608.

Valtionvarainministeriön päätös kuntajaon muuttamisesta Maskun kunnan ja Naantalin kaupungin välillä 8.2.2010/85.

Wilenius, M. (2004), *Luovaan talouteen. Kulttuuriosaaminen tulevaisuuden voimavarana*, Helsinki: Edita.

10 Creativity and post-original

Maritime Centre Vellamo and Kotka-Hamina Region

Saara L. Taalas

On embeddedness of creativity

In February 2009, when Google decided to situate its server factory in Summa, and to redevelop the old Stora-Enso paper mill area in Hamina, in Southeast Finland, into a futuristic park of thousands of internet search engine servers, it sounded like an old industry site was just replaced by a new one. Google's investment of US$200 million into the development of the Summa industrial site came as a relief after the shock in 2007 when Stora-Enso announced its decision to close Summa paper mill and to relocate its paper production closer to markets in Asia and South-America. This decision meant 430 lost jobs in the region and had considerable effects on the industrial networks in the area. In addition, it ended over 50 years of paper-making history in the Kotka-Hamina region in Southeast Finland with the combined population of just over 75,000 inhabitants. However, the development of the Kotka-Hamina region – one of the most important export harbour clusters in Finland – is not just a story of an old industry being hit by globalization.

The development in the region is strongly linked to developing cultural institutions and sites, side by side with the more global Google affair. Maritime Centre Vellamo with a €48 million investment in Kotka's old harbour was opened in July 2008, and a over-€1 million creative industries development programme was introduced in the same year. However, it is difficult to classify the local development in the area of Kotka-Hamina in traditional terms. Kotka-Hamina seems to have embraced both strategies of regional renewal but also established a major creative economy initiative on a local level only to be matched by cities several times bigger in Finland. While the paper industry in the area was slowing down, Kotka-Hamina area was already investing in building a modern cultural centre and preparing for a creative industry development programme. Further, a wind power park was being planned for the Summa area before Google's decision. It added an attractive aspect to Google's decision to invest in the area. If the developments of the recent years in Kotka-Hamina are viewed in parallel, instead of as separate events, the local activity can be interpreted from the perspective of a contemporary move within an understanding of creative from an alternative perspective. A picture of industrial past and present is assembled creating connections and disconnections as a basis for regional economy.

Kotka-Hamina's development is a case of investment in local cultural and creative economy running parallel to the need to create commitment in renewing of economic relations in the area. A change in the industrial futures is difficult to grasp in terms of either traditional cultural policy or solely in terms of the popular cultural industries development approaches alone. Further, the Kotka-Hamina case falls outside the traditional regional development initiatives. To understand the type of activity in Kotka-Hamina, a more systemic view of the relationship of culture and economy needs to be developed. Kotka-Hamina is breaking up the traditional boundaries of cultural and industrial sites through simultaneous development of Maritime Centre Vellamo fostering creative activity in the area linking it to the information flows and clouds, transforming the old harbour side, and seeking out new industrial uses for redundant industrial sites. The Kotka-Hamina development process is communicating a change in industrial and cultural futures and allowing for reinterpretation of the industrial sites and facilities for contemporary markets. To understand such hybrid moves, we need to revisit traditional views of how the relationship between creativity and management is conceptualized, and how this kind of move might be contributing to the ways global changes might be linked to local futures.

This chapter seeks to find ways to understand the linkages of creativity and local economy revitalization through an illustrative case of regional development in Kotka-Hamina. The chapter is structured into three parts. First, a revisit to the creative economy discussion from the perspective of recent work linking creativity and innovation: focusing on historical development of models of creativity and management (Xu and Richards 2007), obsession with newness in creativity and innovation (Styhre 2006), and an alternative reading on creativity in forms of post-original production (Rehn and Vachhani 2006). Second, drawing from the previous, an alternative way of presenting the case of Maritime Centre Vellamo in Kotka is drafted to show it embedded in the other developments in the region to illuminate possible relationships between creativity and economy on a local level. Finally, Kotka-Hamina's recent regional development is visited and creative projects like Maritime Centre Vellamo and Google's server factory are considered embedded in local networks as examples of creativity emerging from reinterpretation of history as cultural forms in both culture and industrial activity to create a local sense of possible futures: Vellamo in Kotka as a Cultural Centre is visited from the perspective of maritime history and post-original reinterpretation of commercial harbour development not only in terms of its economical past, but also as a hybrid cultural form. The Google server factory in Summa in Hamina becomes similarly perceived from the perspective of post-original production of an industrial past into present and connecting to innovative modern technologies of wind power and communication. Both projects and processes have run parallel in the recent years of the Kotka-Hamina region's developments.

Creativity, innovation and the post-original

The question of how creativity can be linked to local governing practices and development as a strategic move is pivotal when considering local projects and programmes. Traditionally creativity is linked to creative individuals.

> The creative economy is based on a new way of thinking and doing. The primary inputs are our individual talent or skill.
>
> (Howkins 2001a)

The most commonly used definition of the creative economy cited above originates from individual creativity, novel ways of thinking, and producing and utilizing creative content innovatively. The source often referred to is *The Creative Economy*, by John Howkins (2001b), which considers new creative activity, combining it with mass production and large audiences as crucial features. Howkins shows that the new creative class and a group of individuals working with creative content, have been considered key to the creative economy. This view challenges the traditional forms of economic activity and emphasizes immaterial production in particular, and it highlights the novel role of rights related to it.

The concepts of creative economy and creative industries are commonly used as synonyms, even though the scope of the latter is considerably narrower and its focus is different. The definition most commonly applied to creative industries is associated with individual creativity resulting in products protected by intellectual property rights and with sectors of the economy that concentrate on utilizing them in 14 separate industries:

> Those industries which have their origin in individual creativity, skill and talent and which have a potential for wealth and job creation through the generation and exploitation of intellectual property.
>
> (DCMS 2001: 4)

The most extensive empirical report on the subject is the report prepared for the Directorate of Culture and Education of the European Commission, where economic activity in the creative sector was approached from the standpoint of value chains of creative products – not through the concept of the creator or creativity as a quality of the individual.

Based on this, a more economical activity-oriented approach and multi-layered definition of the cultural and creative sector was applied in the Economy of Culture in Europe report (Gueller *et al.* 2006). The economic activity is divided into three fields: arts, cultural industries and the creative sector. This approach is based on the accumulated monetary value applied in industrial business economics, wherein economic value is primarily based on the exchange of outputs. This perspective differs fundamentally from the concept of creative industries that associates economy primarily with the economies springing from individual creativity. The approach applies in business economics and, in turn, emphasizes the exchange and utilization of creative content in systemic forms of economy. Nevertheless, the view is utilitarian and focuses on creative content as separately disseminated and used in the monetary markets.

The formal definition of the creative economy is problematic. It emphazises in a rather elitist manner creative people and their abilities, and the activities of one individual in the economy may lead to cross misunderstandings. On the other hand, the individual-skill-centred view on creativity leads to a view of creativity as a scarce resource that is held and controlled by a precious few (Rehn 2009). While creativity as a resource serves quantitative economic analysis well, it does not serve well regional development where it leads to utilitarian focus on specialization and assumptions of a straightforward relationship between ownership and control based on industrial logics as basics for local economy (e.g. Taalas and Rehn 2007). Regional creative projects seem more likely to generate challenges of commitment and support in mobilizing action rather than a fight over direct ownership. Similarly, it seems that while all other resources have been spent, creativity becomes a modus operandi breaking through redundant forms of organization and moving outside traditional ways of acting (Rehn 2009). An insulate view on creativity and innovation tends to break linkages of participation in favour of direct control and ownership. In that light a more processual view of the relationship of creativity and management seems to be a more useful way to move forward.

Xu and Richards (2007: 217) connect creativity and the organizing process: 'characterization of creativity as the process through which individuals and groups arrive at ideas that are new and valued to those individuals, groups and others within their wider communities of practice'. They analyse the relationship of creativity and management through embedded processes of many simultaneous projects that can facilitate creativity of the multiple players, individuals and institutions. Xu and Richards view creative management drawing from several parallel projects and combining effects in the realization. Their view is in the hybrid structures of such strategies. In the present case we could approach Kotka-Hamina from the perspective of a hybrid strategy. However, that would need to simultaneously take a broader and a more specific view on developments. First of all, we would need to take a look at the simultaneous processes taking place in the region at one particular time. Further, we would need to focus on combined effects of such processes as forms of creativity.

Economical activity is built on systemic forms and processes of exchange that typically result from the activities of a number of various actors. The ideas of systemic and processual forms of creativity and of those forms of organization that are created in the markets in close connection with production and consumption form an alternative interpretation of the creative economy.

> [N]ew ecology of learning and thinking... is holistic and radical and provocative, ranging over systems theory, emergent thinking in the arts and sciences, and new ideas about dialogue and collaboration.
>
> (Howkins 2009)

The conceptual shift emphasizes creativity that is innate in human beings; cooperation and its processes; the ethical basis of mutual exchange; the goals, politics and operating models of cooperation; and the evolving consequences of continuous interaction between them, gaining visible forms in the markets. While there is a more recent interest in creativity in processes and ecology type of networks the shift is highlighting a central problem with the relationship between creativity and economy regarding the idea of the new and the novel. If the configuration of ways of thinking and acting is seen as creative, it is not exactly new or even particularly novel.

Most literature on creative economy, as is the idea of creative ecologies, still builds on the idea of newness of the new while process approaches stress on combinations, associations and disassociations of creative processes in addition to its central role in the building of economy. This is in drastic contrast to the views of innovation being an insulate creation resulting in an end state.

The problematic aspect of creativity and processual moves concern the obsession with novelty and the nature of newness of an accomplishment. Styhre (2006) takes a critical view on the newness of the new. Building on Zizek, Styhre develops his point of process actualizing itself virtually by its previous dissociations. In the context of creativity it underlines the influence of the social and cultural embeddedness of creativity within its organization. Styhre's perspective takes up the neglected empiristic point that there is always a pluralism in ways creativity works in organizations. Styhre explores creativity through integrating and assembling components. It brings all components together in multiple ways and creates infrastructures where all the links represent different forms of explanations. The creative process then becomes a form of linking, associating and disassociating. In the context of creativity it underlines the influence of the social and cultural embeddedness of creativity within organization. Styhre's treatise of creativity could be understood as a by-product of processes with constant engagement within a field of action. It may be fruitfully encouraged by the composition of various activities, actions, beliefs, ideas, technologies, conflicts, communications and other resources for assembly. Therefore creation is no longer understood as a transcendental and exceptional event but much more as an act of connecting and assembling to generate the new. As a result, creativity is dependent on collaboration, communication and networking that can be seen as a social accomplishment where heterogeneity in the resources is employed. According to Styhre creativity is an embedded hybrid that is not insulated from the past or the future. It has the ability to bring forth new possibilities or futures by reassembling past, social resources and networks, and other embedded cultural resources. In this sense creativity can be seen in terms of assemblage and renegotiations. While considering a local case of Kotka-Hamina, creativity is purposefully connected to reinterpretations of local industrial sites and cultural heritage for a reassembly. I will be visiting the embeddedness of local creative economy projects among other projects running simultaneously in the Kotka-Hamina area to explore interplay of culture and economy. For the purposes of a short case, I will focus on the post-production of material sites to modify and produce new combinations but also the simultaneous processes of creative unmaking of cultural and industrial resources such as industrial sites like an old harbour or factory to make room for their life after the original use.

In order to meet the purpose of this chapter, it is necessary to link the idea of post-original as an innovation space and forming the basis for contemporary local economy. Rehn and Vachhani (2006) take a step away from the new altogether into the realms of the post-original – production after the original realization that stands in the heart of industrially driven thinking of innovation and much of the creative economy literature. Rehn and Vachhani take the problem to the other side and focus on the ontology of innovation and the problem of valorization and eventness of innovation. They criticize a notion of the original as being an ontologically secure, value-creating event, the oversimplification of the origination of value. Rehn and Vachhani (2006: 312) compare this to Marx's commodity fetishism whereas a creative moment is seen as the sole value-producing event and innovation is turned into a relation of ownership and reduced into a claim of property or money. This way of thinking neglects one of the central aspects of economy, which is reproduction and the question of copying and post-original. Moreover, Rehn and Vachhani engage with the philosophy of Walter Benjamin on the afterlife of the object that could be characterized as the process of ruination, integration, transformation of an object and thus unfolding its hidden meanings, truth or potential. In terms of art, new forms of reproduction create new understanding of art. In terms of innovations, the space of innovation proposed by Rehn and Vachhani is the post-original afterlife of produce. This is particularly useful when considering materials, sites, places and cultural relationships that already exist as in the case of Kotka-Hamina. To engage with this type of thinking we would focus on the reading of local creative projects as parallel projects with interconnections within economy. The Kotka-Hamina region is extensively engaging with post-original production of cultural heritage as well as material sites, in this case a harbour and a factory. Quite specifically industrial sites of the past are not being looked at through the lens of the afterlife. While newness is also produced in the process, it is only to a limited degree when viewed in its embedded setting. It needs to be considered in its setting, gaining meaning as markers of assembly processes (Styhre 2006). It is about the afterlife of space and place, objects and sites that are in the centre of the cultural assemblage of economic relationships in the Kotka-Hamina region. This results in cultural and economic hybridity in forms of combinations, linkages and assembly (Styhre 2006). The afterlife of industrial sites has become one of the prominent sites for contemporary creativity, fostering ways to connect and disconnect to the past and the present allowing for futures. However, focusing on the original use and purpose does not help to understand the nature or consequences of their life after original realization.

Xu and Richards (2007) describe the historical development of management theories and gradual incorporation of humanist and ecologist considerations to move towards creative management as process driven. Styhre (2006) shows how to look at creativity and an act of creation in the light of the empiricist philosophy shifting the focus to embeddedness to social relationships. His work is useful in establishing creativity not necessarily as a transcendental act, something that requires higher intelligence or geniality, but rather as something that emerges at the edges of communications, negotiations or other channels with heterogeneity of resources. Rehn and Vachhani (2006) show the limitations of our understanding of innovations therefore not explicitly filling gaps in the understanding of the relation between creativity and management but creating much more space for the existence of innovations, and thus also for creativity and eventually implicitly enabling more possibilities of how to connect creativity and management. Rehn and Vachhani also take up moral issues, which arise from the application of post-originality when post-original is considered lesser than original. Moralistic tendencies regarding afterlife can hinder the understanding of creativity in connection to management and economy. All authors stress the unlimited nature of creativity in connection to management as is situated in embedded social processes and inherent to all people, not just a precious few. Further, setting the original creation always before and over the one that comes afterwards, the post-original, is a moralist category that might be hindering our view and value in afterlife.

Moralist tendencies might be somewhat surpassed if creativity is looked at from a different angle. Process-centred reading on creativity also raises the question of agency and creativity. The parallel processes, the long history of the new and the post-original perspectives open up alternative avenues to explore the Kotka-Hamina development. The processes of transforming an old commercial harbour or a factory site have many material aspects that are not solely social or cultural. These entities have place and meaning in social worlds but have effects on people on a larger scale. Not just because they are new buildings or a new version of an old factory, but because they represent how it is possible for a place to be transformed. Large material sites are setting limitations and possibilities for a local way of life. Industrial cities are marked by industrial sites and settings in material forms which for a long time have impacted ways of living in many ways. Transforming a factory or harbour site can become a strategy of transformation due to the material sites' hybrid relationship to human activity, both cultural and economical. If creativity is interpreted as a process belonging to the post-original, interest in such creative processes can lead from stories of transforming material sites to analyses of processes of understanding their influence on the changing concept of what is possible for a region. To elevate this aspect in the case of Kotka-Hamina, the story of Maritime Centre Vellamo is written at the same time, taking place at the same time as other processes take place in the same region. Narrating the case of Maritime Centre Vellamo as a process running parallel, seemingly separate projects can be seen in their embedded, local settings.

Post-original Kotka-Hamina

In the early years of Kotka, in the 1870s, there was not yet a need for a port. Sailing ships which arrived to load sawn timber from the nine sawmills in Kotka cast their anchor beside the sawmill or remained in the roadstead to await the loading of timber. The first quay built through public funds, Pakkahuoneenlaituri, was completed in 1879 in the area where Maritime Centre Vellamo is now located. Pharmacist Grahn had a lemonade kiosk built near the quay, and the port soon evolved into a place where the townspeople could meet their friends and see the hustle and bustle of the port.

Another quay was built in the 1880s. A step towards a larger port was taken when a great novelty, the railway, was built to facilitate cargo traffic. The construction of the City Port did not progress without glitches. There were arguments over the ownership of water areas, and also whether or not the port had the correct location in the first place. The arguments had an impact on the construction of the Eastern Quay, with the work started in 1911 and completed as late as 1921. Due to its high costs, the new quay was referred to as Miljoonamölja (Million Quay).

> Cargo traffic at the City Port decreased when the focus in traffic flows in Kotka shifted to the new Mussalo Deep-Water Harbour from 1989 onwards. However, the genuine port appearance of the City Port with the cranes and other port-related items will be retained into the future in the surroundings of Maritime Centre Vellamo.
>
> (Maritime Centre Vellamo 2012a)

The case of Kotka-Hamina is difficult to comprehend from the point of view of the traditional way of looking at creative economy. The region has not previously been characterized by a particular creative community in cultural fields or strong clusters of arts and media as in large cities. The area identifies itself with strong linkages to the industrial era – with a maritime history and trade on one hand, and paper and pulp industries on the other. However, what we see are many projects that seem to be running parallel. The building of Maritime Centre Vellamo 2004–2008 was a central project in the rebuilding of the old harbour area in Kotka. The area followed the investment in the creative sector development by launching a creative industry development programme financed by the European Structural Foundation, the city of Kotka and a local network of actors between 2008 and 2011 that focused on supporting small- and medium-sized creative sector entrepreneurship with a €1.15 million budget that was comparable for regions much larger than Kotka-Hamina, and on a par with larger Finnish cities like Tampere and Turku.

Culture was brought in as a concept of developing the region in terms of space in Kotka's old harbour in the early 2000s when it was decided that the Finnish Maritime museum was to be developed and moved out of Helsinki. The move launched a location competition in the early years of the new millennium when several cities were interested in hosting the museum, most notably Kotka and Turku. In February 2004, when the final decision was reached by the Ministry of Culture, the plan secured €444,000 in permanent yearly operating funding for the museum project in Kotka provided by the Finnish government and some

10 permanent vacancies. The decision to move the museum to Kotka was based on Kotka's commitment to provide a specially built 65,000 m^2 museum space to be opened for the public in 2008. The decision to relocate the museum was followed by the launch of an architectural competition later in the same year, 2004.

The area had already experienced many structural changes over the years. In the 1980s the Finnish ship-building industries were concentrated in Helsinki, Turku and Rauma, through moves by large companies like Valmet and Wärtsilä. In the 1990s the engineering industry was restructuring, and large employers like Alström were laying people off. Since the beginning of the 2000s large forestry industry actors have increasingly been moving their production out of Finland. In 2007, when it was announced that the Summa paper mill was closing down, the area already had experience in engaging local collaboration and bringing in wide networks to combat negative effects of the globalization development. All local and regional actors including the cities of Anjalankoski, Kotka and Hamina, the Kymenlaakso region, Stora-Enso, the regional Finnish Ministry of Employment and Economy Centre (TE), the local government employment centre divisions, the Kouvola area business development centre, the City of Kouvola economic development division, the Southeast Finland's entrepreneurs association, labour unions, the Southeast Finland higher and vocational education institutions, the divisions of local occupational health services, the regional development organization Cursor Ltd and the Southeast Finland Chamber of the Commerce took part in the economy rescue programme put together in October 2006. When the final news of the Summa factory shutdown came out in the spring of 2007, the programme was already running with planning measures of support and pooling resources. Kotka-Hamina region was already preparing for the severe blow.

During 2007 the governmental organization, Invest in Finland, was looking for international companies wanting to locate in Finland. One of these companies was the US internet search engine company Google. In January 2008 Invest in Finland suggested the Summa factory site to Google as one possibility for a new server facility. Summa had the ability to provide enough electricity and sea water to cool the search engine servers. The Nordic climate is suitably cool for operating servers on a large scale factory setting. By the summer the regional development organization Cursor Ltd was already working on two projects to find new users for the Summa paper mill area. One of them was Google with the plan for a server facility promising to employ 50 individuals, the other was Winwind, a wind power turbine company with a factory that would create 250 new jobs. Winwind's new factory was announced in December 2008. Google's new server location was announced a few months later, 13 February.

Vellamo was already in the building stage when the news of the Summa closure became public in 2007. During the launch of the new museum in the summer of 2008 Google was making its decision about relocating to Kotka-Hamina. Maritime Centre Vellamo opened its doors at a time of a big shift for the region's economic relationships. The architectural competition for Maritime Centre Vellamo was launched in 2004, and the final decision to start building the Centre was made by the city council in 2006. After a name competition in 2006 the

Centre got the name Vellamo, referring to the goddess of the sea and wife to the sea god Ahti in Finnish mythology. 'Vellamo' literally means 'to rock with the waves' and is usually pictured as a mermaid. The name has also been a very popular name for sea vessels for centuries in Finland. The building of Vellamo started in 2006.

The total building cost of the Maritime Centre Vellamo was €48 million. The Maritime Centre Vellamo was opened to the public in July 2008. In 2011 over 140,000 visitors were reported at the Centre, of which 60,000 visited the Finnish Maritime Museum (2,000 m^2, temporary exhibitions 200 m^2) and some 10,000 the Kymeenlaakso Museum (2,200 m^2, of which 350 m^2 was used by the Coast Guard Museum) and temporary exhibitions. Vellamo also hosts an Information Centre (500 m^2 with printed materials of 20,000 books and 3,500 volumes of journals and magazines, 22,000 electronic journals and magazines, 260,000 titles of electronic books, hundreds of databases in various sectors). Vellamo is a hybrid space for changing exhibitions, three permanent museums, information centre and conference centre facilities.

Maritime Centre Vellamo has won several national awards for its architecture and construction:

- ceiling project of 2007;
- top attraction in Finnish tourism in 2008;
- steel structure of the year 2008;
- first prize in the tourism series of Finnish championships in marketing by municipalities in 2008;
- Certificate of Honour granted by the Council on Disability and the Unobstructed Kotka team of the City of Kotka for significant efforts in promoting accessibility;
- illuminated item of 2009, Illuminating Engineering Society of Finland, outdoor illumination series;
- first prize in the Väri09 (Colour09) competition by the Master Painters' Association of Finland, Master Painters' Association of Helsinki and Finnish Fair Corporation (Maritime Centre Vellamo 2012b).

In Kotka-Hamina a combination of processes to cope with sudden crisis as well as structural changes were built on the practice of wide collaboration. The strong regional collaboration had already started before the shutdown of the Summa factory as a result of pooling practical measures as the strategic way to handle crisis and to stop the region from falling into despair while one of its largest employers was pulling out completely and laying off all its staff. Since 2006, the areal development organization Cursor Ltd with the cities of the region was facilitating a large scale regional restructuring project when it became apparent that Stora-Enso would be withdrawing completely from the area. The same development agency was active in the development of Maritime Centre Vellamo.

The Maritime Centre Vellamo was the first stage of redevelopment work at the old Kotka harbour site. The new master plan for the further development of the old harbour was launched in the spring of 2011, and spans to the year 2030 with a large scale development plan for the entirety of the old Kotka harbour including housing and commercial development. Vellamo is a central feature in the afterlife of Kotka harbour in a contemporary setting, linking Kotka to immaterial information, art and object history in its setting and its location (cf. Rehn and Vachhani 2006). The re-establishment of the old harbour was taken into strategic focus of urban planning work in Kotka already in early 2000, and getting the Finnish Maritime Museum to Kotka was the first goal. While the permanent tenant of the Maritime Museum was secured, Vellamo plans became viable. Vellamo is not simply a museum site but a combination of maritime history and heritage with contemporary connections to the Information Centre and conference facility, linking contemporary information society, museum and education. It hosts a major national and regional heritage exhibition space bringing under the same roof several museums and providing versatile space for visiting exhibitions. Vellamo is a hybrid space that has many uses and target groups as well as working as the physical centre point for old harbour city planning efforts. Set in the context of other projects and processes taking place, even architectural realizations that are new can be seen in a different light: Vellamo is deeply rooted in the hybrid assembly and disassembly of the old harbour site and local economical relationships from the material past to a more immaterial present, and works to launch future developments (Styhre 2006). In that sense Vellamo is a contemporary cultural site that brings together arts and architecture in combination with a museum and arts collection as well as housing contemporary educational spaces and services. All this contributes to high levels of use and recorded visitor numbers have remained constantly high. The networks of projects and processes produce ideas and technologies of a community that redefines and renegotiates what is valuable, what the rules of exchange are, and what is important to the local actors.

Considering the architectural realization of an exhibition site as a separate project, simply a novel construction project, would not reveal the roles of the material sites and parallel projects. Similarly, when considering the realization of the Maritime Centre Vellamo among other processes, it is revealed that it is not simply a cultural institution but also has an important role in demonstrating the networks of collaboration in developing of the region's economical relationships and production set-ups. Vellamo stands for the movement from an industrial harbour site to the development of a more post-industrial old harbour in Kotka. Similarly, it becomes easier to understand the establishment of Google in Summa through a strong local commitment in cross-sectoral collaboration, and that old production set-ups can be reconfigured innovatively in the process. Together these moves make Kotka-Hamina an interesting case with a pattern of turning towards reconfiguration and with an orientation towards change. Focusing on creativity in processes, post-original innovation and parallel projects can shed light on the dynamics of local creativity in post-original uses.

Revisiting the relationship between creativity and the local economy

The traditional views of creative economy focus on the necessity of newness of ideas and realizations that are based on an individual's capacity for creativity (Howkins 2001a, 2001b, 2009). These views lead to a reading of how markets are constituted based on newness of the produce or creative content as an insulated outcome. The approach emphasized in the current reading of Kotka-Hamina's regional development is, however, that the cultural and creative sectors are not independent systems separated from other sectors in the market economy. Instead, from the perspective of an afterlife, the renegotiation and development processes can be part of engaging something that stands in the heart of the creative economy. To engage with creativity in the economical afterlife – processes of many, multiple outcomes and assemblies, and the focus on post-original – can make room for understanding local developments in their embedded setting. It can also help us to understand the development ideas that are copied from elsewhere but that are worked in their local settings in innovative and creative ways. Kotka-Hamina is certainly not the only region to face the challenges of globalization but their processes and projects are unique in local settings, and allow for study of creative moves in realization.

While the utilitarian project of the creative industries has been largely focusing on creative content – or indeed on the sole creative individual – the systemic creativity in the form of logic for operations and ways of acting for bringing forth possible futures in local settings have been left behind. A viable regional economy proposes great challenges to the industrial economy logic and policy making, as well as challenges functionalist educational systems and employment services of various types. As a result, a more process-focused view is needed. Similarly, it is dangerous to consider creativity in a narrow sense but to recognize it as a permanent part of all market economy. Nevertheless, it is necessary to work on projects that are also specific, material and visible like the Maritime Centre Vellamo to bring forth and mark powerful changes in ways of living. The economy of creative content stresses the role of entrepreneurship and business activities, competitive assets, and the scarcity of competences and resources. Afterlife and processual reading of creativity allows for modification, alteration, and movement to enter as a basis for market economy innovation.

The view on post-original creativity challenges the prevailing discussion in the market economy for the primacy of ownership control's central role to create value when applied to the cultural and creative sectors. Networked organization and cross-sectoral collaboration, ethical principles of co-creation, and a strong future-oriented approach seem to be more important. They also call for participation by the public. In Kotka-Hamina this is to a large degree conceptualized as refusing to be ruled by the negative notions of going under. The social mission is connected to creating a community and creative processes.

As an approach, the afterlife and creative processes shift the emphasis of discussion from creative content as added value toward forms of organization that have been created in the exchange economy of cultural and creative sectors. Such forms of organization include, for example, tight and holistic peer networks, iterative processes of creating information, forms of peer assessment and development, and communal networks of innovators. These forms of organization are largely based on principles typical of the exchange economy, linked with the market economy in alternative ways that mix the traditional models of governing and hybridize organizational boundaries. Cultural networks communicate a will to build futures and to reinterpret old resources in new ways giving room to new uses. In Kotka-Hamina Summa's wind power farm was one reason why Google was interested in developing the old industrial site. Even industrial production technology can communicate a community commitment to future lifestyles.

In September 2011, the tenth Google server farm was opened in Hamina. There cold seawater can be used for cooling the servers, and wind turbines to provide part of the power making this one of Google's most energy efficient server centres. In October 2011 it was announced that Facebook had purchased a green site outside Luleå, Northern Sweden, with an investment plan that aimed to build a server farm. The former Finnish and Swedish paper mills are workable sites for further development into server factories for global actors. The marketing of these sites is already taking place in both countries. However, for these developments to make sense on a local level they need to be linked to the making of local futures in places like Kotka-Hamina. The alternative ways to consider creativity's role in the economy are about renegotiating ways of living and connecting it to all forms of creativity in local networks. It is a profoundly different approach because it does not seek to determine the future outcomes but focuses on communicating and taking steps on new paths into the future in times of eruptions and discontinuance.

References

DCMS (2001) *Creative Industries Mapping Document*, Creative Industries Task Force, London: UK Department for Culture, Media and Sport.

Gueller, G., Geppert, J., Taalas, S. and Toivonen, T.E. (2006) *Economy of Culture in Europe*. European Commission: DG Education & Culture. Available at: http://ec.europa.eu/culture/key-documents/doc873_en.htm (accessed 25 May 2012).

Howkins, J. (2001a) *The Creative Economy*. The Basics. Available at: www.creativeeconomy.com/thebasics.htm (accessed 20 October 2011).

——— (2001b) *The Creative Economy: How People Make Money from Ideas*, London: Penguin.

——— (2009) *Creative Ecologies: Where Thinking is a Proper Job*. Available at: www.creativeeconomy.com/think.htm (accessed 20 October 2011).

Maritime Centre Vellamo (2012a) *From the Toil of Port Work to Museum Experiences. The Colourful Past of the City Port in Kotka*. Available at: www.merikeskusvellamo.fi/en/Building/Location (accessed 21 May 2012).

——— (2012b) *Steel, Glass and Wood. These are what Maritime Centre Vellamo is Made of*. Available at: www.merikeskusvellamo.fi/en/Building/Facts (accessed 21 May 2012).

Rehn, A. (2009) 'After Creativity', in N. Koivunen and A. Rehn (eds), *Creativity and the Contemporary Economy*, Liber: Malmö.

Rehn, A. and Vachhani, S. (2006) 'Innovation and the Post-Original: On Moral Stances and Reproduction', *Creativity and Innovation Management*, 15(3): 310–322.

Styhre, A. (2006) 'Organization Creativity and the Empiricist Image of Novelty', *Creativity and Innovation Management*, 15(2): 143–149.

Taalas, S. and Rehn, A. (2007) 'Tekijänoikeus ja jälkiteollisen talouden omistamisen murros' ['Ownership Revisited – Copyright and the Post-industrial Economy'], in T. Mylly, J. Lavapuro and M. Karo (eds), *Tekemisen vapaus. Luovuuden ehdot ja tekijänoikeus* [*Freedom of Creation – Constraints of Creativity and Copyright*], Helsinki: Gaudeamus.

Xu, F. and Richards, T. (2007) 'Creative Management: A Predicted Development from Research into Creativity and Management', *Creativity and Innovation Management*, 16(3): 216–229.

11 How to develop a region through culture and creativity

The foundation Cultiva in Kristiansand

Trine Bille

Introduction

This chapter will examine a very special dedicated case of using culture and creativity to develop a region, namely the foundation Cultiva in Kristiansand, Norway. The case is very special in the sense that a lot of money has been allocated to the foundation. The foundation has 1.44 billion NOK, and the returns on this capital must be invested in projects that develop the region in economic and social terms by using arts, culture and creativity as instruments. The foundation has existed since 2001 and therefore ten years of practice and experiences can be evaluated. This chapter will examine the strategies of Cultiva and discuss them in the context of the existing knowledge and literature of culture economics, concerning art and culture in urban and regional development. What does the theory and existing empirical knowledge tell us? How can the strategies of Cultiva be evaluated in this context? What are Cultiva's experiences so far? What can we learn from this case? These questions will be addressed in this chapter.

The chapter is structured as follows: first, the case of Cultiva is presented. Second, two overall different policy goals – growth and welfare – are discussed; followed by a presentation of the applied theory. Third, the case of Cultiva is discussed in relation to the theory presented. Finally, a short section concludes the chapter.

The foundation Cultiva in Kristiansand

The foundation Cultiva in Kristiansand is a unique example of a local organization that aims to ensure local development through arts, culture and creativity. And unlike most other local and regional initiatives the foundation has money – lots of money! Actually 1.44 billion NOK, but only the return on the investment of the foundation capital can be used for grants within the purpose of the foundation. The initial capital must not be touched. The official aim of Cultiva is 'to secure jobs and good living conditions[1] in Kristiansand, by providing grants to projects which set up art, cultural and educational institutions or organizations that contribute to innovation, development and competence building within the creative milieu of Kristiansand' (www.cultiva.no).

The Foundation was made possible and created when the municipality of Kristiansand sold a portion of its shares in the energy power plant Agder Energi A/S, which supplied the municipality with substantial capital. Based on a proposal from the former CEO of the municipality, who later became the CEO of Cultiva, the local politicians decided that 1.44 billion NOK of the earned capital should be placed in an independent foundation with the above purposes. The Foundation has its own executive board and management and as such it is formally independent of the municipality, but closely connected since three of the seven members of the executive board are local politicians. The foundation was formally established in December 2001 and the first projects grants were handed out in December 2003. The political process leading to the establishment of Cultiva has been discussed in other studies (e.g. Kiland and Horrigmo 2012; Normann 2007) and is outside the scope of this chapter.

The establishment of Cultiva was conceived as part of a larger strategy for the development of the region Southern Agder and the municipality of Kristiansand. Based on a report 'Tough life in the mild Southern Norway' from 1993 (Røed 1993), which documented a large underperformance measured on different life-condition indicators, a strategy document 'Joint Targes for Agder' (Norman, Knudsen and Røed 1994) was developed, which proposed a number of initiatives. The initiatives were especially based on four important factors to help regenerate and develop the region: competence, art, culture and communication. The most important initiatives based on the strategy report were the creation of Cultiva and another similar foundation 'the Competence Foundation', which has a capital base of 0.7 billion NOK. Furthermore, it was decided that the municipalities in the region should have greater focus on its primary function to create good living conditions for the citizens, and the municipality of Kristiansand also took a number of other specific initiatives, particularly regarding communication, such as broadband development, better infrastructure at the airport, new location plan for the harbour and a new ferry terminal, toll financing of a new road system and a commitment to transform the local college HiA, College of Agder, into a university.

Since 2003 Cultiva has donated approximately 500 million NOK in grants for study programmes, festivals, cultural projects, venture funds, talent grants, a foundation for major cultural centres, etc. in Kristiansand. Quite a lot of money in a municipality with approximately 80,000 inhabitants.

Until now the grants donated by Cultiva have been based on applications. To apply for funds from Cultiva applicants must work within the field of arts, culture or knowledge development within this sector. Cultiva's financial involvement is time limited and can be given both for projects and investments, but Cultiva does not cover permanent operating costs. In addition, the activities must be relevant to the development of Kristiansand, meaning that the primary activities must be located in Kristiansand. In addition, emphasis has been placed on the following criteria when applications have been assessed: the degree of creativity and innovation in the project, that the activity is on a high quality level, that the project contributes to capacity building, networking, internationalization, equality and tolerance and image generating activities which contribute positively to Kristiansand's reputation outside the region.

Policy: between growth and welfare

The purpose of Cultiva is to secure jobs and good living conditions in Kristiansand. This twofold purpose places Cultiva in the middle of an ongoing political debate about arts and culture as 'arts for the arts sake'[2] versus arts and culture used as an instrument for urban and regional economic development (see e.g. Lysgård 2011; Bille 2011b; Cruickshank *et al.* 2011). And it has placed Cultiva in a passionate local public debate, where local artists, politicians, academics and professionals have being discussing the purposes and strategies of Cultiva.[3] The debate about Cultiva has, however, remained local, without a lot of repercussion in the rest of Norway or Scandinavia.

The arts for the arts sake, or the intrinsic value of arts and culture, are closely related to the traditional and original goals in cultural policy, like artistic freedom and production of new art, participation (to increase education and enlightenment, etc.) and preservation of cultural heritage (Duelund and Bille 1994).

The use of arts and culture in economic and social development is, however, not a new theme either. The 'instrumentalization' of arts and culture has been an essential element in the cultural debate and in cultural policy research since the 1980s (see e.g. Duelund 2003). From the mid 1980s and for the following 10–15 years, the focus on the 'instrumentalization' was mainly on public-funded cultural institutions and activities and the economic impact created in the form of employment and turnover based on visitors' consumption. The economic activity created was measured in economic impact studies and used as an argument for public support for cultural institutions and activities like festivals. While these economic impact studies were heavily used for political argumentation, they were also heavily criticized in the academic economic literature (for a critique of economic impact studies, see e.g. Bille Hansen 1993 and 1995; and Seaman 2003).

From the beginning of the millennium the expectations of economic returns and economic development based on culture have increased even more – but based on a broader view of the economic importance of the arts and culture, called *the experience economy*. In the Scandinavian countries the notion 'experience economy' developed from about the year 2000 (Bille 2011a) – mainly in a political context (Birch 2008) – and since then it has apparently been a very popular development policy for many local government authorities and regions.

Bille (2011a) has shown how the Scandinavian version of the concept 'experience economy' was inspired and came about from a mix of three different approaches and theories. First, Pine and Gilmore's book *The Experience Economy – Work is Theatre & Every Business a Stage* from 1999, second, the focus on the *Creative Industries* in the United Kingdom with the first mapping of the creative industries (DCMS 1998 and 2001), and third, Richard Florida's book *The Rise of the Creative Class* from 2002. Even though these three books and theories are very different, and deal with very different issues, they are nevertheless all dealing with art, culture, experiences and creativity as the main drivers of economic development. This quote from a Danish government report from 2003 shows how the Danish and Scandinavian (political) interpretation of the experience economy is closely linked to expectation of economic returns and development based on culture, creativity and experiences:

> Ud af fusionen mellem kultur og erhverv er der vokset en ny form for økonomi [From the merger between *culture* and business, a new kind of economy is growing]. En økonomi, der er baseret på en stigende efterspørgsel efter oplevelser, og som bygger på den merværdi, kreativiteten skaber både i nye og mere traditionelle produkter og serviceydelser [An economy that is based on an increasing demand for experiences and that builds upon the value added that creativity lends to both new and traditional products and services].
>
> (Regeringen 2003: 8 [author's translation])
>
> Samtidig med at der er en generel forventning om vækst i oplevelsesøkonomien [At the same time, the report expresses a general expectation that the experience economy will grow]:
>
> At kultur- og oplevelsesøkonomien er kommet i fokus både herhjemme og i udlandet, hænger i høj grad sammen med, at det er et felt, som fylder stadig mere i økonomien [That the culture and experience economy has come into focus, both at home and abroad, correlates closely with the fact that it is a field that is increasingly expanding within the economy].
>
> (Regeringen 2003: 9 [author's translation])

Because of this expected economic potential, the experience economy has been a very popular development strategy in many cities, regions and countries for the last ten years. The economic potential of the experience economy is closely connected to the market value, but the market value is only one part of the total value of art and culture. The other part is the non-market values. The two kinds of values – the market value and the non-market value – do more or less represent the dilemma stated above: between the 'arts for the arts sake' (the non-market value) and arts and culture as an instrumental tool for economic development (the market value).

Economic theory: between market value and non-market value

There are two different perspectives that can be used when the economic importance of culture is addressed: the welfare economic perspective and the market economic perspective. The market economic perspective is based on market value that can be traded in the market and can be measured in GDP and is centred on economic growth. The welfare economic value is, however, based on the individual citizen's subjective perception of life quality and values, namely individuals' utility. It is recognized that there exists significant values that are not traded in the market (non-market values), but nevertheless represent a substantial value for citizens, and therefore must be considered when the total value of culture is evaluated and public resources are allocated.

Where the welfare economic perspective is about maximizing the society's total benefits and utility by distributing 'the pie' in the best possible way, economic growth is about making 'the pie' bigger. In the following sections I will look more deeply into these two different perspectives.

The market economic value and economic growth

As mentioned earlier the importance of culture for economic growth is an argument which has been widely used in the public debate – both by politicians and people from the cultural sector. The research has dealt with how culture can create market economic value and economic growth. There are three ways in which culture can create market value, and each of them is closely linked to one of the three books and theories mentioned above:

(1) The importance of culture in local and regional development (Florida 2002).
(2) The creative industries: the direct contribution to employment, turnover and export (DCMS 1998 2001).
(3) Broader value creation – experiences, creativity and innovation (Pine and Gilmore 1999).

In the following sections I will take a closer look at each of them, and in the end of this chapter, I will discuss the effects for Cultiva in Kristiansand.

The importance of culture in local and regional development

It is well known that culture can give rise to some indirect economic effects through the generation of activity in a geographical area, for example by attracting tourists, new residents and/or new businesses.

The natural demarcation is a specific *geographic area*, for example a region, as we are to a large extent dealing with relocation and migration patterns, as the economic activity moves from one place to another, when tourists, inhabitants and/or companies choose where to move or locate. In terms of economic value creation, the impact will therefore, among other things, depend on how the geographical area is defined. Tourists from Bergen spending money in Kristiansand have an economic impact on Kristiansand, but not on Norway.

The economic significance of culture is to be found in the external effects which consist of short-term consumption effects and long-term effects. In order to identify the ways in which culture can generate regional (economic) development, it seems therefore convenient to distinguish between short- and long-term effects (see Bille Hansen 1993, 1995 and Bille and Schulze 2006). These economic effects will mainly arise from cultural activities that residents and tourists can enjoy in the region, i.e. theatres, museums, concerts, events, festivals, sport, etc.

Short-term effects: economic impact and tourists' spending

The short-run spending impacts are due to the fact that the arts and culture can attract visitors – local and non-local consumers – who spend money on culture, but often also on related goods and services like food, beverages, accommodation, shopping, etc. If there are visitors who have come to a city or a region because of the cultural activities on offer, their consumption constitutes an increase in aggregate demand that can be attributed to the cultural activities in the area. These kind of short-run spending impacts are mainly based on cultural tourism, but can also be due to the possibility that the region's own population spends less elsewhere. These effects are closely linked to the economic impact studies and the arguments put forward in the 1980s.

When cultural institutions and events attract tourists to an area, the economic effects of the tourists' and the locals' spending can be measured in the so-called economic impact studies. In Denmark, as in several other countries, a large number of economic impact studies have been done to show that public support to culture 'pays off'. In this way it was 'proven' that public investment in culture pays off: the money is coming multi-fold again. This 'good news' was frequently used in political arguments. However, the problem is that the analyses were often made on an incorrect basis and the impact exaggerated (Bille Hansen 1993, 1995). There are several problems.

First, there is the problem of *additionality*. Many studies have not taken into account whether culture creates *new* economic activity. If the inhabitants don't spent money on culture, they will spend it on something else that also creates economic activity. Therefore, one should be interested in the *additional* economic activity generated, but unfortunately, many studies look at the gross – not the additional – economic impact of cultural activities (e.g. in Hjemdahl *et al.* 2007). The activity created might be additional if many tourists are attracted by a cultural institution, because they create value added for the community when they spend money in the local area, but in most cases the local inhabitants' spending is not additional, as they would spend the money in the area anyway.

Second, there is the problem of *alternatives*. If the government had not supported the specific cultural institutions or activities, the government support could be spent on something else that also had created economic activity. Therefore, the interesting point is not to show that culture creates consumption, income and employment – because all economic activity does that. The interesting point is to show whether the supported cultural activities create more economic activity than alternative uses of money.

Third, and most important, the main problem with these analyses and the arguments put forward, is that they do not take into consideration the purpose of cultural activities. The purpose of a library is not to create income, consumption and employment in the local area. If that was the intention, it would undoubtedly be better for the government to support something else than the library. It goes almost without saying that the library's purpose is not to provide jobs for librarians, and a library's value cannot be measured based on how many librarians are employed, and how much these librarians are spending. If the economic impact of culture is used as an important argument for public support, the logical conclusion is that society should support the culture which creates the biggest economic activity: for instance, popular concerts with star performers, which attracts many tourists who spend money in the local area. But when the purpose of public cultural policy is something quite different,[4] the political focus on culture's short-term economic effects can create a failed cultural policy. While at the same time, economic growth is undoubtedly better and more efficiently created in other sectors. This makes the political value of the economic impact studies limited, if they are to form the basis for decisions about competing uses of public resources (Bille Hansen 1993, 1995; Seaman 2003).

Long-term effects: new residents and businesses

The long-term effects are primarily attributable to the fact that cultural offers in a region can attract new residents as well as businesses and investments (cf. Florida 2002).

Cultural activities can attract new residents and businesses to an area, but the question is how important this effect really is. Most studies show that it is not the cultural activities that come first, when people choose in which city or area to live. The primary reason is often love, family, jobs, housing, schools, etc. These factors very often come before sport, cultural and recreational facilities (see e.g. Deding and Filges 2004). A new report from Norway (Vareide and Kobro 2012) has shown that the level of culture in a municipality has no significant impact on the net immigration of people to the municipality. Municipalities with a lot of cultural attractions and activities do not seem more attractive as a place to live as a municipality with only sparse cultural activities.

But also in this case, the arguments need to be a little bit more nuanced. It is clear that what make big cities attractive are the many cultural offerings (along with opportunities for education, job opportunities, etc.). In remote areas, however, it is hardly a new library or similar institution that makes people want to move there. In addition, we always need to look at marginal changes, which mean that one must look at what additional cultural supply means in the form of additional inflow of people or companies to the area.

Richard Florida's (2002) theory of the creative class has gained huge political attention in relation to culture and regional development. Florida has introduced a new perspective on economic growth which is based on the importance of creativity. According to Florida, businesses today move to where the 'creative class' lives because human creativity, both now and in the future, is the single most important resource for businesses. Members of the creative class change jobs frequently, and therefore it is important for businesses to locate in a place that has a 'critical mass' of the creative class which, according to Florida, constitutes about one-third of the workforce in the US today.

Florida argues that it is the ability of cities and regions to attract and retain the creative class labour that will determine their future levels of economic growth. According to Florida it is therefore, crucial for economic growth to construct a 'people climate' that motivates the creative class to move to a certain area. Here, tolerance, as mentioned earlier, is a key factor, but Florida also mentions the option of investment in 'lifestyle amenities' that the creative class really wants and often uses. He mentions parks in cities and towns, bicycle lanes, off-road trails for running, cycling and rollerblading. While art and culture are also potentially significant factors in determining where the creative class decides to live, Florida is not particularly detailed about this.[5]

The biggest and most decisive problem with Florida's analysis is causality – what depends on what? To put it plainly: is it urban growth with rapid economic development that attracts the creative class? Or is it the presence of the creative class that creates economic growth? (See also the critique from Malanga 2004; Bille and Schulze 2006). The positive correlations, which Florida's arguments are based on, do in themselves not provide answers to this question.[6]

When Florida's theory has been so widely used in municipalities and regions as a development strategy, it is probably because it is kind of a feel-good strategy. Culture and creativity is a very positive way to create economic development. But the evidence that the strategy works still need to be seen.

From a national perspective, many of the market economic effects can be characterized as a zero-sum game in the sense that growth in one locality happens at the expense of growth in another locality. Visitors attracted to a municipality because of, for example, a mega concert will spend money in this region rather than in their home municipality. The same applies when culture attracts new residents or businesses. From a national perspective it may seem inappropriate to compete for visitors, residents and businesses in this way. For each individual municipality, however, it can make sense, as it may be necessary to 'keep up' and invest at the same level (or more than) as other municipalities, to follow the development in order to not lag behind.

The creative industries

The focus on creative industries in the United Kingdom with the first so-called 'mappings' of creative industries (DCMS 1998, 2001) is another important approach that forms part of the general understanding of the importance of arts and culture for economic development, and for the Scandinavian understanding of the concept of experience economy. The idea behind this is that the creative industries represent an important area of business industries with associated employment, turnover, value added, exports, etc., and the focus is upon the 'economic size' of the industries measured by the various indicators. One of the questions is which industries to include as creative industries? A common list includes the following industries: publishing, advertising, architecture, art and antiques, arts heritage, handcraft, design, fashion design, film and video, computer games, software, music, performing arts, TV and radio (Towse 2003).

The industries included have been expanded from the more traditional *cultural industries* and activities to *creative industries*,[7] by also including industries like fashion, computer games, restaurants, etc. But the delimitation is by no means clear (as discussed in Bille 2011a), and every country has its own definition (Birch 2008). There are many problems with this approach, and one of them is that the creative sector can become larger or smaller depending on how many or few industries are included in the definition.[8] Besides, several reports have shown that cultural and creative industry in general is a growth sector, but also points to a large variation between industries, with some cultural and creative industries showing very little or no growth at all. The various creative industries are characterized by very different demand conditions, technology, structure, etc., and therefore they are developing very differently, and certainly not all creative industries are growing (see Bille and Lorenzen 2008; Bille 2011b).

Following the model from DCMS, similar studies have been carried out in many other countries; in Scandinavia e.g. Regeringen (2003), Rambøll (2005), Erhvervs- og Byggestyrelsen (2008, 2011), Haraldsen *et al.* (2004, 2008), Menon and Perduco (2011), KK-stiftelsen (2003), and on the EU level (KEA 2007).

This counting of the size of the creative industries makes the most sense in relation to the commercial industries. For government-supported cultural institutions and industries it makes little sense if there are substantial public subsidies and non-market values, because it means that employment effects are not an end in itself.

However, the interesting question is: are special policies, incentives and support mechanisms necessary for the cultural and creative industries? And, if this is the case, how do we create policies that can stimulate the cultural and creative industries in the best possible way?

Bille and DePaoli (2012) have shown that the cultural and creative industries are special in some sense and that the cultural entrepreneurs especially need policies concerning financial start-up help and help to deal with immaterial rights and exports. General business aid measures have not functioned well in Norway as cultural entrepreneurs do not respond to these kinds of initiatives the same way general business entrepreneurs do (De Paoli and Hansen 2010). Deloitte and Bille (2012) have referred to similar results for Denmark.

Furthermore, it can be questioned whether it is right to stimulate the cultural sector actively for the purpose of business development, as the industries have low earnings, and only a few are able make money (see e.g. Abbing 2002). Most artists earn very little, and wages in the industries are low. Public stimulation of cultural industries may thus contribute to channelling young people into industries with low earnings through 'carrots', where the alternatives for these young people are other industries with much higher value creation, greater job security and higher wages.

The government cannot support cultural industries based on the argument that they are growth industries and create employment. In general, it is not a public sector task to support growing commercial businesses, but the government can try to create good conditions for the development of the creative industries, for example, through zoning, inspiration and knowledge (Mathiasen *et al.* 2006). Which strategies to follow in order to stimulate the creative industries in the best possible way is, however, by no means obvious (Bille and De Paoli 2012).

Broader value creations – experiences, creativity and innovation

Finally, the arts and culture can have a broader impact on value creation in other industries (industries in general), by contributing to the development and innovation through creativity, innovation and experiences. There are two different ways that can be distinguished. The first one is a supply side effect and the second one is a demand side effect.

Creativity, innovation and educational effects (the supply side)

First, *creativity* from the arts and cultural sector can spread to the economic sphere, and thereby contribute to economic development in other sectors. The idea is that creativity and innovation in the cultural sector – as fuzzy and undefined as these concepts may be – are essential for both the economic and cultural development.

Most people would agree that the arts and culture are important for the formation of identity, personality, attitudes, job motivation, creativity, etc. – factors which are also important for economic development. In other words, the arts and culture can provide inspiration for creative processes and trigger actions directed towards change and innovation. Artistic and cultural activity in a region can thus indirectly lead to more innovative industrial development through the creativity in the arts sector spreading to other economics activities. Creativity – in the form of innovation and breaking through boundaries – is something universal, and impulses from the arts can be important for actors on the business stage – and thus for economic growth. In this way, arts and culture may act as a key driver in the development of society. Educational and creativity effects can occur in the long run and are obviously very difficult to verify or to measure, partly because we do not know the transmission channels through which such creativity and personality spill-over could materialize. It is thus necessarily a somewhat vague concept. However, this does by no means indicate that it is irrelevant. Rather, it is probably one of the arts and culture's most important economic functions.

The experience economy by Pine and Gilmore 1999 (the demand side)

Second, *the experience economy* (as developed by Pine and Gilmore 1999) explains how most companies can create huge economic gains by connecting to experiences, for example through branding, marketing and production of products and services that blend experience and functionality. The special Scandinavian version of the experience economy is closely linked to arts and culture and creative industries, as the assumption is that it is these industries that particularly contribute to creativity and experience elements of 'ordinary' products and services.

The concept of the experience economy was first introduced in Pine and Gilmore's book *The Experience Economy* from 1999. Here the market is central and experiences are defined as a new source of value creation for businesses, an add-on to various consumer products and services. In the book, Pine and Gilmore predict that experiences will be a decisive factor in the development of products, service and marketing, and that companies' future success will depend on their ability to build a universe of experiences around their products and services. Using metaphors from the theatre they show how companies can stage experiences – *Work is Theatre & Every Business a Stage* – as the book's subtitle reads. Since 1999, new books have been published that follow the same approach; e.g. Pine and Gilmore (2007) and Boswijk *et al.* (2007).

The concept of 'experience economy' has had a huge influence on cultural policy – especially in Norway, Denmark and Sweden. But unlike the original contribution by Pine and Gilmore (1999) it has been closely linked to the arts and culture and creative industries, as explained earlier, and the experience economy is interpreted much more broadly including the two other dimensions mentioned above (culture as urban and regional development and the creative industries approach), linking not only to the single company but to society in general.

As Bille and Lorenzen (2008) conclude, the biggest growth potential is probably to be found in the *broad value creation.* The number of 'ordinary' companies which potentially can be linked to 'creative' companies is very large. But it is not possible to determine, for example, what proportion of Danish industry might benefit from being marketed through Danish films, or from integrating elements of Danish film or video productions in their products. Because the number of unexploited opportunities in the experience economy for such alliances is probably high, a challenge exists to identify the problems and barriers for this kind of value creation.[9]

Both these effects (the supply side and the demand side effects) are however very difficult – if not impossible – to measure and quantify at an aggregated level, and they are thus very difficult to 'prove' (Bille 2011a). But even though they are difficult to measure, they may nevertheless have broad implications for the development and innovation in businesses and industries in general. Other market values can be measured far better (like the size of the creative industries and short-term spending effects in economic impact studies), and probably therefore they form a much more frequent basis for political reasoning.

The welfare economic perspective

Having discussed the market economic perspective in detail, I will turn to the welfare economic perspective, which takes a rather different approach. Basic welfare economic theory assumes that society's total utility is to be maximized. And society is made up of individuals/consumers. Society therefore needs to produce goods and services that maximize social benefits. In general this is done through the market mechanisms, which in most cases are well suited to regulate supply and demand. However, it is not the case for all goods and services that the market is good to regulate supply. This applies not for public goods, like national defence, street lighting, etc. For these kind of goods and services it is difficult and inappropriate to exclude anyone from using them and therefore difficult to introduce user fees (Stiglitz 2000). Without user fees, there are no private providers who want to produce the goods and services, because everyone benefits from them, whether they pay for them or not. Most cultural supply is not 'pure public goods' in the economic-theoretical meaning, but private goods with external effects. They are private goods because each cultural consumer can be charged when buying a book, watching a play or a movie or visiting a museum, and is willing to pay for this private experience. But a lot of culture has broader effects on the economy because the whole community can benefit from the cultural activities – it's not only the users who benefit. These external benefits like existence value, bequest value, prestige value, education value and option value are difficult and sometimes impossible to internalize within the market (Frey and Pommerehne 1989; Throsby 2001). Many studies show that people are actually willing to pay for these values through their taxes – even for cultural activities that they never use (see e.g. Bille Hansen 1997 for an analysis of the willingness to pay for the Royal Theatre in Copenhagen and Noonan 2003 for an overview). This is the main argument for public subsidies to the cultural sector (Frey and Pommerehne 1989; Throsby 2001).

Discussion of Cultiva

The two main goals of Cultiva must be weighed in relation to one another: securing jobs and good living conditions, when funds are allocated to different projects and activities.

The executive board of Cultiva has a difficult task and a huge responsibility in relation to spending the money in the best possible way to benefit the inhabitants of Kristiansand. It requires constant vigilance, development and monitoring. Cultiva is working in a very complex setting where the transmission mechanisms – and the knowledge about what ultimately comes out of it – are neither very clear nor transparent, and most of the effects will probably first show up only in the longer term. Moreover, the research evidence in this area still remains limited.

From 2002–2010 the total return on capital was 520 million NOK. The Foundation has spent approximately 170 million NOK on grants to projects and used approximately 44 million NOK on administration and operations. The foundation has mainly focused on building infrastructure: local education, competence centres for creative industries, strategically important festivals and events, establishment of seed and venture funds, funding of cultural facilities and scholarships for talented young people. About 40 million NOK has been invested in the development of festivals and events, such as the Quart Festival, Punkt Festival and Opera Island. About 20 million NOK has been allocated to the establishment of competence centres for cultural industries, such as South Norwegian Film Centre (Sørnorsk Filmsenter), Agder Centre of Arts (Agder Kunstnersenter) and SØRF (Competence Centre for Rhythmic Music). About 30 million NOK has been spent on the development and establishment of education and knowledge creation, like grants to study programmes at University of Agder, vocational education at Noroff and the Southern Science Park (Sørlandets Kunnskapspark) at the University of Agder. Due to some legal issues 350 million NOK was in May 2010 transferred to the creation of the new and smaller foundation: 'The foundation for major cultural facilities in Kristiansand'. The bulk of this amount has been used for the building of a large scale theatre and concert hall in Kristiansand, named 'Kilden'.

In this chapter I have highlighted three different approaches by which culture can create *market value*: culture in urban and regional development; creative industries (the direct contribution to employment, turnover and export); and broad value creation through experiences, creativity and innovation. Besides, I have pointed out that the *non-market value* of culture, based on citizens' utility and willingness-to-pay can be quite substantial.

Relating the two main purposes of Cultiva to these two perspectives, the market economic perspective and the welfare economic (non-market) perspective, one can roughly and for the sake of simplicity connect the market economic perspective to the purpose of securing jobs, and the welfare economics perspective to the purpose of good living conditions (the two perspectives and goals are of course interrelated in more complicated ways).

Until 2011, the strategy of Cultiva has been based on the concept of experience economy[10] (in the Scandinavian broader sense, as the concept has been explained and developed in this chapter). It means that Cultiva has focused on the creation of market value, and again Cultiva has chosen a broad strategy, aiming at all three approaches, mentioned above.

However, looking at how Cultiva actually has prioritized its resources, the vast majority of funds are actually spent on projects that can be attributed to the objective of good living conditions, including: 'Kilden' (the new theatre and concert hall), Sor Arena (a large football arena) and the Quart Festival. These institutions and events can of course create economic impact (measured by economic impact studies) if they attract a lot of tourists from outside Kristiansand. But these institutions and events may create quite substantial non-market value, and in this way Cultiva has contributed significantly to investments, which rarely can exist on market terms, but which require public support. And if the citizens of Kristiansand are happy about 'Kilden' and want to pay for it through taxes (as Cultiva's funds are public funds), it is actually a good investment (in the same way as the public funds for the Royal Theatre in Copenhagen has been argued in Bille Hansen (1997)) – even if it is not a good investment in terms of job creation.

Concerning both the market and the non-market value created, unfortunately, no formal evaluation of Cultiva's projects and grants have been conducted, and therefore we can only guess.[11]

Culture in urban and regional development

Cultiva has supported several institutions and activities that may contribute to the short-term spending effects in Kristiansand by attracting tourists (people living outside the Kristiansand area). Especially 'Kilden' and the different festivals have the potential to attract outside visitors. Kristiansand was, however, already very attractive for visitors – mainly because of its beautiful nature and the cliffs along the coastline, and because of a major commercial attraction, namely Kristiansand Zoo and Amusement Park (Dyreparken Kristiansand). The number of additional visitors (and related jobs) that Cultiva has created remains therefore an open question.

It is, however, more questionable how many new inhabitants and companies have moved to Kristiansand because of the increase in cultural offerings. Even though the former strategy by Cultiva was highly inspired by Richard Florida's (2002) theory, there is no evidence that Kristiansand has attracted more people from the creative class than it would have done without Cultiva, and there are no indications that is has done better in this respect compared to the other three big cities in Norway: Bergen, Stavanger and Trondheim (counting Oslo as an exception) (Tinagil 2009; Isaksen 2005).

The creative industries

Cultiva has done quite a lot to build framework conditions and support commercial industries from the cultural and creative sector in order to make them settle and develop their businesses in Kristiansand. Cultiva has had a special focus on companies within the music, film and media industries. Initiatives like top-finance of new movies and establishment of seed and venture funds have been among the instruments, but the actual outcome has not been measured and is difficult to access.[12]

Broad value creation

Cultiva has not directly supported projects that use culture, creativity and experience to increase innovation and value added in other business and sectors outside the creative industries. Primarily because there have been no applications in this area. However, Cultiva has contributed to many projects that may have increased educational and creativity values in Kristiansand – and by doing so Cultiva may have made an important contribution to the development and innovation outside the creative industries. Cultiva has contributed to several new study programmes at the University of Agder (in Kristiansand), conferences, knowledge building and dissemination. The short-term effects of these projects may be limited, but some effects will probably show up in the longer term.

As stated earlier, the spending of public resources like Cultiva's, must always be evaluated in terms of additionality and alternatives.

As mentioned above, there are reasons to believe that Cultiva has contributed to value added in Kristiansand – especially by attracting new visitors to the area and by contributing to a broader value creation in the long term by adding substantial educational and creativity values.

When it comes to alternative spending of the money, this exercise shall in principle be done for every single project Cultiva supports (which is beyond the scope of this chapter), but it is also possible to state some general remarks on the idea of Cultiva as a whole. The question is whether the citizens of Kristiansand would have had more pleasure from the funds Cultiva possesses if they had been spent on something other than the establishment of Cultiva.[13] The most obvious alternative was that the money could have gone into the municipality's total operating budget. Would that have created a larger impact on jobs and good living conditions in Kristiansand? The question is difficult to answer and remains open. But the question could also be put like this: what would have happened in Kristiansand without Cultiva? Artists and cultural industries are in general urban in character and therefore, especially in a country like Norway, that has big geographical distances (but also elsewhere), it can be important to try to ensure that all development is not concentrated in Oslo, but that favourable development also occurs in the other regions (Røed *et al.* 2009).

In the spring of 2011 the executive board of Cultiva chose a new strategy that focuses on projects aimed at children's and young people's living conditions and creative development, and Kristiansand's attractiveness for families. Whether this strategy is appropriate is beyond the scope of this chapter to assess. Besides, in the autumn of 2011 the situation in financial markets led to negative real returns on the assets and the foundation has from 2012 put a stop on all funding and grants given from Cultiva. As of 2012, and for a foreseeable future, Cultiva will concentrate on asset management in order to build a buffer capital.

Conclusion

The purpose of this chapter has been to examine the strategies of Cultiva and discuss them in the context of the existing knowledge and literature of culture economics, concerning art and culture in urban and regional development. What does the theory and existing empirical knowledge tell us? How can the strategies of Cultiva be evaluated in this context? What are Cultiva's experiences so far? What can we learn from this case? There are several things that can be pointed out.

The executive board of Cultiva really has a difficult task in relation to spending the money in the best possible way to benefit the inhabitants of Kristiansand, and to weigh the two main purposes in relation to one another: secure jobs and good living conditions. Cultiva is working in a very complex setting where the transmission mechanisms – and the knowledge about the ultimate outcomes – are neither very clear nor transparent, and most of the effects will probably first show up only in the longer term. Moreover, the research evidence in this area still remains limited. A formal evaluation of Cultiva could probably have helped

Cultiva to prioritize funds, and could have increased the general knowledge of how arts, culture and creativity can be used – or not used – to create local and regional development.

Vareide and Storm (2010) have looked at development of the region of Kristiansand compared to other regions in Norway. The analysis shows that over the last ten years, the Kristiansand region has had a very strong development in terms of attraction of visitors and attraction of companies. The number of jobs in the Kristiansand region has grown by 21.6 per cent from 2000–2009. It is far above the average on a national basis, which was 10.4 per cent during the same period. Businesses in the Kristiansand region had a formidable increase of 25.8 per cent in the number of jobs after 2000. In particular, it is the number of jobs in industry and technological services that has grown in Kristiansand. The degree to which Cultiva has contributed to this positive development remains an open question.

This chapter has shown that the inherent dilemma between the intrinsic values of culture versus the instrumental use of culture as a development tool is an ongoing debate – in politics as well as research. The dilemma is hot stuff – as the local debate around Cultiva has also shown.[14] Part of the dilemma also relates to the question of quality. If arts and culture are supported because of their intrinsic value, the question of quality is crucial. However, if the goal is economic development, the question of quality is secondary compared to support for projects and activities that create development.[15]

The dilemma can to some degree be discussed and analysed in economic terms by looking at the market economic perspective versus the welfare economic perspective. Economic theory will tell us, that the welfare economic perspective is the most important argument for public support to culture. Taking this to the two-fold purpose of Cultiva: securing jobs versus good living conditions; the primary purpose for a public foundation like Cultiva must be to make the citizens of Kristiansand happy – to increase utility, happiness[16] and well-being.

With all the funds Cultiva possesses it has the potential to do a lot for Kristiansand – probably especially in terms of good living conditions, happiness of the citizens and probably also economic development in the long term through creativity, innovation and educational effects.[17] Whether this potential has been reached remains an open question and outside the scope of this chapter. There is still a lot to be learned about the Cultiva case and the use of culture and creativity in economic development.

Notes

1 'Good living conditions' is a vague concept. It can be interpreted in a narrow sense linking closely to certain life-condition indicators like crime, use of drugs, suicides, etc., or in a broad sense linking to the population's general utility and happiness. The last interpretation will be used in this chapter.

2 'The arts for the arts sake' is a tricky concept, because it actually implies that the arts provide no utility at all. This is not coherent with the economic approach. In this

chapter 'the arts for the arts sake' means the intrinsic value of arts and culture and the utility it gives people.

3 The local newspaper www.fedrelandsvennen.no has published numerous articles about Cultiva, and the local debate can be followed here.

4 Economic benefits are in general side-effects of cultural policy – not the intended goal. The intended goals are rather goals like production of new art, participation, education and preservation.

5 Bille (2010) has, based on Danish data, investigated which cultural activities the creative class uses more than others.

6 See Andersen *et al.* (2009) for a Danish analysis of Florida's theories.

7 'Cultural industries' is the original term, but following the reports from DCMS (1998, 2001) the popular term has been 'creative industries'. However, Hesmondhalgh (2002) argues – among others – that 'cultural industries' is a more proper term than 'creative industries'.

8 See Bille and Lorenzen (2008, chapter 3) for a critique of this approach.

9 It is this approach a new Center for Culture and Experience Economy in Denmark is working with. The centre has received a grant of 50 million DKK over a period of four years, starting in 2009, and it has just been evaluated by Deloitte and Bille (2012).

10 See strategy documents at www.cultiva.no.

11 A pre-evaluation report has been done by the University of Heidelberg (Then *et al.* 2010), but unfortunately no real evaluation of Cultiva's activities has been conducted.

12 In the Norwegian city Tromsø a new foundation INTRO has been established, focusing mainly on developing business within the creative industries (www.introfondet.no), and other cities like Stavanger seem to follow the idea.

13 It must be remembered that the initial capital may not be touched.

14 It is interesting that the same passionate debate has not evolved around the Competence Foundation – the other foundation established at the same time and with the same background as Cultiva. Probably because the grants to arts and culture (and the arguments for giving them) is hot stuff, compared to grants to knowledge institutions and educations.

15 This also differentiates Cultiva from the cultural policy conducted by state and municipalities in the sense that Cultiva has no formal obligations concerning quality of the arts supported. While artistic quality is of course one of the prime goals in public cultural policy.

16 See Frey and Stutzer (2002).

17 See also the *Value Creation Circle* by Then *et al.* (2010).

References

Abbing, H. (2002) *Why are Artists Poor? The Exceptional Economy of the Arts*, Amsterdam: Amsterdam University Press.

Andersen, K.V., Lorenzen, M. and Bille, T. (2009) *Den danske kreative klasse – Hvor bor den? – Hvem består den af? – Hvad betyder den for det danske samfund?*, Aarhus: Klim forlag.

Bille, T. (2010) 'Cool, Funky and Creative? – The Creative Class and Preferences for Leisure and Culture', *International Journal of Cultural Policy*, 16(4): 469–499.

——— (2011a) 'The Scandinavian Approach to the Experience Economy – Does it Make Sense?', *International Journal of Cultural Policy*, 18(1): 93–110.

——— (2011b) 'Kunstens balancekunst mellem velfærd og marked', in H.C. Garmann, Johnsen (ed.), *Kunstens Form og Kulturens Bruk*, Kristiansand: Portal.

Bille, T. and De Paoli, D. (2012) 'Approaches to Stimulate and Support the Cultural Entrepreneur – the Case of Denmark and Norway', in G. Haggort, A. Thomassen and

R. Kooyman (eds), *Pioneering Minds Worldwide. On the Entrepreneurial Principles of the Cultural and Creative Industries*, Delft: Eburon Academic Press.

Bille, T. and Lorenzen, M. (2008) *Den danske oplevelsesøkonomi – afgrænsning, økonomisk betydning og vækstmuligheder*, Copenhagen: Samfundslitteratur.

Bille, T. and Schulze, G. (2006) 'Culture in Urban and Regional Development', in V. Ginsburg and D. Throsby (eds), *Handbook of the Economics of Arts and Culture*, Amsterdam: Elsevier.

Bille Hansen, T. (1993) *Kulturens økonomiske betydning – state of the art*, Copenhagen: AKF Forlaget.

——— (1995) 'Measuring the Value of Culture', *Journal of Cultural Policy*, 1(2): 309–322.

——— (1997) 'The Willingness-to-Pay for the Royal Theatre in Copenhagen as a Public Good', *Journal of Cultural Economics*, 21(1): 1–28.

Birch, S. (2008) *The Political Promotion of the Experience Economy and the Creative Industries – Cases from UK, New Zealand, Singapore, Norway, Sweden and Denmark*, Copenhagen: Samfundslitteratur.

Boswijk, A., Thijssen, T. and Peelen, E. (2007) *The Experience Economy – A New Perspective*, Amsterdam: Pearson.

Cruickshank, J., Lysgård, H.K. and Normann, R. (2011) 'Kulturen og den instrumentelle tenkemåte – Eksemplet Kristiansand', in H.C. Garmann Johnsen (ed.), *Kunstens Form og Kulturens Bruk*, Kristiansand: Portal.

Cultiva. Documents available at: www.cultiva.no.

DCMS (1998) *Creative Industries Mapping Document*, Creative Industries Task Force, UK, London: Department for Culture, Media and Sport.

——— (2001) *Creative Industries Mapping Document*, Creative Industries Task Force, UK, London: Department for Culture, Media and Sport.

Deding, M. and Filges, T. (2004) *Derfor flytter vi – Geografisk mobilitet i den danske arbejdsstyrke*, Report 04:19, Copenhagen: Socialforskningsinstituttet.

Deloitte and Bille, T. (2012) *Kultur- og oplevelsesøkonomien i Danmark. Evaluering af aftale fra 20. juni 2007 om styrkelse af kultur- og oplevelsesøkonomien i Danmark*, Copenhagen: Deloitte.

De Paoli, D. and Hansen, T. (2010) *Competence About Public Measures Directed Towards the Cultural Industries – an Evaluation of the Norwegian Art Council and State Innovation Bureau*, Oslo: Norwegian Department of Commerce.

Duelund, P. (2003) *The Nordic Cultural Model*, Copenhagen: Nordisk Kultur Institut.

Duelund, P. and Bille Hansen, T. (1994) *Hvor står vi nu?*, Copenhagen: Klim.

Erhvervs- og Byggestyrelsen (2008) *Vækst via oplevelser*, Copenhagen.

——— (2011) *Vækst via oplevelser*, Copenhagen.

Florida, R. (2002) *The Rise of the Creative Class – and How it's Transforming Work, Leisure, Community and Everyday Life*, New York: Basic Books.

Frey, B.S. and Pommerehne, W.W. (1989) *Muses & Markets. Explorations in the Economics of the Arts*, Oxford: Basil Blackwell.

Frey, B.S. and Stutzer, A. (2002) 'The Economics of Happiness', *World Economics*, 3(1).

Haraldsen, T., Hagen, S.E. and Alnes, P.K. (2008) *Kulturnæringerne i Norge. Muligheder og utfordringer – en oppdatering av kartleggingen fra 2004*, Østlandsforskning, Lillehammar: ØF-report no. 1212.

Haraldsen, T., Flygind, S.K., Overvåg, K.D. and Power, D. (2004) *Kartlegging av kulturnæringerne i Norge – økonomisk betydning. Vækst- og udviklingspotensial*, Østlandsforskning, Lillehammar: ØF-report no. 1010.

Hesmondhalgh, D. (2002) *The Cultural Industries*, London: SAGE Publications.

Hjemdahl, K., Hauge, E.S. and Lind, E. (2007) *Festivaler på Sørlandet. Kultur i kraftformat*, Agderforskning, Kristiansand: FoU-report nr. 4/2007.

Isaksen, A. (2005) *Den kreative klasse og regional næringsutvikling i Norge*, NIFUStep, Oslo: Arbeidsnotat 22/2005.

KEA European Affairs (2007) *The Economy of Culture in Europe*, Brussels: European Commission.

Kiland, C. and Horrigmo, A.M.J. (2012) *Policy endring i en lokalpolitisk kontekst – regimer, mulighedsvindu eller lederskap?*, Forthcoming in Norsk Statsvitenskapelig Tidsskrift, Oslo.

KK-stiftelsen (2003) *Upplevelsesindustrin 2003. Statistik og jämförelser*, Stockholm: KK-stiftelsen.

Lysgård, H.K. (2011) 'Kulturforståelsen i byutviklingsdiskursen. Antagonismer i konstruksjonen av en kulturbasert utviklingsdiskurs', in H.C. Garmann Johnsen (ed.), *Kunstens Form og Kulturens Bruk*, Kristiansand: Portal.

Malanga, S. (2004) *The Curse of the Creative Class*, City Journal, Winter 2004.

Mathiasen, S.B., Poulsen, C.F. and Lorenzen, M. (2006) *Rammebetingelser for Københavns kreative brancher*, Imagine..., Copenhagen: Copenhagen Business School.

Menon and Perduco (2011) *The Role of the Cultural Industries for Norwegian Economy*, Report no. 9, Oslo: Menon Business Economics.

Noonan, D.S. (2003) 'Contingent Valuation and Cultural Resources: A Meta-Analytic Review of the Literature', *Journal of Cultural Economics*, 27(3)–(4): 159–176.

Norman, V., Knudsen, J.P. and Røed, H. (1994) *Felles mål for Agder. Et tiltaksprogram for Sørlandet, Aust-Agder and Vest-Agder*, Kristiansand: Aust-Agder and Vest-Agder.

Normann, R. (2007) *Democracy in Development – A Critical View on Regional Governance*, Trondheim: Norwegian University of Science and Technology, Department of Industrial Economy and Technology Management.

Pine, B.J. and Gilmore, J.H. (1999) *The Experience Economy – Work is Theatre & Every Business a Stage*, Boston, MA: Harvard Business School Press.

Pine, B.J. and Gilmore, J.H. (2007) *Authenticity. What Consumers Really Want*, Boston: Harvard Business School Press.

Rambøll Management (2005) *Oplevelsesøkonomi Hovedstadregionen – Perspektiver og forslag fra seks kreative brancher*, Copenhagen: Rambøll Management.

Regeringen (2003) *Danmark i kultur- og oplevelsesøkonomien – 5 nye skridt på vejen*, Copenhagen.

Røed, H. (1993) *Surt live på det blide Sørland*, Kristiansand: Agderforskning.

Røed, H., Hilde, K. and Hjemdahl, K.M. (2009) *Kultur og det regionale Norge*, Kristiansand: Agderforskning, FoU-report no. 5/2009.

Seaman, B. (2003) 'The Economic Impact of the Arts', in R. Towse (ed.), *A Handbook of Cultural Economics*, Cheltenham: Edward Elgar.

Stiglitz, J. (2000) *Economics of the Public Sector*, London: W.W. Norton & Company.

Then, V., Münscher, R., Seegelken-Lautenschläger, C. and Eggersglüss, C. (2010) *Cultiva, Sørlandets Kompetencefond. Impact measurement Approach*, Final report, Heidelberg: Centrum für soziale Investitionen und Innovationen (CSI).

Throsby, D. (2001) *Economics and Culture*, Cambridge: Cambridge University Press.

Tinagil, I. (2009) *Norway in the Creative Age. Citisense 2009*, Oslo: Abelia og Statens Vegvesen.

Towse, R. (2003) 'Cultural Industries', in R. Towse (ed.), *A Handbook of Cultural Economics*, Cheltenham: Edward Elgar.

Vareide, K. and Kobro, L.U. (2012) *Skaper kultur attrative steder?*, Bø: Telemarksforskning, TF-notat no. 1/2012.

Vareide, K. and Storm, H.N. (2010) *Næringsutvikling og attraktivitet Kristiansandregionen*, Bø: Telemarksforskning, TF-notat no. 39/2010.

12 Site-specific strength

The regional power of historical plays and place sponsoring

Anne-Britt Gran

Entrance: a Norwegian context

Norway finds itself in the midst of a cultural and political golden age: the government is investing significant sums in national cultural institutions such as the Norwegian National Opera and Ballet, and right around the corner a new National Museum, while investments are being channelled into a number of regional cultural facilities. While budgets earmarked for culture are being heavily cut back in many European countries, funds for culturally related projects are being augmented slowly but surely because the sitting government under Jens Stoltenberg has as its goal to bring the cultural budget up to a level of 1 per cent of the national budget. During the period between 2005 and 2012 the culture budget has grown by 3.7 billion crowns (€1 is approximately 8 Norwegian crowns), which represents an increase of 73 per cent. The growth of the culture budget is currently greater than growth in the national budget as a whole. This focus on culture goes under the name 'Culture Boost', a boost that is of course very well received by those involved with culture.

At the same time as the government flexes its cultural muscles, in local and regional political contexts significant cultural focus is being put on culture: new local and regional cultural centres are getting funding – with or without government support. There has been an explosion of festivals during the last decade and historical plays are enjoying a resurgence. In a survey from 2008, 75 per cent of culture directors in Norwegian municipalities report that they have one or more festivals in their township during the course of the year (Aagedal *et al.* 2009). The 317 culture directors who took part in the survey could report 822 festivals and historical plays in their townships. Old factories, abandoned industrial areas and empty churches are used as cultural arenas, and urban pockets are aestheticized to create a sense of well-being and to improve the public perception of the area. In this same survey, 30 per cent of the municipalities report that they have undertaken such changes in disused industrial areas, and 48 per cent report that they have used churches as cultural arenas.

On a national level, there has been a 50 per cent growth in the number of people employed in the creative industries during the period from 2000–2009, compared to a growth of employment in industry and commerce of 31 per cent (Espelin and

Gran 2011). In the category 'cultural activity', in which art institutions and artists find themselves, growth in employment was a remarkable 201 per cent during this period. Growth in value creation is 8 per cent greater in cultural activities than in Norwegian industry and commerce in general.

A substantial culturalization is taking place in Norwegian society, at national, regional and local levels: belief in the creative power of culture, its significance for economic growth and its role as the fuel and engine of local and regional development is considerable. The tendency is not typically Norwegian; we can find a similar revitalization of belief in the power of culture in a number of greater and lesser European areas and regions (Lindeborg and Lindkvist 2010).

To the extent that something uniquely Norwegian can be found in what is happening in Norway, there is the fact that Norway is at present a very rich petroleum nation and the sitting government has chosen to use a greater portion of its budgets to give the country a cultural boost. Both smaller and larger areas of the society can benefit from this, since both the number of funded projects and the size of the funding have increased. For this reason cultural life in Norway finds itself in an especially privileged position now, compared to many other countries in Europe. In 2012 Norway is a little oasis of cultural focus in a larger international context.

In this chapter I will take a closer look at one example of the local and regional upswing, represented by the theatrical genre of the historical play.

The approach to the issue and theoretical perspectives

Historical plays are dramas about historical events or legends staged outdoors. I call these plays *site-specific*, from the concept 'site-specific art' because the content of the play is closely linked to a site through specific historical events that happened there. Many local inhabitants are involved in the production of the performance, and on stage you will find both known professional actors and amateurs from the region.

All in all there have been more than 350 historical plays in Norway from 1954 until today. Between 70 and 80 historical plays are performed each summer, while other plays are performed every second year or more rarely.

The place plays a vital role in the play. We ask: why has this rather old-fashioned looking theatre phenomenon become so popular in the era of globalization and digitalization? What is the significance of the aesthetic genre, 'historical play' and the repetition of the plays in a local context? What kind of power do the plays have in a local, regional and global context?

Different theoretical perspectives will be used: theories about theatre versus rituals, staging versus authenticity (the theatre anthropology discourse), theories of cultural financing (the sponsorship discourse) and theories about globalization (the homogenization–heterogenization discourse). These theoretical perspectives are related in a certain dialectical way: the globalization perspective can explain both the popularity of the theatre genre, historical play and the local cultural sponsoring, while the theatre anthropology perspective can explain the 'fitness' of the genre, historical play, in a global context and why local firms prefer to sponsor these plays. I will seek out a theoretical overlap in the explanation and understanding of the phenomenon of the historical play – from within and from without. Combining these perspectives in such a way will hopefully provide new insight about cultural power in local and regional places today.

'Local' here refers to the concrete place where the play is performed, such as Verdal in Nord-Trøndelag. 'Regional' refers to a larger geographical area, which coincides with the county (e.g. Nord-Trøndelag) or extends over several counties. The historical plays recruit amateur participants, volunteers, sponsors and the public from both the actual place and from a larger geographical entity. There is no theoretical point here in making a strict distinction between the local and regional levels.

A play and its place

To explain and exemplify the genre, historical play, we will use the first and best known of plays in Norway: *The Play of King Olav the Holy One* (Spelet om heilage Olav), also called The Stiklestad Play. Since the first night in 1954 more than 800,000 people have seen the performance on a bright summer evening in Verdal in Nord-Trøndelag.

This is not a traditional case study, but rather The Stiklestad Play is used as an example – the archetypical example – of a theatrical genre. What is analysed and put into focus is the phenomenon 'historical play' and its role in a local, regional and global context (Gran and Ohrem 1996; Ohrem 2005).

Stiklestad is located in Verdal in Nord-Trøndelag County and was the scene of the single most famous battle in Norwegian history.[1] The battle of Stiklestad, 29 July 1030, represents the Christianization of Norway, as well as the introduction of monarchy. The battle of Stiklestad is looked upon as a turning point in the history of Norway. Verdal is apparently the only municipality in Norway to keep its borders and local names unchanged as far back as we know. Verdal municipality's coat of arms is a yellow cross on a red background. In the battle of Stiklestad, King Olav Haraldsson and his army were said to have used shields marked with a similar cross. Today, Stiklestad is a centre of activity consisting of an open air theatre, a church, a cultural centre and a number of museums. The main museum was moved to Stiklestad in the 1950s, and the cultural centre was finished in 1992.

The play of St Olaf King of Norway (Olav Haraldsson) is the largest and oldest Norwegian outdoor play. The first performance of the play took place on 29 July 1954, called St Olaf's day or Olsok. Olsok (19 July–29 July) in Stiklestad is a ten-day long festival built around the play, St Olaf King of Norway. The four performances form the basis of the festival, in addition to a Middle Age market, lectures, art exhibitions, concerts, theatre, children's activities, etc. The national heritage museum in Stiklestad consists of 30 well-kept antiquarian buildings from the seventeenth century and after. The national heritage museum is also the arena for different events during all seasons of the year. In this study we will focus only on the historical play performed in the summertime and not the whole heritage museum.

A historical play should fulfil one or more of the following criteria:

- be based on local historical material;
- be played in the open air;
- be anchored geographically to the location of the theatre;
- be presented regularly;
- have amateur actors or a mix of amateurs and professionals.

The Stiklestad Play contains all these elements, and therefore it is typical of the genre, but it is untypical in other ways: it is based on a historical event which is more important on a national level than most of the other historical plays are, and it is a part of a large heritage museum supported by the state with almost 20 million crowns. The play of St Olaf King of Norway plays an important role locally, regionally and nationally in Norway, and it is called the mother of the genre, historical play.

The play between theatre and ritual

Theatre anthropology is a discipline influenced by the anthropologist Victor Turner and developed by the theatre director and scholar Richard Schechner (Schechner 1985 and 1988; Turner 1991). According to Schechner all kinds of performances exist somewhere between theatre and ritual, the axis 'theatre–ritual' is understood as a *continuum* rather than an *opposition*. A performance or an event is never either-or theatre or ritual but somewhere between them on the axis. This was of course a provocative point of view, because for a long time theatre had been studied and treated as an art form and an aesthetic object, while ritual had been studied as habits belonging to primitive cultures typical to the 'rest' and not the West. Putting western high theatre tradition together with low ritual habits in the same theoretical framework is the benefit of theatre anthropology. The concept of performance unites them, and the use of a continuum instead of the classical opposition challenges the historically invented distinction between western theatre and primitive rituals, as if the classical outdoor Greek theatre was not also a ritual. Schechner presented a model of this performance continuum, in Figure 12.1 only relevant aspects are included (Schechner 1988: 120). This model is both relevant and useful in analysing the genre, historical play.

Theatre, illusion and entertainment

The village of Stiklestad is staged as a historical drama, not only the outdoor play, but everything that is happening there: the festival, the market and the building of new (old) buildings like the Stiklastadir farm. Everything mimics the idea of the real Middle Ages, the real Vikings and the real battle. The aim is to look as realistic/authentic as possible, and to get the audience/the tourists absorbed in the

Efficacy ⟷	Entertainment
Ritual	Theatre
results	fun
symbolic time	emphasis now
audience believes	audience appreciates
collective creativity	individual creativity

Figure 12.1 The continuum ritual–theatre.

illusion of being in the Middle Ages and being entertained by it. Of course it looks theatrical; it is, after all, a representation of another age, but the staging is based on the illusion principles of 'looking like' the real thing. This is realistic theatre in the tradition of the Russian director Konstantin Stanislavskij who represents the staging of an illusion. This principle tries to hide the theatrical instruments involved; I will call it hidden and unspoken theatricality (Gran 2004). This theatricality is found in its old-fashioned form in both realistic theatre and film, based on the principle 'as if it were real'. The actor has to play Hamlet as if he was Hamlet, and the ketchup needs to look like blood if that is what we want the audience to believe. The hidden theatricality implies mimesis of a true reality, and it represents the seemingly authentic. The aim is to get the audience absorbed in the stage, forgetting it is theatre. The more the acting and staging are hidden, the more the seeming authenticity is effective on us and the more entertaining it feels.

In order to have the largest roles played in a realistic and believable fashion, professional actors are brought in. Ten of the central roles are played by professional actors and many of our most profiled actors have, over the years, guested Stiklestad. Functions also covered by professionals include instruction, choreography, musical direction, production and sound. The professional actors and other professionals make up the theatrical certainty of the play's artistic quality, of the entertainment aspects and of the audience appreciation. As a theatre production the play belongs to the fine arts, and to a theatrical illusion – an illusion is not the real thing. The yearly ritual of The Stiklestad Play is a real thing.

Ritual, authenticity and efficacy

The ritual and authentic aspects of the play are: the place itself – the site-specific Stiklestad battle; the role of the amateurs and volunteers; and the yearly repetition of the play (see Figure 12.2).

Site-specific-Stiklestad

The origin of the place and play is the historical Stiklestad battle in 1030. The authenticity of this fact is the ground on which everything else is built; it is the identity of the place and play, the true essence of Stiklestad. This true essence is put on stage every year, and thousands of people join the event.

Local amateurs and volunteers

The Stiklestad Play is performed by 350 actors and extras, including a full symphony orchestra and male choir. This meeting of professionals and amateurs has characterized the production of The Stiklestad Play since its first performance in 1954 and the cooperative effort of the professionals and amateurs serves as a foundation for the strength of the genre of historical plays. The professionals maintain the aesthetic dimension and artistic quality and amateurs from the area provide the authentic connection to the place and an authentic acting style. In a theatrical context, amateurs are often looked upon as more authentic than schooled, professional actors.

The Stiklestad Play is only made possible through a volunteer effort involving 700 people who work with strong engagement, competence and determination. Volunteer activity at Stiklestad is the glue of the whole event and time put in by the volunteers is estimated at between 10 and 11 years.

The repetition aspects

The annual recurrence of the play gives it an atmosphere of rituality and brings a dimension of cyclicality to an otherwise linear and modern experience of time. The recurrence and the substantial presence of amateurs and volunteers glue the event together in an old-fashioned way that brings to mind the old sociologist, Tönnies' description of 'Gemeinschaft' (Tönnies 2010). The play becomes a shared activity that gathers people together across generations and creates a sense of belonging and a collective experience. It is a local ritual where the community is the result.

The power of the historical play lies in being between theatre and ritual, between realistic theatre and a local and regional yearly ritual, between professional actors and amateurs, between staging images and authentic site-specificity. The influential post-structural critique of theatre based on essence, ritual and authenticity (Derrida 1967, 1978), may be philosophically 'true', but has no relevance in the critique of ritual theatre and historical plays as being metaphysical and primordialistic (Gran 2000). The way these plays work and function in a local context, shows that essence, identity and authenticity have a practical and pragmatic relevance and make a difference – even when staged.

Regional economic power – culture sponsoring

The play most certainly has had a spin-off effect on the cultural life and the business community in Verdal. The play was a direct cause of the location of a national centre of culture in Stiklestad. The business community supports the play of St Olav, King of Norway, through *Stiklestadsleidangen*, an agreement between

The Stiklestad Play between:

Theatre and entertainment ⟷	Ritual and results
- staging the place	- identity of the place
- theatrical: a representation, image	- authenticity, essence, depth
- staging the Middle Ages as an illusion of the real age	- based on the historical battle in 1030 where St. Olaf, the king of Norway, died
- professional actors entertain	- amateur actors and volunteers give results as community and intergration
- individual creativity	- collective creativity
- linear time; new mise-en-scène	- cyclical and symbolic time; repetition

Figure 12.2 The Stiklestad Play between ritual and theatre.

a group of companies and the cultural centre concerning the development of Stiklestad and the financing of the play. A 'leidang' was a system presumed to originate from Håkon the Good (*c.* 950 AD) concerning the organization of a fleet for naval defence. The 'leidang' was originally a tax paid by the farmers to provide ships, crew and provisions. Today *Stiklestadleidangen* is a way of sponsoring the heritage centre and the play, and the involvement of private business is typical of the financing of historical plays in Norway.

It is not just the genre of theatre that gives the historical plays their regional energy; the method of financing the plays, itself, also helps shape the plays' regional strength. How then are the plays financed?

There is a governmental subsidy scheme currently at 3 million Norwegian crowns under the auspices of the Norwegian Amateur Theatre Council. A ceiling of 300,000 Norwegian crowns exists, however, which is not enough to cover the costs of these productions. The arrangers of the historical plays are consequently dependent on local public funding (county and municipality) and private sponsors in order to set up the annual performances.

For many years I have been working with the research topic of culture sponsorship in Norway (Gran and Hofplass 2007; Gran and Vaagen 2010). In some of the studies we have done surveys with as many as 2,000 managers, which gives us the possibility to compare the 19 counties in Norway. One of the most surprising and important results of this research was that the involvement in arts and culture sponsorship was largest in the north and west of Norway – not in the capital, Oslo, where most of the public art institutions are and where most of the artists live.

The impression created by the media of cultural sponsorship was that this was something that took place among the large cultural institutions in the capital city of Oslo by the major sponsors in the oil, banking and industrial sectors. No systematic surveys in the area had been carried out until we conducted one in 2004 (Gran and Hofplass 2007). Several times since then, we have conducted similar studies for Art & Business Norway and the results have been the same every time.

Figure 12.3 shows the percentage share per county of companies that have sponsored or cooperated with the cultural sector in the 19 counties of Norway in 2009: the capital, Oslo, and the neighboring county of Akershus are at the bottom of the list.

What makes sponsorship more common and popular among firms in regional counties than in the capital county?

Theories of sponsoring – a missing link

Sponsoring has traditionally been looked upon as either generous philanthropy or strategic marketing and corporate communication (Martorella 1996; McNicholas 2004). Sponsoring – targeting both sports, culture and humanitarian objectives – has, in traditional marketing, been regarded as a market channel that is very accurate in relation to different target groups. Research in the field has put focus on the branding of a product or company, methods for measuring effect, the development of stakeholders, case studies of individual sponsors with focus on the company, consumers' attitude to sponsoring companies and overview studies of a country's cultural sponsoring with focus on cash flow and companies' preferences for sponsoring objects (Head 1998; Meenaghan 1998; Jiffer and Roos 1999; Prendergast *et al.* 2010).

These approaches, naturally, tell us very little about the geographical zones of sponsorships. Moreover, sponsor research has been dominated by sports

Percentage of firms in Norwegian counties that have sponsored or cooperated with the cultural sector during the last 12 months (performing art, music and fine art – not sport):

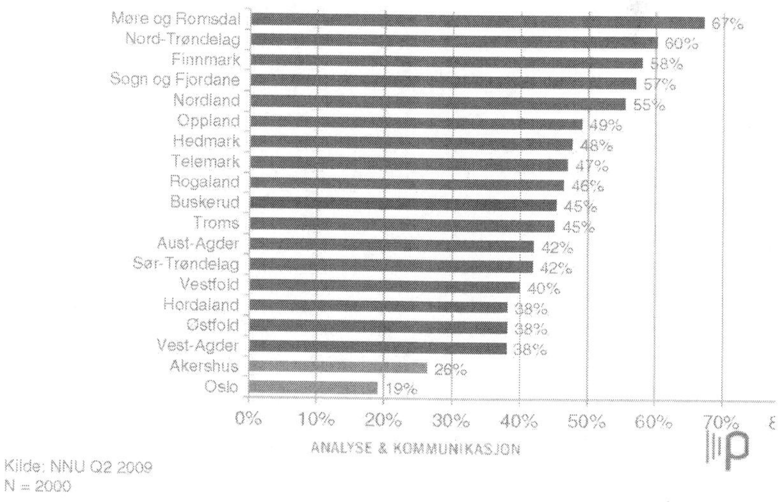

Figure 12.3 Percentage of sponsors in Norwegian counties.

sponsorship, an even more commercial sponsor market than cultural sponsorship. Primary focus has been put on the sponsorship company's yield from the sponsorship, which is a result of research being anchored in marketing disciplines and not cultural disciplines.

With regard to case studies, research has had a primary interest in *large* companies that sponsor *large* cultural institutions/festivals and not small and middle-sized companies and cultural institutions that are important for culture at a local level and at the site (Rectanus 2002; Sarstedt *et al.* 2010).

The importance of cultural sponsoring for culture at a local level and for city and site development is lacking in the journals that have covered the field of sponsorship during the last few years, such as, for example, the *Journal of Business & Marketing*, *Journal of Advertising Research*, *Journal of Sponsorship* and *International Journal of Arts Management*.

National overview studies find geographical differences with regard to cash flow/liquidity where the largest cities with the largest cultural institutions and festivals are the financial winners (Mermiri 2010). These national studies might give the impression that there is little sponsorship in more peripheral districts. It is first when the share percentage of companies that sponsor culture in relation to the number of companies that exists in the area (here, in the county) that a new pattern emerges in the sponsor market: in this context, the largest *share percentage* of companies that sponsor culture is *outside* the largest municipalities.

The logic of local sponsorship

The geographical aspects of cultural sponsorship can contribute to casting new light on the private financing of historical plays and the regional strength it has. In the surveys we have conducted 'sponsoring' is not defined in the questionnaire such that company managers have replied with what they themselves regard as sponsorship activities. Moreover, we ask whether they have sponsored and/or cooperated with cultural organizations such that different forms of cooperation and bartering (swapping of products and services), including the purchase of services, is included.

We take a closer look at motives for sponsoring and which players in the culture sector sponsors prefer to finance. In marketing studies, most focus is of course on marketing motives and consequently questionnaires are made with marketing answers. When we began measurement of the Norwegian sponsorship market in 2004, we did just the same, inspired by international studies. The questionnaires regarding companies' motives for sponsoring have thus had the following as response alternatives: branding, product advertising, corporate social responsibility, relationship marketing, internal care and motivation of employees and top management's personal interest in the sponsor object (McNicolas 2004). With this we don't capture companies' interest in local cultural affairs and development of the local community.

In a web survey of 637 executives from 2007 we introduced a series of new response alternatives with regard to motivation for sponsoring. There were two alternatives that especially changed the whole picture, and they were the motives for 'strengthening local culture' and 'strengthening the local community/region where the company is located' (Gran and Hofplass 2007). More than 80 per cent of the sponsoring companies responded that these motives were important/very important, while 78 per cent responded, 'to show the company's social commitment', and 63 per cent responded that marketing 'the company's name and products' was important/very important. In fifth place among the motives was 'personal interest for art and culture', which is a motive we also find among international studies.

We had precisely the same tendency confirmed in a web survey of 748 companies in 2010: the most important motive was 'to strengthen the local community/region where the company is located' (80 per cent), followed by 'to strengthen local culture' (75 per cent), to 'show the company's social commitment' (73 per cent), 'marketing the company's name and products' (55 per cent) and 'personal interest in art and culture' (53 per cent) (Gran and Vaagen 2010). Both of these surveys showed that large companies (over 100 employees) are more marketing oriented, while small and middle-sized companies are more charity-oriented and concerned about the local community.

It is in light of the fact that eight out of ten companies respond that strengthening the company's local community and region as the most important motive for culture sponsoring that I choose to introduce the concept of 'place sponsoring'. It is not culture exclusively that is financed in these sponsorships; it is, in principle, the place itself that is to be made attractive for both those whose interest lies in culture and for the employees.

What is it then that companies prefer to sponsor? With regard to the extent to which the sponsor object is a professional activity, an amateur activity or a semi-professional activity (both professionals and amateurs), it is the amateurs who are the winners. Six out of ten executives say that they have sponsored amateurs during the course of the last year, while fewer than three out of ten have sponsored professional activities or semi-professional activities.

This discovery was also a very surprising one because what we knew from the media and culture field was that the large professional cultural institutions were the preferred sponsor objects. And they are just that for the large national and international companies, but these turned out to not be representative for sponsor companies in Norway. In the districts in Norway there is clearly more amateur activity to sponsor than there are professional activities or semi-professional activities. When so many companies choose to support and cooperate with amateurs, this can be seen as a direct connection to the motive of 'strengthening the local community/region where the company is located'. Amateurs in both the music and theatre sectors maintain and strengthen local cultural activities that the company and its employees benefit from. The networks in smaller towns are often tight and transparent, such that direct contact between amateur activity and the company's management does occur. Cooperation between professionals and amateurs makes historical plays semi-professional, something which one out of four of the companies had sponsored.

Many amateurs in music and theatre participate in the historical plays during the summer, so sponsoring local choirs, orchestras and acting groups is also indirect support of the historical plays.

With regard to the extent to which companies prefer to sponsor institutions, groups or ensembles, individual artists or temporary cultural arrangements, the pattern is the same. It is groups and ensembles as well as temporary arrangements that are the most popular. Six out of ten companies have sponsored such players, while only two out of ten have sponsored institutions (Gran and Hofplass 2007).

The historical play is a temporary arrangement consisting of primarily amateurs and some professionals who activate the population of the place – and in some places the company's own employees are most likely part of the production. Historical plays release a wave of interest in sponsor activity in the districts of Norway because the genre appeals to the motives of the companies to sponsor: management wishes to support local cultural activities, primarily through amateur activities, and a desire to strengthen the local community where the company is located.

When analysed in the perspective of resource dependence in the context of organizational theory, we can say that historical plays are a local environment resource for the companies and the companies are a local financial resource for the plays; together they enjoy geographical gains (Pfeffer and Salancik 1978; Gran and Hofplass 2007). Local sponsor objects have a focus in the local community that is not found in the larger sponsor objects in larger cities. They are primarily motivated by their own self interest in marketing, company communication and transfer of competencies. When Mercedes sponsors the Norwegian National Opera and Ballet or when DNB (The Norwegian Bank) sponsors the National Theatre, Oslo as a place is not important. When local and regional companies sponsor historical plays, the place plays a major role in the sponsorship.

Large companies' marketing motivated sponsoring in large cities and the small and middle-sized companies' sponsoring in the districts appear as two completely different things. Marketing motivated sponsoring can be interpreted as an expression for a kind of global business logic, independent of place, while culture sponsoring in the districts of Norway is first and foremost place sponsoring.

A global context and theories of globalization

Neither the genre of the historical play nor the financing of them is enough to explain their regional strength. The substantial growth in both historical plays and regional festivals of all types during the last few decades must also be seen in a larger socio-political context, which comes under the name of globalization.

Globalization has been on the agenda of political scientists and humanists over the last few decades. The discourse has had to do with the role of the nation state in globalization, of the relationship between the global and the local, of the meaning of globalization for the development of identity with regard to art and culture and for the site as a concrete, local place. Many theories and models have been developed in different subject areas in order to understand and explain globalization and its consequences (Featherstone 1990; Appadurai 1990; Robertson 1992; Gupta and Ferguson 1997; Held and McGrew 2000 among others). To properly place historical plays in this globalization discourse, we must first look briefly at several different theoretical positions. These positions will not be systematized in relation their relevant subject areas, but rather in relation to theoretical *figures* that operate across different subject areas and their traditions. These are: the colonial figure, the dialectical figure and the deconstructive figure. The presentation of them will have a certain *idealtypischen* character, since there has not been opportunity to go into depth with regard to the different variants of each figure. The choice of using the theoretical figure is completely decisive with regard to how one can understand historical plays in a global context.

The colonialistic figure is the one we find with theoreticians who maintain that globalization has primarily to do with homogenization, be it of economic systems (capitalism), of modernization or of cultural expression (Wallerstein 1990; Appadurai 1990). These theoreticians put focus on the processes that are of a homogenizing nature and globalization is presented as a colonialistic process in which Western phenomena enfold and outstrip local and national differences. In its early phases, this process was also understood to be a form of American cultural imperialism (Hollywood) and a McDonaldization of food culture and public space. The colonialistic figure has been significantly modified since then, particularly because homogenization turned out to have met more local opposition than previously expected (Castells 1997). I believe that this theoretical figure still has validity and it is especially relevant for use when the goal is to identify homogenizing elements in the globalization process. This is so because, when globalization is not identical with homogenization, there are nonetheless homogenizing processes in it – for example in the new social media, such as Facebook, that are in use worldwide.

I choose to divide the dialectical figure into a strong and weak variant. The strong dialectical figure is tied to theories that would have globalization meeting explicit local, national, ethnic and religious resistance. Globalization is understood here as a threat or a strong challenge to local variations and an unwanted process of secularization. The answer to this threat of globalization is a strengthening or revival of local, national, ethnic or religious traditions.

Friedman's concept of 'localization', which is an equivalent of 'globalization', can be interpreted as a dialectical figure, despite his seeing it rather as an interplay (Friedman 1990, 1994).

I would also like to link Adam Smith's concept of an 'ethnic revival' to the strong dialectic in globalization, despite Smith not having done so himself (Smith 1981). The ethnic revival started in the 1950s according to Smith and it revealed itself as a political organization in Bretagne, Catalonia and Quebec and as black racial identity in the US and the UK. Smith regards ethnic revival as an extension of the concept of national identity from the 1800s; it is nationalism that is the driver in ethnic revival, and not globalization. If one understands globalization as a threat against both ethnic groups and nation states, one can just as well understand ethnic revival as an answer to globalization understood as homogenization. With or without Smith's blessing, I thus see ethnic revival as a strongly dialectical globalization figure. The revival concept covers the meaning of reliving and renewal in which reliving points back to tradition and origins while renewal points to the future.

Here we will understand the strong dialectic as such: globalization is the homogenizing motor in the development of societies, and localization and ethnic and religious revival are its counterforce. When I describe this as a strong dialect figure, this is because the counterforce is understood as explicit, desired and deliberate.

The weak dialectical figure has to do with those phenomena that experience a renewed and strengthened significance under global conditions. It is not a matter of active and expressed resistance against globalization, only an unexpressed and continued protection of existing traditions and place-specific characteristics. The weak dialectal figure relates to those phenomena that experience a strengthened significance under global conditions. It is an enhancement of the value of that which has always been there, an intensification of the significance of what is close and familiar because one suspects that it can disappear; that the most secure sense of belonging was nonetheless transitory.

The position has something in common with the phenomenological approach to the meaning of place in anthropology and cultural geography even if the approach in itself is not dialectical (Feld and Basso 1996; Gray 2000). The main point of this approach is that places are an elemental social experience and our perception of reality is necessarily tied into specific places. Virtual global and non place-dependent identities and relationships have no significance within such a phenomenological understanding of the importance of the place. Included in the weak dialect is the understanding that this experience and the significance of place become even more important under global conditions. The place provides an anchoring and solid ground for our existence, which the placeless, homogenizing globalization does not do. There is no direct protest in the weak dialectic, only a new appreciation for what existed before globalization changed the world.

The deconstructive figure emerges from French post-structuralism and the concomitant American postmodernism. Jacques Derrida's criticism of structuralism as a metaphysical philosophy, and his deconstructive device for revealing this metaphysics, has had enormous influence in many disciplines (Derrida 1967). In discourse on globalization, we find influence from post structuralism in the deconstruction of binary oppositions such as global–local and centre–periphery. One major thesis here is that such dichotomies have collapsed. In the continuation of the postmodern mentality that dominated a good deal of the 1980s and 1990s, such concepts as 'glocalization', hybrid and heterogenic identities and 'de-territorization' are introduced in the discourse of globalization (Robertson 1992; Bhabha 1983, 1994; Young 1995; Tomlinson 1999; Giddens 1999).

Individual or cultural identities are no longer identical in a global world, but hybrid. The development of identity is freed from tradition and origins, and specific places no longer have relevance for perceptions of reality: virtual reality rules. Especially suspicious was the tying together of identity and place, in this theory, and that identity seems to emerge from the place and its history. In the universe of deconstructive theory, the difference is always already shot into the identity, which means that a clean and unsullied identity based on origin and proximity is impossible. Looking back, one can see that the deconstructive figure more or less ran amok in all other theories than the strictly philosophical; Derrida, after all, criticized only metaphysical eminences in philosophic *texts*, and to transfer this criticism to ethnic and marginal identity projects based on origin and belonging to a place is a theoretical short circuit.

Here we can presume a more pragmatic position and regard the different theoretical positions in the globalization discourse as different perspectives through which one can perceive globalization. Rather than discuss which theoretical figures are closest to the truth about globalization – globalization is identical with homogenization, or identical with the dialect between the local and the global, or identical with the collapse of dichotomies – we will confine ourselves to looking into which of the theoretical positions are most relevant and useful for the task of understanding historical plays and their regional power. The choice of perspective has to do with both the object of research that is to be analysed and the researcher's theoretical anchoring and preferences. To what extent the chosen perspective is useful and relevant and whether it sheds new light on the analysed object of research is up to the reader and other researchers to decide. The perspective and its application can be seen as a theoretical proposition.

Historical plays and the theoretical figures

Among the three theoretical globalization figures, I find the dialectic to be the most relevant with regard to understanding historical plays' local and regional strength. This does not at all mean that the two other theoretical figures are completely unsuitable as perspectives with regard to historical plays. The colonialistic figure could, for example, be used to show how the dramaturgy itself in the plays is fundamentally Aristotelian; a classic power – belief – and love conflict is established and this is resolved in the final act. This is, after all, a dramaturgy that Hollywood has utilized very effectively in entertainment movies, and it can be argued that historical plays are also influenced by American popular culture. This originally Greek and significantly Western dramaturgy becomes, like American popular culture, a homogenizing power in the worlds of both film and theatre. The traditional, and almost cliché presentations of Vikings in the plays could very well be said to belong to a global interpretation of the Norwegian Viking as a place-specific version of this figure. In this perspective, one could say that the historical plays obtain a regional power from the effective use of the instruments of popular culture. The plays provide no aesthetic resistance – the form is already recognized because this dramaturgy has colonialized dramaturgy. When I do not choose this theoretic figure as my major perspective, it is because it is not suited to perceive historical plays as a genre that finds itself between theatre and ritual and the local culture sponsoring.

The deconstructive figure could have been used for the genre of historical plays itself. One could have argued that it is a hybrid that has arisen in the wake of the theatre-ritual, staging-authenticity dichotomy having broken down. One could further have used the perspective to argue that the younger generation's participants experience a heterogenic and hybrid development of their identity through a mix of a global internet virtual reality and a place-oriented history. It is perfectly possible, but I find this approach least relevant. The historical play genre came about with the Stiklestad Play in 1954; at that point in time the deconstructive thought process was not in play. With the growth of historical plays we observe in the 1990s, this can certainly fit in with globalization, but not with the deconstructive, de-territorialized version of it. Historical plays represent what in every way the Western, cosmopolitan, postmodern academics distance themselves from. When I, along with a philosopher colleague of mine, carried out a research project on historical plays in the 1990s, this was regarded as a completely anachronistic activity; what one should have been researching was urban postmodern theatre that undertook deconstruction of moribund Western dichotomies.

I find the dialectical globalization figure the most relevant for the task of explaining both the success of the historical play genre and the local private form of sponsoring. It is the dialectic between the global and the local that makes the historical play so powerful, and this applies to both the strong and the weak dialectic. Strong and weak are tied into the dialectic itself, much or little direct opposition, and little to the regional power the dialectic engenders.

The rise of historical plays like the Stiklestad Play can be understood as both a form of *geographical localization* and as *site-specific revival*; as a reliving and renewing of the place's importance.

The strong dialectic is tied into the threat of rural depopulation of the Norwegian districts. Globalization has resulted in a heavy tendency towards urbanization, which has made the districts extremely vulnerable to a rural drain of younger people. Young people in Norway want to study in the larger cities and will later also live and work in the largest cities (which strictly speaking are not big, but are nonetheless biggest in a Norwegian context). The process of homogenization is tied into the privileges made available by an urban, cosmopolitan culture with an expansive range of art and culture, restaurants, cafes and bars and a differentiated labour market. What the Norwegian country township has to offer of such attractions is very limited. Local and regional sponsorship activity can be interpreted as an answer to this threat of rural depopulation: strengthening cultural activities at the place also strengthens the local community where the company is located and can hopefully contribute to a reduction in the numbers leaving the districts. The threat of rural depopulation is used explicitly by the government to defend its funding of culture in the districts.

The strong dialectic that has to do with the threat of rural depopulation can also be used in the choice of the actual genre of the historical play; one chooses to promote a historical play at the place because it involves a number of amateurs and volunteers and because it activates the place's history itself. One hopes that a sense of community and care with regard to the place will hinder the flow of people away from the district. A number of festivals have been organized in Norway for the same reason; a large volunteer effort is necessary for this and a successful festival can create greater pride in the place.

Cultural arrangements, such as historical plays and festivals, are used to profile the place in the context of tourism, and this can create highly sought after jobs during the summer season. Belief in the so-called experience economy (Pine and Gilmore 1999) and the creative class (Florida 2002) has had a significant impact in the Norwegian districts, and this belief, or more precisely the *need* for this belief, can also be understood as a direct answer to the threat of rural depopulation.

The weak globalization dialect can be used to understand the appreciation itself of the historical play genre, the significance of *live* theatre and love for the place as a horizon of experience. The notable increase of the number of historical plays in the era of globalization can be seen as an expression of a revival of them and a new appreciation of both their ritual and theatrical sides. The ritual is tied into local volunteer engagement, participation of amateurs and the regular repetition of the plays, which create and intensify a sense of local identity that is shared across generations, something that fewer and fewer activities do. This has to do with a shared activity, practical cooperation, predictable repetition, cyclical experience of time and a kind of sanctification of the place. The plays can, in the weak globalization dialect, be seen as a ritual revival, a reliving and renewing of ritual qualities in life.

The theatrical aspect is tied into the plays' *live* presentation on a physical stage, and to the content in them, itself. The live performance, like the live concert, has enjoyed a significant revival in our digitalized era: the reception of live people, who present a message here and now on the same physical place as you, is experienced with new potency when consumption of culture is something that more and more takes place 'in your pocket' – from the cell phone or the net tablet. There is no active resistance in this globalization figure, only a strengthening of the worth of the aspect of *live*. Here one can talk about the performing art form's *live revival* in a globalized and digitalized era.

The dimension of content in the historical plays can be understood as a site-specific revival, which involves a reliving and renewing of the local place and its significance. The place and its history play a major role in these plays, and in this way the place provides a potential horizon of experience and platform for identification for people in an age of globalization.

Sortie: a site-specific-strength

After having shed light on and analysed the phenomenon of the historical play in the perspective of theatre anthropology, culture sponsorship and globalization, we can answer the question regarding what kind of local and regional power the plays have. This power is inscribed in a strong and a weak globalization dialectic as noted above. We can divide the power into three dimensions:

(1) A performative power that has to do with the historical play's theatrical and ritual genres, with *live revival* and with *ritual revival*.
(2) A power of place sponsoring that has to do with the sponsors' interest in strengthening the place as an attractive residence and to reduce the number of people leaving.
(3) The power of *site-specific revival*: the historical plays inscribe themselves in a battle to save the place as a residence, and they are the reliving and renewal of the place's significance as a horizon of experience. They represent a geographic *localization*.

Above all I would describe these power dimensions as *site-specific-strength* because they contain the core itself of the historical play phenomenon in a global age and because the expression has such a beautiful alliterative ring in English: site-specific-strength.

Note

1 Turid Hofstad, 'Stiklestadspelet – tradisjon og nyskaping'. Available at: www.spelhandboka.no/kalender.asp?s=hofstad (accessed 26 November 2012).

References

Aagedal, O., Egeland, H. and Villa, M. (2009) *Lokalt kulturliv i endring*, Oslo: Fagbokforlaget.
Appadurai, A. (1990) 'Disjuncture and Difference in the Global Cultural Economy', in M. Featherstone (ed.), *Global Culture: Nationalism, Globalization and Modernity*, London: Sage Publications.
Bhabha, H.K. (1983) 'The Other Question', *Screen*, 24.
——— (1994) *The Location of Culture*, London: Routledge.
Castells, M. (1997) *The Power of Identity*, Oxford: Blackwell Publishers Ltd.
Derrida, J. (1967) *L'écriture et la difference*, Paris: Seuil.
——— (1978) 'The Theatre of Cruelty and the Closure of Representation', in A. Bass (ed.), *Writing and Difference*, Chicago: University of Chicago Press.
Espelin, A. and Gran, A.-B. (2011) *Kulturnæringens betydning for norsk økonomi. Status og utvikling 2000–2009*, Oslo: MENON-report.
Featherstone, M. (ed.) (1990) *Global Culture: Nationalism, Globalization and Modernity*, London: Sage Publications.
Feld, S. and Basso, K.H. (1996) *Senses of Place*, Santa Fe: School of American Research Press.
Florida, R. (2002) *The Rise of the Creative Class – and How it's Transforming Work, Leisure, Community and Everyday Life*, New York: Basic Books.
Friedman, J. (1990) 'Being in the World: Globalization and Localization', in M. Featherstone (ed.), *Global Culture: Nationalisme, Globalisation and Modernity*, London: Sage Publications.
——— (1994) 'Modernitetens implosjon', in O. Hemer and R. Araeen (eds), *Kulturen i den globala byn*, Lund: Ægis.

Giddens, A. (1999) *Runaway World. How Globalisation is Reshaping our Lives*, London: Profile Books.

Gran, A.-B. (2000) *'Hvite løgner / sorte myter' – det etniske på modernitetens scene*, Oslo: Unipub forlag.

——— (2004) *Vår teatrale tid*, Oslo: Dinamo Forlag.

Gran, A.-B. and Hofplass, S. (2007) *Kultursponsing*, Oslo: Gyldendal Akademisk.

Gran, A.-B. and Ohrem, S. (1996) 'Spillet om spelet. Lokale spel, ny-ritualisme og nasjonal kannibalisme', in S. Bjørkås and P. Mangset (eds), *Kunnskap og kulturpolitikk: Utviklingstrekk i norsk kulturforskning*. KULTs skriftserie nr. 56, Oslo: Norges forskningsråd.

Gran, A.-B. and Vaagen, H. (2010) *'Kultur og næringslivsundersøkelsen 2010'*, Status 2010, Oslo: Report Arts & Business Norway.

Gray, J.N. (2000) *At Home in the Hills. Sense of Place in the Scottish Borders*, New York and Oxford: Berghan Books.

Gupta, A. and Ferguson, J. (eds) (1997) *Culture, Power, Place. Explorations in Critical Anthropology*, Durham: Duke University Press.

Head, V. (1998) *Successful Sponsorships*. London: Director Books.

Held, D. and McGrew, A. (eds) (2000) *The Global Transformations Reader: An Introduction to the Globalization Debate*, Cambridge: Polity Press.

Jiffer, M. and Roos, M. (1999) *Sponsorship – A Way of Communicating*, Stockholm: Ekerlids Forlag.

Lindeborg, L. and Lindkvist, L. (2010) *Kulturens kraft för regional utveckling*, Stockholm: SNS Förlag.

McNicholas, B. (2004) 'Arts, Culture and Business: A Relationship Transformation, a Nascent Field', *International Journal of Arts Management*, 7(1): 57–69.

Martorella, R. (ed.) (1996) *Art and Business. An International Perspective on Sponsorship*, London: Praeger.

Meenaghan, T. (1998) 'Current Developments and Future Directions in Commercial Sponsorship', *International Journal of Advertising*, 17(1): 3–28.

Mermiri, T. (2010) 'Arts Sponsorship: The Facts, Trends and Potential', *Journal of Sponsorship*, 3(4): 307–320.

Ohrem, S. (2005) *Spillet om stedet: historiske spel i Norge*, Sandefjord: Purgatorio Forlag.

Pfeffer, J. and Salancik, G.R. (1978) *The External Control of Organizations. A Resource Dependence Perspective*, New York: Harper & Row Publisher.

Pine, B.J. and Gilmore, J.H. (1999) *The Experience Economy – Work is Theatre & Every Business a Stage*, Boston, MA: Harvard Business School Press.

Prendergast, G.P., Poon, D. and West, D. (2010) 'Match Game: Linking Sponsorship Congruence with Communication Outcomes', *Journal of Advertising Research* (June 2010): 214–226.

Rectanus, M.W. (2002) *Culture Incorporated: Museums, Artists, and Corporate Sponsorships*, Minneapolis: University of Minnesota Press.

Robertson, R. (1992) *Globalization. Social Theory and Global Culture*, London: Sage Publications.

Sarstedt, M., Schwaiger, M. and Taylor, C.R. (2010) 'Art for the Sake of the Corporation: Audi, BMW Group, DaimlerChrystler, Montblanc, Siemens, and Volkswagen Help Explore the Effect of Sponsorship on Corporate Reputations', *Journal of Advertising Research* (March 2010): 77–90.

Schechner, R. (1985) *Between Theatre and Anthropology*, Philadelphia: University of Pennsylvania Press.

Schechner, R. (1988) *Performance Theory*, New York and London: Routledge.

Smith, A.D. (1981) *The Ethnic Revival in the Modern World*, Cambridge: Cambridge University Press.

Tomlinson, J. (1999) *Globalization and Culture*, Cambridge: Polity Press.

Tönnies, F. (2010) *Gemeinschaft und Gesellschaft*, Darmstadt: WBG.
Turner, V. (1991) *From Ritual to Theatre*, New York: Performing Arts Journal Publication.
Wallerstein, I. (1990) 'Culture as the Ideological Battleground of the Modern World-System', in A. Appadurai (ed.), *Global Culture. Nationalism, Globalization and Modernity*, London: Sage Publications.
Young, R. (1995) *Colonial Desire: Hybridity in Theory, Culture and Race*, New York and London: Routledge.

13 In culture we trust

Beliefs in culture as an instrument for development in the Stavanger region

Hilmar Rommetvedt

The Norwegian 'oil capital'

In 2008, the Stavanger region served as European Capital of Culture (ECOC) together with Liverpool. The European Capital of Culture event was an important part of the development strategy of the Stavanger region. As we shall see, the ECOC event reflected widespread beliefs in the importance of culture for regional development.[1]

Stavanger is the centre of Rogaland County in the south western part of Norway and is the fourth largest city in the country. The ECOC event was organized by *Stavanger2008*, an inter-municipal enterprise set up and owned by the two neighbouring cities of Stavanger and Sandnes together with Rogaland County. 128,000 of the 5 million Norwegians live in the city of Stavanger. If we include the neighbouring city Sandnes and two other municipalities bordering on Stavanger, we get a total of 229,000 people. The County of Rogaland has a total of 443,000 inhabitants (as of 1 January 2012).[2]

Oil exploration in the Norwegian part of the North Sea started in the middle of the 1960s, and since then Norway has become a major exporter of oil and natural gas. Stavanger is the centre of the Norwegian petroleum industry and the city is frequently referred to as the 'oil capital' of Norway. The two petroleum-related government agencies, the Petroleum Directorate and the Petroleum Safety Authority, are located in the city together with the headquarters of the national oil company Statoil and the manager of the direct financial interests of the Norwegian State, Petoro. Furthermore, the Norwegian and in some cases also the European headquarters of numerous international oil companies such as BP, ConocoPhillips, ExxonMobil, Shell and Total, and international oilfield services companies such as Baker Hughes, Halliburton, Schlumberger and others, are located in the region.

No doubt, the Stavanger region has prospered on the Norwegian petroleum industry. Oil was discovered at a point in time when the traditional shipping and canning industries in Stavanger faced severe problems. The region was in need of new industries and in the 1960s local politicians managed to convince international oil companies to settle down in the city (Egeland 1984). Since then, Stavanger has developed from one of the poorer cities in Norway into one of the richest (Rosenlund 2000).

The challenge ...

However, in the second half of the 1990s the Norwegian oil production levelled out and since the peak at the beginning of the millennium, the production has been reduced by more than 40 per cent, from 181 million Sm^3 in 2001 to 104 million Sm^3 in 2010. To some degree the decrease in oil production has been compensated by a substantial increase in the production of natural gas and condensate, but these resources are not as valuable as oil. The total production of petroleum peaked in 2004 and has been reduced by 13 per cent, from 263 million Sm^3 at the top to 230 million Sm^3 in 2010. The prognoses for the future show that the production in general, and of oil in particular, will decrease even though the recovery of discovered resources is expected to be improved and new resources have been discovered (NPD 2012: 23, 135).

Norway prospers on petroleum resources, but the industry and the government have to deal with huge fluctuations in the petroleum prices. As we can see from Figure 13.1, the petroleum sector's shares of GDP and state revenues vary substantially. The economic and political consequences were most dramatic in the 1980s when the petroleum sector's share of state revenues dropped from 21 per cent in 1984 to 1 per cent in 1988. In 1986 the Norwegian government resigned after losing a vote in Parliament on proposed retrenchment measures (Rommetvedt 2003).

... and the response

By the end of the millennium Norway was facing new challenges. The decreasing oil production and the experiences with dramatic fluctuations in oil prices demonstrated that the centre of the petroleum industry, Stavanger, was vulnerable and that it would be wise to make the region less dependent on the petroleum

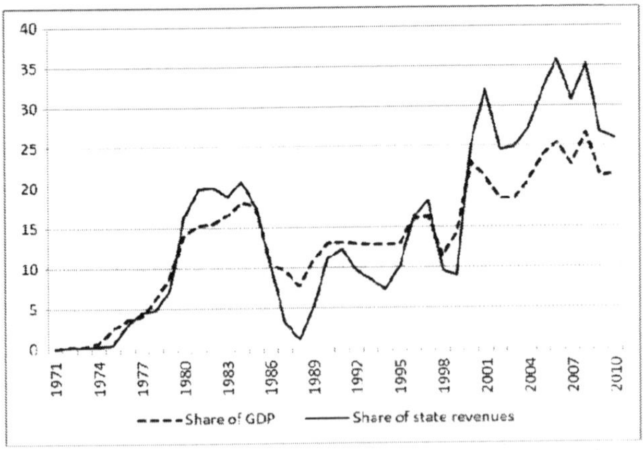

Figure 13.1 The Norwegian petroleum sector's shares of Gross Domestic Product and state revenues (%) (NPD 2012).

industry and more attractive to new businesses and highly skilled professionals and workers. (Later, it turned out that the immediate threat was superseded by new increases in oil prices and large investments in the petroleum industry, but that was not how the situation was perceived by the end of the twentieth century.)

Local and regional politicians took the long-term challenge seriously, and the response to the challenge, or at least an important element in the response, was *culture*. In 2001 the local council of Stavanger decided to bid for the status of European Capital of Culture in 2008. The final application from the Stavanger region to the European Union describes the challenge and the answer with these words:

> Since the end of the 1960s, the region has experienced rapid growth closely linked to the North Sea oil and gas industry. However, our dependence on oil and gas resources also makes us vulnerable to market fluctuations and declining oil and gas reserves.
>
> Culture has its own intrinsic value, but it can also be an instrument in promoting new business opportunities, education and health. Most people, including politicians and business leaders agree that culture is an important part of the new diversification that must be developed in response to the challenges that our vulnerable region is facing.
>
> [...]
>
> We will use Stavanger2008 to fulfill a wish to contribute towards promoting the region as a location for new businesses and progressive solutions, determined to meet any of the challenges that the future may hold. We wish to create an environment that values and attracts talent and initiative.
>
> (Stavanger2008: Part 2, 6–8)

These views were shared by the man in charge of sponsoring from Sparebank 1 SR-bank, one of the four main sponsors of Stavanger2008. He gave the following motivation for the sponsorship of the bank:

> This is an investment for us. Culture creates growth. ... This is a great opportunity for the region, and we, as the region's bank, see it as natural to participate as an important contributor. ... We believe that Stavanger2008 will motivate the existing cultural life of the region. This will have a long-term impact ... on both culture and industry ... Cultural life creates business growth. The more and the better cultural experiences a region can offer, the more attractive the region is for new establishments. ... Cultural life has to flourish if the region is going to succeed as a business magnet.
>
> (Pahr-Iversen 2007: 46, my translation)

The statement was given in an interview with the monthly magazine *Rosenkilden*. The magazine is published by the Stavanger Chamber of Commerce and Industry. The Chamber established its own 'Resource group for culture and industry' in 2002, and it was an eager advocate for the Stavanger region as ECOC in 2008.

Stavanger as ECOC was not the only element in the regional strategy for diversification and increased attraction. Other elements include the construction of a new Viking football stadium which was opened in 2004, the establishment of the fifth Norwegian university in 2005, and the municipal take-over and new plans for cultural activities in the former Tou brewery buildings. And not least, 1225 million NOK have been invested in a new concert building which opened in September 2012. The landmark building with red concrete and glass facades includes a concert hall for Stavanger Symphony Orchestra and acoustic music with 1,500 seats, a hall for multiple uses with seats for 850 people or standing places for 1,900 people, and an outdoor amphitheatre for 10,000 people.[3] Continued support for the regional theatre and arts museum, and for cultural events such as international jazz and chamber music festivals, yearly weeks of literature, an enormously popular '*Gladmat*' or 'happy food' festival, and many more, could be mentioned in this context.

The importance of culture in the strategy for regional development is clearly reflected in local government allowances to culture. Figure 13.2 shows the net running expenses per inhabitant of the largest Norwegian cities together with the twin cities of Stavanger and Sandnes.[4] As we can see, Stavanger is on top of the list, well above the other major cities and the national average.

The belief in culture as an instrument for economic development is also expressed by central government. In 2005, the Norwegian government presented

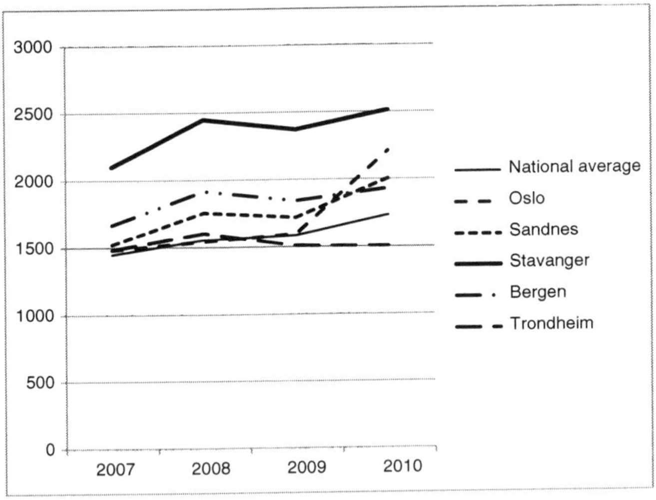

Figure 13.2 Local government allowances to culture in the largest Norwegian cities. Net running expenses in NOK per inhabitant.

a Report to the Parliament on 'Culture and Industry'. The Report, which refers explicitly to Richard Florida's book *The Rise of The Creative Class*, argued that 'culture and cultural industries can play an important role in regional development' and that 'cultural initiatives may bring in creativity and dynamics, which can lead to the establishment of different culture based industries as well as other enterprises in the region'. In other words, 'Culture can contribute to the creation of new work places' (St meld. nr. 22, 2004–2005: 18, my translation).

As a follow-up to the Report to the Parliament, a *handlingsplan* or 'action plan for culture and industry' was published in 2007 by the ministries of trade and industry, local government and regional development, and cultural affairs. The plan states that: 'Design, art and culture, entertainment and experience industry have become more important parts of the economy, both in Norway and internationally' (Handlingsplan 2007: 5, my translation). Furthermore:

> There are many good examples from all over the country of how culture and experiences are used actively in order to develop exciting and attractive places. ... Pursuing business development also based on culture, experience and leisure time will contribute to the identity and attractiveness of the place. Culture based industries make the locality an interesting place of residence and they may create a place where people want to live, work or visit. And when the circle is closed, this may lead to a wish for establishment among other industries as well.
>
> (Handlingsplan 2007: 7, my translation)

An updated action plan for culture and industry is supposed to be completed in 2012.

From Norwegian 'oil capital' to European Capital of Culture

The economic arguments above fit well with the claim of Beatriz Garcia that 'by the mid 1980s, the emphasis of cultural policy as a mechanism to enhance community development and encourage social participation was progressively substituted by an emphasis on the potential of cultural policy as a tool for urban economic and physical regeneration' in the age of city marketing and city branding (Garcia 2004: 315). Palmer *et al.* point out that '[t]he vast majority [of European Capitals of Culture] have been very heavily geared towards increasing tourism'. However, the wealthy Stavanger region 'had the luxury of being able to focus almost entirely on culture, which was arguably the original intention of the ECOC'. The mission of Stavanger was 'to focus firmly on culture which is in complete juxtaposition with its partner ECOC city, Liverpool, whose bid was based on economic regeneration'. Stavanger 'had a different aim, that of opening up minds and imaginations' (Palmer *et al.* 2011: 48–56).

The Stavanger region's first ECOC application shows, nevertheless, that the cultural goals were accompanied by economic goals:

> Stavanger2008 will challenge the traditional divisions between economy and culture; the material and the immaterial; between publicly funded and commercial, profit-making activities. This interplay between different types of cultural activities is decisive in retaining professionals and for attracting new talent to fields such as technology, communication, art and science.
>
> (Stavanger2008: Part 1, 15)

On the web page of Stavanger2008,[5] the vision for the region as European Capital of Culture was 'expressed through the concept "Open Port"':

> This can be understood both in the English sense – 'an open harbour', – and in its Norwegian meaning of 'an open gate'.
>
> The OPEN PORT vision for the programme offers opportunities to join in for everyone – to those who have never thought of themselves as 'creative' right through to those for whom the highest forms of art are daily bread.
>
> Open Port – openness towards the world – is about challenging the region and its people to be even more open and inclusive towards each other, art, ideas and opportunities.

The following objectives were listed:

- Ensure a broad and enduring cultural lift, especially for children and the young.
- Promote quality, innovation and diversity in the arts.
- Contribute to the establishment of enduring networks in the fields of arts and culture.
- Contribute to cultural curiosity and tolerance.
- Enhance regional identity and pride.
- Contribute to further development of industry and commerce.
- Contribute to the construction of cultural and physical infrastructure.

And finally, the following values were set for 'how the cultural capital will be developed and executed':

- Tolerance and freedom of speech
- Hospitality and accessibility
- Cultural heritage and development
- Innovation and quality
- Environment and aesthetics.

(Stavanger2008)

The intrinsic value of culture, cultural objectives and values such as openness and tolerance may seem more articulate in Stavanger than in other capitals of culture.

The Selection Panel (2004: 7) which evaluated the nominees for European Capitals of Culture in 2008 was 'impressed with the daring Programme that Stavanger was proposing, commenting that the artistic quality was excellent, including a remarkable contemporary programme of challenging nature'.[6]

A number of 'warm-up' events were organized in 2006 and 2007, and by the end of 2008 a total of 160 projects comprising 1,100 + events had been carried through (Miller *et al.* 2009: 36). Palmer *et al.* (2011: 56, 59) concluded that 'Stavanger delivered a high quality, innovative cultural programme' and that the programming was 'excellent' compared to other European Capitals of Culture.

In other words, it may seem as if the contribution of Stavanger2008 to the 'further development of industry and commerce' fused into a 'higher unity' with the 'intrinsic value of culture' and the 'high quality, innovative cultural programme'. High quality culture should make Stavanger more attractive to the 'creative class' and thus smooth the region's transition to the post-oil era.

The data: surveys among citizens and leaders

As we have seen, the belief in culture as an instrument for regional development was clearly expressed in the Stavanger region's bid for the status of ECOC in 2008. But how widespread is the belief in culture?

Data from four large scale surveys carried out in the Stavanger region before and after the year as ECOC in 2008 may give at least part of the answer to this question. The surveys include two that were carried out among the *citizens* of the region: one that was completed before the launch of the Stavanger2008 programme in October 2007, and one after the event in the winter 2009; and two that were carried out among regional *leaders*: one in 2007 among local politicians, leading civil servants and business managers, and one in 2010 among business managers only. The surveys among the citizens combined telephone interviews with a postal follow-up questionnaire, while the surveys among the leaders combined telephone interviews with electronic follow-up questionnaires.

It should be noted that the definitions of the 'Stavanger region' in the surveys are somewhat different. The citizen surveys included respondents from the whole county of Rogaland, but here we focus on respondents from a smaller region comprising the municipalities of Stavanger, Sandnes, Sola and Randaberg. One may say that this was the core area of the European Capital of Culture in 2008, even though quite a few of the Capital of Culture events took place in other municipalities in Rogaland. The leader surveys were carried out in two larger regions including Stavanger and thirteen other municipalities in Rogaland. The larger regions were quite similar, but two of the municipalities in the first leader survey were substituted by two other municipalities in the second survey. Furthermore, it should be noted that the first survey included business leaders in firms with five or more employees while in the last leader survey the limit was set at ten employees. (One should bear in mind that most Norwegian enterprises are small or medium sized.) In spite of these differences, the major trends to be shown in this chapter should not be affected.[7]

The importance of culture in general

The respondents in both the leader surveys and the citizen surveys were asked: 'How important would you say that increased support for cultural life is for' a variety of reasons (listed in Figures 13.3 and 13.4). The question was asked in general, without reference to Stavanger as ECOC in 2008.

Figure 13.3 clearly demonstrates a strong belief in culture as an instrument for regional development among local politicians, civil servants and business leaders in the Stavanger region in 2007. Overwhelming majorities of the three groups of leaders agreed that increased support for cultural life is 'very' or 'fairly important' for the development of creativity and innovation in professional life (64–83 per cent), for the region's attractiveness vis-à-vis new workers and students (82–91 per cent), for the region's ability to attract new businesses (70–90 per cent), for the quality of life among the inhabitants of

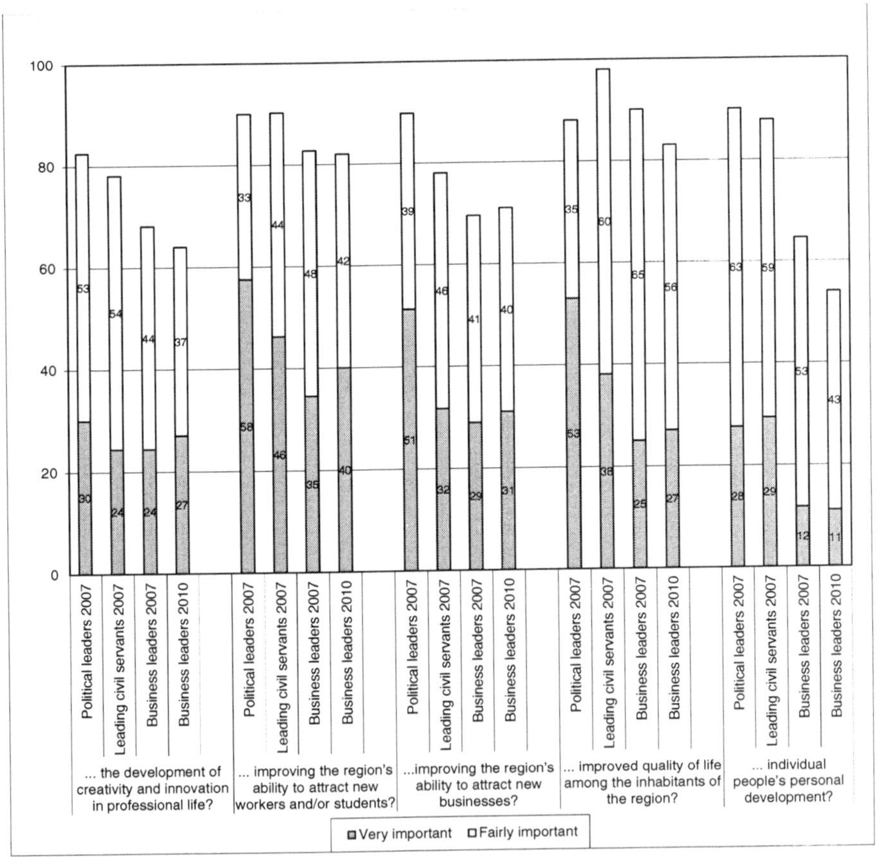

Figure 13.3 How important would you say that increased support for cultural life is for . . . ? Per cent of leaders in the larger Stavanger region (N 2007 = 276–278, N 2010 = 133–134).

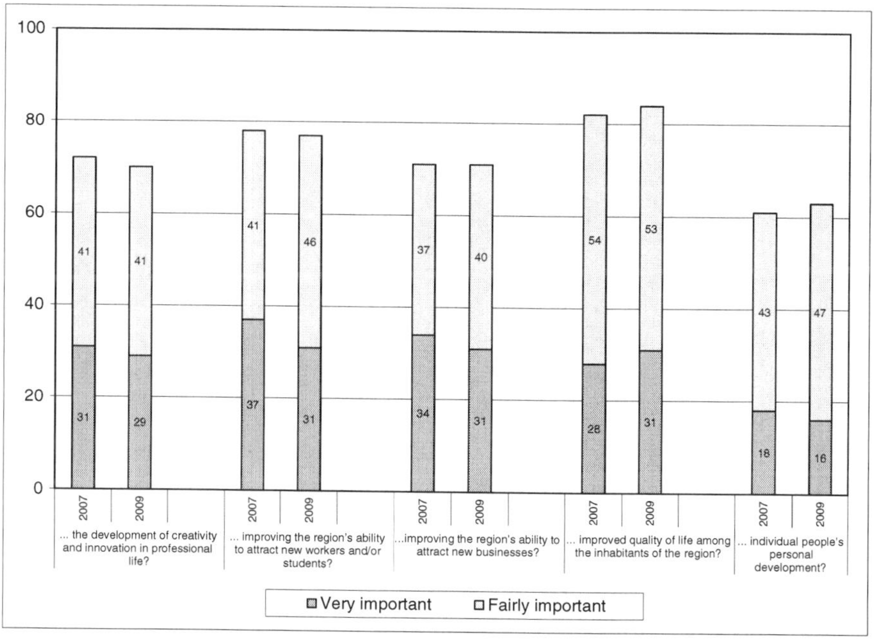

Figure 13.4 How important would you say that increased support for cultural life is for ...? Per cent of citizens in the smaller Stavanger region (N 2007 = 633–641, N 2009 = 612–617).

the region (83–98 per cent), and for the personal development of individuals (54–91 per cent).

The politicians and civil servants were generally more supportive of culture than the business leaders. This trend is most pronounced with regard to how important increased support for cultural life is for individual people's personal development. Political leaders and civil servants agree significantly more than business managers that support for culture is very or fairly important for the personal development of individuals. Business leaders seem to be more engaged in regional than personal development.

Unfortunately, we do not have data on the assessments of the political leaders and civil servants after Stavanger's year as ECOC. However, in the case of business leaders, we do have data on their assessment of the importance of culture in 2010. Figure 13.3 shows a certain decline in the business leaders' assessments of the importance of culture for the quality of life and personal development, but the assessments of culture in relation to creativity and innovation, and attractiveness vis-à-vis workers, students and new businesses were very stable compared to 2007.

The questions about the importance of increased support for cultural life in general were also asked in the citizen surveys in 2007 and 2009. The results are shown in Figure 13.4.

Again we see that clear majorities of the citizens agreed that increased support for cultural life is important for the various reasons listed in the figure. Culture was perceived to be most important for the quality of life among the inhabitants of the region (82–84 per cent), followed by the ability of the region to attract workers and students (77–78 per cent), creativity and innovation (70–72 per cent), ability to attract new businesses (71 per cent), and finally personal development (61–63 per cent).

If we compare Figures 13.3 and 13.4, we see that the assessments of the citizens are most similar to those of the business leaders. However, we find practically no change in the citizens' assessments of culture in general after the accomplishment of the ECOC events in 2008.

The impact of Stavanger2008: expectations and experiences

The questions above were related to support for cultural life in general. However, the surveys among the citizen in 2007 and 2009 raised a number of questions related to the ECOC events in particular. In 2009, 75 per cent of the respondents living in the 'core area', Stavanger, Sandnes, Sola and Randaberg, stated that they had participated in at least one of the Stavanger2008 events; 42 per cent of the citizens had been members of the audience at three or more events, and 9 per cent said that they had participated both as performers, organizers or volunteers, and as members of the audience. Only 25 per cent said that they had not participated in any of the ECOC events (Berg and Rommetvedt 2009: 19). The level of participation clearly indicates that Stavanger2008 succeeded in attracting broad strata of the population. A closer analysis shows that background variables such as sex, age, education and income had limited impact on participation (Fitjar *et al.* 2011).

The support for the event was massive among the citizens both before and after 2008. 73 per cent of the respondents in 2007 and 74 per cent in 2009 agreed that it was the right thing to do for the Stavanger region to bid for the status as ECOC. 64 per cent of the respondents in the 'core area' agreed that the region's year as Capital of Culture had given them experiences they would otherwise not have had (Berg and Rommetvedt 2009: 33, 43).

The respondents were also asked if they agreed or disagreed with a number of propositions regarding possible effects of the Stavanger region as ECOC. The responses to the propositions of interest are shown here in Figure 13.5[8]

Here we see that at least before the event, vast majorities of the citizens agreed completely or partly that the Stavanger region's year as ECOC would have a variety of positive effects. In 2007, 88 per cent of the respondents agreed that the European Capital of Culture event would give the region important new impulses and strengthen the cultural life of the region. Furthermore, large majorities of the citizens agreed that Stavanger2008 would make the region better known in Norway and in Europe (85 and 75 per cent respectively), and that it would attract tourists to the region (77 per cent). A smaller majority, 52 per cent, believed that the year as Capital of Culture would 'contribute to attracting people from other parts of the country to come and look for employment in the region'.

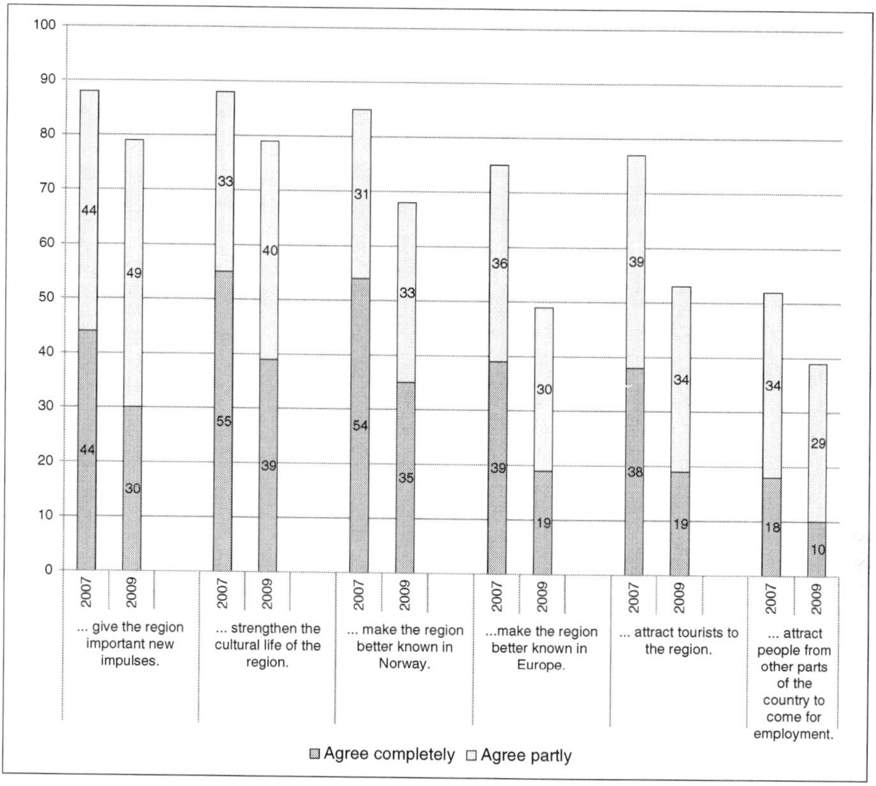

Figure 13.5 Expected effects of the Stavanger region as European Capital of Culture 2008. Per cent of the citizens in the smaller Stavanger region (N 2007 = 1193, N 2009 = 1254–1256).

No doubt, the expectations beforehand were enormous and the results in Figure 13.5 indicate that according to the assessments of several of the citizens, the event did not live up to the expectations. We see that in 2009 there was a decline in all the percentages of the respondents who agreed that Stavanger2008 would have the expected effects: make the region better known in Europe, −26 percentage points; attract tourists, −24 percentage points; make the region better known in Norway, −17 percentage points; attract people from other parts of Norway, −13 percentage points; and give new impulses and strengthen cultural life, −9 percentage points each. However, we also see that even after the event there was a majority of the respondents who agreed that Stavanger2008 would lead to four of the six proposed effects.

Concluding remarks: Stavanger2008 and beyond

As we have seen, the belief in culture as an instrument to promote regional development is a widespread phenomenon in the Stavanger region. Vast majorities of the citizens, leading politicians, civil servants and business managers in the region believe that increased support for culture in general and the event as ECOC in 2008 were important for the attractiveness of the region. The strongest beliefs in culture are found among local politicians and leading civil servants.

It seems appropriate to argue that the high expectations we found before the ECOC event in 2008 were unrealistic. The assessments made by the citizens after the event seem to be somewhat more realistic. Some of the citizens have realized that a single year of culture, and even a year as ECOC, is not enough to change the attractiveness of the region. However, we have also seen that in the aftermath of the ECOC event, most of the regions' citizens and political leaders, civil servants and business managers still believed that increased support for cultural life in general is important for the development of the region.

The belief in culture is reflected in the willingness of the local authorities to allocate money to cultural infrastructure and activities. Large investments have been made in culture, not only the year as ECOC, but also in, among other things, the new concert hall. The yearly net allowances from the local council of Stavanger are considerably higher per capita than the national average and that of other larger cities in Norway.

At the time of the application for the status of ECOC and when increased investments in and allowances to culture were made, the Stavanger region seemed to face the challenges of a not too distant transition to a post-oil era. The challenge was acknowledged by the leading decision-maker of the region. However, after the 2008 event a number of new major oil and gas fields have been discovered in the North Sea. The oil capital's need for diversification seems at least to have been postponed by increasing (but still fluctuating) oil prices and new large investments in the petroleum industry. On the other hand, attention is drawn towards a new problem with regard to the attractiveness of the Stavanger region, the costs of housing.

In Norway in general and Stavanger in particular, there is a strong tradition of owning one's own house or flat. Housing prices and rent expenditures in Stavanger have reached almost the same level as in Oslo, one of the most expensive cities in the world. Consequently, political attention may be drawn from culture towards more acute problems such as booming housing costs. However, the long-term impact on the beliefs in culture as an instrument for regional development remains to be seen.

Notes

1 This chapter draws upon material from within Rommetvedt (2008) together with data from surveys in the Stavanger region in 2009 and 2010. I would like to thank my colleagues Christin Berg, Rune Dahl Fitjar and Gunnar Thesen for excellent assistance and advice. For further information on the scientific research on Stavanger as European Capital of Culture in 2008, see www.iris.no/S2008.

2 Source: Statistics Norway, www.ssb.no/befolkning.

3 See www.stavanger-konserthus.no/1217842.

4 Source: Statistics Norway, http://statbank.ssb.no/statistikkbanken/selectvarval/Define.asp?MainTable=Kostra2K5099K1Ko&SubjectCode=17&planguage=0&nvl=True&mt=1&nyTmpVar=true.
5 See www.stavanger.kommune.no/SVG2008ENG/index.html.
6 See www.ec.europa.eu/culture/pdf/doc1155_en.pdf.
7 For details on the design of the citizen surveys, see Berg and Rommetvedt (2009) and Fitjar, Rommetvedt and Berg (2011). Data from the leader surveys have been provided by Rune Dahl Fitjar. For further information on the design of the leader surveys, see Fitjar and Rodríguez-Pose (2011a, 2011b).
8 For assessments of the impacts on cultural organizations and cultural production, see Bergsgard and Vassenden (2011) and Bergsgard *et al.* (2010).

References

Berg, C. and Rommetvedt, H. (2009) *Stavanger-regionen som europeisk kulturhovedstad – slik innbyggerne ser det* (The Stavanger region as European Capital of Culture – the citizens' views), Stavanger: International Research Institute of Stavanger.

Bergsgard, N.A. and Vassenden, A. (2011) 'The Legacy of Stavanger as Capital of Culture in Europe 2008: Watershed or Puff of Wind?', *International Journal of Cultural Policy*, 17(3): 301–320.

Bergsgard, N.A., Jøsendal, K. and Garcia, B. (2010) 'A Cultural Mega Event's Impact on Innovative Capabilities in Art Production: The Results of Stavanger Being the European Capital of Culture in 2008', *International Journal of Innovation and Regional Development*, 2(4): 353–371.

Egeland, K. (1984) *Myndighetenes møte med oljevirksomheten. Lokalpolitikk og oljeetablering i Stavanger-området* (Authorities facing the petroleum industry. Local politics and the establishment of petroleum activities in the Stavanger area), Oslo: Universitetsforlaget.

Fitjar, R.D. and Rodríguez-Pose, A. (2011a) 'Innovating in the Periphery: Firms, Values and Innovation in Southwest Norway', *European Planning Studies*, 19(4): 555–574.

——— (2011b) 'When Local Interaction does not Suffice: Sources of Firm Innovation in Urban Norway', *Environment and Planning*, 43(6): 1248–1267.

Fitjar, R., Rommetvedt, H. and Berg, C. (2011) 'European Capitals of Culture: Elitism or Inclusion? The Case of Stavanger2008', *International Journal of Cultural Policy*, forthcoming, published online 23 August 2011.

Florida, R. (2002) *The Rise of the Creative Class – and How it's Transforming Work, Leisure, Community and Everyday Life*, New York: Basic Books.

Garcia, B. (2004) 'Cultural Policy and Urban Regeneration in Western European Cities: Lessons From Experience, *Prospects for the Future, Local Economy*', 19(4): 312–326.

Handlingsplan. Kultur og næring (Action plan, culture and industry, 2007) Oslo: Nærings- og handelsdepartementet, Kommunal- og regionaldepartementet og Kultur- og kirkedepartementet.

Miller, M., Tjomsland, N., Hansen, M.E., Robberstad, K.H., Aae, B. and Wrapson, A. (eds) (2009) *Our Story*, Stavanger: Stavanger2008.

NPD (2012). *Facts 2012. The Norwegian Petroleum Sector*, Stavanger: The Norwegian Petroleum Directorate.

Pahr-Iversen, H. (2007) 'Kultur og næring – hånd i hånd' (Culture and business – hand in hand), *Rosenkilden*, 11.

Palmer, R., Richards, G. and Dodd, D. (2011) *European Cultural Capital report 3*, Arnhem: Association of Tourism and Leisure Education (ATLAS).

Rommetvedt, H. (2003) *The Rise of the Norwegian Parliament*, London: Frank Cass.

——— (2008) 'Beliefs in Culture as an Instrument for Regional Development: The Case of Stavanger, European Capital of Culture 2008', in L. Malíková and M. Sirák (eds),

Regional and Urban Regeneration in European Peripheries: What Role for Culture? Bratislava: Institute of Public Policy.
Rosenlund, L. (2000) *Social Structures and Change: Applying Pierre Bourdieu's Approach and Analytic Framework*, Working Papers 85/2000, Stavanger: Stavanger University College.
St.meld. nr. 22 (2004–2005) *Kultur og næring* (Report to the Parliament on Culture and Industry), Oslo: Kulturdepartementet.
Stavanger2008 (not dated) *European Capital of Culture. The Application*. Stavanger: Stavanger2008. Available at: www.stavanger.kommune.no/SVG2008ENG/indexde08.html?event=about.showElement&id=541&catId=12 (accessed 1 August 2012).

14 Culture and value creation

An economic analysis of Vara Concert Hall and the Nordic Watercolour Museum

John Armbrecht and Tommy D. Andersson

Introduction

To value and evaluate is deeply rooted in our society. This may relate to whether we think it is worth travelling into town to go to an art gallery or whether we decide to purchase an annual subscription to a concert hall. This fundamentally economic approach permeates politicians' thinking, as well as decisions on community initiatives that are often made after considering what value will be obtained from the investments made by society.

With regard to cultural policy initiatives, these are often taken after careful assessments of what investments are required in the form of financial support. But the natural follow-up question of what value is created by these financial investments is rarely answered satisfactorily. Although the value may be discussed in terms of the number of visitors, the number of performances or total ticket revenue, such indicators do not provide a satisfactory estimate of the cultural value created.

International economic research has made substantially more ambitious attempts to estimate the value created by cultural activities. These methods, which have not previously been tested in Sweden, are worth applying as a way of making a more accurate and nuanced assessment of the cultural yield created through cultural policy.

In this chapter it is the intention to estimate the economic value of two cultural institutions. Vara Concert Hall and the Nordic Watercolour Museum on the island of Tjörn have been chosen as objects of study and will first be presented. The chapter presents a more general discussion of the effects of culture and then formulates this in an economic model. The study and the results for the two cultural institutions are then presented. Finally the results are discussed in relation to similar studies and to the need to value culture.[1]

Vara Concert Hall and the Nordic Watercolour Museum

There are several reasons why Vara Concert Hall and the Nordic Watercolour Museum were chosen as study objects. The primary reason is that both cultural institutions are physically well defined. Most of the population of Västra Götaland are familiar with the concert hall and the museum through the media, word of mouth or visits, which makes it easier for the respondents to have their own views on the cultural institutions. Vara Concert Hall and the Nordic Watercolour Museum are also both located a relatively long distance from the major towns and cities in the region, which makes it easier to draw conclusions on their attractiveness to visitors.

There is a difference between the cultural institutions in the motives behind, and initiatives for, their establishment. In Vara it was the municipal executive board that decided to invest in culture as a strategy for improving the quality of life in the municipality. On Tjörn, the initiative was the dream of the Nordic Watercolour Society to create a centre for Nordic watercolour art, work, research and teaching on watercolour techniques, papers and paints. Another difference is that the Watercolour Museum is relatively specialised in what it offers, which results in less breadth but greater depth, while Vara Concert Hall attempts to offer a broad range of performances.

Vara Concert Hall

The first plans were submitted in Vara in 1996. Few people thought that anything would come of them, but on 1 January 1998 Västra Götaland Region was born, and the Municipality of Vara gained a new position at the centre of the region. Construction of what was then still known as the 'Future House', estimated to cost around SEK 80 million, started in 2002. The new centre for culture, schools and conferences was officially opened on 5 September 2003, under the name Vara Concert Hall (Vara Konserthus).

> Vara Concert Hall brings together Friday clubs and Saturday chats over coffee with performances for families and for schools. Classical music meets jazz, country, pop and rock. Dance, theatre, musicals and stand-up comedy are all on offer. There is no need for everyone to go to everything, but there's guaranteed to be something for everyone!
>
> (Vara Concert Hall 2012, our translation)

The Bohuslän Big Band and the VOX vocal quartet, who perform at the concert hall as well as in other parts of Västra Götaland Region, are part of the Vara Concert Hall organisation and also act as its ambassadors. The concert hall is the second home of the Gothenburg Symphony Orchestra. The concert hall in Vara is a venture managed mainly by the municipality, but has also been supported by Västra Götaland Region. Every year around 50,000 people visit the Concert Hall to enjoy one of the 100–150 annual performances.

Nordic Watercolour Museum

The Nordic Watercolour Museum opened in 2000, and the museum's website reads as follows:

> The Nordic Watercolour Museum is a unique meeting place for art, set in a barren yet beautiful landscape. It is a centre for art based on water, pigments and light. Exhibitions by Nordic and international artists and courses and paint experiments for children and adults in the children's studio and experimental workshop provide many rich opportunities for anyone to actively engage with art.
>
> (Nordic Watercolour Museum 2012, our translation)

The museum has an exhibition room for permanent and temporary exhibitions, but also guest studios, children's studios, an experimental workshop with technical equipment for artistic work, teaching and research, an assembly room for dance, theatre and conferences, a restaurant ('Vatten') and a museum shop, all located in the same main building.

The exhibition rooms mostly house temporary Nordic and international exhibitions, but the Nordic Watercolour Museum also has its own permanent collection of Nordic contemporary watercolour art. The collection consists of more than 700 works, and the museum regularly acquires new pieces. The aim is to provide a broad range, to be an exciting Nordic cultural project and to be a Nordic centre for contemporary art, research and education focused on watercolour techniques. Between 150,000 and 230,000 people visit the Watercolour Museum annually.

The operational activity of the Nordic Watercolour Museum is funded by the Swedish Government, the Cultural Committee of Västra Götaland Region, the Development Committee of Västra Götaland Region and the Municipality of Tjörn, but also through the museum's ticket sales and sponsorship.

Effects of culture on individuals and society

Social science research has devoted great interest to studying the significance of culture. Areas that have been the object of research include the impact of culture on education and knowledge, mental and physical health, attitudes and behaviour and social relationships and networks.

Art and cultural experiences can be regarded as a form of communication between the artist and audience intended to appeal to the *individual's* emotional, intellectual and aesthetic senses. Cultural institutions offer quality experiences rather than an ordinary experience. Cultural experiences capture our thoughts and contribute to shifting the focus away from the present to other places and times. We interpret art with existing knowledge and consequently develop new knowledge. Art challenges and develops our thinking, which contributes to *learning and cognitive development.* By being forced to relate the expressions and images of art to our own lives, we are constantly challenged to face new experiences.

Art can also help people to communicate with others by offering a different language that enables them to understand one another better. We can think ourselves into new, unfamiliar situations. Eisner (2002) studied children and students and found that positive effects occur after repeated occasions of consumption. Some of the most important lessons that art can convey, according to Eisner (2002), are that:

- Art teaches individuals that problems can have more than one solution.
- Art promotes individuals having more and greater perspectives.
- Art clarifies that not everything can be expressed through words and language.
- Art teaches individuals to think in and through different materials.
- Art gives us experiences that we cannot gain from other sources.

According to Cortines (1999), art instruction combined with traditional school teaching leads to pupils achieving a higher level of academic education than pupils who do not receive art instruction.

Culture is also considered to have effects on *attitudes and behaviour.* Research in this area shows that a change in behaviour is a process that begins with individuals gaining belief in something. These beliefs turn into attitudes, intentions and finally actual behaviour. A change in attitudes affects individuals' ways of thinking, which then has an impact on behaviour. Art that communicates and convinces individuals about the benefits of a multicultural society can, for example, influence their behaviour (Deasy 2002; Fiske 1999; Wright *et al.* 2006).

Health-related effects of art are an area of research that has attracted attention, particularly in the past decade. The approach to analysing the impact of culture on health is interdisciplinary, and research is undertaken in various areas such as neurobiology, psychology, medicine, public health, humanities and artistic research. Both general well-being and mental, physical, intellectual, emotional, social and spiritual health has been the object of scientific analysis in this area of research (Fiske 1999; Folkhälsoinstitutet 2005).

The social effects *for society* created by culture are explained by theories on *social capital.* According to Bourdieu, social capital is the sum of the resources, actual or virtual, that accrue to an individual or a group through social networks (Bourdieu and Wacquant 1992: 119). Social capital can thus generally be said to mean that effects such as networks and social contacts arise, but it can also lead to effects such as improved municipal infrastructure, employment and increased range of services (Cavaye 2004). An improvement to the infrastructure and other functions of society can, in turn, lead to improved social interaction, municipal organisation and increased trust. Studies conducted by the Australian Expert Group on Industry Studies (AEGIS) show that cultural institutions reduce social exclusion, improve self-esteem and self-confidence and contribute to community health (AEGIS 2004).

The term *cultural capital* has been used in several areas of research. The term has probably been most widely used in sociology, where Bourdieu (1973) considers cultural capital to be a personal asset that is inherited, is acquired and is present among individuals in different groups (networks). Bourdieu's definition of cultural capital means that groups (often with a specific socio-economic background) differ from other groups in their aesthetics and knowledge of art and culture. Studies of cultural capital and the education of individuals strengthen the hypothesis that high cultural capital and socio-economic status are positively correlated to study results (Dumais 2002).

In contrast to Bourdieu, Throsby (1999) considers cultural capital also to exist in a physical form. A cultural heritage building has particularly great value. The cultural value supplements the physical value. Certain objects like paintings are predominantly of cultural value, while their physical value is negligible. Their cultural value accounts for virtually the whole of their economic value.

A number of researchers consider cultural capital to be of significance to the economic performance of municipalities and regions (Barro 1999; Barro and Sala-i-Martin 2004; Becker 1974; Lucas 1988; Sala-I-Martin 1997). Hayami and Ruttan (1985) studied the correlations between existing resources, cultural capital, technology and institutions. They found in their study that the correlation between resources and technology and between cultural capital and technology/institutions is relatively strong. The creative industry has become something of a buzzword, and Ache (2000) believes that cultural institutions contribute to developing *creativity* and a *creative environment.*

Two dimensions will be used to summarise the discussion above on the effects of cultural institutions on *individual* and *society*. Culture has *instrumental* effects (i.e. relatively concrete and often measurable effects) both on the individual and on society. Culture has effects, for example, on health and behaviour. Culture also enriches the individual and society through *intrinsic* values that are more introspective and difficult to measure. The pleasure and happiness an individual can gain from cultural experiences are intrinsic, like the cultural capital of society.

The effects of cultural institutions can therefore be classified according to whether they principally affect either the *individual* or *society*. The second dimension describes whether the effect is *instrumental* or *intrinsic.* The model is shown in Figure 14.1.

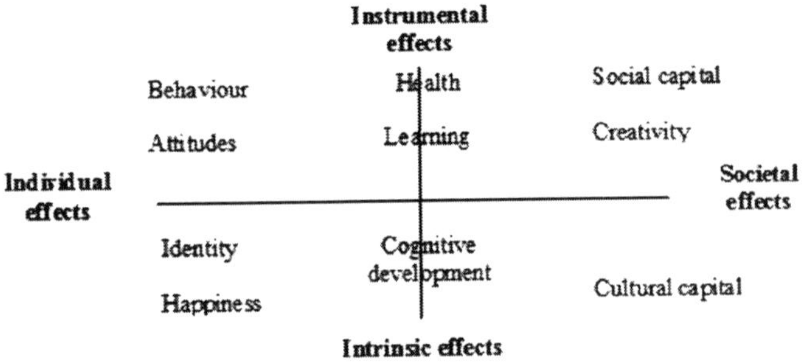

Figure 14.1 Effects of culture on the individual and on society (McCarthy *et al.* 2004).

Value of cultural institutions – an economic model

In line with the model above, the economic model will differentiate between the value that culture creates for the visitor at the individual level and the value created at the level of society. The individual value to a visitor who experiences a performance or art exhibition is called *use value*. Great societal value is created that is not necessarily associated with all citizens taking part in cultural activity, as well. But the value may consist in society developing positively as a result of the existence of culture, and therefore cultural and social capital, in society. This economic value is termed *non-use value*.

Use value

The use of culture creates *direct use value* for the visitor. This value may, for example, be pleasure in having seen an interesting play, a good feeling because the performance has set an individual on a different train of thought or given him or her a sense of relaxation after a day at work, and so on. Different performances create different value for different individuals. Use value also includes *indirect use value* generated by experiences that do not directly have anything to do with art. This may, for example, be satisfaction at having been able to spend an evening with one's friends and family, at a performance or exhibition, or a sense of boosting one's identity by meeting people and being seen in cultural contexts.

Non-use value

An evident form of economic value created by a museum or concert hall is the value of monitoring and developing art and music, but several altruistic values that are less self-evident are also created. These altruistic motives can apply both to those who are alive today and to those will be alive in the future.

Altruistic motives for future generations create value that corresponds well to the term *bequest value*. Mitchell and Carson (1989) describe *bequest value* as that which arises when someone sees a value in preserving access, for example to a cultural resource, so that it can be experienced by future generations (Mitchell and Carson 1989: 65). Hansen (1997) notes that the Danish population is prepared to pay tax to preserve the Royal Theatre in Copenhagen for future generations. Ruijgrok (2006) describes bequest value in his study, in which a cultural area in the Netherlands consisting of fortresses, churches and other buildings is partially preserved.

Another term that describes an economic value of cultural institutions is *existence value*. Throsby believes that people regard the mere existence of a cultural resource as valuable to themselves and to society even if they do not themselves utilise this cultural resource. Throsby gives the example of the pyramids in Egypt, which most people consider to be of value to preserve even if they themselves have not seen them or do not plan to see them. The existence value of culture in a region also affects the region's image and the sense of pride the region's inhabitants feel in living in a region containing cultural assets (Throsby 2001:78–79).

Similar to bequest and existence value, *option value* is regarded as constituting a third type of non-use value. In relation to culture, Ginsburgh and Throsby (2009; Throsby 2001, 2010) believe that option value can be defined as a desire to preserve the possibility of visiting the cultural institution oneself one day in the future and making use of the culture it offers.

It should be pointed out that non-use value exists both among people who have visited the cultural institution and among those who have not. The valuations of all individuals must be included to determine the existence, option and bequest values of culture.

The economic model describes the total economic value (TEV) by adding together the *use values* and *non-use values* (Bateman and Willis 2001). The value of culture can therefore be defined in an economic model as shown in Table 14.1.

Using the economic values as described above we can now link back to the previous model (Figure 14.1) on the effects of culture. Figure 14.2 shows approximately which parts the economic values may cover. Figure 14.2

Table 14.1 An economic model based on use and non-use value (Garrod and Willis 2001)

$$\text{TEV} = \underbrace{\text{DUV} + \text{IUV} + \text{OV}}_{\text{use value}} + \underbrace{\text{EV} + \text{BV}}_{\text{non-use value}}$$

TEV = total economic value	OV = option value
DUV = direct use value	EV = existence value
IUV = indirect use value	BV = bequest value

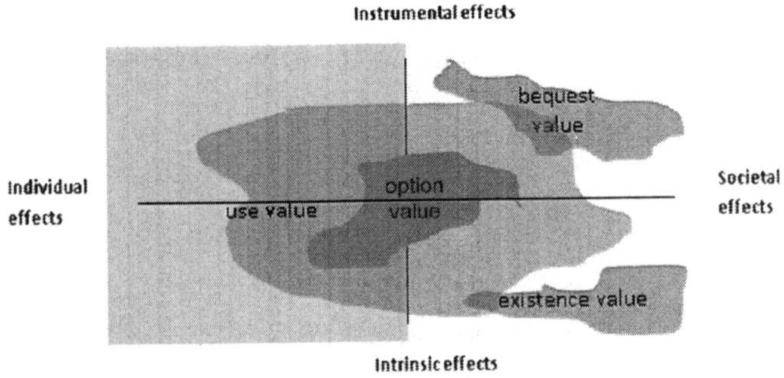

Figure 14.2 A synthesis of economic and non-economic terms (Garrod and Willis 2001; McCarthy *et al.* 2004).
Source: Armbrecht (2009).

also indicates that we do not anticipate being successful in fully covering the value of culture.

Economic values and financial flows

The above discussion of economic values may appear confusing as the link to cash flow is not clearly mentioned. The focus in this study is on estimating an economic value as accurately as possible, which may differ substantially from a financial value (i.e. cash flow). On the other hand, it is naturally the case that, when economic values are created, these are also linked in most cases to financial flows. This applies, for example, when a concert visitor experiences use value during a concert for which he or she has paid and travel for (incurred financial expenditure). If he or she additionally has an enjoyable time with friends at a restaurant or concert (indirect use value), this is also associated with financial outlay (e.g. the restaurant bill).

Regarding non-use values, the link in a shorter time perspective is to tax payments and public financial grants for culture. There might also perhaps be a greater willingness to pay tax, and citizens experience great non-use value through access to cultural value. In a longer-term perspective, the link consists in the region becoming a more attractive place to live and work. This results in higher economic activity in the region and consequently higher tax payments.

Measurement of economic value

The description of the study method here will be very brief. For further details, see the licentiate thesis (Armbrecht 2009).

The survey questions

The *Contingent Valuation Method* (Mitchell and Carson 1989: 65) was used to estimate use values and non-use values, and *willingness-to-pay* was estimated using two types of questions:

(1) Use value:
  What is the highest amount you can imagine paying for . . .
  a the ticket? (Direct use value)
  b the whole experience from leaving home until you get back home? (Direct + Indirect use value)

(2) Non-use value:
  What is the maximum amount you can imagine paying in tax per year to . . .
  a have an opportunity in the present situation to enjoy cultural experiences in the museum/concert hall? (Option value)
  b preserve the museum/concert hall and its value for future generations? (Bequest value)
  c preserve the museum/concert hall when you consider all aspects? (Total value including existence value).

In addition to the above questions on the valuation of culture, a number of questions were asked that provided insight into what influences the valuation of cultural experiences and cultural institutions.

The interviews

The data presented in this chapter consist of 1,847 responses. A total of 997 interviews were conducted to estimate use value (583 in Vara and 414 at the Nordic Watercolour Museum). The study consists of another 500 telephone interviews with residents from both municipalities (250 each). Additionally, 350 residents from the region were interviewed using telephone interviews. The regional residents were asked about the concert house and the watercolour museum.

Results of the studies

Use value will first be presented for the average visitor, with comments based on a deeper statistical analysis which is not shown here in detail (see Armbrecht 2009). A similar examination is then made of non-use value. Use and non-use value are finally aggregated to calculate the total economic value generated by Vara Concert Hall and the Nordic Watercolour Museum.

Use value for Vara Concert Hall

Table 14.1 shows the average experienced use value (i.e. direct + indirect) for one visit (including any peripheral activities such as food and drink in connection

Table 14.2 The visitors' average willingness to pay and consumer surplus for a visit to the Concert Hall

		Willingness-to-pay	Total expenditure	Consumer surplus
Local visitors(Vara)	Mean value	SEK 534	SEK 208	SEK 326
Regional visitors	Mean value	SEK 526	SEK 243	SEK 283

with a visit). Visitors consider the value of the experience to be greater than the price. The willingness to pay for the visit to the Concert Hall averages SEK 534 for *local visitors* (i.e. visitors who live in Vara or Tjörn respectively) while the average expenditure is SEK 208. Local visitors thus have an average *consumer surplus* of SEK 326 (the difference between 534 and 208) per performance (Table 14.2).

Regional visitors (i.e. all visitors not living in Vara or Tjörn) value the experience on average somewhat lower, at SEK 526, while spending somewhat more, SEK 243. The average consumer surplus for regional visitors is SEK 526 – 243 = 283.

Use values for the Nordic Watercolour Museum

The willingness to pay for an experience at the Nordic Watercolour Museum averages SEK 389 for visitors from Tjörn and SEK 480 for regional visitors, while the expenditure is SEK 202 and 301 respectively. The average consumer surplus for visitors from Tjörn is SEK 187, and for regional visitors it is SEK 179.

The three columns describe:

(1) economic value of the whole experience (willingness to pay for the whole experience);
(2) financial outlay generated by the visit (total expenditure for the whole experience);
(3) the economic surplus that is the part of the economic value not revealed in financial effects in terms of business economics (consumer surplus). The consumer surplus remains in the 'visitor's heart' but is a complete and important part of the economic value of the experience.

Table 14.3 The visitors' average willingness to pay and consumer surplus for a visit to the Watercolour Museum

		Willingness-to-pay	Total expenditure	Consumer surplus
Local visitors(Tjörn)	Mean value	SEK 389	SEK 202	SEK 187
Regional visitors	Mean value	SEK 480	SEK 301	SEK 179

Comments on use values from the concert hall and the watercolour museum

- The differences that exist between locals and non-locals are not significant, with one exception: the expenditure of those travelling to Tjörn is significantly higher than the expenditure of those who live on the island of Tjörn.
- There are weak but significant correlations between use value in Vara Concert Hall and age (negative), education (positive), annual income (positive) and gender (higher for men).
- There is only a significant correlation between use valuation and age (negative) for the watercolour museum.
- The consumer surplus among inhabitants of the municipality is found to be greater (although not significantly greater) than among regional visitors for both the cultural institutions. This is fair, in a way, as the inhabitants of the municipality also pay for the cultural institutions through their taxes.

Non-use value for Vara Concert Hall and the Nordic Watercolour Museum

The population of Vara has a willingness to pay for the non-use value of Vara Concert Hall of SEK 309. The population of Tjörn makes an equivalent valuation of SEK 314 for the Nordic Watercolour Museum (see Table 14.3). The average option value is SEK 136 for the Nordic Watercolour Museum and SEK 122 for Vara Concert Hall. The average existence value is SEK 70 for the Nordic Watercolour Museum and SEK 38 for Vara Concert Hall. The average bequest valuation is SEK 108 for the Nordic Watercolour Museum and SEK 149 for Vara Concert Hall.

In addition to the inhabitants of the municipalities of Vara and Tjörn, a stratified random selection of the population in Västra Götaland Region was interviewed (see Table 14.4).

The value ascribed by the population of Västra Götaland to the non-use value of Vara Concert Hall is SEK 203 per individual, while the value ascribed by the population of Vara to the concert hall is SEK 309. Similar values were also estimated for the Nordic Watercolour Museum, where the non-use value of the

Table 14.4 Willingness to pay of municipal inhabitants for Vara Concert Hall (VCH) and the Nordic Watercolour Museum (NWM)

	VCH valued by inhabitants of Vara				NWM valued by inhabitants of Tjörn			
	OPTION VALUE	BEQUEST VALUE	EXISTENCE VALUE	TOTAL VALUE	OPTION VALUE	BEQUEST VALUE	EXISTENCE VALUE	TOTAL VALUE
Mean value	SEK 122	SEK 149	SEK 38	SEK 309	SEK 136	SEK 108	SEK 70	SEK 314

museum for the population of Västra Götaland is SEK 158 per individual, compared with the population of Tjörn, which values it at SEK 314.

Comments on non-use values from the concert hall and the watercolour museum

- The average non-use value of Vara Concert Hall for an inhabitant of Vara is significantly higher than for an average inhabitant of Västra Götaland. The option value and bequest value are also significantly higher.
- The average non-use value of the Nordic Watercolour Museum for an inhabitant of Tjörn is significantly higher than for an average inhabitant of Västra Götaland. The option value, bequest value and existence value are also significantly higher.
- Non-use values thus co-vary in a significantly negative way with distance between place of residence and cultural institution.
- The differences between the non-use value of Vara Concert Hall and the Nordic Watercolour Museum for an average inhabitant of Västra Götaland are not statistically significant. Nor are there any significant differences between option value, bequest value and existence value.
- Individuals who have visited the cultural institutions ascribe significantly higher non-use value to them than those who have never visited them.
- Non-use value co-varies in a significantly positive way with other leisure interests: 'Going to the theatre' and 'Going to classical music concerts'.

Aggregate values for Vara and Tjörn

The average willingness to pay for use and non-use value for Vara Concert Hall and the Nordic Watercolour Museum can be added together at municipal and regional levels to provide an insight into the socio-economic welfare contributions of the cultural institutions. This is done using relatively simple mathematical operations: average use value, as described above, is multiplied by the number of visitors during the year, and average non-use value, also discussed above, is multiplied by the number of inhabitants over the

Table 14.5 The willingness to pay of the population of Västra Götaland for Vara Concert Hall (VCH) and the Nordic Watercolour Museum (NWM) does not show any significant differences between the cultural institutions

Population of Västra Götaland values VCH					Population of Västra Götaland values NWM			
	OPTION VALUE	BEQUEST VALUE	EXISTENCE VALUE	TOTAL VALUE	OPTION VALUE	BEQUEST VALUE	EXISTENCE VALUE	TOTAL VALUE
Mean value	SEK 84	SEK 90	SEK 29	SEK 203	SEK 68	SEK 61	SEK 29	SEK 158

Table 14.6 Aggregate use value for Vara Concert Hall

	Willingness-to-pay**	Total expenditure**	Consumer surplus**
Local visitors (Vara)	SEK 3,900,000	SEK 1,500,000	SEK 2,400,000
Regional visitors	SEK 14,600,000	SEK 6,700,000	SEK 7,900,000
Total	SEK 18,500,000	SEK 8,200,000	SEK 10,300,000

age of 16 in the municipalities of Vara, Tjörn and in the region of Västra Götaland.

The aggregate value is based on average value and 27,800 regional visitors, as well as 6,700 visitors from the municipality during the year.

Table 14.5 shows that the aggregate use value is greater for regional visitors (regional visitors: SEK 14.6 m; local visitors: SEK 3.9 m). Visitors who do not come from Vara also benefit from the consumer surplus to a greater extent than the population of Vara. The difference is not due to a greater willingness to pay per visitor but to the number of regional visitors being four times greater than the number of visitors from Vara.

The same picture is found for the Nordic Watercolour Museum in Table 14.6. Compared with regional visitors, the total use value for the local population is smaller.

The aggregate value is based on average value and 111,500 regional visitors, as well as 38,500 visitors from the municipality during the year.

Non-use value can also be aggregated for the populations of Vara, Tjörn and Västra Götaland. The aggregate willingness to pay for the non-use values of the Concert Hall and the Watercolour Museum is shown in Table 14.7.

Table 14.7 Aggregate use value for the Nordic Watercolour Museum

	Willingness-to-pay**	Total expenditure**	Consumer surplus**
Local visitors (Tjörn)	SEK 11,781,000	SEK 7,777,000	SEK 3,388,000
Regional visitors	SEK 44,712,000	SEK 33,567,000	SEK 13,050,000
Total	SEK 56,493,000	SEK 41,344,000	SEK 16,433,000

Table 14.8 Average and aggregate non-use values for Vara Concert Hall (VCH) and the Nordic Watercolour Museum (NWM)

	Inhabitants of Västra Götaland	Inhabitants of municipality of Vara	Inhabitants of municipality of Tjörn	Aggregate for the municipality	Aggregate for the region	Total willingness-to-pay
VCH	SEK 203	SEK 309		SEK 4,084,290	SEK 261,360,000	SEK 265,444,290
NWM	SEK 158		SEK 314	SEK 3,831,520	SEK 199,320,000	SEK 203,151,520

The aggregate values at municipal and regional level are obtained by multiplying the values in the first three columns in Table 14.7 by the number of inhabitants over the age of 16 in Vara (13,000), on Tjörn (15,000) and in Västra Götaland (1,320,000). The number of inhabitants in Västra Götaland explains the high non-use values obtained for the region (Table 14.8).

Comments on aggregate values for the concert hall and the watercolour museum

- Total expenditure for the experience (Tables 14.5 and 14.6) show the direct financial effects the cultural institutions have generated, i.e. SEK 8m for Vara and SEK 41m for Tjörn. More than 80 per cent of these financial effects come from regional visitors.
- The use value and consumer surplus for regional visitors (totalling around SEK 59m and 21m respectively) should be regarded as a goodwill gift from the municipalities of Vara and Tjörn to visitors. This goodwill is materialised for example as tourism in the region and as an advantageous favourable image for the destination.
- The inhabitants of the municipalities of Vara and Tjörn value their cultural institution in both cases at around SEK 4m per year. This means that it is felt that the municipality's budget should include a substantial sum to support the cultural institutions.
- Although the inhabitants of Västra Götaland have a significantly lower non-use value per inhabitant (mainly explained by distance away from the cultural institution), because of the large number of inhabitants in the region the total sums of non-use value show that there is a willingness to invest tax funds equivalent to more than SEK 200m for Vara Concert Hall as well as for the Nordic Watercolour Museum (Table 14.7).
- It is important to bear in mind that the value measured by this study does not include non-use value at national and international level (the Watercolour Museum also has explicit *Nordic* objectives). Both Vara Concert Hall and perhaps, in particular, the Nordic Watercolour Museum are likely to also have national and Nordic significance.

Analysis and discussion

When the analysis is done at municipal level, the use value is found to be the dominant type of value. In the case of Vara Concert Hall, use value accounts for 82 per cent of the total annual economic value (Figure 14.3). This proportion is higher still in the case of the Nordic Watercolour Museum.

It is worth noting that the bequest value accounts for the greatest non-use value. There appears to be great concern for future generations in Vara, and there is a strong willingness to offer a society containing culture to the next generation. The same applies to Tjörn.

Of the total annual economic value of SEK 22.6m created in the municipality of Vara by the concert hall, regional visitors take a use value of SEK 14.6m 'away

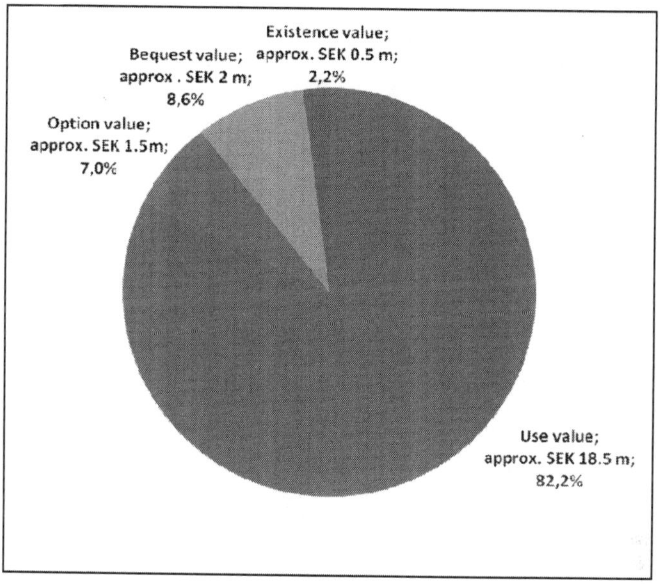

Figure 14.3 Breakdown of the total annual economic value of SEK 22.6m for the municipality of Vara of the concert hall in Vara.

with them'. However, they leave SEK 7.9m behind in expenditure on the visit, for example in ticket purchases. Analyses of regional visitors show clearly that culture is not subject to any municipal boundaries, and inhabitants of other municipalities obtain a greater yield from the cultural institutions than the inhabitants of the municipality concerned.

The cultural institutions thus also create great economic value in adjacent municipalities, which is revealed in non-use values which are, conversely, greater the closer someone lives to the cultural institution. This is in stark contrast to public funding, which is largely provided by the cultural institution's own municipality with, at best, small contributions from neighbouring municipalities.

If the perspective is broadened to the whole of Västra Götaland Region, the inhabitants of the region show a high non-use value and consequently also a very strong willingness to support the cultural institutions, as is apparent in Figure 14.4, showing the breakdown of the total annual regional economic value of SEK 269m for the Nordic Watercolour Museum.

The use value is high (SEK 56m per year), depending on how many visitors experience great value from the visit. In addition, the 'option value', i.e. the possibility of getting there and having access to an outstanding watercolour museum, is valued highly. The option value is estimated at SEK 92m per year by the population of Västra Götaland. The bequest value reflects a desire to offer future generations a society that provides art and culture.

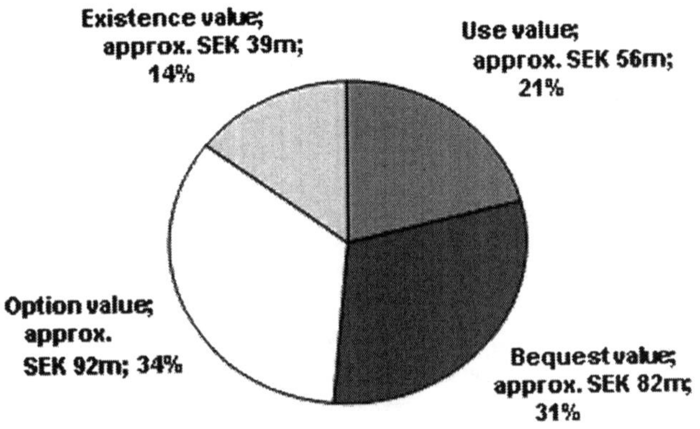

Figure 14.4 Breakdown of the total annual economic value of SEK 269m for Västra Götaland Region of the Nordic Watercolour Museum.

Conclusions

A comparison with other international research shows that the non-use value in these studies from Tjörn and Vara is consistent with previous similar studies. Hansen (1997) found that the average non-use value per Danish citizen for the Royal Theatre in Copenhagen was DKK 101. As in this study, the values in the study by Hansen (1997) are estimated using the *contingent valuation* method. As the aggregate value is measured at national level (and is therefore multiplied by the number of inhabitants in Denmark), it is not surprising that the aggregate non-use value for 'The Royal Theatre' is greater.

Santagata and Signorello (2000) studied the willingness to pay for maintenance of a network of cultural and historical monuments in the central parts of Naples. Although the maintenance in reality only cost just over SEK 24 per inhabitant each year, the willingness to pay on average was between SEK 85 and SEK 130. The willingness to pay to preserve the cultural heritage town of Fés Medina in Morocco from falling into disrepair was found to be SEK 294 for non-users and SEK 686 for users (Carson *et al.* 2002).

It is common to all three study objects that the economic value exceeds the financial resources invested. This is consistent with the analysis by Noonan (2003) of most *Contingent Valuation* studies in cultural economics. Noonan (2003) found that the estimated value of a cultural resource on average exceeds the operational costs by around 120 per cent. The annual operational costs for Vara Concert Hall were around SEK 20 m and for the Nordic Watercolour Museum around SEK 16 m, which is significantly less than the socio-economic value created in the municipality and only a fraction of the value created in the region. To summarise, it is apparent from the comparisons that the results and the aggregate values for Vara and Tjörn are reasonable.

An interesting difference between the results of this study and other international results is that both Schulze and Ursprung (2000) and Hansen (1997), in the studies of the 'Zurich Opera House' and 'The Royal Theatre' in Copenhagen, found that specific types of value such as education and annual income influenced the amounts of money people would be willing to contribute to the tax funding of cultural institutions. The results from Vara Concert Hall and the Nordic Watercolour Museum do not show any correlation between these variables and non-use value.

There were weak correlations between the variables of annual income, gender and education, as well as use value, i.e. these values appear to influence how valuable a performance or exhibition is experienced as being, but the willingness to support the cultural institutions, i.e. the non-use value, is not affected.

The results can therefore be interpreted to show that both Vara Concert Hall and the Nordic Watercolour Museum succeed in appealing to a broad public, and it is apparent from the results of the study that individuals from different socio-economic strata value having these cultural institutions in society.

The initial question in this chapter related to whether it is possible to value the yield of culture and set it against the investments made to fund culture. It is for others to decide whether this way of valuing the yield of culture is relevant to political decisions. As researchers it is our belief that we have opened up a field with potential to develop work on many interesting issues in Sweden, and at the School of Business, Economics and Law in Gothenburg we intend to undertake further work in this field of research in the next few years.

The results of the study that has been presented point to valuations that are on a par with other international studies of cultural values and of environmental economic values. It is also evident that there is a great willingness among the population of Västra Götaland to financially support culture. Of the sub-values analysed, *bequest value*, i.e. concern that future generations should be allowed to grow up in a society with culture, is prominent.

If use and non-use values are used as an indicator of the yield of culture, the yield is quite clearly far greater than the financial investment made in culture. We therefore note in conclusion that we appear to have found, in culture, an economic golden egg.

Note

1 The authors wish to express their gratitude towards IKON, an Interreg IVA-project, part of the European Regional Development Fund for financial support.

References

Ache, P. (2000) 'Vision and Creativity – Challenge for City Regions', *Futures*, 32(5): 435–449.

AEGIS, A.E.G.o.I. S. (2004) *Social Impacts of Participating in the Arts and Cultural Activities: Report on Stagetwo-Evidence, Issues and Recommendations*, Sydney: University of Western Sydney (report to the Cultural Ministers Council via the Department of Communication, Information, Technology and the Arts, Canberra).

Armbrecht, J. (2009) *Att värdera det ovärderliga: en studie om kulturinstitutioners värde*, Göteborg: Centrum för turism, Företagsekonomiska institutionen, Handelshögskolan vid Göteborgs universitet.

Barro, R.J. (1999) 'Human Capital and Growth in Cross-Country Regressions', *Swedish Economic Policy Review*, 6: 237–277.

Barro, R.J. and Sala-i-Martin, X. (2004) *Economic Growth*, Cambridge, MA: MIT Press.

Bateman, I.J. and Willis, K.G. (2001) *Valuing Environmental Preferences [Elektronisk resurs] Theory and Practice of the Contingent Valuation Method in the US, EU, and developing Countries*, Oxford: Oxford University Press.

Becker, G.S. (1974) 'A Theory of Social Interactions', *Journal of Political Economy*, 82(6): 1063.

Bourdieu, P. (1973) 'Cultural Reproduction and Social Reproduction', in R. Brown (ed.), *Knowledge, Education and Cultural Change*, London: Kegan Paul, 71–112.

Bourdieu, P. and Wacquant, L.J.D. (1992) *An Invitation to Reflexive Sociology*, Chicago: University of Chicago Press.

Carson, R.T., Mitchell, R.C. and Conaway, M.B. (2002) 'Economic Benefits to Foreigners Visiting Morocco Accruing from the Rehabilitation of the Fés Medina', in S. Navrud and R.C. Ready (eds), *Valuing Cultural Heritage: Applying Environmental Valuation Techniques to Historic Buildings, Monuments and Artifacts*, Cheltenham: Edward Elgar.

Cavaye, J. (2004) *Social Capital: a Commentary on Issues, Understanding and Measurement*, Melbourne: Observatory PASCAL.

Cortines, R.C. (1999) 'Introduction', in L. Longley (ed.), *Gaining the Arts Advantage: Lessons from School Districts that Value Arts Education*, Washington, DC: President's Committee on the Arts and the Humanities and Arts Education Partnership (p. 4). Available at: www.pcah.gov/pdf/GainingArtsAdvantage.pdf (accessed 18 August 2008).

Deasy, R. (2002) *Critical Links: Learning in the Arts and Student Academic and Social Development*, Washington, DC: Arts Education Partnership.

Dumais, S.A. (2002) 'Cultural Capital, Gender, and School Success: The Role of Habitus', *Sociology of Education*, 75(1): 44–68.

Eisner, E.W. (2002) *The Arts and the Creation of Mind*, New Haven: Yale University Press.

Fiske, E.B. (1999) *Champions of Change: The Impact of the Arts on Learning*, President's Committee on the Arts and the Humanities, Washington, DC: Arts Education Partnership, Washington, DC.

Folkhälsoinstitutet (2005) *Kultur för hälsa – En exempelsamling från forskning och kultur*.

Garrod, G. and Willis, K.G. (2001) *Economic Valuation of the Environment: Methods and Case Studies*, Cheltenham: Edward Elgar.

Ginsburgh, V. and Throsby, D. (2009) *Handbook of the Economics of Art and Culture. Vol. 1*, Amsterdam: Elsevier North-Holland.

Hansen, T.B. (1997) 'The Willingness-to-Pay for the Royal Theatre in Copenhagen as a Public Good', *Journal of Cultural Economics*, 21(1): 1–28.

Hayami, Y. and Ruttan, V.W. (1985) *Agricultural Development: an International Perspective*, Baltimore: Johns Hopkins University Press.

Lucas, R.E. (1988) 'On the Mechanics of Economic Development', *Journal of Monetary Economics*, 22(1): 3–42.

McCarthy, K.F., Ondaatje, E.H., Laura, Z. and Brooks, A.C. (2004) *Gifts of the Muse: Reframing the Debate About the Benefits of the Arts*, Santa Monica: RAND Corporation.

Mitchell, R.C. and Carson, R.T. (1989) *Using Surveys to Value Public Goods: The Contingent Valuation Method*, Washington, DC: Resources for the Future.

Noonan, D. (2003) 'Contingent Valuation and Cultural Resources: A Meta-Analytic Review of the Literature', *Journal of Cultural Economics*, 27(3): 159–176.

Nordic Watercolour Museum (2012). Available at: http://akvarellmuseet.org/Kultur_Default.aspx?id47012 (accessed 6 August 2012).

Ruijgrok, E.C.M. (2006) 'The Three Economic Values of Cultural Heritage: a Case Study in the Netherlands', *Journal of Cultural Heritage*, 7(3): 206–213.

Sala-I-Martin, I. (1997) 'Just Ran Two Million Regressions', *The American Economic Review*, 87(2): 178–183.

Santagata, W. and Signorello, G. (2000) 'Contingent Valuation of a Cultural Public Good and Policy Design: The Case of Napoli Musei Aperti', *Journal of Cultural Economics*, 24(3): 181–204.

Schulze, G.G. and Ursprung, H.W. (2000) 'La Donna e Mobile – or is She? Voter Preferences and Public Support for the Performing Arts', *Public Choice*, 102(1): 129–147.

Throsby, C.D. (1999) 'Cultural Capital', *Journal of Cultural Economics*, 23(1–2): 3–12.

——— (2001) *Economics and Culture*, Cambridge: Cambridge University Press.

——— (2010) *The Economics of Cultural Policy*, Cambridge: Cambridge University Press.

Vara Concert Hall (2012). Available at: www.vara.se/omoss.4.58aef784115b28a58298000324.html (accessed 6 August 2012).

Wright, R., John, L., Alaggia, R. and Sheel, J. (2006) 'Community-based Arts Program for Youth in Low-Income Communities: A Multi-Method Evaluation', *Child and Adolescent Social Work Journal*, 23(5): 635–652.

15 Brilliant combinations of art and nature

Learning points from the world of opera and classical music

Per Frankelius

Introduction

An opera arena right in the middle of nature – in a large old limestone quarry? Margareta Dellefors got this idea, believed in it and promoted her vision. The vision came true, and several hundred thousand people have enjoyed its magic. It became an injection for Dalarna's regional brand as well as for Sweden. The music has flowed. The scene has been crackling with activity. People have enjoyed the new combination of nature and art. But huge amounts of energy were used to realize the dream.

Perspective, aim and method

The research presented here is not about the 'nature of art' such as the nature of different paintings, which is a common theme in existing literature. Neither is this research about the 'art of nature' in the sense of art describing nature (compare Martin 2011). The focus here is creation processes resulting in *hybrids* between nature and art. I will try to describe how such a process can occur and evolve – and what it can lead to.

In order to access the inner being of art-nature processes, in-depth studies at the *micro level* are required. It also requires *process perspectives* in the sense of studying a series of events over time – not just processes in the sense that 'A leads to B' (compare Frankelius 1999).

But the creative process is just part of the core of this chapter. I will foremost analyse an example of *results* from such a process and discuss the related concepts of culture, art and nature, and conclude with a model, which has been named 'The Dalhalla Concept'.

One aim of the chapter is to discuss building blocks for a theoretical model, or framework, for future research of development processes on the boundary between nature and art. Normatively speaking, the aim is to carve *useful perspectives* that can be strategic tools for both enthusiasts and policy-makers interested in art and/or regional development. It also aims to bring forward an analysis of how the concepts of culture, art and nature relate to each other.

The basis for this research journey in search of new understanding and new models is a case study that began 31 August 2001 with a personal conversation with Margareta Dellefors. The last interview for this text was completed 28 May 2012. Mostly they have been semi-structured and open-ended interviews, conducted on the Dalhalla site, in Dellefors' apartment, in my apartment and over the telephone. Besides Dellefors I have talked to many other people, such as Håkan Ivarson (former CEO of Dalhalla Production AB), Maria Norrfalk (County Governor in Dalarna) and Lena Adelsohn Liljeroth (Swedish Minister of Culture).

I have visited Dalhalla many times, and my Leica camera has been an important research tool. I photographed different concerts and details in and around the arena. I have also used archival material, in particular material that Margareta Dellefors had collected over the years, including letters, applications, legal documents and articles.

The connection between art, culture and nature

The word *culture* (Swedish 'kultur') has a meaning which varies in different contexts and languages (Frankelius and Vogel 2009). One should distinguish between its aesthetic meaning (when referring to the expression of such things as literature, performing arts and music) and its anthropological meaning (when referring to people's customs, practices, values, etc. in a broad sense). The aesthetic aspect of culture ('kultur') can be looked upon as a subset of the broader anthropological meaning. See Figure 15.1.

There is a connection between nature and art. Aristotle pointed this out when he defined art as a result of the process in which someone in a skilful way *imitates* nature (Aristotle 335BC). The history of art is filled with masterpieces on that theme. Immanuel Kant was in some opposition to Aristotle's perspective, as he

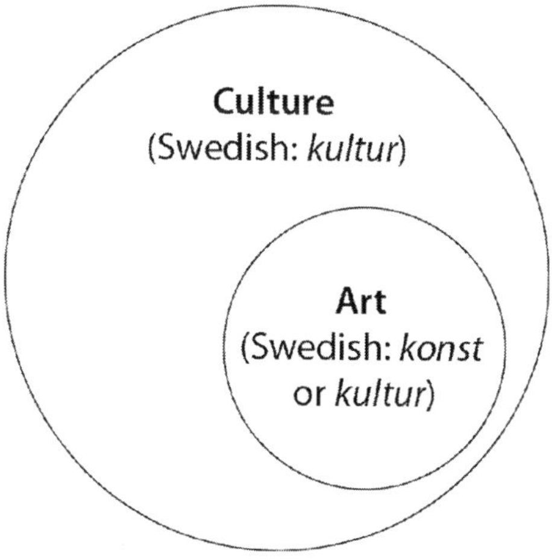

Figure 15.1 The concepts of culture and art as set and subset.

seems to have defined art (or at least culture) as being somewhat *higher* than what nature itself can do or express (Kant 1790/2007).

A synthesis between Aristotle and Kant's perspective would be to use nature in combination with art such as in music and performing arts to pave the way for experience hybrids where both the art and nature (in the natural world sense) are included as ingredients. Several art activities in modern society are in fact about clever combinations of art and nature, where the art is created by means of a mix of such things as music and nature, or theatre and nature. One mission in this research is in fact to uncover some important aspects of nature from an art perspective, as well as to present a definition of nature in this context.

For the successful combination of art and nature to become reality, requires processes that may be more difficult and more complex than one might think. Now let's look into one such a process.

The Dalhalla case: from wild visions to sweet outdoor tones

When Carl Linnæus travelled in Dalarna in 1734, he noticed that people around the town of Rättvik made their living partly with the help of limestone. He wrote: 'The parish of Rättvik burn limestone and sell it all over Dalarna region' (Linnæus 1734: 63, my translation). Notice that Linnæus focused not on nature in and of itself, but on the economic use of nature (compare Frankelius 2007, 2011).

In 1898, a more industrial enterprise started to dig out limestone from the place. The name of this company was Kullsbergs Kalkförädlings AB, and the name of the quarry by tradition was Draggängarna. The company had its good times, but in 1991 the business around the limestone quarry ceased. A gigantic hole was left in the bedrock after centuries of digging. What would become of this monument from the heyday of mining? Could it perhaps, as someone suggested, be used as a swimming lake or a municipal rubbish dump?

Another idea was hatched on 18 May 1991 by an opera singer, later a radio producer, named Margareta Dellefors, then aged 65. The idea was to create a summer stage for opera in the enormous quarry. To create a new unique summer stage was a thought that she had had for a long time.

Dellefors had been responsible for the opera production department for Swedish public radio since 1980, a job that included reportage visits to different festivals around Europe, such as Verona, Bregenz, Glyndebourne and Savonlinna. On the last day of March 1991, Dellefors retired from Swedish Radio – now she was free to do new things.

Dellefors reconstructs the moment of imagination: 'As soon as I saw Draggängarna I knew: this is the place for the international opera festival. I had been looking for, for some quite time.' She also commented on it in this way:

> What to do with an industrial ruin – in this case a limestone quarry no longer in use? To the district county of Rättvik this was an obvious problem. To me

> it was no problem at all. Draggängarna was the answer of a dream that I had had for quite some time. Love at first sight. Go ahead and do it.

From the citation we can see that Dellefors was very dedicated and motivated. This aspect will be integrated in the theoretical model at the end of the chapter.

This is how Dellefors was connected with the limestone quarry: 'I started trying to find a place for an international music festival in Sweden, but maybe something different. I have a summerhouse in Rättvik and knew that there, in the beginning of the last century, were a few limestone industries.' For some years she had been asking different people for tips about a good place. In November 1990, she explored the woods around Rättvik searching for old quarries. She had a local map, but she did not find any of them. They were well hidden, partly for safety reasons. The active searching for opportunities is part of the common theme in this story, and we will take care of this in the model-building following the case description.

One of the people Dellefors asked was Rättvik's cultural director, Åsa Nyman, around New Year's Day 1991. On 18 May, Dellefors got the strategic information about the site Draggängarna from Nyman. They went by car to the quarry the same day.

When she arrived at the place, she sang, recited poetry and noticed the marvellous acoustics, both regarding reverberation and silence. The cliffs had different pastel colours because of different kinds of rocks in vertical lines – black, pink, blue, white and brown. At the bottom there was an emerald-coloured lake, never ceasing, because it was under groundwater level. The dimensions of the limestone were powerful. Here were all the natural conditions needed for the stage, she had dreamed of. And she thought: 'It need only be furnished.'

In the theoretical analysis I will come back to this interesting example of how a person perceives opportunities in the interface between art and nature. I will also come back the essence of nature in this art context.

Starting the work

Lots of activities started after that first impression. 'I got a kick from the very first moment I set eyes on it. To be sure I invited lots of friends – conductors, musicians, singers – people whose judgement I could trust and started to work for my, as I thought, splendid idea.' Dellefors wanted second opinions – confirmation – from people she trusted. At the same time, she wanted to market the project to opinion leaders: 'As I had a long career behind me in the Swedish music world I knew people and organizations I thought could be of value for my idea. And most of them knew who I was.' One should remember Dellefors had been an opera singer for 15 years.

After having taken photos of the place, she magnified the best one and went to a bookshop to buy clear sheets of plastic. She wanted to visualize her vision by drawing on the photos taken. She drew a stage in the middle of the lake, and a grand stand opposite it. This pedagogical trick was used at a meeting with a construction company in September 1991, and later in December with decision-makers from the municipality Rättvik.

Apart from herself and opinion leaders in the music sector, there were many more people to convince in this very early part of the process, not the least the locals: 'Everyone in the little country town of Rättvik considered me more or less crazy, but as I presented letters and documents from musical and well-known Swedish authorities I did manage to overcome the first scepticism'.

The period between the first visit in May 1991 and the first written project plan on 9 July 1992 was about intense marketing, including hundreds of contacts, speeches and meetings. In fact, personal marketing is a recurrent theme in this story, and probably in many other innovative creation processes in the art field. Therefore I will have this as one important building block in the coming model.

The reputation of the project began to spread. The very first article on the Dalhalla project was written by Carl-GunnarÅhlen in the Swedish newspaper *Svenska Dagbladet* (one of Sweden's largest morning newspapers) in July 1992.

On 6 August Dellefors managed to convince some decision-makers in the municipality and the county council, to come and see the quarry with their own eyes. It happened to be a chilly day, but Dellefors started to sing an opera aria and the men were noticeably impressed by the acoustics of the quarry. 'Imagine if I had not been able to sing', said Dellefors afterwards. Maybe they could help with some money, Dellefors thought, but still no decisions were made.

The hunt for capital

A lot of money was needed for the project, and the main problem was finding and persuading sponsors. In retrospect, about 50 million Swedish crowns (about US$7.5 million) would be needed to fulfil the dream. But Dellefors concludes: 'The first 100,000 were actually the most difficult to get.' She needed to convince a lot of people of her vision. The perfect marketing concept for that, she thought, was to arrange a trial concert that would, at the very least, prove the musical potential. Such an event costs a lot of money. Dellefors recalls: 'After about two years I managed to raise the necessary money to hold a trial concert, which would prove among other things the extraordinarily good acoustics Dalhalla has.' Thus, the fund-raising process was crucial. The problem was that many observers did not believe that Dellefors was serious. She reflects:

> Suspicions always arise when something new is initiated. 'We cannot do this, it has never been done before', 'We must do this, because, that is what we always have done', 'Opera – that is something where people only shout and you can't hear a word of what they are singing', 'And who does she think she is, wanting to come here and tell us, what we shall do'.

Others thought it was a nice idea, but would never dream of investing money in such a project. Dellefors encountered resistance from sceptics everywhere including experts in engineering and economic matters. Articles in newspapers were also written about the impossibility of the project. Furthermore, opera is something foreign for most people, particularly people in Dalarna, the folk music capital of Sweden. However, she did arouse great enthusiasm in a few. In January 1993, the County Administrative Board decided to support the project with 50,000 crowns. Then the Municipality also decided to support it with the same amount.

Thanks to this money Dellefors was able to hire experts to examine the limestone quarry and the site as a whole in detail. The fascinating hole was found to be 400 m long, 175 m wide, and as deep as 60 m. Its walls were nearly vertical and the acoustics were on par with Greek amphitheatres. The acoustic quality of the limestone quarry was something that Dellefors noticed directly. She also understood that this was a very important aspect of the place. Another important aspect was that it was located far from the noise of cities, roads and factories. In the analysis I will come back to this focus on the genuine touch.

The trial concert

In May 1993, it was time for a meeting: 'I invited the local people to the library hall in Rättvik on Tuesday 25 May. I talked about all the possibilities and what it could also mean economically for little Rättvik.' She got unexpected support: 'One person – totally ignorant of classical music or opera – was curious enough and asked some very important questions: Roland Pettersson.' He was a local automobile dealer and embraced the idea even though he himself had never set foot in an opera house or heard a classical concert. He also helped her with the coming trial concert. The meeting was made known through advertising in *Rättviksnytt* and *Leksandsbladet*, two free papers delivered to every household in the area. And the library hall was crowded.

Altogether, Dellefors was able to gradually awaken commitment among numerous people, both private individuals and foundations. But even so, a lot of money was needed.

A project group was appointed in the spring of 1993, with Dellefors as project leader. On 18 June 1993, the planned trial concert was held with a specially invited audience. Dellefors explains: 'I chose people who were connected with music and opera in particular and music writers and critics and of course people connected with state organizations who supported culture with money.' In total, there were 200 people on the list. The concert was successful. To take the edge off the criticism that the idea did not suit Rättvik's folk music culture, Dellefors spiced up the programme with traditional fiddlers and birch-bark horn blowers. She will never forget this concert:

> The local people had contributed with big bowls full of wonderful wild summer flowers and were all there in their national costumes. Birgit Nilsson, our world-famous soprano, sat there in her mink coat on the first bench. I introduced the programme by singing the first lines of Elisabeth's greeting aria from Tannhäüser, 'Dich teure Halle, grüss ich wieder'.

Dalarna's own orchestra DalaSinfoniettan, and eight young singers sang opera arias, folk music was played, and a choir of 200 singers from the ongoing international choir week sang 'Hallelujah' from *Messiah* by Handel.

The trial concert was a vital ingredient in the marketing strategy: The aim was to prove the substance in the project for everyone that mattered in Swedish music life. That included not only musicians and opera managers, but also the head of the Royal Academy of Music. In fact, part of the problem was convincing the members of the project group that Dellefors really *had* the important contacts she talked about. The key word here is *verification*, and that is important probably in early phases of most innovative processes.

The concert was covered by the national and local press as well as television. The biggest newspaper in Scandinavia, *Dagens Nyheter*, wrote: 'It is simply brilliant. A limestone quarry in the middle of the forest as a giant opera arena.' *Expressen* wrote: 'The conditions for a unique mega stage, far more beautiful and more interesting [than the Globe Arena in Stockholm] is as evocative as it is realistic.' *Falu Kuriren* wrote: 'What comparisons can be made to this enchanting place and evocative environment.'

Increased intensity in the project

The next Monday, 21 June 1993, after the trial concert, Dellefors applied for the protection of the name Dalhalla. She sent the application in her own name. It was registered 29 June. As sender of the application, however, she wrote the address of Rättvik municipality. Now a strange thing happened. Dellefors says:

> Behind my back two executives in Rättvik asked the Patent and Registration Office to get my application back and then they wrote their own names on it. Then they sent it back to the Patent Office. Thus depriving me of my rights to the brand.

She invested lots of time in collecting information on specific targets for her fundraising process. 'I sat down in the library and looked through big books for foundations that might be interested in investing money in Dalhalla.' Notice, once again, that Dellefors made huge efforts in searching for opportunities by means of smart information channels – an aspect, which will be part of the coming model building. She then contacted each prospect with a tailored proposal. After the first contact, Dellefors continued her actions. 'When I had sent a request, a proposal or an application to potential donors I always continued to update them about the progress of the project'. Her 'relationship marketing' was both comprehensive and personal. 'I do not know how many applications I have written. It must be a couple of hundred.' Every success during the early process was used to promote later steps to fulfil the vision. We can call this relay race marketing.

Dellefors continues: 'After the important and successful trial concert I invited people to become members in the Society of Friends of Dalhalla. It soon amounted to more than 3,000 members. Our world famous Wagner soprano Birgit Nilsson, my great friend, consented to be our honorary chairman.'

The first years Dellefors mostly worked alone on the project, but then one helping hand arrived in December 1992, the architect Erik Ahnborg. He got in touch after having read an article in the 22 November issue of the Swedish newspaper *Svenska Dagbladet* about the opera vision for the limestone quarry. Ahnborg is the man behind the famous concert hall in Stockholm, Berwaldhallen. Dellefors felt that he was the right person to help her fulfil her vision. She showed him the photo with the amateur drawing of her vision overlaid on top of it. By September 1993 he had made new professional drawings of Dalhalla as an opera arena. These drawings were a prerequisite for all further processes. Ahnborg became an important project companion.

In December 1993 Dalhalla got one million crowns from Boverket, a state organization that supports art projects.

As the information about the Dalhalla project spread, mixed reactions followed. On 18 February 1994 a critical article in the regional press was published. The article questioned the plausibility of the vision of creating an opera stage in the middle of a folk music county like Dalarna. But the project continued.

The many problems alternated with success. Positive news came on 21 February when the County Administrative Board of Dalarna, despite local criticism in the media, decided on a grant of a further 500,000 crowns.

In the spring 1994, Dellefors had enough money, totalling about 4 million SEK, to start rebuilding the limestone quarry into a festival arena. With pomp and circumstance the first dynamite blast was fired 13 May – with Birgit Nilsson at the detonator.

A provisional stage was built on the lake, with a channel between the stage and the audience, and they installed seats for 1,620 people.

In this spring, 1994, the project also had the resources to plan and conduct an opera concert that was to take place on 23 July. The 1,600 concert tickets sold out in no time. Part of the reason was that Dalhalla had now got recognition from the state, as the Ministry of Culture had contributed 250,000 crowns. In their press release they described Dalhalla as the Verona of the north, an attribute that is still connected to Dalhalla.

A few other concerts also took place that summer, and were seen by a total of about 3,000 people. Autumn 1994 and spring 1995 were periods of extensive planning activities, which included, as usual, marketing.

Official inauguration of Dalhalla

In the summer of 1995, the audience capacity was expanded to 2,670 seats. Parking places were arranged and a protected path was laid down into the quarry. The stage, with an aesthetic roof of sailcloth, was placed on a peninsula in the emerald-coloured water, far down in the quarry. About 40,000 tons of limestone were blasted and used as material for the stage. The 11 m broad channel between stage and audience was ready. The dream was becoming a reality.

The official inauguration of Dalhalla took place on 21 June 1995 with a major opera concert that was broadcast on Swedish television. Unfortunately, that very day the area suffered an awful storm and the concert had to be stopped halfway through. Despite (or partly because of?) the disaster Dalhalla soon became known throughout Sweden and its fame spread abroad like wildfire. Since Dalhalla already had become internationally known, there were journalists there to cover the event. For instance Stephen Pettitt from the British newspaper *The Independent* wrote the following in its report of the inaugural concert:

> Soaked and shivering in our orange plastic ponchos, we had nevertheless seen and heard enough to be convinced that Dalhalla – as Dellefors has wittily re-christened the former Draggängarna – has an immensely promising future. ... First among Dalhalla's many virtues is its quiet location, close to the small town Rättvik and the beautiful Lake Siljan. Then there is the sheer sight of it. You approach down a long, narrow lane that takes you down deeper and deeper into the forest. Suddenly a twist in the lane and there it is, and almost sheer-sided rectangular arena a quarter of a mile long, 175 metres wide and 60 metres deep. A natural stone platform juts out into the flooded bottom of the pit. How can mere humans fill such a great void with sound and without amplification? But as soon as Kamu had disembarked from the rowing boat that had brought him to the platform and launched into the overture to Wagner's Die Meistersinger, it was plain that there was no difficulty. Partly because the water acts as an acoustic reflector, the sound strikes the 2,500 souls seated across the pond with a surprising immediacy. The balance is miraculous too, and the acoustic has a lovely varnish and a languishing distant echo that adds mystic aura, perfect for Wagner.
>
> (Pettitt 1995).

The television broadcast was very important. Dellefors confirms: 'The Swedish television did manage a whole planned programme, even if the total concert did not take place. From the very beginning TV has shown a lot of Dalhalla, which of course has been of gold's value, as you don't exist if you are not on the telly.'

1995 was the break-through year. Besides the concert in June, Dalhalla also cooperated with the festival Music at Siljan, Rättvik. Dances, and a jazz concerts were organized. Dellefors produced the programme 1995, and not least also planned the next season. This planning process was a mix of her own thinking and external impulses. Let us now look more closely into this.

Towards the staging of the opera Ring of the Nibelungs

The staging in 1996 of a short version of Wagner's opera *Ring of the Nibelungs* was a triumph. This big event took years to plan and complete. Dellefors tells:

> I read an article in the magazine *Musikdramatik* written by the editor Torbjörn Eriksson. It described how in 1994, Iceland celebrated their

> 50 years of freedom as a republic. Part of the festivities was a performance of Richard Wagner's Ring of the Nibelungs in a short version of 4 hours.

This special version was partly arranged by Lars Lönnroth, professor of literature at the University of Gothenburg (Sweden) and specialist in the Nordic languages. Two storytellers held the show together. And Dellefors reflected: 'This seemed to be interesting and also viable for us.' She saw this as an opportunity to fulfil the dream of an opera arena at Dalhalla and she went into action: 'Already in January 1995 I contacted Iceland.' The work for this project was enormous. A lot of money was needed. Many people and organizations had to be coordinated, and marketing was vital. Dellefors comments:

> I started the marketing work for this coming event already in autumn 1995. With the help of Bengt Göransson (former minister of culture) we got a distinguished opportunity. He offered the big ABF conference centre for us to organise a seminar under the heading 'Richard Wagner – genius and monster in the same person'. The seminar took place 25 November. We started at 9 in the morning and finished at 5 in the afternoon. We had advertised in Stockholm newspapers and the hall was crowded. The Court singer Birgit Nilsson made the introduction, and was interviewed by Musikradion's Tom Sandberg. On request, she delivered her famous Ho-jo to-ho from the Valkyrie, and the high C hit the roof like a rivet.

This marketing effort was thus a 'marketing of marketing tool'. Dellefors marketed the event that in turn was a marketing tool for the actual big opera event the following year. And she got results not only from potential visitors. The day before the seminar she received information about the decision by the foundation Crafoordska stiftelsen (in Lund, Sweden), to contribute one million crowns for the opera event planned for the following year.

She succeeded. The first special version of the Wagner opera was performed in the summer of 1996, and it was a sensation. Imagine three enormous people on stage – the Rhine maidens – about 3 m high. One would think that they walked on stilts, but that was not the case. Under the singers were three young music students from the Falun Conservatory, well hidden by the costumes. They moved according to the director's instructions with help from numbers written on the stage.

The lighting was a masterpiece in itself. Carl-GunnarÅhlen wrote in the Swedish newspaper *Svenska Dagbladet*:

> When light setter Thomas Mirstam transforms the rock wall behind the lake, the orchestra podium and the acoustical sails, into by far the world's largest circular horizon, it's so awesome that you gasp. At least two, maybe up to three acres of blazing light and colours and shapes fill the visual field. No other outdoor stage or Cosmonova can compete with something similar. ...

> After Saturday's performance even the harshest sceptics should be convinced that it is actually possible to play opera in Dalhalla.

The Viennese opera magazine, *Der Neue Merker*, named Dalhalla the most powerful opera stage in Europe, partly because of visual effects towards the end that had never been made in such a beautiful way. Also CNN came to this event, and produced a five-minute reportage, shown all over the world.

Other leading publications, many of them opera-related, also wrote about Dalhalla. Brian Kellow, the chief editor of the premier opera magazine in the United States, *Opera News*, wrote an article about the new original arena Dalhalla and pointed out the fact that one really could perform opera entirely acoustic. The German magazines *Orpheus* and *Opernglas* wrote articles. The well-respected English magazine *Opera Now* was also among the magazines that wrote about Dalhalla. I interpret this to mean that opera experts considered the Dalhalla phenomenon original – as a new innovative thing in the opera world.

Established business looking for its form

The great event of 1997 was a longer version – full-evening show – of the *Nibelungen Ring*. During the year they played four operas and six concerts of classical music. The level of the art content was always high in Dellefors' productions. This aspect is part of the model that will be derived later.

The workload was increasing. In May 1996, a company called Dalhalla Produktion AB was established, wholly owned by the Society of Friends. This company was to take care of the productions. The company appointed a CEO, Nils Aittamaa. From this point on, Dellefors became the Art Manager, and could concentrate on art content. Unfortunately, cooperative problems emerged and deepened during 1997.

At the end of 1997, Dellefors told the steering committee of Dalhalla that they had to choose between her and Aittamaa. She won this ultimatum. She then suggested that Håkan Ivarson should be the new CEO. At the time, he was the manager of the orchestra DalaSinfoniettan. He was approached in January 1998 and was employed part-time from 9 March the same year. Dellefors continued to be responsible for art direction.

In 1998 a total of 22 events were staged (including four operas, four opera concerts and four classical music concerts). All of the events were very well attended. It also meant that a great number of the locals had discovered something new: opera and classical music.

Dalhalla towards becoming an institution

During 1999, Dalhalla became institutionalized and from that year forward begun to receive an annual sum of money from the Ministry of Culture. At the annual meeting on 14 May 1999 Dellefors and Ivarson presented a strategy for continued development. The strategy included formulation of a business mission (statement) and plans for expansion. Let me cite just two sentences: 'Dalhalla shall be an international festival arena offering music events of high quality, with music dramaturgy as the centre of gravity. The programmes shall have a character, that harmonizes with the natural conditions and the unique environment.' Once again we see here that Dellefors combined art and nature.

The big thing in 1999 was a concert with the mega opera star José Cura. This time it was the artist himself who approached Dellefors (through his agent). He had probably heard of Dalhalla via the CNN reportage. This event was very complicated. For example, the Philharmonic Orchestra of London was engaged. Here is Dellefors' comment on all this: '160 different letters and faxcs, and as many from his agent, were needed to fulfil this guest appearance.' It is hard to imagine all the work and all the details that she attended to over the years, but this example gives us a sense of her achievement – and illustrates her dedication!

Of course, there were also many practical problems – some of them unexpected. In the summer of 1999, for example, a tornado destroyed the sail-roof. Dellefors comments:

> It happened on 13 August 1999, the very same evening we were giving our own version of Richard Wagner's Ring. Part of the scenography and the light depended on this roof. We played it anyway without the roof and it still was a success.

During the process Dellefors accumulated knowledge about subjects of many different kinds, like the behaviour of the wind: 'One of the difficulties with a "hole" as an amphitheatre instead of one built upon the ground is that the wind always tends to find its way downwards.'

The fundraising process was always in focus. And she was sometimes very successful. Dellefors fills in: '11.4 million Swedish crowns were given by a rich couple in the neighbourhood.' She managed to get more and more money from sponsors. The Barbro Osher Pro Suecia Foundation, based in San Francisco, gave Dalhalla 2 million crowns for opera productions (in the years 2000 and 2002). Later, the Barney Osher foundation also donated money and a first-class theatre text machine. During 1999, Dellefors also managed to get a main sponsor, the petroleum company OK/Q8. Another important part of the financing process was Dellefors' ability to round up pro bono help from professionals such as a first-class architect. To manage economic issues seems to be critical in the creation of novel concepts in the art field, and this fact will be integrated in the model later on.

By June 2000, Dalhalla had become a well-developed opera arena. They had a big concert on 7 June with the Swedish King and Queen as invited guests. At this time, Dalhalla had 4,000 seats, and heating for the orchestra pit and the artist's building behind the stage from geothermal power 180 m down. A stable roof was supported by pylons secured 26 m down in the ground, a roof that further improved the acoustics and was perfect for the various types of light scenography. The stage was 42 m wide and 18 m deep and had a professional lighting system. In the middle of the stage area was a small section whose height level could be adjusted by hydraulics.

Changes, problems and the 'bomb' in the mailbox

In the spring of 2001, the Swedish retail clothing company Hennes & Mauritz arranged a fashion show at the site. This was something that marketed Dalhalla internationally. Journalists and top models, including Grace Jones, were flown in from all over the world. The company's annual report mentioned Dalhalla in three places and pictures from the event were over two full pages.

Since 1998 Dalhalla has continually been used for events other than what the arena was originally intended for. Despite Dellefors protests, pop concerts began to dominate. As we shall see below, this new orientation from opera and classical music to pop music was something that had serious consequences.

In 2003, Dalhalla had existed for 10 years. There was a big jubilee concert. Events at Dalhalla were covered extensively by television and newspapers. That year the prestigious magazine *Magazin Festival* in Vienna ranked Dalhalla number three of the best outdoor stages (after Verona and Orange). It wrote: 'It does not matter if you go to Verona or Dalhalla – it becomes a memory for life.'

Behind the scenes, however, there were great problems. In 2001, Dalhalla had been on the brink of bankruptcy, but was saved by a loan from the county council thanks to Dellefors and former Chairman of Dalhalla Bengt Göransson (former Minister of Culture).

In the same year, Dellefors, on her own initiative, left her position as artistic director, but would, according to a new employment contract remain as artistic consultant. After the near-bankruptcy incident she was re-hired unanimously by the board as artistic director, but with some restrictions. The new employment contract was dated March 2002.

Late on Tuesday evening, 3 June 2003 a letter was thrown into the mailbox of Margareta Dellefors' apartment in Stockholm. It stated that she had been removed as the artistic director of Dalhalla; in other words, she was fired. This was the culmination of a struggle that locally had become known as the opera war. The core of the disagreement was whether Dalhalla should focus primarily on opera or turn to more popular genres. But according to Dellefors, it was more about a personal issue. She commented:

> I lived in Stockholm most of the time, something that undermined my position. Behind my back plans were made. I begun to understand that I had three handicaps: My gender (I was the only woman on the board), my age, and being a Stockholmer.

The conflict soon became known also outside of Dalarna and people in the Swedish art world started to react. Everyone was aware that Dalhalla got its big government grants because of its focus on primarily classical music and musical theatre, but that the focus had now been shifted. A letter written by Sweden's three opera directors and some other music personalities was submitted in person on 12 May 2003 to the Association Friends of Dalhalla (and its Chairman, the former deputy prime minister). This letter was also sent simultaneously to Dalhalla's Office for distribution to members of the association at the coming annual meeting 24 May. That never happened. Largely because of this, the annual meeting became chaotic.

The board of directors of Dalhalla's production company thought that Dellefors herself was behind the attempt to replace the board. Dellefors denied this, but she maintained that classical music and opera should dominate Dalhalla's programming. Such declarations had also been the message to several of the largest donors before they made their decisions regarding financial contributions. Dellefors' argument was that, while it was perhaps possible to earn more money by taking in popular music, in the long run it was important to uphold Dalhalla's identity, the Dalhalla brand. She continued: 'Instead of broadening into a 'tour place', Dalhalla should be broadened by also bringing in dance and theatre.'

How did Dellefors feel about this letter? 'It was a very big shock to me.' She had expressed her views at the board meeting in October 2002, and became a 'whistle blower'. She realized the disastrous economic future because of, among other things, the growing administrative costs and the increasingly expensive popular productions.

In 2004, Dalhalla (again) was near bankruptcy. Dalhalla's economy continued to go up and down over the years. Rescue operations, especially from the municipality, have helped to save the business. The Dalhalla brand was so strong and was of great importance for the municipality.

On 17 June 2006 a bronze bust of Dellefors, that had been donated by the approximately 2,000 people who had left the association Friends of Dalhalla', was unveiled. However, the friction between Dellefors and Dalhalla was and still remains a hot topic of conversation.

2008 was a dark year for Dalhalla when it lost one in four visitors. In the summer of 2009 the programme (which was a surprise) once again contained an opera at Dalhalla – Mozart's Magic Flute. It was well received. The five performances attracted 15,000 visitors in total. That year Dalhalla broke even. The cost of the Magic Flute was, according to budget, about 20 million SEK. A new roof was built for 8 million SEK. That roof, however, proved to be 'an acoustic disaster', condemned by several experts. Moreover, the annual administration costs approached the nine million level.

In late 2009, the CEO Håkan Ivarson publicly announced that he would leave after the following season. In 2011 operations halted on the whole, and Dalhalla had no opera performance at all. There was a concert version of Donizetti's L'Elisir d'amore, however it was entirely dependent on electronic amplification.

During 2012 both problems and positive things happened. The private company Rättvik Event, backed with a rich person from the gaming industry) bought most parts of Dalhalla in the spring. A lot of turbulence was behind the scenes of this. Göran Ericsson became new art manager at Dalhalla – and he loves opera! The programme during the summer, however, was mostly about popular music including heavy metal. And for example the event 16 June with James Morrisson had an 'embarrassingly small audience' according to one of the visitors. But also positive things happened: On 11 August a 'Dalhalla aid gala' was arranged with opera promotion as the main message. 'The plan', according to Dellefors, 'is to set up a new full-scale opera production in 2013'. Sedulous may win!

Despite everything: a brilliant creation

In summary, Sweden and the world got a new opera and music stage. Since its inauguration, several performances and concerts have taken place in Dalhalla. People have made pilgrimages there to be part of something they had never before experienced.

Rättvik and Dalarna got a new attraction that has strengthened the whole region. Over the years Dalhalla has been visited by about 100,000 people per year, to see about 25 different concerts or go on guided tours.

Dellefors received all kinds of prizes. She was awarded the title 'Entrepreneur of the Year' 2001 by the Confederation of Swedish Enterprise. That same year she received the medal 'Illis Quorum' from the Swedish Government for meritorious services. She received the King's Medal of the eighth magnitude in 2001. She was especially happy about the medal she received from the Musical Academy of Stockholm for 'classical music promotion.'

As late as 2010 Dalhalla was invited to participate in a major international exhibition of what can be done with quarries. The project was led by the internationally renowned architect and professor Vincezo Pavan. He wrote the following 28 October 2010 in an email to Dellefors:

> The exhibition in Verona was very good, and the project on quarries recoveries was appreciated by architects and also by other people. . . . Your project Dalhalla is always followed by architects, public administrators and also by the Italian press. I attach one page of Republica, the main newspaper in Italy, with an article about the exhibition, where Dalhalla is in evidence. In the catalogue you can see some quarries in Italy used for music and theatre spectacles, but nothing can be compared to Dalhalla, for cultural quality and precise organization. I hope this event in Verona will give a contribute for the operatic activities in Dalhalla.

It is worth noting that Pavan despite having a world-famous outdoor stage at home (Verona) considered Dalhalla as something truly original. He also pointed specifically to the artistic quality of Dalhalla and especially opera. Furthermore, the basic theme of his project was nature's interaction with human creations. In a magnificently illustrated work, coupled with the exhibition, Dalhalla got eight pages of space (Pavan 2010).

Part of what happened during the key years are summarized in Figure 15.2.

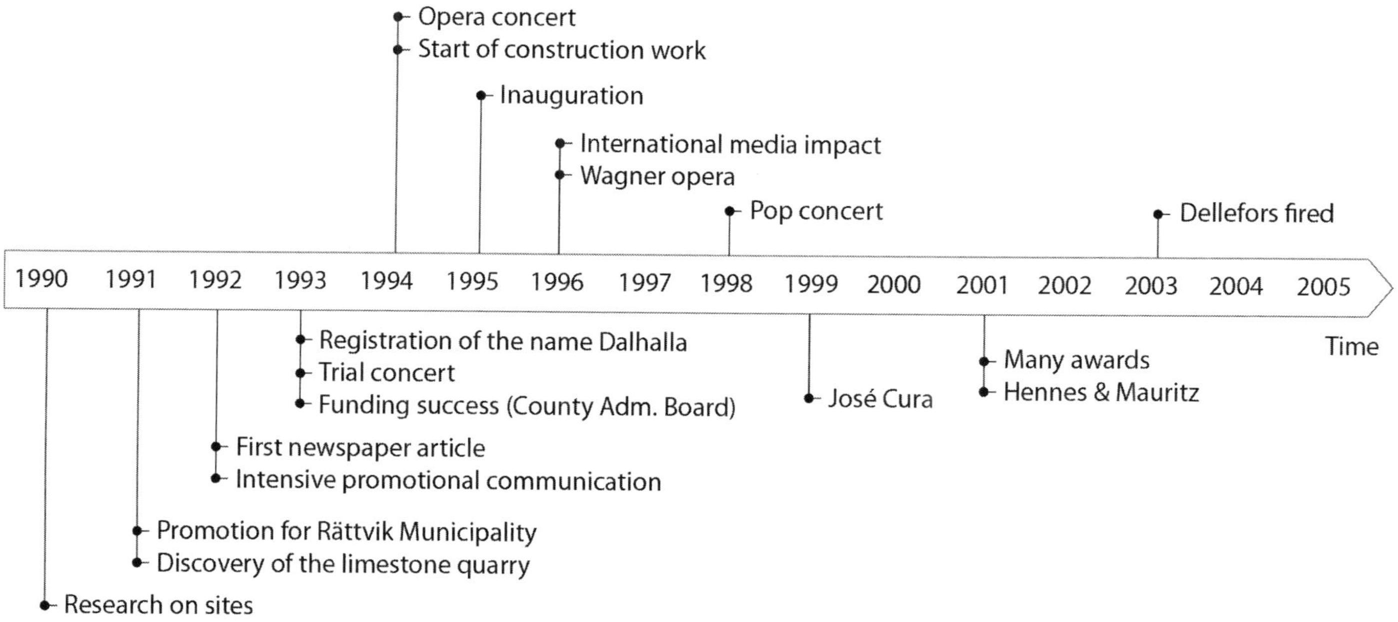

Figure 15.2 Overview of the Dalhalla creation process. (Note that important things also occurred after 2005, for example the Bronze statue 2006 and the Verona exhibition 2010, and the Dalhalla aid gala in 2012).

Discussion and conclusions

There are many learning points that can be derived from the case Dalhalla. One such is linked to the chapter introduction, where it was argued that nature can play a large role in art. Let's now dig a little deeper into the question of what I mean by nature in this context.

The essence of nature

Carl Linnæus, in his 'Systema Naturae' from 1735, spoke about nature in terms of three realms or kingdoms – rock (or mineral), plants and animals. But one could add both water kingdom and air kingdom. When it comes to water it has of course different guises and roles in relation to art. In the case Dalhalla water was important in the form of a lake and in the form of rainfall.

The reason for Dellefors' fascination with the place that came to be Dalhalla was its natural conditions. The mountain, with all its layers shifted in different pastel colours, was part of this. At least as interesting was the water in the form of the emerald green lake. In fact, this particular lake – in line with Dellefors' vision – was converted to become both lake and canal in front of the stage – is part of what makes Dalhalla so unique. Dellefors told how they took advantage of this natural resource:

> This natural flow has proved to be Dalhalla's main stenographic asset. When we did Wagner the water ditch was the Rhine. I Nebuchadnezzar it was the Euphrates River. In Aida it was the Nile. In the Flying Dutchman it was the water of the Norwegian coast. No stage has anything similar.

In particular there is a strong link between acoustics and nature. It's nature's materials and shapes – including water – which makes the acoustics of Dalhalla so extraordinary.

All around Dalhalla there are forests that contribute to the feeling that it is far out in the wild. Birdsong also makes a strong impression. Natural factors have been influential in two ways. First they inspired Dellefors' own innovative process. Second, nature has had an impact on all the visitors who came to Dalhalla.

As mentioned water plays a role not only by the lake. The uncertainty about whether or not it will rain is perhaps something that makes Dalhalla visits always feel a little exciting? Maybe it's the rain that makes us understand the contrast between the different weather conditions and why we get so excited when the evening sun casts its rays on us? Furthermore, attending concerts in the rain can also be positive. With the right clothes – and Dalhalla offers thousands of raincoats if needed – concerts in the rain can be very pleasant. The rain may in fact contribute to the drama and art experience.

I am now ready to define nature in the art context: Nature consists of specific sites with specific surroundings, and is made up by rock, plants, animals, water and air; and appears in different colours and shapes in a way that creates a specific acoustics and a special atmosphere.

Synthesis of art and nature: a model

The core of the Dalhalla case was an *innovative vision*. This vision was of a very specific kind. Through the case we can conclude that there was a strong link between art and nature in the innovative vision. The experience of Dalhalla, from a visitor's point of view, consists of a *combination of music, performing arts and nature*. This is the core of the model presented in Figure 15.3.

It has been shown that the phenomena I am talking about do not materialize by themselves. It requires entrepreneurship and it is, in particular about overcoming resistance and problems: *barriers*. They are of very different kinds.

The rocket fuel for making the innovative vision come true consists of *time resources*, *network resources* and not least *competence*. But overall, Dellefors' creation was boosted by her *dedication* to fulfilling the vision. By dedication I mean the act of binding oneself (intellectually and emotionally) to a course of action over a longer time period. Motivation is just a part of dedication, because it not always includes action, and because motivation also can be connected with small and temporal activities.

One of the important support processes is *continuous searching for opportunities*. While Herbert Simon (1945) argued that people are irrational because of lack of information, the Dalhalla case illustrates that lack of information is not an inflexible element.

Another support process is marketing. An important part of marketing is *verification* in early phases of innovative processes. Another phenomenon identified in the case is *relay race marketing*. That means one activity is marketed and that activity, after being fulfilled, in turn becomes a new marketing tool for further steps.

It has not escaped anybody's notice, that *economy management* was very important. In fact this is a vital support process to fulfil innovative visions like Dalhalla.

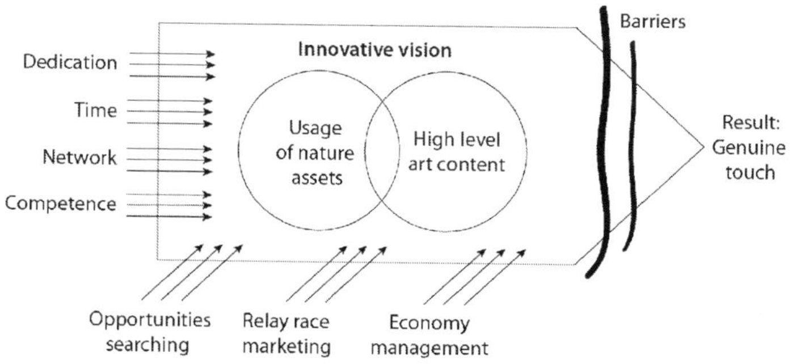

Figure 15.3 The Dalhalla Concept.

The result from the process has both positive and negative sides from the creator's point of view. In Figure 15.3 I focus on the positive side. The result became something original with *genuine touch*. Dellefors had the idea of letting what is genuine and true always come first. Instead of faking rivers as decoration, it was to be pure water. Instead of microphones and amplifiers voices were heard directly. When she and the architect designed the stage roof the preservation of the natural acoustics was the first and foremost criteria.

A concluding remark

There are many other optional perspectives one can use for analysing cases like Dalhalla. For an analysis on innovation aspects, for example, see Zander and Scherdin (2011). However, the philosopher Friedrich von Schelling may form the foundation for the completion of this chapter.

In his *System der Naturfilosophie* published 1799 the point of departure was the process of nature. Nature had, said Schelling, once begun with inanimate matter and then developed into the most amazing forms. Man was thus a manifestation of nature's process. According to Schelling, one can not logically speak in terms of 'man and nature' because man is a fully integrated part of nature. Among nature's top spectacular creations are man and his or her creativity at producing art and other things, according to Schelling.

Schelling saw nature as everything, and therefore culture (including art) was a subset of it.

References

Aristotle (335BC) *Poetics – Theory of Poetry and Fine Art* (translated by Samuel H. Butcher, Dover Publications, 1951).

Dellefors, M. (2008) *Dalhalla: Kampen för ett brott* (Dalhalla: The struggle for a quarry), Stockholm: Carlsson.

Frankelius, P. (1999) *Företagande över tid – Kontextuellt perspektiv och visuellt beskrivningsspråk* (Enterprise over Time – A Contextual Perspective and a Visual Language of Description) (Volume I of Doctoral Dissertation), Jönköping: Jönköping International Business School.

——— (2007) *Linné i nytt ljus – Den första översättningen av Systema Naturae samt ny analys av Linnés perspektiv* (Linnæus in a new light: The first translation of Systema Naturae and a new analysis of Linnæus perspective): trans. of Latin parts: Bertil Aldén, Malmö: Liber.

——— (2011) *'Sustainable Innovation: What Can We Learn from Linnæus and his Integration of Nature and Economy?'*, Research paper presented at the 56th Annual ISCB World Conference, Stockholm, Sweden, 15–18 June 2011.

Frankelius, P. and Vogel, O. (eds) (2009) *Värdeskapande möten* (Value-creating meetings), Malmö and Stockholm: Liber.

Kant, I. (1790; edition 2007) *Critique of Judgement* (translated by James Creed Meredith), Oxford: Oxford University Press (original title: *Kritik der Urteilskraft*).

Linnæus, C. (1734) *Iter Dalekarlicum* (The Dalarna Journey), New edition with eds A. Casson and J. Jacobsson, Stockholm: Gullers, 2007.

Martin, C. (2011) 'Art: Taking the Long View of Nature', *Nature*, 473(12 May): 152.

Pavan, V. (2010) *Architetture Di Cava (The Architecture of Quarries)*, Verona: VeronaFiere.

Pettitt, S. (1995) 'Dalhalla, Sweden', *Independent*, 29 June. Available at: www.independent.co.uk/arts-entertainment/music-dalhalla-sweden-1588865.html (accessed 11 December 2012).

Schelling von, F. (1799) *System der Naturfilosophie (The System of Nature Philosophy)*, Halle.

Simon, H. (1945) *Administrative Behaviour*, New York: Macmillan.

Zander, I. and Scherdin, M. (eds) (2011) *Art Entrepreneurship*, Cheltenham, UK and Northampton, MA, USA: Edward Elgar Publishing.

16 An innovation lost

The Ice Dome Concert Hall Project in Piteå

Hans Gelter and Jennie Gelter

Introduction

In a mode of amazement and anticipation I walk in the dark night along a snow path guided by candle lights behind beautifully designed ice blocks. I walk towards a huge snow structure shaped as a double-dome pile of snow. In itself not sensational, but now in the cold of subarctic northern Sweden, magically illuminated by a full moon above us, this snow-pile grows into a mystic world of the arctic. I open the wooden door and enter a strange magic world of snow and ice in different colourations of blue, turquoise and green, and I know I'm part of a very special cultural experience – a music concert on ice instruments in an ice dome concert hall! And when the ice-music begins we all know we are part of a very unique historical experience. It fills my heart with joy and excitement that our little township of Piteå in peripheral northern Europe has realized an artist's dream with this ice construction and unique concert. But how could Piteå end up having such an extraordinary experience production?

The story of the Ice Dome Concert Hall in Piteå is an amazing story of a man's innovative dream in a world of slow bureaucratic structural organizations of financing and project planning, ending up in the lost future of this extraordinary innovation.

Background

Since the establishment of the Icehotel™ in Jukkasjärvi in 1990, snow and ice as a resource for innovation in culture and tourism has been on many agendas in northern Scandinavia. The Icehotel has become one of Sweden's strongest trademarks beside Volvo and IKEA and is used as a raw model for cultural innovation within winter tourism and experience production. Despite the rhetorical high expectations on innovations from snow and ice, there have so far been only a limited number of true creative innovations developed based on snow and ice (Gelter 2008, 2010). Copycats using snow and ice within the original concept of igloos for living (i.e. ice hotels, snow hotels, igloo-villages), and transformations of these into snow chapels, snow/ice bars and snow/ice restaurants as well as snow castles in different shapes, are numerous

(Gelter 2010). The copycatting of the Icehotel is interesting as Sweden still only has one ice hotel while Norway has at least three and Finland at least seven (Gelter 2010), and the number is growing worldwide.

In arctic, subarctic and high altitude areas, winter markets and winter carnivals as well as snow and ice festivals based on snow and ice carving competitions and on art performances in winter settings are common (Gelter 2010). Besides these traditional cultural manifestations based on snow and ice, in Scandinavia we have only found three new innovative cultural projects based on snow and ice. These are the Ice Music Festival – Geilo, the Ice Globe Theatre in Jukkasjärvi and the Ice Dome Concert Hall in Piteå, of which the latter two did not develop into economically sustainable projects.

Regional development and innovation in the creative and cultural area is expected to occur according to a model of triple helix cooperation between the public, private and academic spheres (Etzkowitz and Lyedesdorff 1997; Leydesdorff and Etzkowitz 1998). This theoretical model has been used as a base for governmental and EU-founded projects and developed by the Swedish Knowledge Foundation (*KK-stiftelsen*) into a FUNK model for a professional development of 'cultural resources' into business (Nilsén 2006). FUNK stands for the Swedish words of *Forskning* (research), *Utbildning* (Education), *Näring* (Business) and *Kultur* (Culture). The model expects the organized cooperation of these four sectors to 'absorb' ideas and innovative initiatives as cultural raw material 'out there' in the cultural society, and through the processes of networking, cooperation and common projects to incubate and refine them into professional business. Although innovation has become a buzzword among politicians and decision-makers, and become a base for regional development strategies, empirical data for successful FUNK processes are still too rare to pinpoint success factors in regional development according to this model.

Maybe more interesting than learning from success stories such as the Icehotel, would be to learn from promising creative and innovative projects that did not succeed, and to identify factors and processes that prevented the innovation from becoming a success. So far research about innovations in the cultural and creative industry have not paid much attention to this research approach. This can be illustrated by the Ice Globe Theatre in Jukkasjärvi, where the Icehotel in a bold venture without any cultural or innovative funding built a copy of the Shakespeare Theatre in London out of snow and ice. This unique cross-border production, where completely different concepts are combined into a new, innovative concept for success, mixed classic Shakespeare theatre with Sami culture, snow and ice, cold climate and northern lights, into a fantastic experience concept, that however, did not develop into an economically sustainable production. So far no scientific analysis of this great cultural project has been conducted. The aim of this chapter is to present and analyse a similar innovative project that failed to become a success story for regional development: the story of the Ice Dome Concert Hall in Piteå.

Prelude to the Ice Dome Concert Hall

Innovative use of snow and ice in the cultural context is limited and most often restricted to snow constructions or as a stage for traditional cultural performances (Gelter 2008, 2010). An interesting cross-border innovation is to use ice and snow to produce music. There are only a few musicians in the world that use snow and ice for their music. One of the most famous is the Norwegian percussionist Terje Isungset (Isungset 2008a). Together with Bengt Carling he created a battery of ice instruments that performed on television for the whole world during the millennium New Year celebration. Fascinated by the potential of this music art, he constructed string instruments in snow, and produced a CD album of ice music, 'Iceman Is', recorded at the Icehotel in Jukkasjärvi (Isungset 2008b). A special recording studio was built in a room at the Icehotel with 1 m thick walls for sound isolation. Since then Isungset has performed in several ice music concerts around the world such as in Québec City, The Ice Globe Theatre in Jukkasjärvi, the Sapporo Snow Festival in Japan, in Helsinki, and in Narvik and Geilo in Norway. Ice music as an annual festival was established in 2006 at the Geilo Ice Music Festival. This unique festival is held annually at the first full moon in January at a frozen waterfall on the 1,930 m high mountain Hallingskarvet. The festival consists of music and dance performances inside and outside an ice igloo with instruments made from snow and ice (www.isfestival.no), and is dedicated to nature, as nature determines the conditions and date for the festival.

Ice music has the potential to become a cross-border cultural innovation unique for regions of snow and ice, such as northern Scandinavia. Ice music as a cultural phenomenon is, however, still mostly unknown. It also has yet to be accepted as 'real music', and is thus scientifically and artistically unexplored. In Sweden ice music started in 2003 when the Swedish Polar Research Secretariat held the SSW 2003 Arctic Science Summit Week in Kiruna between March and April 2003 (Polarsekretariatet 2008). As part of the conference programme 'Science as Art', an experiment was conducted as part of an empirical research project about ice music. The experiment was based on cooperation between the Swedish Polar Research Secretariat, the Royal College of Music in Stockholm and the ice sculpture artist Tim Linhart from New Mexico, USA. An ensemble of six musicians from the Royal College of Music, 'Voices of Ice', performed on ice instruments constructed by Linhart at the Ice Globe Theatre in Jukkasjärvi (Polarsekretariatet 2003). On 16 March, the ensemble performed a piece called 'Ice Music Fantasy for soprano, speaker, ice instruments and an audience with warm mittens' composed by Karin Rehnquist, and 'Of Ice and Frozen Circles' by Bill Brunson. The ensemble consisted of Gunilla von Bahr on flute, Ulrika Bodén vocals, Olle Hagson on contrabass, Jonny Axelsson on percussion, and Åsa Åkerberg and Susan Barett on cello. Two additional performances were given 1 and 2 April. To construct the ice instruments for these concerts, Tim Linhart had been working since the beginning of February. He used his own developed technique where he mixes fresh powder snow with water that he pastes together into instruments.

This ice instrument concert became a success. When, the same year, the Swedish Queen Silvia celebrated her 60th birthday on 23 December, she was invited by her family to stay overnight at the Icehotel in Jukkasjärvi. In association with this a performance of ice music was arranged at the Ice Bar in the Icehotel, with her favorite flute player Gunilla von Bahr (The Royalty Forum 2003). For this occasion Tim Linhart again built his ice string instruments, and again the performance was a success.

After these successes Tim Linhart decided to more actively establish ice music in Sweden, after his successful years in the USA. Tim Linhart constructed his first ice instrument in 1997 in the form of a 3 m high bass cello. He got the idea from his friend Luthier Tony Sutherland, a guitar builder, during a camping trip. They were talking over the campfire about how an ice violin would sound. After this Linhart became obsessed by the idea of ice instruments (Vail Daily 2005). Before then Linhart had been working as an ice sculptor in the Rocky Mountains. To get access to a free ski pass for the season at Taos Ski Valley, New Mexico, and to be able to be a 'ski bum', he created snow sculpture at the ski resort. During ten years of snow sculpturing he developed his own technique that extended the strength of snow constructions beyond the expected and he discovered thus a fantastic flexible construction material. This inspired Linhart to start building ice instruments and to dream of his ultimate snow construction – a fully functional airplane made out of snow and ice (personal communication)!

During his construction work of fantastic sculptures at the ski resort, he discovered the technique to mix fresh powder snow and water into 'slush', not unlike the technique of clay sculpting (Advice ibice 2008). With this technique he developed the skill to construct string instruments with walls only a few millimetres thick, but strong enough not to break under the pressure of the strings. The biggest challenge was to tune the string instruments without breaking the fragile snow constructions. An additional challenge is the influence of the heat from the musician and the audience during a concert, as a change in temperature quickly alters the tuning of the ice instruments.

Linhart's first instrument was the 3 m bass cello with piano strings. He waited with excitement for the first tone, which sounded like sweet music, but after adjusting the strings a bit more the next sound was a loud bang and the instrument exploded into a thousand pieces. But Linhart was captured by his idea and decided to build the world's first ice orchestra, and coined the word 'Ice Lutherie' for building music instruments of ice. During the winter of 2000 Linhart built an igloo on top of Beaver Creek at an elevation of 3,500 m. Here he constructed five instruments, and hired Colorado's Symphony Orchestra to perform an ice music concert in a excavated amphitheatre in the snow, claimed to be the first in the world. During 2001 there was an ice music festival at Taos Ski Valley with the name 'Fiddling While Rome Burns' that resulted in one of the first ice music CD recordings, called 'Kiss My Ice Music'. It included music from Mozart to 'Ice Cello Blues' (Vail Daily 2005). Although these ice music concerts were successful and attracted nationwide media attention in the USA, Linhart could not find financiers to continue to develop his ideas about ice music. Therefore the invitation from the Swedish Polar Research Secretariat in 2003 made it possible for him to continue his work. Before the conference in Kiruna, Linhart visited Gunilla von Bahr at the Royal College of Music in Stockholm, to learn about playing the flute in order to be able to develop ice flutes. Ice flutes together with ice percussion instruments complemented his earlier developed ice string instruments. The concerts at the Icehotel in Jukkasjärvi ended with the recording of the CD 'Voice of Ice', which also included the traditional Sami music style joik, together with ice instruments. Inspired by the attention Linhart received in Sweden, he continued with his next bold idea – to build a 54-pipe organ completely out of snow and ice!

During his instrument construction time at the Icehotel, Linhart met the Swedish snow- and rock sculptor Birgitta Johansson, whom he later married. To fulfil his dream of constructing a full scale organ, he needed to learn about organ construction. Luckily the organ building company *Grönlunds Orgelbyggeri*, was located in Birgitta's home town Luleå. Tim Linhart managed to persuade Yngve Bergkvist, the founder of the Icehotel, to let Linhart continue to build ice instruments at the Icehotel, including an ice organ. Yngve Bergkvist being fully occupied with the success of the Ice Globe Theatre, did not pay too much attention to this and let Linhart do his construction work in an extension area to the Ice Bar in the Icehotel. Bergkvist also agreed to give Linhart free board, but no salary. Linhart started his work by spending two weeks in Luleå to learn how to construct an organ. *Grönlunds Orgelbyggeri* provided Linhart with copper pipes in different sizes as templates for the ice pipes of the organ. Around the pipes Linhart packed his 'slush' snow to form ice pipes. The workers at the organ company were sceptical to the whole idea at first, but when they heard the sound after blowing air through an ice pipe they changed their minds and became enthusiastic. Linhart then spent three months in Jukkasjärvi to construct the 54 pipes. After a while he acquired an assistant Daniel Rosenbaum from Australia, who was a trainee at the Icehotel.

This whole unique project of constructing a full scale organ in snow and ice was initiated solely by a visionary artist and got no attention or funding during the three months of construction. To survive, Linhart luckily had a sponsor in the USA that was fascinated by Linhart's visions and provided finance for travelling and other costs. Before starting his construction work, Linhart contacted the School of Music in Piteå at the Luleå University of Technology, as the School of Music which is the most northern in Europe, has a famous organist Professor Hans-Ola Ericsson. The School of Music promised to arrange the concert production and provide musicians and the school's media department was to document the concert with sound and film recordings. The School of Music was unprepared for this request, however, as it came in the middle of a school term, and the whole concert production had to be hastily organized by student and teacher volunteers. Planning courses and major activities such as concerts, usually take a long time in the academic world.

During the last weeks before the concert both students and teachers became involved in the construction of the concert room at the Icehotel. It became a race against time where about a dozen volunteers from the School of Music were involved in the construction and preparation work. After three months of hard work for Linhart the organ was ready for a concert on April. That evening two concerts were performed for an audience of about 450 people. After the evening the wonder that was the ice organ was allowed to melt away and return to the Torne River.

The ice music for the concert was composed by Jan Ferm, the organ was played by Professor Hans-Ola Ericsson and the other ice instruments were played by students from the School of Music in Piteå. The concert as well as the composition of the ice music was themed by an experience production student Jennie Lindström (now Gelter) based on the interaction of arctic mythology, the northern lights and the sounds of ice music (Lindström 2004). The theme was the 'Re-emergence of Ymer in the shape of the ice organ'. The storytelling of 'how the Ice giant Ymer emerged from snow and ice and together with the northern wind Bore creates the mystic music of snow and ice' formed the basis for the music compositions, improvisations, lighting of the instruments and concert area as well as the costumes of the musicians. The compositions by Ferm were called 'Improvisation on Ymer', 'Awaiting Ymer's re-emergence', 'The dance of Aurora Borealis', 'Ymer's re-emergence' and 'Snow and Ice'. In addition Hans-Ola played 'Improvisation on snow and ice' and 'Improvisation on the cold'. This world unique concert was much appreciated by the audience as well as by the musicians; as all understood that a similar concert would probably never occur again. It was a once in a lifetime experience!

The whole ice organ project is interesting from an innovation and regional development perspective, as it was a kind of inverted FUNK-process. Here a visionary artist by himself initiated and almost 'forced' research and education (School of Music in Piteå) and business (Icehotel and Grönlunds) into a development project, instead of, according to the FUNK-model, a public organization based on FUNK-partners refine a cultural idea to make it into an innovative business success.

Although the project through the two concerts was an experiential success, in economic terms it was financially unsuccessful, or even a disaster. The stakeholders (the Icehotel, the School of Music and the artist Linhart) committed considerable resources, while the revenues due to modest concert fees from the two concerts were minimal. In addition, the media attention, which could have compensated the limited economic returns by its attention value, was also limited, consisting of only small notices in the local press. Again this was due to the lack of a professional organization (within FUNK) for media promotion that could see and promote the unique innovation potential of the project. One important practical lesson from the two concerts at the Icehotel was that the design of the concert room was not adapted for the ice instruments in close proximity to the audience. During the second concert the tuning and sound of both the organ and ice instruments started to drift due to heat from the audience in the restricted area. Linhart concluded that lack of ventilation in traditional igloos is not suitable for ice music concerts. He quickly developed a new visionary idea – a special constructed Ice Dome Concert Hall (Figure 16.1).

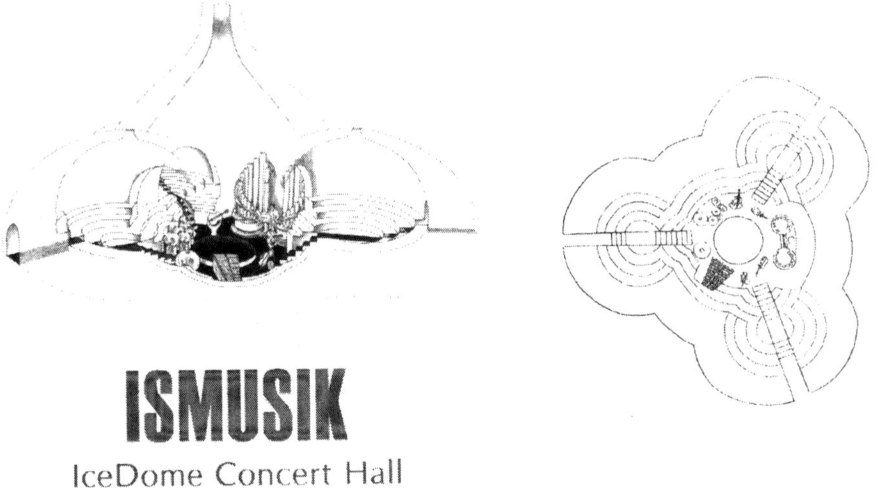

Figure 16.1 Vision of the Ice Dome Concert Hall, drawing by Tim Linhart (with permission from Linhart).

From Icehotel to Ice Lab and Concert Hall

At the evaluation meeting of the project with the stakeholders, Linhart presented his idea about a concert hall in snow and ice. After the economical troubles with the Ice Globe Theater at the Icehotel, Yngve Bergkvist was not interested in another risky project. We (Gelter 2007) therefore suggested taking the concept to the School of Music in Piteå in the form of an 'IceLab', where music students can be trained on ice instruments and research and development in ice music and ice concerts can be conducted before a full scale concert hall was constructed. Everyone at the meeting agreed that the natural place for an Ice Dome Concert Hall was in association with the world's most northern School of Music. Our vision was that the IceLab would develop the concept during some years and then a magnificent Ice Dome Concert Hall would be built on the sea ice outside the resort Piteå Havsbad, to become an attraction complementing the Icehotel in Jukkasjärvi. The resort Piteå Havsbad had initiated a process of developing winter activities called '*Winter Wonderland*', and the municipality of Piteå had just started a winter festival '*Vinter I Piteå*' (Winter in Piteå). Developing ice music at the School of Music in Piteå would fit perfectly into these development processes and make the destination a world class winter attraction. The trio of the LumiLinna Snowcastle of Kemi by the Gulf of Bothnia in northern Finland, the Icehotel in Jukkasjärvi and the Ice Dome Concert Hall in Piteå would create a common attraction for unique winter experiences in Northern Scandinavia. As the CEO of Piteå Havsbad as well as the representatives for Piteå Municipality and the School of Music in Piteå were enthusiastic about this innovative development concept, this emerged as a perfect opportunity for a triple helix process according to the FUNK-model for local and regional development.

The Ice Concert Hall at the School of Music in Piteå 2005

During the spring of 2004 meetings were held in Piteå to plan for developing the IceLab in the shape of a larger igloo where Tim Linhart could construct his ice instruments. At the School of Music in Piteå discussions were initiated about which courses could be involved in the IceLab. The enthusiasm among music teachers and most music students was, however, subdued as 'ice music' was outside the box of traditional music education and music culture. This was also expressed by Linhart stating that 'Musicians are among the most difficult to sell the concept of ice music to'.

After a period of local lobbying in Piteå, an informal and loose cooperation emerged between the School of Music and the Municipality of Piteå with its division Culture and Leisure as the coordinator (Lenndin 2004). Despite the innovative approach of the project, neither the development organization for the experience economy, MUIP (*Mötesplats Upplevelseindustrin I Piteå*, Meeting Place for the Experience Industry, Piteå) an organization sponsored by the Swedish Knowledge Foundation (*KK-stiftelsen*), nor other development agencies engaged in the project. As with the musicians, most people did not take ice music and ice instruments seriously, and could not see the cultural and touristic potential of this development project.

So only a limited budget of 105,000 SEK (approx. € 10,700) was raised by the Municipality of Piteå, Piteå Havsbad and School of Music in Piteå, through course resources within the education programme of Experience Production. None of the music courses actively engaged in the project. Tim Linhart was hired by the municipality, and was also invited to be a guest teacher to educate about snow constructions and ice music for students at the Experience Production programme. The Municipality of Piteå also provided a trainee to help Linhart with snow sculpting in the city's centre and at Piteå Havsbad, as a small compensation. The deal with the School of Music was that Linhart together with students from Experience Production would construct some ice instruments to be performed at a concert during the 'Vinter-i-Piteå' festival between 23 and 27 February 2005. Piteå Municipality also arranged a freezing room to preserve the ice instruments for coming years, and together with personnel from Piteå Havsbad, ice blocks were harvested from Piteå River for the instruments, and 60 m^3 of snow was piled up for an igloo construction at the School of Music.

Linhart accepted these offerings and started to negotiate with the Icehotel to rent a balloon they use in constructing their snow igloos. Instead the Icehotel offered to sell Linhart a balloon with a 8 m diameter and a height of 4.5 m that they did not need any more. With resources from his sponsor in the USA Linhart bought this balloon and together with his trainee started to construct his Ice Concert Hall in the form of a double igloo, instead of the planned single igloo for the 'IceLab'. Instead of fiddling around for some years with students and researchers, Linhart developed his own plans of a full scale ice music concert, based on his extensive experience in this field. This new turn surprised everyone associated with the development project who quickly had to adjust to the new conditions. Instead of teaching and learning about snow construction and concept development for ice music concerts, the Experience Production students were engaged by Linhart in the construction of the snow concert hall. The double igloo was constructed for an audience of 100 people with the ice instruments in the centre, and the seating elevated around so the heat from the audience would not reach the ice instruments. To lead the heat away from the instruments a hole was made in the roof.

Due to the informal arrangement of the development project, a plan and organization was again lacking for organizing the concerts, as well as how the music teachers and students would be involved and prepared for the concert. As the whole concert hall emerged premature to the plans of a slow development project through the concept of an IceLab, nobody was leading this new development into a full-scale concert hall and ice music concert. The Culture and Leisure department of the municipality of Piteå could only manage the manpower and machinery to provide snow and ice for the construction work, while teachers at the Experience Production programme due to lack of time and resources, only could inspire their students to engage in the project outside their courses. As the date for the concert approached, Linhart became more and more upset about the limited involvement by the School of Music, and threatened to bring up music students and teachers from the Royal College of Music in Stockholm that were involved in the concert for the queen at the Icehotel. So a few days before the concert some voluntary students from the School of Music in Piteå became involved and started to practise on the ice instruments, and a programme of two concerts with different music styles was planed. Media students were again engaged to film the concert and sound engineer students record them. This time, due to lack of time during the school term and a lack of extracurricular work, no experienced production students were involved in the concert production.

The first concert was held at midnight on 26 February 2005, and was according to the local press a magical experience with an excited audience. The concert was limited to 40 minutes in order to limit the amount of heat in the igloo. The second concert was held the next day on a Sunday afternoon and was rigged for filming and sound recording. Having not been properly acknowledged for his work, Linhart, within minutes of its start, abruptly stopped the concert. His motivation was that the quality of the music was too poor, as the music students had not practised on the instruments long enough. This became big news within the music world around the globe and the project suddenly received global media attention. Linhart's action resulted in a strong reaction from the project coordinator at the municipality who fired Linhart directly and the dean at the School of Music broke all formal cooperation with Linhart, and at the same time defended his students as being just students and not yet professional musicians. This resulted in a catastrophe for the whole development project, and at a crisis meeting with all the stakeholders, Gelter suggested that the Experience Production students association (UPAP) should take over the Ice Dome Concert Hall to continue all the work that had been invested in the project. The municipality that formally owned the concert hall and the ice instruments agreed to the proposal, as well as the dean of the School of Music.

Together with Linhart the students continued to plan for an additional six concerts in association with a small snow festival called '*Snöyran*' that the students created, to be held during the Easter holidays 25–27 March in the same year. Linhart invited professional musicians from southern Sweden and abroad to play together with some music students from the School of Music in Piteå that had become interested in ice music. At these concerts the ice instruments consisted of an ice xylophone, bubble drums, ice cello, ice guitars, ice trumpets and the world's first violin in ice played by Sofia Csakany from Romania. In addition, experimental organ pipes were played by Christina Rödder from Germany. On Good Friday two blues concerts were planned, on Easter Eve two concerts with modern music mixed with folk music and on Easter Sunday the festival was planned to end with two classical music concerts. On Easter a church service was also planned in the concert igloo as well as children's activities for families organized outside the igloo by the students. Unfortunately unusually warm weather with 10° C caused problems with the instruments, and the wet snow and slush outdoors caused by the sunny weather did not attract families to the planned activities. Nor did the concerts fill up the concert hall igloo. There were only 50 people at the first concert and the following concerts also had only a few visitors. So, once again the concerts barely covered the costs for salaries and Linhart himself paid for the musician's travel expenses out of his own pocket. The festival arrangement was also an economical disaster for the UPAF as the costs for the festival exceeded the returns.

The Ice Dome Concert Hall at Piteå Havsbad

After these two less successful attempts, the Ice Dome Concert Hall in Piteå could have been put to an end. But the business development office at Piteå Municipality now regarded the project as so unique and innovative that the experience and knowledge gained during the Ice Dome project shouldn't go to waste. Therefore, they again contacted the CEO at Piteå Havsbad who also saw the Ice Dome Concert Hall as a potential attraction for international guests during the low winter season. The Ice Dome Concert Hall could become a complement to their main winter attraction, the icebreaker Arctic Explorer, which attracts about 2,000 international visitors annually. These two stakeholders agreed upon a test project to be conducted in the first year in order to learn the construction process, and then a full scale production in the second year. Linhart now intended to build the ice concert hall according to his original plans (Figure 16.1), a three dome igloo for the audience surrounding a central 15 m high onion shaped dome for the ice instruments with a 'chimney' to conduct the heat from the audience out of the hall. Linhart immediately prepared for this next step by sewing the onion shaped balloon at a hot-air balloon factory. During a kick-off meeting between Piteå Municipality, Piteå Havsbad and snow construction researchers from the Luleå University of Technology, it was decided due to safety reasons and the lack of empirical data on such snow constructions, that Linhart's vision of the concert hall would not be built the first year. To Linhart's disappointment the stakeholders instead agreed upon building a four-igloo dome with the capacity for 200 concert guests. But due to the lack of the central onion shaped heat-chimney, only 150 guests at a 45 minute concert were allowed.

It was decided that Piteå Havsbad would coordinate the project, and they invested 500,000 SEK, and Piteå Municipality invested another 100,000 SEK for the construction work. The aim was not to make a profit the first year, but rather to learn the construction process. By freezing the ice instruments in a freezer they could be preserved for the next season, thus speeding up the construction phase. The original idea to put the concert hall on the sea ice was abandoned due to construction problems in association to the changing sea level and sea ice conditions. Eleven professional musicians where hired from Sweden and Switzerland as well as music students from the School of Music in Piteå. Six concerts were performed during an ice music festival at Piteå Havsbad 16–19 April, 2006. During the opening concert 120 guests experienced the exotic music event and in total 850 gusts visited the ice music festival. The concept created a great amount of interest and the Munich symphony orchestra, as well as the rock band KraftWerk, were interested in giving concerts in the coming season.

In evaluating the costs in relation to the income from the concerts, the owner of Piteå Havsbad suddenly decided not to continue the project unless external funding could be guaranteed. They did not want to make the same financial mistake as the Icehotel did with the Ice Globe Theatre in Jukkasjärvi, and did not have the patience to wait for the long-term indirect financial returns of a developing winter season attraction.

End of the Ice Dome Concert Hall story in Sweden

During evaluation meetings with stakeholders in the spring and summer of 2006 where the future of the project and different funding options were discussed, Linhart perceived a diminished interest in his ideas among the stakeholders in Piteå as well as a problem with the limited winter season due to weather conditions at the coast of Swedish Lapland. During that summer Linhart took a road trip through central Europe to find a new location and new sponsors for his concert hall and ended up in Schnalstal in northern Italy. Next to the mountain hotel Granwand at 3,000 m elevation on top of the Val Senales glacier, Linhart started to construct a new Ice Dome Concert Hall, only 500 m from the mountain cable car station. Here Linhart constructed probably the world's largest man-made glacier cave by filling a natural hole in the glacier with man-made snow covering his 23 m high central onion shaped cupola and side igloos according to his original plans (Figure 16.1). The whole Ice Dome Concert Hall was thus completely buried in the glacier. At this high altitude location the concert hall can be in use the year round. With the help of a refrigerated truck Linhart took the ice instruments from previous concerts in Piteå preserved in the freezer room, to his new concert hall in Italy. The new Ice Concert Hall in Schnalstal opened on

18 February 2007 and was used for some years. But again the artist and the stakeholders disagreed on different issues, this time about the safety of the construction, and all future concerts were cancelled. Today the world's largest man-made 'cave' still remains in the glacier, but is closed for visitors. After an attempt in 2010 to establish the Ice Dome Concert Hall as an attraction at Beaver Creek ski resort in Colorado, where 77 concerts were given for audiences totalling 10,000 people, the concerts were successful but the investors did not see the greatness of the project. Linhart is now back in Sweden, trying to convince the Municipality of Luleå, north of Piteå, to take up his dream.

Conclusions and reflections on the project

What can we learn from this story about the Ice Dome Concert Hall in Piteå? Like the Ice Globe Theatre in Jukkasjärvi, the Ice Dome Concert Hall was a spectacular and innovative development project suitable for the far north of Scandinavia. Both of these projects contributed to the development of the cultural sector in a new and innovative way, using the unique local resources available in northern Sweden, such as snow, ice and cold. Both of these cross-border projects were therefore unique in their combination of traditional culture (theatre and music) with snow and ice, resulting in an exotic experience.

Unlike the Ice Globe Theatre that has so far not been scientifically described and analysed, we now have the historical record of the Ice Dome Concert Hall by the authors' close association to the project. A descriptive analysis is of course not enough to get the whole picture of the project, but can function as a starting point for further analysis, such as stakeholder analysis, experience outcome analysis, artistic analysis etc. of the project. But the main goal of this study is to try to pinpoint the importance of analysing innovative projects that despite a potential high impact value on local and regional development, still fail. Identifying factors and processes that lead to the failure of the process may teach us to avoid these traps in future similar projects.

Despite any deeper analysis of the Ice Globe Theatre, one apparent common factor for the failure of the two projects was the economic sustainability of these projects. As the production costs for advanced snow constructions are high, the season short and the number of audience members at each performance restricted, the return on the investment becomes a critical factor. Unlike other 'fine arts' projects and facilities in the cultural sector in Sweden, these two projects had no cultural funding from the government. Nor had they any external risk capital, EU-funding or other support other than the local stakeholders. The physical restrictions and the short season limit the total number of guests that can attend such productions. Thus if the admission fees alone have to cover the production costs they would have to be considerably higher than the modest ticket prices that were charged. This implies that these kinds of ice concerts should be regarded as very exclusive and expensive experiences and marketed and priced accordingly. Exclusive experiences, however, create high expectations of the artistic performance (far beyond music students), high quality concert productions and design. But the measure of success cannot just be determined financially, such as the return on investment of construction costs. Indirect gains by such projects may, for example, be an increased number of hotel nights and thus an extension of the tourism season for stakeholders such as Piteå Havsbad, as well as new categories of tourists to the destination. For the municipality and the destination of Piteå and Swedish Lapland, the value of a world class attraction and 'Unique Selling Point' (USP) will be difficult to measure economically.

From a triple helix perspective we can learn that from the stakeholders' point of view, 'crazy' ideas from artists and others have to be processed in a professional way into commercial production. Here the FUNK-model (Nielsén 2006) on a theoretical basis could be one way to execute this, but then there needs to be a synchronized FUNK-organization in place to extract good ideas and process them into innovative development projects. Neither in Jukkasjärvi or Piteå was there such an infrastructure to manage the innovative cultural development processes. Such an organization must have the preparedness, resources, knowledge and interest to engage in such processes. As the situation was in Piteå, neither the university (School of Music), the municipality of Piteå, or the private stakeholders (Piteå Havsbad) had the financial and manpower resources to manage the Ice Dome Concert Hall project in a full scale and professional way. Without a project management organization and proper resources, any project is likely to fail. As the stakeholders were dependent on external financing, such as EU-funding, and the Academy was dependent on resources for research and artistic development, such funding processes that have an extensive application and decision-making process for funding approval, they are therefore not suitable for a quick absorption and processing of innovative suggestions from driven artists and entrepreneurs.

This leads to the third lesson from the project. Innovators such as artists and entrepreneurs have limited patience with the slow processes of investigation, planning, and testing ideas, which is a common procedure in triple helix processes. In both the ice organ project and the Ice Concert Hall project the artist was pushing the project without taking the time to lay the ground work of his ideas among the stakeholders. He wanted quickly to fulfil his visions and ideas. The sceptical attitude in the academic world of 'crazy ideas' such as ice instruments and onion-shaped concert hall constructions, despite their extensive and long time praxis of development, and the academic need to 'test' and scientifically learn before going into business, was thus in contrast to Linhart's extensive practical experience of ice and snow constructions. He didn't need to test his ideas in an IceLab as he knew by praxis that they would work, and he wanted to express his art form – ice music – as quickly as possible in full scale concerts as he had been doing this for decades. Here also different cultures clashed, such as the meeting of the 'American action culture' with the 'Swedish negotiation and meeting culture', as well as the meeting of the impatient innovative entrepreneur with the slow administrative institutions.

Also the business stakeholders, here Piteå Havsbad, have a limited patience in testing and developing without proper financing, as the return on investment is often a demand of sustainable business. In tourism and the cultural field, businesses rarely have resources for research and developmental testing. Both the Icehotel and Piteå Havsbad withdrew from the concert hall project as they didn't see the economical profit in engaging in the development process. This could have been compensated if business developing agencies took an active financial role in the development and testing process. Again slow bureaucratic processes in such agencies, such as in project applications, may have hindered their direct involvement in this development project. Thus our conclusion is that a better pro-activity on the part of business developing agencies and other stakeholders in triple helix cooperation for development of the cultural sector is strongly needed in order to be able to catch and process 'crazy' and exciting innovative projects without too long application and administrative processes. Instead of waiting for such slow processes among the triple helix stakeholders (academy, municipality and company), Linhart took his idea, his knowledge and entrepreneurial drive and left the country of bureaucratic meetings to find better grounds to develop his artistic ideas. At the same time the idea of an annual international ice music festival was taken over by Geilo in Norway. Thus Piteå, Swedish Lapland and Sweden lost the opportunity to develop and refine a unique and interesting cultural innovation based on cross-bordering music and snow and ice.

References

Advice ibice (2008) Available at: http://adviceibice.com/main3.cfm?idEDC716B9-1372-5A65-3B4DC8A9089F4988 (accessed 20 February 2008).

Etzkowitz, H. (2003) 'Innovation in Innovation: The Triple Helix of University – Industry – Government Relations', *Social Science Information*, 42(3): 293–337.

——— (2008) *The Triple Helix: University-Industry-Government Innovation*, London: Routledge.

Etzkowitz, H. and Lyedesdorff, L. (eds) (1997) *Universities and the Global Knowledge Economy. A Triple Helix of University – Industry – Government Relations*, London: Routledge.

Gelter, H. (2004) *Projekt: Gestaltning av Piteå vinterstad i snö och is*, Projekt Piteå Tillväxtråd Handel, Turism & Arrangemang 2004-10-18.

——— (2007) *Evenemangsforskning för hållbar evenemangsturism – IceLab och TestLab Acusticum*, CTU-rapport, Luleå: Luleå tekniska universitet.

——— (2008) 'Snow and Ice as a Resource for Innovative Tourist Experiences in Northern Sweden, the Case of Ice Theatre and Ice Music Hall', in M. Breitling (ed.), *Proceedings TTL The Vienna Symposium on Polar Tourism – Contribution of TU Wien to the International Polar Year 2007–2009*, TTL Technology, Tourism, Landscape TU Interfaculty Cooperation Centre, Vienna University of Technology.

——— (2010) *IglooEvents och IglooCamps. Resurs för innovative vinterupplevelser och säsongsförlängning av traditionella sommardestinationer, såsom Norrbottens skärgård*, Projektrapport 2010-01-10, Piteå: Mötesplats Upplevelseindustrin i Piteå.

Icefestival (2008). Available at: www.icefestival.no (accessed 20 February 2008).

Icemusic (2008). Available at: www.icemusic.de/mainTim.html (accessed 20 February 2008).

Isungset, T. (2008a) *Iceman*. Available at: http://home.online.no/~isungz/ (accessed 20 February 2008).

——— (2008b) *Iceman Is*. Available at: http://home.online.no/~isungz/is.htm (accessed 20 February 2008).

Lenndin, P. (2004) *PM: Projekt: Gestaltning av Piteå vinterstad i snö och is*, P; 2004-12-21 Piteå Kommun, Kultur och Fritid.

Leydesdorff, L. and Etzkowitz, H. (1998) 'The Triple Helix as a Model for Innovation Studies', *Science and Public Policy*, 25(3): 195–203.

Lindström, J. (2004) *Isorgelkonsert, Icehotel. Isorgelprojekt*, Utbildningen Upplevelse-produktion, LTU, 2004-02-10.

Nielsén, T. (2006) *FUNK, En tillväxtmodell för upplevelseindustrin*, Stockholm: Stiftelsen för Kunskaps- och Kompetensutveckling.

Polarsekretariatet (2003) Available at: www.polar.se/assw/infofiles/Pressmeddelande%201.pdf (accessed 20 February 2008).

——— (2008) Available at: www.polar.se/assw (accessed 20 February 2008).

The Royalty Forum (2003) Available at: www.theroyalforums.com/forums/f185/queen-silvias-60th-birthday-celebrations-december-2003-a-1506.html (accessed 20 February 2008).

Vail Daily (2005) Available at: www.vaildaily.com/article/20050219/NEWS/102190011 (accessed 20 February 2008).

17 'Finding the Spiritus Loci'

Cultural planning in the Kronoberg Region

Lars Lindkvist, Erica Månsson, Sunny Sandström and Lisa Öberg

Introduction

In Sweden, cultural policy has mainly been built on the national cultural policy objectives and has been separated from other political areas. In Kronoberg County, southern Småland in Sweden, the politicians felt that art and culture should be seen as a part of regional development as a whole. They also wanted to establish a broader concept of culture than the traditional view of culture as art. The questions the politicians posed were: how do we support culture in the right way and in the right place? Where are the known and unknown cultural resources?

Critics of cultural policy point out that the traditional cultural policy within art and cultural institutions has failed to integrate with other, more highly prioritized, areas of politics and planning. These areas include education, health, housing, environment, employment, transport and communication and other social aspects of land use and development. The cultural planning method is basically that of the social planner and its point of departure is to look from a bottom-up perspective at which cultural resources can be found in the city/municipality/region and how they can be used to develop the area and strengthen its identity. In Kronoberg County the entire process from analysis to strategy has been completed and the county works according to the integrated cultural strategy. Culture was previously used as a perspective to develop tourism, but as a result of the cultural planning model culture is also used to develop social care, infrastructure, trade and industry. Our claim in this chapter is that the cultural planning method has been proven to be useful for regional development in Kronoberg and could be used in other places and regions as well. It is about finding something unique that can then be developed to increase the dynamics in the region/place.

Kronoberg County is made up of eight municipalities with a total of 182,000 inhabitants. The county is characterized by small-scale industry, agriculture and woodland, low unemployment and a high degree of self-sufficiency. A large proportion of the region's businesses are small companies – 75 per cent have fewer than 25 employees. Migration, in particular of young people, takes place from the countryside to the city. At the same time the county is affected by an ever faster changing society and there are increasing demands for greater input from citizens. The need for more flexible forms of organization is increasing and in the region there are divergent political opinions on the scale of public financing for cultural policy. This resulted in a question of how to find new cultural expressions and regional development in Kronoberg.

The fact that cultural planning focuses on the place, has a bottom-up perspective and sees culture as a part of the development of a place, fitting in well with the political ambitions from the perspective of regional development. Cultural planning crosses the boundaries between the public sector, the private market and civil society. It connects art and culture with just about all parts of the political sphere. This way of working also includes a strong desire to counteract social exclusion, a question that seems more pressing in England and the US but which also affects certain areas of Scandinavia. The method also strongly emphasizes the citizen's perspective.

There are other examples of municipalities and regions/counties in Sweden (including Gothenburg, Malmö, Uppsala and Lund) that have been inspired by cultural planning, but none of them have completed the careful survey that is a basic requirement for the application of the model. Kronoberg County is the first in Sweden to do so.

Cultural planning thus builds not on the idea of 'culture as art' but on a wide range of cultural resources. In Kronoberg cultural planning included:

- art, media activities and cultural institutions;
- culture among young people, ethnic minorities and other special interest groups;
- cultural heritage, including archaeology, gastronomy, local dialects and rituals;
- local and external notions of a place, as expressed in jokes, songs, literature, myths, tourist guides, depictions in the media and traditional wisdom;
- the natural and built environments, including public and open spaces;
- the variety and quality of leisure facilities, food and drink, entertainment and cultural activities;
- the range of local products and talents in handicrafts, production and services.

Culture as a factor in regional development

The cultural aspect of local and regional development work has long been discussed and the Inquiry on Cultural Policy in Sweden has now launched the concept of 'aspect policy' for this more comprehensive view of culture that spans sectors. Cultural planning is an example of aspect policy and in short is about mapping cultural resources in a broader sense, using both quantitative and qualitative methods. That which is found to be unique can then be developed to provide greater dynamics in the area.

The background is that in 2005 the Swedish Arts Council, the National Archives, the Swedish National Heritage Board and the Swedish Film Institute completed a study to establish which roles are assigned to culture in regional development programmes (Kulturrådet 2005). The study emphasizes the following roles: culture as an experience industry, living environment, business, profiling and marketing and finally as a developer of creativity. Foghagen and Johansson (2007) point out that the goals of cultural programmes are unclear because qualitative effects, such as the effects on living environments, are mixed with quantitative effects, such as an expansion of the experience industry. It is also difficult to determine the long-term effects of cultural and development programmes as there are no reliable ways to measure these effects.

The KRUS Project (Culture in Regional Development Strategies) draws the following conclusions regarding the role of culture and its value for regional development in Sweden during the 2000s.

- The concept of culture is rarely defined, but culture is generally seen as a positive factor in terms of development.
- Cultural environment and cultural heritage are said to be significant for development and growth, while the cultural infrastructure within the liberal arts, museums and libraries are not equally emphasized.
- Compared to sustainable growth, the role of culture and its value is vaguely defined. Furthermore, a certain shift has taken place compared to the amount of value with which culture is accredited in the regional growth programmes from the period 2003–2006. Issues of diversity and entrepreneurship are now of increased importance (Remmare 2008).

Johannisson (2006) makes a distinction between the *aesthetic* and the *anthropological* concept of culture. The concept of culture has broadened, from what was in the beginning an aesthetic view that primarily encompassed the traditional arts: music, literature, the visual arts, architecture and the study of its practitioners, to an anthropological view that includes the ways of life of different individuals and groups. The anthropological view includes for example religion, science, politics, clothes and food. During the 1970s and 1980s, according to Johannisson (2006), two other aspects developed: the *sociological* and the *instrumental* concept of culture. The sociological view has freedom as its goal. The instrumental, or *market-oriented* view as Johannisson prefers to call it, sees culture as a way of achieving economic growth. The purpose of culture, according to this definition, is to function as a competitive advantage for geographical places.

The instrumental, market-oriented, view of culture has become more common. An instrumental way of looking at culture means placing culture in relation to the good of society. According to this view, one can see different 'uses' and 'values' in culture, and the main goal of culture is to be a tool for achieving these values. This view can be expressed in many different ways, depending on which value one is aiming to achieve. One instrumental aspect of culture is culture as a location factor (Nilsson 2003). This means that the availability of cultural attractions in a place is a crucial factor in influencing people and business and industry to settle in the area. This aspect is based on culture's ability to attract people and companies.

Working with growth and development is a question of survival for all regions. In order to survive, a region must show that is it worthy of its inhabitants, companies and visitors. Culture has thus acquired a new task in society. The availability of a rich variety of cultural offerings in a place has long been seen as an important factor in attracting young people and new businesses to an area. In order to become competitive as a region, one also needs to look at the cultural assets. Florida (2002, 2012) emphasizes that it is important for the growth of a region that it can offer an environment that is attractive to creative people. Specific factors that attract the creative classes are experiences such as art and culture, openness to diversity and above all the potential to have their identity as creative people confirmed.

The idea that culture can be beneficial for the economic growth in cities and regions has been increasingly recognized since Landry and Bianchini (1995) wrote about the Creative City. Power (2002) describes how interest in culture and its function as an economic instrument has increased in the Swedish economy. Evans and Foord (2008) focus on how culture can be leveraged and utilized as an economic driver and Kunzmann (2004) describes how previously culture has been neglected from a spatial planning perspective. As a result, the economic benefits that culture can bring about were nowhere to be found. However, global economic competition has led to culture receiving increased attention for its ability to contribute to urban and regional development. Kunzmann (2004) sees culture as a phenomenon that is rooted in and created by the history and identity of the place where the culture exists. Spatial planning is therefore about critical thinking in terms of a place's ability to make room for action.

Scott (2004) sees cultural focus as a contribution to the development of a new economic climate. This so-called 'cultural economy' is the main force behind increased economic growth and decreased unemployment. Therefore, it is important to plan for culture as an economic driving force from a societal perspective.

Place marketing

Kunzmann (2004) discusses the idea that culture can strengthen the local identity of a particular place or community. In light of increased globalization, the local identity has become an issue for cities and regions as a tool to differentiate themselves from other places in order to attract new residents as well as visitors through tourist attractions and the like. Culture has shown itself to be a good channel for place differentiation. Kunzmann (2004: 387) sees the cultural content as 'the last bastion of local identity'.

There are various theories and opinions about how local cultural identity should be highlighted. According to Scott (2004), there is not, nor should there be, standardized solutions for how culture should be used as an identity-building tool. The identity-building effort should originate from what is unique about a particular place or area. When cultural and creative industries are being established, it should be with reference to what already exists in terms of uniqueness and historical value in the surrounding area, so that they can build upon that to achieve the best results.

Competition between places has increased. In order not to lose out in this competition, places are being marketed as products. There is talk of the profile and image of a place. *Place marketing* means, just as the name suggests, the marketing of a geographical place. The aim is to mediate a positive image of the place to various target groups. These groups can include tourists, businesses, potential migrants to the area and the local population. Examples of groups that may work with place marketing are tourist organizations and the municipality's communications unit. With the help of place marketing, various agents try to bring out that which is unique for the place (Aronsson 2007; Ek and Hultman 2007; Murray 2001).

Place marketing is of course nothing new – it has been in use for hundreds of years (Murray 2001), but particularly in the last decades, it has become more common and more important for places to work actively with marketing and brand building (Kotler *et al.* 1993). There may be several reasons for this. For example, as globalization increases people are becoming less attached to a place. Competition between places has increased as it has become easier for people to move. In the past the identity of an individual was more closely tied to a place because of work and family; nowadays it is more common to move and travel. Regions must therefore increasingly take good care of their inhabitants, as well as attract new ones.

To plan for tourism associated with culturally based activities requires a cautious and thoughtful approach (Fernandes 2011). Cultural tourist attractions and activities should be locally rooted and go hand-in-hand with the local conditions in order to be sustainable in the long run. Fernandes (2011) emphasizes how important it is that the relationship between culture, tourism and society's inhabitants works in such a way that everybody is satisfied. If instead, too much focus is placed on economic gain through tourism and the needs of the local residents are neglected, there is an imminent risk that the cultural identity values will be lost.

Kunzmann (2004) argues that cultural activities and initiatives whose primary goal is economic gain should be viewed with scepticism. Furthermore, that a balance between efforts to support local identity and investments on a global level, is required. Therefore, there is a required awareness about what the local identity stands for and what message it should relay as well as the need for politicians to allow themselves to be open and creative in terms of profiling and marketing.

Scott (2004) emphasizes the importance of place marketing based on cultural heritage and cultural activities. This is often done in places that want to renew themselves by revitalizing old local traditions. By drawing upon cultural resources value is created and people become attracted to the area. It can even serve to attract new residents who can support themselves in professions associated with these cultural resources. Markusen (2006) sees cultural planning as a way to attract new residents which over time, through the domino effect, will attract more and more residents. This, argues Markusen (2006), would not only benefit the cultural sector, but also other branches and sectors of society that contribute to increased economic development and growth for society in general.

Cultural planning

In some aspects place marketing and cultural planning coincide. A major similarity between the two concepts is that both try to use what is unique for a place and develop it. One difference, however, is that place marketing tends to focus on image and the external perspective while cultural planning goals are focused more on identity and the internal.

Evans (2001: 7) describes cultural planning as 'a cultural approach to Town Planning which uses an infrastructure system of Arts Planning'. In other words, cultural planning is a way of looking at city planning and regional development from a cultural perspective. Cultural planning uses a broader definition and doesn't just see culture as art. Instead, it applies the anthropological concept of culture, where culture is seen as a way of life. The aim of cultural planning is to find the unique aspects of a place/region and develop these as a way of hopefully growing and developing as a region.

Evans and Foord (2008) see cultural planning as a method to nurture and strengthen cultural initiatives so that culture can grow and hopefully bear fruit. When culture is planned correctly not only can it cultivate economic gain but also a richer cultural life and inspiration for those people who partake of it. Cultural planning is seen as a process that through consultation and decision-making can for example, help a region to identify cultural resources and assets, and analyse from a strategic perspective how they can be used to build a stronger society, both economically and socially (Evans and Foord 2008).

Colin Mercer (2006) argues that the point of departure for cultural planning is that culture is whatever counts as culture for those who are affected by the survey. That means that for some people culture is sitting in front of a painting and enjoying the central perspective while for others it is sitting in a park enjoying nature.

The organizations *2010 Legacies Now* and *Creative City Canada* have together developed a guide for working with cultural planning (*Cultural Planning Toolkit* 2010). In the guide, cultural planning is described as a way of working that sees all aspects of a society's cultural life as assets that can bring many advantages to society if used in the right way. Culture is seen as a resource for the development of society.

> Understanding culture and cultural activity as resources for human and community development, rather than merely as cultural 'products' to be subsidized because they are good for us, unlocks possibilities of inestimable value. And when our understanding of culture is inclusive and broader than the traditionally Eurocentric vision of 'high culture,' then we have increased the assets with which we can address civic goals.
>
> (*Cultural Planning Toolkit* 2010: 1)

According to Iordanouglou (2008) where place marketing and cultural planning differ is above all in their problem formulation: which problems can be solved by using and increasing the cultural resources? Within place marketing, culture is about what creates attraction and what can influence the competitive relationship between different places. It's all about brand image, the transformation of place and the creation of so-called 'mega events', large-scale one-time events. Within cultural planning, marginalization, social polarization and suburbanization are higher on the agenda than economic growth.

Cultural planning is a cross-sectional and holistic approach to the administration and planning of local society. Its base is a humanistic user perspective where local people articulate their experiences. Cultural planning wants to change and improve local society as a whole, and not just the culture that characterizes the place, which is no small feat.

Why use cultural planning in Kronoberg County?

The project of developing a new cultural strategy in Kronoberg County, southern Småland, was a political initiative based on questions such as: Who will decide the cultural policy objectives? What concept of culture do we want to use? Why does the budget not reflect our broader concept of culture? What is happening at grass roots level? Which unique cultural recourses are there in Kronoberg, southern Småland?

The elected representatives wanted to move away from their roles as passive administrators, where they paid out funds and maybe provided a summary once a year for a number of cultural organizations. Cultural policy discussion in Kronoberg often centred on the division of money and those who participated in this discussion were mainly those who lived on the money in question. Cultural policy debates at the national level tend to have the same fixation on detail, focusing on grants and technical details such as broadcasting rights. It is primarily agents that are dependent on these subsidies, for example theatres, that receive the most attention in the media, not their customers or users.

At the regional political level in Kronoberg new questions were asked: Why are we involved in cultural policy and what do we want to achieve? Which methods can be used to pursue an active cultural policy? The politicians read, attended seminars, cogitated and worked seriously with the question: How should we work with cultural policy and who should be involved? In the process that followed a decision was made to work with the concept of cultural planning.

That cultural planning method that focuses on the place, has a bottom-up perspective and sees culture as a part of the development of a place, fitting in well with the political ambitions from the perspective of regional development. That the method also was seen as practical with a manageable toolkit made it even more attractive. It was decided that a survey would be conducted of the region's cultural resources from a cultural planning perspective. The politicians needed cultural mapping at a local level – what is going on in the region and how do we develop?

A problem in Kronoberg was that there were no run-down neighbourhoods and no industry in decline. Manufacturing was thriving, unemployment levels were the lowest in the country, but new manpower was needed. The labour market was and is based on small companies and is strongly segregated between men and women. The politicians needed to make the county more attractive to residents and visitors. The main questions, which would become the basis of political priorities, were: What is unique in this place and how can we develop it?

Survey of cultural resources in Kronoberg

With the help of Lia Ghilardi from London, a consultant with long experience in cultural planning processes, a survey of the cultural resources in Kronoberg was conducted. The main focus was on the following areas:

- the existing cultural infrastructure in the county, which includes public access, the calendar of events, etc.;
- the attractiveness of public places;
- the region's historical, creative, architectural and anthropological character;
- the development of local talents;
- the local and external image of the place (as portrayed in films, songs, stories, tourist guides, travel brochures, literature).

The following questions formed the basis of the survey:

- Which known cultural resources can be found in the area?
- Which as yet unrecognized cultural resources can be found in the area?
- Which cultural resources could be established with the right encouragement and planning?
- How can each of these resources be useful for the development of individuals and the region as a whole?

Since the cultural department of the Regional Council of Southern Småland (Kronoberg) is small with only two employees others were asked to help with the survey. A wide range of organizations and consultants were contacted to help with the work. Some of them were very positive about the initiative, others were deeply sceptical. The organizations were given different assignments and could thus influence the shape of the new cultural strategy in the county. Here are some examples of assignments and reports that were written:

Smålands Museum: cultural – historical characteristics and identity

The county museum, *Smålands museum*, was given the task of illuminating the special mentality of Kronoberg County and its inhabitants from a cultural – historical perspective. The idea was to identify special characteristics associated with the place. Smålands museum also discussed the identity of Småland in its report.

Disability movement: social and physical accessibility

The disability movement and Kronoberg County Council hired an independent consultant to conduct an inventory of the access to cultural meeting places from a broader perspective, in other words, not just cultural institutions but also restaurants, cafes and other cultural meeting places. The focus was on disabilities other than physical handicaps, such as social and psychological disabilities. The consultant conducted in-depth interviews, observations and a number of quantitative studies. The work on the concept of accessibility resulted in a discussion that then became the basis for further initiatives.

Småland people on film

How are Småland and its people depicted on film? That was the task given to the regional resource centre for film, *Reaktor Sydost*. A report was produced that showed the strong position Småland had and has as a brand, especially when it comes to Swedish films. This report contributed to a better view of the image of Småland, which was an important part of the survey.

Quality of life from a multicultural perspective

An independent research organization, the *Institute for Regional and Local Democracy*, was given the task of working with 'Quality of life from a multicultural perspective'. Workshops were conducted with people from the 'million programme' area of Araby[1] where questions of quality of life were discussed. One conclusion was that the area's bad reputation contributed to the decline of quality of life.

Young people's view of Ljungby

The Interactive Institute conducted a project, Ljudstråk, where young people described their hometown of Ljungby with the aid of digital stories. The youths described their roads and places in the town, using sound narratives which afterwards could be borrowed from the tourist office. The places the young people came up with were not the same as the ones the city planners had considered.

How do young people organize themselves?

The youth organization *Tech Group* completed a substantial survey of the way young people organize themselves and what they do during their leisure time. They interviewed more than 200 high school students from the Ljungby and Tingsryd municipality. The young people had a number of different opinions but generally what they lacked were meeting places and others wished for more music venues.

Many pointed out that a specific restaurant/music venue in Växjö was important to them when it came to staying put in the county: *Kafé de Luxe* with its music arrangements was what stopped them from moving to a larger town. The restaurant was later awarded a prize as 'Creative Culture Entrepreneur' by the Regional Council in Kronoberg. Experiences gained from the study were also used in the development of new rules for subsidies for youth organizations. Among other changes a system with 'fast cash' was introduced so that these organizations could be provided with subsidies faster.

Stories and myths in Småland

How is Småland depicted in tales and myths? That was the question in the assignment given to the Museum of Legends, *Sagomuseet*, in Ljungby. There is a very strong story-telling tradition in Småland. The Museum of Legends collects local stories and regularly brings them to life at festivals and other events. The report, among other things, discussed the strong story-telling tradition in Småland and the images of Småland that are invoked by the traditional folktales.

ALMI

ALMI is a state-owned company whose job it is to promote competitive small and medium-sized business and stimulate the set up of new businesses in order to promote growth in business and industry. ALMI looked at the number of cultural employers in the county – a survey that formed the basis of a larger initiative in the creative sector later on. ALMI also looked at culture in the business sector in Småland in terms of values, self-image and so on. This turned into a study that had a lot to say about the future of the county. ALMI chose to present the values using various sayings, which was very telling. Examples included: 'He who cries after too much often loses the whole deal.' 'Every man to his own trade.' ALMI pointed out the lack of risk-taking and innovation among small companies in the region – something that they found crucial for the future in a society that is becoming increasingly globalized.

Results of the strategy's first years

The gathering of survey material lasted six months and 25 different reports were written. Secondary material such as material from various media and statistics were analysed. In addition, observations were carried out in cafes and public spaces. Workshops were organized with various groups, such as young entrepreneurs in the entertainment industry. At the same time, seminars on culture and development in general and cultural planning in particular were organized primarily for elected officials and people within the cultural field. There were also regular meetings with all the groups that had been given assignments in this process, which led to many new contacts and projects.

All the material was analysed and it proved difficult to find a common thread in the exciting material. One basic stipulation during the analysis was to not become too absorbed in what was already well known (such as the area known as the

Kingdom of Crystal and Linnæus' birthplace at Råshult). Instead the idea was to challenge the views the participants had of the area. In the end, a cultural strategy was created and written based on the rich material, focusing on the following unique conditions in Kronoberg, the region of southern Småland:

- entrepreneurship/diversity;
- story-telling tradition;
- strong media and IT sector;
- Småland as a brand;
- the power and competence of young people;
- the storm Gudrun[2] and the effects of climate change.

The cultural strategy also stresses the regional leadership's role, which was taken to be that of providing visions, goals and strategy suggestions. The regional leaders role should primarily be to facilitate and to transgress boundaries, for example by breaking the boundaries between commercial and publicly financed culture. As culture is a factor in regional development, part of the task is to place a cultural perspective on other political areas.

The cultural strategy was approved by members of the newly formed Regional Council of Southern Småland in May 2006. The cultural strategy was launched with a great culture festival where amateurs and professionals collaborated with music, theatre, acrobats and cultural debates. The local press gave the launch a great deal of attention and started a new discussion on culture.

What was seen as the most important result was the strong focus on cultural policy and the role of politics. Cultural policy on a regional level came to deal more with strategic questions than with funding and cuts that used to dominate the debate. Culture came to be an important part of the county's strategic development.

All organizations receiving funding from the Regional Council of Southern Småland had to work in line with the cultural strategy. Agreements were brokered with cultural organizations based on the following concepts: accessibility, attraction, impossible meetings. 'Impossible meetings' is a concept used to stimulate non-traditional cooperation in order to access the resources of, for example, marginalized people who seldom get their say.

While the work on the cultural strategy was in progress a Regional Development Plan (RDP) was drawn up in the county. A great number of the results from the cultural planning survey were incorporated into the regional plan, among them the concepts of impossible meetings and the focus on meeting places.

Cultural planning in Kronoberg today

It has been almost ten years since the County Council of Kronoberg started to search for a simple, efficient and understandable method to use for regional development. At first the method was aimed toward the cultural strategy but very soon it turned out to be a good instrument for other policy areas too. In 2007 the

Regional Council of Southern Småland was established as a member organization for cooperation between municipalities and the Regional County Council. This has improved the conditions for cooperation between different areas of policy as they are now part of the same organization. This makes some of the previous obstacles in cultural planning less of a problem today. Today's work with cultural planning has taken three paths: *participatory processes in 'Samverkansmodellen' for making arts and culture policy*; *increasing citizen participation when working with cultural heritage*; and *cultural planning and public transport.*

Cultural planning and 'Samverkansmodellen': a model of cooperation in the area of culture

Experiences from cultural planning have recently come in handy since today's work with arts and culture at the regional level is very much connected to the ongoing reform at the national level. During 2011 politicians in Kronoberg County, as well as a majority of Swedish regions, are making preparations to implement the new state model *Samverkansmodellen*, a model of cooperation in the area of culture. This means new authority for regional counties in policymaking and in funding arts and culture. General terms for the model are to be carried out by the county in cooperation with local authorities, professional cultural workers and non-profit associations. County councils are also prompted to have a strategy on how they work according to national cultural policy objectives and how they will support state-funded culture.

The new reform is well received and accepted in Kronoberg County. Previous experiences working with cultural planning now make implementing the reform a natural step in developing cultural policy. The timing is also good. The general election was held in 2010 and the political representation on cultural policy was strengthened in numbers by 2011 with a new cultural board at the Regional Council of Southern Småland. Cultural planning seems to be an established method of making arts and culture policy in Kronoberg County and a follow up on previous cultural mapping was a good way of starting work when new cultural policy was needed.

Among lessons learned from cultural planning is the importance of clarifying roles and responsibilities on regional and local levels and the new working model focuses on dialogue and cooperation with different stakeholders. Also, regional policy has to be operational to make a difference in a three-year period. The objective for the planning process was to make it a participatory process, a kind of 'open source', easy to follow and contribute to. Also, the dialogue and cooperation needed to be structured into a working model for implementation, follow-up and evaluation of arts and culture policies.

The result has been a Regional Cultural Plan for Kronoberg County based on a distinct citizen perspective where those who are responsible for the implementation of the plan are identified. Today the implementation work is under way and it can be concluded that the first decisions regarding the budget and operations are in line with the plan's intentions. The cooperation model that was designed to develop the culture plan, and that is based on the cultural planning method, was put into practice and further developed in order to implement the plan. On behalf of the Government Agency for Cultural Analysis, a comparative case study of two regions, Jämtland and Kronoberg, was conducted with the general purpose of studying if and how the cooperation model has changed the regional cultural policies' form and content. It was especially focused on Kronoberg's citizen perspective as one that differentiates itself from other regions.

Cultural resources in the county, the existing cultural infrastructure and public access to it needed to be surveyed in order to make new policies. To conduct a survey, thematic working groups were set up consisting of representatives from local authorities, professional cultural workers and non-profit associations. Meetings were designed as participatory processes. Several hundred people were involved in the process during 2011. To stay in contact and keep the stakeholders up to date with ongoing work, to share information and to encourage participation, social media has been used. During the planning process nearly 7,000 people visited the blog.

The process has provided knowledge at the regional level when it comes to policymaking. The regional policymakers have clarified their role and responsibilities and are about to take action. The role of local authorities still needs to develop and a majority of the municipalities are not ready to completely benefit from the ongoing regional development. The most important outcome from the work is that it has set up a working model based on the process of collaboration and dialogue.

Increasing citizen participation when working with cultural heritage

Knowledge about cultural resources in the county, and public access to existing cultural infrastructure, is essential when directing an institution. Erica Månsson, one of the pioneers in bringing cultural planning to Kronoberg, became the director of *Kulturparken Småland* (Culture Park Småland). Culture Park Småland AB was founded in 2009 as a result of the cultural planning process and is owned by the Kronoberg County Council and the Municipality of Växjö. It is a new meeting place for culture where new ideas and old traditions from Småland are combined in a new cultural arena. Culture Park Småland AB has three major aspects: the development of Museum Park which is a venue that attracts many people, and serves as a place for people to engage in cultural activities; the development of the Småland cultural heritage, as a way to bring cultural heritage alive and make it accessible to many; and to serve as an umbrella for various organizations operating cultural activities in Småland. The entire organization of Culture Park Småland is now engaged in a process to increase the level of citizen participation. This process is backed up by the new regional policy on arts and culture as a way of supporting methods for participatory processes.

As a result, the operation has reached new target groups and more people. Culture Park Småland's work has been recognized by the Association of Swedish

Museums with the distinction Sweden's Museum of the Year 2012. The prize was motivated by the Culture Park's work to bring together collections, archives and exhibitions into a flexible whole that focuses on its audience. In addition, the new working methods to get more residents involved and the wish for more openness was emphasized. Furthermore, research study of the regional leaders in Kronoberg has been initiated in order to study the ongoing development work on the participation processes of two institutions in two neighbouring regions, Culture Park Småland and Regionteatern Blekinge Kronoberg (the Regional Blekinge Kronoberg Theatre).

Cultural planning and public transport

All Swedish counties are required to develop a programme for public transport. In Kronoberg County ongoing policymaking on public transport is influenced by cultural planning and the method contains six phases or steps: why; mapping; analysis and conclusions; vision and goals; actions; and follow-up. There are some key answers to the question why: in order to keep up low costs the traffic does not suit the passengers very well, the companies do not earn any money and the capability for change is low. The number of people using public transport has decreased in many parts of Sweden. It is easy to identify many weaknesses but also some strengths. The reactions to the survey are mixed – people are surprised by the facts, some are angry, and some find it interesting.

The most critical and important step is the analysis and conclusions. What are all these facts telling us? What can we learn from the mapping? Civil servants, passengers, local and regional politicians, they all have their own interpretation of the mapping. More people must be involved in the development of public transport – not just the experts on traffic planning. The vision and goals are expressed in a different way now when more aspects on public transport have been discovered. There is a change in perspective: how can buses and trains be there for the passengers?

The planning process has not yet carried out all the steps but so far the experience is that cultural planning can also be used for transport policy. Cultural planning is not promoted as a concept because it can raise some resistance towards the method. However, elements of the method are used and the different steps are easy to explain in a way that makes many people comfortable with the process.

Lessons learned from the strategy process and what it can lead to

The regional development strategy has been revised. Cultural aspects and experiences from the survey were taken into account to a great extent. In general, the experiences from the cultural planning process can be summarized as follows:

- new bottom-up perspective provided a new view of the county;
- the fact that external consultants were used provided a new perspective;

- the fact that the method crosses several sectors is seen as a great advantage and challenges previous ways of working but can also make the method difficult to work with.

Cultural planning does not solve all the problems of culture and development but it is an excellent tool for local environmental scanning and for focusing on cultural policy. It can be applied practically, does not require too many resources, and gives a cultural dimension to development work in general. Cultural planning demands that the survey continues because the surrounding environment changes rapidly.

The project was initiated by politicians and the combination of strategic questions and definitions of culture were very useful – culture was elevated on the agenda in general. The effects also spread to a certain extent to the municipal level.

In Kronoberg a very wide survey was conducted, which is good from the perspective that one can find unknown resources – if one narrows the survey one might only find what is already known. The information was then sent on to those concerned but it was hard for them to understand the material when they had not worked with it themselves.

One problem with working at a regional level is that it tends to end in a survey without changes being implemented. It would be desirable to continue the process in several places in cooperation with the municipalities. The project should have been anchored more thoroughly in the municipalities. Maybe more time should have been spent considering the different regional and local roles.

Another difficulty that emerged during the process was the project's connection with business and industry. The method prescribed a broad partnership with private, non-profit and public agencies but in Kronoberg it proved difficult to incorporate the private sector to any great extent. Perhaps this is a sign that culture and business are a long way from each other in Sweden.

One important aspect when one starts such a large project is of course timing. Kronoberg's cultural strategy was approved only a few months before elections took place and this meant that it was not implemented immediately. Power changed hands, regional tasks were reorganized, and the Regional Council of Southern Småland was formed. Eventually they accepted the same cultural strategy and politicians continue to work on its implementation, but time was lost.

To sum up, the cultural planning method has proved to have the following advantages:

- strategic focus;
- covers different sectors;
- clear method from beginning to end;
- requires cooperation;
- citizen perspective;
- challenges accepted views.

And the disadvantages that were experienced:

- difficulty working with different sectors;
- leads to results over which one has no control;
- hard to explain – the term 'cultural planning' is difficult to translate;
- unclear what is regional and what is local responsibility.

The general view was that the work was intensive but also a great deal of fun. Many new projects, contacts and ideas were developed during the process, which made it well worth the effort. Even though the method has advantages and disadvantages, Kronoberg County is going to continue working with the cultural planning model.

In order to develop the method in a Swedish context, SKL (Swedish Association of Local Authorities and Regions) and the Regional Council of Southern Småland have formed a national network for cultural planning. The network has produced a handbook on cultural planning (Lundberg and Hjorth 2011).

Notes

1 The 'Million Programme' is the colloquial name of an ambitious housing programme launched in Sweden during the period 1965–1975. The aim was to solve an acute housing shortage by building a million houses and flats in a short period of time, while at the same time increasing housing standards. In total just over one million new residences were constructed, accounting for 25 per cent of all residences in Sweden today. Nowadays the Million Programme is often associated with 'concrete suburbs' where crime and racial segregation are rife.

2 In January 2005 southern Sweden along with Great Britain, Ireland and Denmark was hit by the storm Gudrun.

References

Aronsson, L. (2007) 'Bilder av platser', in L. Aronsson, J. Bjälesjö and S. Johansson (eds), *Kulturell Ekonomi – Skapandet av värden, platser och identiteter i upplevelsesamhället*, Lund: Studentlitteratur.

Cultural Planning Toolkit (2010) Available at: www.2010legaciesnow.com/fileadmin/user_upload/ExploreArts/Toolkits/CulturalPlanning_Toolkit.pdf (accessed 23 March 2012).

Ek, R. and Hultman, J. (eds) (2007) *Plats som produkt. Kommersialisering och paketering*, Lund: Studentlitteratur.

Evans, G. (2001) *Cultural Planning. An Urban Renaissance*, London: Routledge.

Evans, G. and Foord, J. (2008) 'Cultural Mapping and Sustainable Communities: Planning for the Arts Revisited', *Cultural Trends*, 17(2): 65–96.

Fernandes, C. (2011) 'Cultural Planning and Creative Tourism in an Emerging Tourism Destination', *International Journal of Management Cases*, 13(3): 629–636.

Florida, R. (2002) *The Rise of the Creative Class – and How it's Transforming Work, Leisure, Community and Everyday Life*, New York: Basic Books.

——— (2012) *The Rise of the Creative Class – Revisited: 10th Anniversary Edition – Revised and Expanded*, New York: Basic Books.

Foghagen, C. and Johansson, S. (2007) 'Konstruktionen av ett världsarv – samspelet mellan kultur, ekonomi och lokal utveckling', in L. Aronsson, J. Bjälesjö and S. Johansson (eds), *Kulturell Ekonomi – Skapandet av värden, platser och identiteter i upplevelsesamhället*, Lund: Studentlitteratur.

Iordanouglou, D. (2008) 'Leka med elden – kulturpolitik och strömningar i tiden', in K. Lundberg (ed.), *Kultur i omvandling – Antologi om kulturpolitik och kulturens nya roll*, Stockholm: SKL publikationer.

Johannisson, J. (2006) *Det lokala möter världen – Kulturpolitiskt förändringsarbete i 1990-talets Göteborg*, Göteborg: Valfrid.

Kotler, P., Haider, D.H. and Rein, I. (1993) *Marketing Places. Attracting Investment, Industry and Tourism to Cities, States and Nations*, New York: Free Press.

Kulturrådet and others (2005) *Kulturen i tillväxtprogrammen – en innehållsredovisning, Stockholm: Kulturrådet, Riksantikvarieämbetet*, Riksarkivet: Svenska Filminstitutet.

Kunzmann, K.R. (2004) 'Culture Creativity and Spatial Planning', *The Town Planning Review*, 75(4): 383–404.

Landry, C. and Bianchini, F. (1995) *The Creative City*, London: Demos Publishers.

Lundberg, K. and Hjorth, K. (2011) *Att fånga platsens själ. Handbok om cultural planning*, Stockholm: SKL Kommentus Media.

Markusen, A. (2006) 'Cultural Planning and the Creative City', paper presented at annual meeting of the American Collegiate Schools of Planning, Fort Worth, Texas.

Mercer, C. (2006) *Cultural Planning for Urban Development and Creative Cities*. Available at: www.kulturplan-oresund.dk/pdf/Shanghai_cultural_planning_paper.pdf (accessed 23 March 2012).

Murray, C. (2001) *Making Sense of Place: New Approaches to Place Marketing*, Stroud: Comedia.

Nilsson, S. (2003) *Kulturens nya vägar – Kultur, kulturpolitik och kulturutveckling i Sverige*, Malmö: Polyvalent.

Power, D. (2002) "Cultural Industries" in Sweden: An Assessment of their Place in the Swedish Economy', *Economic Geography*, 78(2): 103–128.

Remmare, P.-O. (2008) *Kultur i regionala utvecklingsstrategier och program – en lägesrapport*, Stockholm: Institutet för tillväxtpolitiska studier, Nutek, Riksantikvarieämbetet, Riksarkivet, Statens kulturråd, Sveriges Kommuner och Landsting.

Scott, A.J. (2004) 'Cultural-Products Industries and Urban Economic Development: Prospects for Growth and Market Contestation in Global Context', *Urban Affairs Review*, 4(39): 461–490.

18 Cultural entrepreneurship and creative points of intersection

The Island of Furillen

Lars Lindkvist

Introduction

Gotland is Sweden's largest island and the largest island in the Baltic Sea. It is located about 90 km east of the Swedish mainland and about 130 km from the Baltic States. The province includes the tiny Karlsö Islands in the west and the small islands of Gotska Sandön and Fårö to the north. Swedish filmmaker Ingmar Bergman lived and died on Fårö and several of his films were filmed there, among them *Through a Glass Darkly* (1961), *Persona* (1966), *Hour of the Wolf* (1968), *Shame* (1968), *The Passion of Anna* (1969), and *Scenes from a Marriage* (1972), as well as Liv Ullman's *Faithless* (2000), based on a Bergman screenplay. The Bergman Festival is a week-long tribute to the filmmaker held on the island every June. In 2012, the ninth edition which consisted of 52 different programmes was held. Ticket sales were high and the festival was attended by a large audience.

Another island is Furillen, or Furilden, off the northeast coast of Gotland. It is around 2,000 m wide and 5,300 m long. Until well into the 1990s Furillen was a military zone, the location of the radar stations known as 'Katten' and 'Renen'. Foreigners were not allowed to visit the area or moor boats there at the island. On the island there was an old limestone quarry with a factory that had been disused for 30 years.

Twelve years ago the photographer Johan Hellström and his family came to the island and decided to create something new and different, a combination of art, design and entrepreneurship. With a vision of changing the limestone factory into a design hotel in harmony with nature, Fabriken Furillen was created: a hotel, restaurant, bakery and conference venue.

What emerged was a minimalistic design hotel with Scandinavian industrial art products in collaboration with the architect Andreas Forsberg, and with connections to designers and design companies Mattias Ljunggren, Mats Theselius, Alvar Aalto and Bang & Olufsens electronics, Orrefors glass products, Hästens handcrafted beds and Skeppshult bicycles. The mix of top Nordic brands with soft luxurious interiors creates a high-class retreat amidst the wild coastline.

With the factory as a base, the development of Furillen continued with the creation of Studio Furillen: a 'culture cube' for inspiration and creativity; a studio, a gallery, a meeting place and a starting point for journeys that have never been made before. It can also be seen as a demonstration of what Swedish architecture can accomplish when stretched to its limits. By creating spaces for unexpected meetings the island would be developed and creativity would flow.

Through interviews with significant actors over many years and secondary analysis of data collected by others I try to answer the question of what drives the entrepreneurs in Furillen, Johan Hellström in particular, to describe the problems he has overcome in terms of a sceptical environment, and to interpret what lessons can be learned from the project he launched. The study points out the value of arts and culture for creating creative points of intersection, which in turn can lead to the development of a site.

Johan Hellström emphasizes, both in words and deeds, the importance of trying, learning from mistakes and looking forward. He underlines how important it is to believe in an idea 100 per cent in order to be able to convince others. Many companies are started by an entrepreneur who has economic incentives as a goal; however, for Johan Hellström as a cultural entrepreneur the most important goal is to realize an idea. After ten years as an entrepreneur on Furillen Johan Hellström wants to share the following three lessons in my interview with him in June 2011:

(1) You can never get anyone else to believe in an idea if you do not believe in it 100 per cent yourself.
(2) Work with bureaucrats and politicians, not against them. Include them at an early stage in the plans and processes. It is only when civil servants, politicians and business people work together in the long term that sustainable development is created.
(3) Look to the future. Don't dwell on what has been and don't fret over things in the past that could have gone better.

With these lessons as a starting point I will be analysing the situation on Furillen with the help of the following theoretical concepts:

(1) culture entrepreneurship and art entrepreneurship;
(2) creative meeting places and points of intersection.

Cultural entrepreneurship

The term entrepreneurship is, and has long been, central with economic literature (Hébert and Link 2009). For Swedberg (2006) the ability to combine things in new ways is at the core of both entrepreneurship in general as well as cultural entrepreneurship. Swedberg (2006) is based on the pioneer Joseph Schumpeter's first German edition from 1911, 'The Theory of Economic Development: An inquiry into profits, capital, credit, interest and the business cycle' in which he presents his views not only on the entrepreneurship but also on cultural entrepreneurship:

> the economic entrepreneur who works in the creative industries can, for example, be conceptualized as someone who makes combinations, where art

> is one of the elements in the entrepreneurial combination. Or the artist who is interested in economic success may be conceptualized as someone who tries to link up his or her work with other elements in some combination that works.
>
> (Swedberg 2006: 249)

Sarasvathy (2001) argues that an entrepreneurial problem can be solved in two different ways. The first alternative is based on causation, where there is a given goal and by choosing between different means the goal can be reached. In the second alternative effectuation is in focus; here the means are given and the focus lies on choosing between the different effects that can be achieved by a combination of means. If the entrepreneur sees effectuation as the most important aspect it would be possible to create a company in an entirely different genre, by combining the available opportunities in a more successful way.

Sarasvathy (2001) uses the example of an entrepreneur who wants to start an Indian restaurant. When focusing on causation the entrepreneur researches what the restaurant market looks like and formulates a strategy so that she can reach that market in the most appropriate way. If the entrepreneur instead works on the assumption that effectuation is central and tries to think in new ways, the result could instead be that she opens a travel agency focusing on India, or another business with indirect ties to the original idea. The process of effectuation thus encourages greater creativity than a process that is driven by causation.

Sarasvathy (2001) argues that successful entrepreneurs focus more on creating alliances and networks while in the start-up phase instead of trying to find competitive advantages by him or herself. Recently created successful businesses concentrate on creating relationships and create strategic alliances with other interested parties in order to reduce uncertainty. Thus uncertainty contributes something positive by encouraging the search for new knowledge rather than using existing knowledge (Aldrich and Martinez 2003; Bjerke 2007).

Howort, Tempest and Coupland (2005) see an entrepreneur as a risk-taker who coordinates resources in an innovative way. The authors state that it has even been suggested that entrepreneurs are more awake and aware of opportunities. However, they believe that entrepreneurship is a dynamic concept and argue that the definition of an entrepreneur should be based to a greater extent on what an entrepreneur does.

Based on a study of entrepreneurs within the music industry, Darmer (2008) draws the conclusion that they are not primarily motivated by a profit interest but rather have a broader view of their entrepreneurship. It is about taking risks based on the ultimate satisfaction of being able to produce and offer a new product or service to other people.

Since the end of the 1990s, cultural entrepreneurship has been established as a specific study area. Mangset (2009) does an interesting deconstruction of the term cultural entrepreneurship. He begins by emphasizing the Austrian historian Andrea Ellmeier (2003) who describes the rise of a new creative work force, called cultural entrepreneurs who are characterized by seeing that the dividing line between consumption and production is unclear and by readily taking advantage of every opportunity they see within art, music and media, and the combination thereof. Cultural entrepreneurs make no distinction between work and leisure. They combine individual and collaboration oriented values and gladly enter into creative communities (Leadbeater and Oakley 2001). According to Leadbeater and Oakley (1999, 2001) cultural entrepreneurs' primary goal is not financial gain, but rather to retain the feeling of independence, creativity, ingenuity and fantasy.

Lounsbury and Glynn (2001) see cultural entrepreneurship as necessary for the business world in general, not only for cultural and creative industries. It is especially about story-telling that contributes to new ideas and activities being legitimized and therefore gaining access to necessary financial resources. Mangset (2009: 34) connects story-telling and legitimacy with the culture sector where 'stories about cultural entrepreneurship can have a kind of therapeutic legitimizing and motivational function for overburdened actors within culture politics and culture life' (my translation). In his review of cultural entrepreneurship, Mangset (2009: 225) calls for more empirical examples where the starting point is small stories about how cultural entrepreneurs work and what they contribute.

Art entrepreneurship

Art entrepreneurship has also been established as a research field in recent years (Phillips 2011; Scherdin and Zander 2011a). Art entrepreneurship is defined as 'how artists and people engaged in artistic activities perceive of new art ideas, how these ideas are transformed into tangible objects of art and artistic expression, and how they are ultimately accepted or rejected by the general public' (Scherdin and Zander 2011a: 4). They see similarities between artists and entrepreneurs in their mutual emphasis of the idea that beneath uncertainty and risk new expressions and unexpected combinations can be found. However, they also see three significant differences between them in the context of art: '1) it maintains a particularly pronounced focus on creativity and the production of novelty... 2) it is concerned with the introduction of novel ideas and concepts that are de-coupled from immediate utility or profit motives... 3) the artist's communication and persuasive efforts must rest on other means than proof of practical usefulness or profit potential.'

Scherdin and Zander (2011b) also describe the importance of story-telling and legitimacy building measures. 'In reality, new art ideas and initiatives often face severe resistance among certain groups of external evaluators. Overall, art and artistic processes represent an arena that seems particularly suited for empirical study of legitimacy' (ibid: 173). Even other researchers, whose starting point is the idea that the typical entrepreneur is not perceived as alone and stubborn, see the influence on and by external stakeholders in the entrepreneur process as an important field of study.

Another term that Scherdin and Zander (2011b) emphasize in their studies of art entrepreneurship is 'hijacking' where new ideas and concepts are kidnapped by temporary collaboration partners or other interested parties. As a result they lose control over the development and the result is different from that which was intended. This is seen as an area that is worth more study, which I allude to in the study of the development of Furillen.

Creative meeting places and points of intersection

Törnqvist (2009) points out that creative processes require support from the environment that surrounds them. All environments, be they geographical, institutional or network-based, can include both circumstances that promote and that hinder creativity. Törnqvist (2009) sees it as important that the concept of individual creativity is complemented by the concept of collective creativity. Throughout history there have been places where creativity has flourished, such as Athens, Vienna and Florence, and where we clearly see the effects of the surroundings on creativity. This still holds true today.

Scott (2006) sees geography and 'the creative field' as important for the development of entrepreneurship. He defines the creative field as 'all those instances of economic effort and organization whose spatial and location attributes, at whatever scale they may occur, promote development- and growth-inducing change' (Scott 2006: 3). While creative destruction makes up a central element in the development of entrepreneurship, at the local and regional level it is the creative field that is of special interest. The geographical aspect is seen as an active ingredient in the promotion of economical growth and development. Scott emphasizes the interdependence between different stakeholders and actors that are influential in the development of the creative field. It is this association in the form of meeting places and points of intersection that I will allude to in my interpretation of Furillen's development.

Frans Johansson (2004) talks of the importance of using impressions from others in the surrounding world in order to be able to hatch an idea in his book *The Medici Effect: Breakthrough Insights at the Intersection of Ideas, Concepts and Cultures*. He stresses that it is important for the innovative and creative entrepreneur to utilize different ways of thinking in order to create a point of intersection, which can lead to an innovation. Points of intersection can be said to exist everywhere, but in essence they are actually found in our brains. The point of intersection corresponds to a place that increases the chances of unusual combinations. The explosions of fantastic innovations that can be found are what Johansson calls the Medici Effect, referring to the creative climate when the Medici family reigned over Florence.

With help from the theoretical concepts, cultural entrepreneurship, art entrepreneurship and creative points of intersection I will now proceed to describe and interpret the growth of the cultural meeting place, Furillen.

Start-up of Furillen Fabriken Hotel

> Furillen looks more like a moon – grey and barren. And yet this island, an extension of northeast Gotland, is seen as a longing for a personal paradise island. [The author] Håkan Nesser has built his dream house here. [The rock group] The Hives are planning to take over an old military barracks. On the island's eastern side Björn Ulvaeus [of ABBA fame] wants to create his next musical. On this barren island 700 fashion, music and advertisement photo shoots have taken place. Among others Bo Kaspers Orkester and the Cardigans have used the island as a backdrop for music videos and album covers. There are no road signs on the island but that which characterizes the island, a desolate limestone factory and two grey slimy slagheaps, lie beside the hotel Fabriken, the core of Furillen. For many of Sweden's successful creators Furillen is a paradise island.
>
> (Åkesson 2009, my translation)

The road to what is today a much talked about hotel and cultural meeting place has been long. Twelve years ago when Furillen was a military area patrolled by bloodhounds, which encouraged tourists and Gotlanders to stay away from this barbed wire enclosed area, Johan Hellström came to Furillen to photograph winter clothes for a mail order catalogue in the middle of summer. The white slagheaps of crushed limestone looked so much like snow and that it made it possible to create a winter atmosphere in pictures taken a week before midsummer. Children from the village acted as extras; they put on winter clothes and snowboarded on the white slagheaps. Thanks to these special conditions the limestone factory and its special atmosphere became world famous among fashion photographers.

In 1999, the old limestone quarry and factory building were put up for sale. One option was to change the factory to an EU-financed fish factory but this was never explored. This opened up new opportunities for the Hellström family when Johan Hellström had become tired of all the travelling and wanted to do something else. As a photographer of advertisements and fashion, the world was Hellström's workplace, with 260 travel days a year.

After many years as 'summer Gotlanders' Johan Hellström, his wife Anna-Karin and their two daughters decided to move from Gothenburg to the east coast of Gotland. They bought the old limestone quarry and its surrounding land and changed the old factory building in a way that you can feel the wing beats of history. You should really notice that you are in an old workshop with attached canteen (Brulin and Emriksson 2005).

Hellström stresses that the design of the hotel, both interior and exterior, should not stick out from Gotland's natural beauty. 'No matter how beautiful and aesthetically appealing the design, nature is stronger', he says. Johan Hellström had no previous experience in the hotel and restaurant business but after many years as a world traveller he had strong opinions on what he wanted as a guest. 'I have noticed that many hotels have so many distracting offers for the guests that the guest disappears. Instead I wanted to create space for cooperation with nature' (Figure 18.1).

The Hellström family bought the limestone quarry from the cement company Cementa AB. The last limestone was taken from Furillen in the early 1970s. Johan Hellström thinks it is important that the old slagheap is kept as it was. 'It is a monument to time and reminds us that we cannot destroy as much as we used to 50 years ago. I want to turn the negative into something positive.'

The renovation of the limestone factory that was to become a hotel started in the limestone quarry workers' dining room. After renovating five rooms and adapting the interior decoration to the surrounding area, room and board was offered mainly to visiting photographers and their entourages who came to the island for photo shoots.

This worked so well that the Hellström family decided to expand the venture. One condition for the success of the photographs as guests was the change from analogue to digital technology, and the new broadband technology that allowed pictures to be sent to customers around the world. Over time the conference facilities have grown to encompass 15 year-round jobs. Today, the result is a conference hotel with 18 rooms and a restaurant. It is a mixture of simplicity and luxury, with specially made Hästen handcrafted beds and Skeppshult bicycles, both in limestone grey.

Appreciation from stakeholders within the business

The travel and experience business has drawn attention to Fabriken Furillen in various contexts. Every year, RTS, the Swedish Travel and Tourist Industry Federation, awards 'TRIP awards' in three categories: 'Comeback of the Year', 'Stand-Out of the Year' and 'Best Use of Marketing and Distribution'. In 2007,

Figure 18.1 Furillen Fabriken Hotel (photo: Johan Hellström).

the award for 'Stand-Out of the Year' went to Fabriken Furillen for the following reason:

> With a very interesting new way of thinking, an unusual new creativity and a huge amount of enthusiasm the company have created a unique product. They dared and believed in what they were doing, and have developed into a very solid company with strong growth.
>
> (RTS 2007)

On the same day that Johan Hellström accepted the prize in Stockholm in June 2008, a new issue of the American travel magazine *Condé Nast Traveller* came out, with an entire spread dedicated to Fabriken Furillen.

Painful dialogue with politicians

Today Johan Hellström owns the greater part of the island. He has bought all the available land on Furillen, 500 hectares, in order to develop the island's potential and is now involved in a continuous dialogue with politicians and bureaucrats about his ideas for Furillen. This has not been a completely pain-free process – over the years Johan Hellström and the authorities have had differing opinions on the development of Furillen. In the middle of March 2007 Johan Hellström warned all 15 regular employees at Fabriken Furillen that their positions may not be secure because of the lengthy time involved in dealing with appeals which stopped him from continuing to develop the company. The company is based on green tourism and as a part of this Johan Hellström applied for a building permit for five so-called 'hermit huts' around Furillen, where guests can stay without electricity and running water. Continual appeals against the building permit from two neighbours in summerhouses meant that Johan Hellström was not getting any further with the project. While waiting for the result of the appeal, Johan Hellström decided to freeze the company temporarily and put it on ice.

After a long appeals process Johan Hellström was finally awarded a building permit for the hermit huts. These were spartan buildings designed by an architect and located individually in the landscape, for people who want to escape daily life with its often hectic tempo. Here there are no mobile phones, only sea and silence. Food is eaten at the hotel, or delivered to a designated place in the area where the guest picks it up.

In the summer of 2007, five huts were placed on the island. They were painted and decorated, and can be booked by those who want to live close to nature. The County Administrative Board on Gotland has identified a number of important biotopes on Furillen. Information material describing the flora, fauna and characteristics of the various biotopes has been gathered and can be found at the hotel and in the hermit huts. The information is illustrated with photographs taken by photographer and hotel owner Johan Hellström. The hermit huts are rented out for 5,000 kronor for the first night, 500 kronor for the second, 50 kronor for the third, and the fifth night is free. The idea is that the guests will stay several nights, thus being given the opportunity to relax.

In June 2007 Johan Hellström of Fabriken Furillen sent an open letter to, among others, the residents and summer guests on Furillen, inviting everyone who had ideas on how to develop the island to present their opinions. His interest in development issues led him to decide to become director of the newly formed Furillen Development AB in August 2008 and to work with development questions full-time. With the hotel as the focal point more and more new projects were initiated on the island. The new projects can be seen as points of intersections between architecture, art and music.

Architecture: AQ Arkitekters studio building

From the beginning the joint name for three developments that were planned to take place on the eastern side of Furillen was Furillen Studios. All three had a surface area of between 500 and 600 m^2. Here Björn Ulvaeus's new studio was planned to lie side by side with AQ Arkitekter's studio building and Studio Furillen, a 'Culture Cube' where artists, architects, performers and authors can work on creative projects in peace.

AQ Arkitekter's establishment on Furillen are planned to consist of a studio building including a satellite studio, drafting rooms and living quarters totalling 600 m^2 where colleagues, associates and commissioners can meet and work together. Construction of the building, which is intended to create a space for the architects, engineers and creative people of the future, were planned to start in September 2009. Because of the planning of the construction of Björn Ulveaus's studio and the 'Culture Cube' a new decision about when to start the project has been delayed to autumn 2012.

Together with Johan Hellström, the architect Andreas Forsberg plans to develop other projects on the island. Aside from his own office Andreas Forsberg has drafted plans for other buildings in Furillen. When building these projects it has been considered important to work with 'surgical precision' during every building project on Furillen, in order to be able to easily restore the landscape around the building site. Endangered beetles may not be threatened and distracting noises from the wind power station should not be heard too close to the planned music studio. It is a slow puzzle that is taking shape, where Furillen is used to experiment and test new things. For Andreas Forsberg it is the exposure on the island that makes it easier for him as an architect to reach the core of his thoughts.

Art: Studio Furillen the 'Culture Cube'

Alongside the planning of AQ Arkitekter's new studio, another creative studio measuring 600 m^2 has been built. Here artists, architects, performers and authors can come to pursue their creative work in peace. The first spade of earth for the project – which first went under the working name Kulturkuben (the 'Culture

Cube'), was dug in the middle of March 2009. Over time the name 'Culture Cube' has changed to Studio Furillen (Figure 18.2).

In an atrium house designed for all manner of creative activity, artists and cultural workers will be able to work and live in connection with projects. There are studio and gallery spaces, areas for photography and film recording, material rooms, a library, writing places, a kitchen, separate kitchenettes, a spa and four bedrooms with a total of seven beds. The area can be divided up in several ways.

The man behind the project is industrialist Mikael Blomqvist of Michano AB. This industrialist from Blekinge (southern Sweden) has invested 30 million kronor in the Studio Furillen, which will function as both workshop and accommodation for visiting artists. Here an artist will be able to stay and create in the middle of a forest grove. Mikael Blomqvist has been convinced of the potential of the place since he saw it for the first time. For him it was the combination of its location on Furillen, the surrounding natural landscape, and this sculpture of a building which is unsurpassable and will clearly promote all forms of cultural activities. Michael Blomqvist wants to participate in building a creative environment in the barren landscape of Furillen. He has international contacts in the art world and counts on making room for famous artists as well as talented aspirants in the Cube.

Building Committee Chairman in the region Gotland, Lars Thomson, supports the idea and looks favourably upon the development:

> It is the combination that is going to make it a unique place. Music, architecture and art are going to contribute to Furillen's appeal. The 'Culture Cube' will attract famous artists to rent spaces in which to work but also to exhibit their art. This means that Johan Hellström's vision of a creative centre is now becoming a reality.
>
> (Daun 2009)

Figure 18.2 Studio Furillen 'The Culture Cube' (photo: Ake E:son Lindman).

The building is a square structure with a inner courtyard/atrium built for creativity where cultural workers are able to go in order to retreat and find an outlet for their creativity. At the same time they have access to food and drinks at Johan Hellström's Fabriken Furillen only a kilometre away.

The Studio Furillen has a shell of rust-coloured iron and absolutely no windows. With the help of mechanics, parts of the walls can be folded out, creating entryways and allowing observation. The doors can be opened in all four directions and within them is the next shell made up of glass walls that let in light from every direction and that reflect the surrounding forest. The architect Andreas Forsberg describes his vision with the building:

> Studio Furillen tries to both preserve the strong feeling and character to be found on Furillen and at the same time create something completely new. To be both closed and open. Simple yet complex. A distinct, strong character that is discreet and unobtrusive. The idea for building the studio on Furillen was born during a trip with Mikael Blomqvist to Sea Ranch in California in November 2008. Back home in Sweden sketching began immediately. Just after New Year a building permit was granted and planning got under way. Construction of the 500 m^2 studio commenced in spring 2009 and shortly after came another inspirational trip, this time to Tokyo, Japan. Planning continued in the autumn as construction progressed. All the beams were cast in concrete and prefabricated concrete wall elements were used as a framework. The roof structure was steel with a surface layer of sedum. In spring 2010 detailed planning of the building began. The facade was clad with sheets of Corten steel. In November 2010, the building was complete, two years after the first sketch.
>
> (Forsberg cited in Studio Furillen 2012a)

In October 2011 the Swedish architectural magazine *Arkitektur* presented their *Debutpris 2011*, an award which is handed out every other year to promising young architects, to Andreas Forsberg at AQ architecture for Studio Furillen with the following motivation:

> In the barren Gotland landscape on Furillen, an impressive Corten atrium house has been placed. A forward-thinking hybrid between studio, gallery and holiday cottage for a patron of the arts. A house demonstrating an attention to detail that few architects deliver in their lifetime.
>
> (Studio Furillen 2012b)

The Studio Furillen 'Culture Cube' was originally planned as part of Furillen Studios where Bjorn Ulveaus's studio would have been included along with AQ Arkitekter's studio construction. After the rejection of Ulveaus's studio, AQ Arkitekter adjusted the plans to better meet the needs of the creative people within different areas. In addition, Fabriken Furillen wants to create a sculpture park on a peninsula adjacent to Studio Furillen where they want to build twenty sculpture environments.

Music: Björn Ulvaeus's studio construction

The man behind what was thought to become the third new establishment on Furillen was the world famous ABBA-musician Björn Ulvaeus. According to the newspaper *Dagens Nyheter* he fell for the silence of the place, which provides unique opportunities for creative practice. Björn Ulvaeus had planned on building a studio building with accommodation, a place to live for composing, making music and creating. Construction was to start once a decision had been made by the Environmental Court.

> In the final phases of writing a musical or a film you want to be able to retreat somewhere, alone or in the company of fellow creators, somewhere where you can be left in peace in an environment that lends itself to thought and creativity. This can also be the case at the start of a project; you may want to rehearse with actors or come up with a whole new idea in an undisturbed environment. It should preferably be a place where you can be provided with just about anything and where there are plenty of beds. This is where the combination of the hotel Fabriken and Furillen is unbeatable. I hope that people in the future will talk about musicals, films, songs and novels that came into being on Furillen.
>
> (Ulvaeus cited in Olsson 2008)

On 17 September 2009 the Environmental Court proclaimed that Björn Ulvaeus was allowed to build on Furillen. The background was that the Swedish Environmental Protection Agency had lodged an appeal against the planning office's decision to allow Ulvaeus an exemption from the beach protection law (which states that no buildings may be erected within 100 m of the waterline).

However, in April 2010, the Superior Environmental Court decided to deny an exemption from the beach protection law. According to the Superior Environmental Court, the area's protection value is very high and there is a strong interest in protecting the active outdoor life as well as the future needs of the area. The Superior Environmental Court did not consider the motivations to be serious enough to meet the requirements necessary in order for construction to be allowed. This decision cannot be appealed.

The decision raised strong feelings on Gotland. While many Gotland residents, in various letters to Gotland newspapers, see it as important that the beach protection law should apply to everyone regardless of who is seeking an exemption, there are others who are very uncertain about the decision. In a comment regarding the Superior Environmental Court's decision, Gotland's new governor Cecilia Schelin Seidegård expresses regret that Gotland will lose Bjorn Ulvaeus.

> It is very possible that he could have meant as much for the island as Ingmar Bergman has... Bjorn Ulvaeus is an extremely good creator and his work on Furillen would have been really exciting and added value to Gotland. Although I'm regretful, we must accept the way in which the Super Environmental Court has interpreted the law. Johan Hellström is a fantastic entrepreneur and I hope he continues to look for other alternatives.
>
> (Israelson 2010)

Bjorn Ulvaeus declares that he has had enough and is abandoning his dream of a studio on Furillen and accepts the decision. Johan Hellström isn't dwelling on what happened either even if he regrets that Björn Ulvaeus's dreams didn't work out. However, the development of Furillen is continuing in a different way.

New stakeholders and co-owners

Andreas Forsberg is currently drafting other projects that he and Johan Hellström want to realize on Furillen. But first they have to wait on the realization of the new detailed building plan. In part they are working on so-called 'squares', small groups of houses that can be used either for living in or as studios. A second project is a 'barracks', where the idea is that companies can buy their 'own' creative premises. Another project involves so-called 'spinning sun houses', where the houses turns automatically (or are turned manually) depending on the position of the sun (see sketch in Figure 18.3).

A water availability study by the Royal Institute of Technology found that there was enough fresh water for the island's current businesses, housing and future development. A complete solution with a new water treatment plan will be in place where the aim is to make Furillen self-sufficient with renewable energy.

Figure 18.3 Spinning sun houses (drawing: Andreas Forsberg).

The big projects in Furillen Studios alone are expected to yield at least fifty new jobs in the building industry. No exact figures on the total cost of Furillen Studios are known, but several million kronor are involved. In my interview in June 2011 Johan Hellström declares about the future:

> We cannot predict what it will look like here in ten years time, or even in a year's time. A year ago I didn't even know that Björn Ulvaeus wanted to build a studio here. What we have on Furillen is a unique combination of nature, daily life, the establishment of exciting businesses and modern housing. I am looking forward to this. Sparks will fly in all these unexpected encounters.

In the fall 2011, the auto brand Lancia Delta was introduced in Sweden. Prior to this launch, Lancia placed the new cars out in some of Sweden's most mystical and exciting places. One of these handpicked places was Furillen. Lancias marketing director, Lina Gooch, explains why:

> Furillen is a culturally charged place that is associated with many of the values that Lancia itself wants to communicate. A place full of creativity and a self-assured attitude with connections to culture and design.
>
> (Gooch cited in Lancia Press 2011)

Lancia is also leaving behind a more lasting impression in the form of a permanent music stage built with the help of their funding. 'The stage creates yet another place of culture in the Furillen industrial area with its slag heaps of limestone and the sea as a backdrop. It's an effort to provide current and future musicians the opportunity to protect the world's music in a different place', said Johan Hellström in my interview in June 2011. 'The seating capacity, made up of limestone benches, is 200–250, however that number can be multiplied if necessary. Furillen will symbolise culture, creativity and exciting encounters. We can now build a stage suitable for music at Furillen. The stage is built over the old signal box and done in rusty Corten steel in order to blend into the environment.'

More creative venues were created on Furillen when the Fotografiska Museet in Stockholm opened as a local branch at Furillen. In a storage building, in a wooden tower with 15 m high ceilings and 120 m^2 of floor space, a spectacular photo gallery has been created in collaboration with the Fotografiska Museet. The first exhibitor was the actor and stand up comedian Henrik Schyffert who sent 200 photos to Fotografiska Museet, of which ten were chosen. The exhibition was a public success. The first week of the exhibition in July 2011, attracted 2,500 visitors to Fabriken Furillen.

Another project was a film made in 2011 which is a mix between the life and architecture of Manhattan and Furillen which was unveiled at Crown Princess Victoria's visit to New York on 1 November 2011.

In October 2011, Nobis AB which includes first-class hotels and restaurants, among which are Operakällaren and Stallmästaregården, announced that they will launch a professional and creative collaboration with Furillen AB. As of 2012 Nobis AB will be in charge of the hotel and restaurant operations on Furillen. Johan Hellström will be one of the people responsible for the future concept and development of the whole Nobis group. In a joint press release (Nobis 2011) their mutual plans are described:

> I have liked Furillen ever since Johan Hellström began his project on Gotland over ten years ago. Over the last few years I have followed and seen how Furillen's new way of thinking has spread throughout the world by way of media and 'storytelling'. There are so many who talk about ideas but so few who turn them into reality. I am so happy that we can now unite these two strong and unique brands and together development a common future.
>
> (Sandro Catenacci CEO Nobis AB)

'We already have firm plans that we and other creative businesses will be able to work year round on Furillen', say Johan and Sandro (Nobis 2011). The merging of Furillen AB and Nobis AB will mean both joint ownership and a shared responsibility for the operations.

In an interview in a Gotland newspaper in April 2012 Johan Hellström emphasizes the importance of combining different skills, that is to say to achieve creative points of intersection, in his collaboration with Nobis star restaurateur Stefano Catenacci, who among other things is responsible for the banquets and gala dinners served at the Royal Palace in Stockholm. 'To combine my knowledge and experiences with Stefano's can be very good. When Stefano makes contact with Gotland it's going to be fantastic for the whole Island. It's about authenticity and daring to believe in your work', says Hellström. Both Johan and Stefano talk a lot about the overall experience and showing off Furillen's unique attributes. 'Johan is real idea man but he also implements his ideas', says Catenacci (Olsson 2012).

Hellström will seek permission from the building committee to expand the hotel Fabriken Furillen with six new rooms. The construction is identical to an earlier six room expansion of the hotel. There is a high demand for the available hotel rooms at Fabriken Furillen, even if all the guests are not fully satisfied. On a scale from 1 to 10, the average visitor review on booking.com is 8.5. A sign of the ambivalence that characterizes the customer reviews is the latest review that I found on the internet from 15 July 2012. There Frank, a father with small children, writes, 'People who are artistically inclined and like design, photography and nature are going to love this hotel, myself included! People who are looking for comfort and conveniences and the regular top hotel feeling are going to be disappointed.'

Creative meeting places, points of intersection and cultural entrepreneurship

It is in the intersections between different areas of knowledge that the best opportunities for a creative environment can be found, and it is here that it is possible to create an explosion of new innovative ideas. People and teams achieve these points of intersection by bringing together concepts from one area with the concepts of another. At the point of intersection the team or individual can combine concepts from different areas and generate ideas that take an entirely new direction. The point of intersection corresponds to a place that increases the chances of unusual combinations. That is what is happening on Furillen. According to Mikael Blomqvist, it was the combination of nature and culture that was the reason he decided to have the Studio Furillen 'Culture Cube' erected as a centre for artists and performers. It is expected to 'promote all forms of cultural activity'.

Johan Hellström talks about the value of spark formation when different people and perspectives meets. 'Torekov (in western Sweden) has been the home of finance while Österlen (in southern Sweden) has long been a hub for highly-cultured people. On Gotland there's still a mix and that's what I want. When different people get together, sparks can fly' (Daun 2012: 60, my translation).

On Furillen one can see how the combination of factors can form something unique, a point of intersection. The beautiful environment creates ideas and provides inspiration while at the same time providing somewhere to stay. By gathering together the hotel and conference facilities, studio and gallery spaces, areas for photography and film recording, excellent conditions for finding different points of intersection are created. But in order to reach these points of intersection one must also be prepared to break down one's barriers of association.

Johansson (2004) also argues for the importance of motivation in this context. Without motivation there is no driving force to move the idea forward and develop it. It is important not to let a fear of failure be a barrier to creating something new and different. If one fails, one should learn from the failure and not make the same mistake again. The failure should be seen as a new opportunity to learn. It is important to dare to take a chance on one's ideas to the fullest extent and to dare to fail. Johan Hellström on Furillen also emphasizes that it is important to 'look to the future and not dwell on things in the past that could have gone better' but instead turn these failures into positives experiences.

For cultural entrepreneurs and companies in the creative industries it is important that they learn from their mistakes in order to come up with something even better, since innovation and new ways of thinking are important parts of today's creative industries (Bilton 2007). They have to create innovative products while at the same time marketing themselves in a creative and alternative way so that we consumers will notice them.

Johan Hellström as well as Andreas Forsberg and Michael Blomqvist, can be seen as just such persons; they had a clear vision of how Furillen could be developed from a limestone quarry into a unique creative meeting place. They are not afraid to fail and work hard at making sceptical stakeholders, litigious neighbours and civil servants that stand on principle realize the value of a change on the island.

When I interpret the development on Furillen based on earlier completed entrepreneurial concepts, I find that it is about solving entrepreneurial problems based on 'effectuation', and thus the search for new knowledge, instead of 'causation', and only not just about considering the already existing alternatives (Sarasvathy 2001). By creating new unexpected relationships between new partners in conversation, new opportunities become possible. The primary goal is not to achieve maximum profit but rather the satisfaction of seeing new possibilities and combinations. To a great extent it is about cultural entrepreneurship the sense that through more temporary projects taking advantage of opportunities and using one's social capital through networks (Leadbeater and Oakley 2001). On trips throughout Sweden the Furillen entrepreneurs have, through story-telling, succeeded in making sceptical stakeholders enthusiastic (Mangseth 2011). For the hotel project Fabriken Furillen, network creation is obvious in light of the new collaboration with Nobis AB. It is important, however, that the founder Johan Hellström is aware of the risk of 'hijacking' (Scherdin and Zander 2011b), meaning that the original idea could be kidnapped by new collaboration partners and as a result become something other than what was intended.

Conclusion

The site of Furillen can be seen as a creative point of intersection. Just being there generates a feeling of creativity, something that the entrepreneur Johan Hellström realised already from the beginning. Creating a conference venue that could be used by people who wanted to work alone, or work with others in different projects, either at the beginning or at the end of the project, is an example of innovative thinking and a creative business concept. Many famous Swedish creators have noticed the project Fabriken Furillen and developed it to include other cultural areas. The goal, according to Johan Hellström, was for 'sparks to fly between all the unexpected encounters'. In this endeavour it is also important to listen to the civil servants and politicians involved. It is only when civil servants, politicians and business people work together in the long term that sustainable development is created.

Projects such as Fabriken Furillen and Studio Furillen are based on certain assumptions on how the future will develop and it is not unusual for some of these assumptions, made during the initial phase of innovative ideas, to turn out to be wrong. This can be a problem when one finds oneself at a point of intersection where the risk of an uncertain future can be greater than acting within tried and tested areas.

It goes against the grain to turn the idea of building a hotel and conference venue in the middle of an island made of limestone off the coast of Gotland into reality. No one believed that the limestone quarry would have such potential. The same thing occurred in the case of Dalhalla, described by Per Frankelius in Chapter 15 in this book. These two ideas, which have grown independently of each other, show in a useful way that it is possible to combine culture and nature and at the same time increase employment opportunities within the cultural and creative industries.

References

Åkesson, J. (2009) Furillen – drömmen om en egen måne, *Dagens Nyheter*, 3 August 2009. Available at: www.dn.se/livsstil/reportage/furillen—drommen-om-en-egen-mane (accessed 31 July 2012).

Aldrich, H.E. and Martinez, M. (2003) 'Entrepreneurship as Social Construction: A Multi-level Evolutionary Approach' in Z.J. Acs and D.B. Audretsch (eds), *Handbook of Entrepreneurship Research: An Interdisciplinary Survey and Introduction*, Boston, MA: Kluwer Academic Publishers.

Bilton, C. (2007) *Management and Creativity: From Creative Industries to Creative Management*, London: Blackwell Publications.

Bjerke, B. (2007) *Understanding Entrepreneurship*, Cheltenham: Edward Elgar.

Brulin, G. and Emriksson, B. (2005) *Design för ett nytt arbetsliv. Gotland i omvandling*, Stockholm: Atlas Förlag.

Darmer, P. (2008) 'Entrepreneurs in Music: The Passion of Experience Creation' in J. Sundbo (ed.), *Creating Experiences in the Experience Economy*, Cheltenham: Edward Elgar.

Daun, E.C. (2009) Kulturbubbla på Furillen. *Gotlands Tidningar*, 13 February 2009. Available at: www.helagotland.se/nyheter/artikel.aspx?articleid=4833581 (accessed 31 July 2012).

Daun, C. (2012) 'Vattendelaren', *Filter*, 26: 42–62.

Ellmeier, A. (2003) 'Cultural Entrepreneurialism: On the Changing Relationship between the Arts, Culture and Employment', *International Journal of Cultural Policy*, 9(1): 3–16.

Hébert, R.F. and Link, A.N. (2009) *A History of Entrepreneurship*, London: Routledge.

Howort, C., Tempest, S. and Coupland, C. (2005) 'Rethinking Entrepreneurship Methology and Definitions of the Entrepreneur', *Journal of Small Business and Enterprise Development*, 12(1): 24–40.

Israelson, E. (2010) 'Ulvaeus kunde blivit en Bergman'. *Gotlands Tidningar*, 28 April 2010. Available at: www.helagotland.se/nyheter/artikel.aspx?articleid=5980446 (accessed 31 July 2012).

Johansson, F. (2004) *The Medici Effect: Breakthrough Insights at the Intersection of Ideas, Concepts, and Cultures*, Boston, MA: Harvard Business Press.

Lancia Press (2011) *Lancia smyglanseras på mytiska Furillen* (Press Release), 6 July 2011. Available at: www.lanciapress.se/press/article/120 (accessed 31 July 2012).

Leadbeater, C. and Oakley, K. (1999) *The Independent. Britain's New Cultural Entrepreneur*, London: Demos.

——— (2001) *Surfing the Long Wave. Knowledge Entrepreneurship in Britain*, London: Demos.

Lounsbury, M. and Glynn, M.A. (2001) 'Cultural Entrepreneurship: Stories, Legitimacy, and the Acquisition of Resources', *Strategic Management Journal*, 22: 545–564.

Mangset, P. (2009) 'Fortellinger om kulturelt entreprenørskap', in P. Mangset and S. Røyseng (eds), *Kulturelt entreprenørskap*, Bergen: Fagbokforlaget.

Nobis (2011) *nobis + furillen = sant* (Press Release), 6 October 2011. Available at: www.nobis.se/newsitem.asp?newsID=1816 (accessed 31 July 2012).

Olsson, M. (2012) Stjärnkrögaren på Furillen, *Gotlands Tidningar*, 13 April 2012. Available at: http://gt.helagotland.se/nyheter/artikel.aspx?articleid=7612047 (accessed 31 July 2012).

Olsson, R. (2008) Furillen blir platsen för nya musikaler, *Gotlands Allehanda*, 30 October 2008. Available at: http://ga.helagotland.se/nyheter/default.aspx?articleid=4407083 (accessed 31 July 2012).

Phillips, R. (2011) 'Arts Entrepreneurship and Economic Development: Can Every City be "Austintatious"?, *Foundations and Trends in Entrepreneurship*, 6(4): 239–313.

RTS (2007) *Sätra Brunn, Furillen och Lotus Travel vinnare av rese- och turistnäringens TRIP Award 2007* (Press Release), 8 November 2007. Available at: www.rts.se/pls/nvp/Document.Show?cid=4100&mid=342 (accessed 31 July 2012).

Sarasvathy, S.D. (2001) 'Causation and Effectuation: Toward a Theoretical Shift from Economic Inevitability to Entrepreneurial Contingency', *Academy of Management Review*, 26(2): 243–263.

Scherdin, M. and Zander, I. (2011a) 'Art Entrepreneurship: and Introduction' in M. Scherdin and I. Zander (eds), *Art Entrepreneurship*, Cheltenham: Edward Elgar.

——— (2011b) 'Emerging Themes and New Research Openings', in M. Scherdin and I. Zander (eds), *Art Entrepreneurship*, Cheltenham: Edward Elgar.

Scott, A.J. (2006) 'Entrepreneurship, Innovation and Industrial Development: Geography and the Creative Field Revisited', *Small Business Economics*, 26(1): 1–24.

Studio Furillen (2012a) *The Architect*. Available at: www.studiofurillen.com/the-architect.html (accessed 31 July 2012).

——— (2012b) *Press, September 28, 2011*. Available at: http://www.studiofurillen.com/press.html (accessed 31 July 2012).

Swedberg, R. (2006) 'The Cultural Entrepreneur and the Creative Industries: Beginning in Vienna', *Journal of Cultural Economics*, 30(4): 243–261.

Törnqvist, G. (2009) *Kreativitet i tid och rum. Processer, personer och platser*, Stockholm: SNS Förlag.

19 Fragile creativity

Lessons from the rise and fall, and rise again, of Sweden's biggest rock festival

Tobias Nielsén

The great example

For almost thirty years, what seemed to be impossible was real. A small non-profit association had grown from being some teenager's playground to the biggest rock festival in Sweden, and it all took place in the small industrial municipality of Hultsfred with only 5,000 inhabitants, which implied that the number of people gathered in the town increased by six times during some of the festivals. The spin-off effects were huge in comparison. Students and companies moved here, a vivid 'creative cluster' flourished and many local stores took advantage of the economic value of tourism and the young population.

On the national level, Hultsfred was one of the great examples of the wonders of creative industries (Nielsén 2008; Power and Hallencreutz 2005). Here was a small town that had been badly affected by de-industrialization and a steady decline in its population – but that had found new hope thanks to a rock festival and its spin-offs. The leading business daily put one of the founders, Putte Svensson, on the cover of its weekly supplement; he was also named 'entrepreneur of the year' and received other nominations. Thousands of politicians and civil servants have visited in order to learn, either from the festival or from building 'the cluster centre' Rock City – a live venue, restaurant and a centre for educational programmes, academic research, freelancers and small entrepreneurs. The whole milieu was something most small towns can only dream about – tourism and music industries with activities the whole year around, a creative mini cluster constantly fuelled by young people and the civil society acting for the good of the home region.

Everybody acted like the success would last forever, not thinking about the extraordinary risk a big live event actually implies. Inside the organization Rockparty, a non-profit association with employees as well as members with different views of the strategic direction, not everybody was happy. The question of whether it should work strategically as a 'cluster motor' for this specific town and region (see Power and Hallencreutz 2005 for a discussion on cultural industry cluster building), or rather focus on its own activities, music events and other related activities for youths was under debate.

The story of the festival and Rockparty is therefore very much about failures and disputes as much as it is about successes.

Eventually the financial losses became too great and the association Rockparty was not able to be saved. It went bankrupt in 2010, only a couple of weeks before that year's festival was planned to take place. The German entertainment company FPK Scorpio bought the trademark and other assets and is now organizing a festival with the same name – although differently: on a smaller scale, with its headquarters not based in Hultsfred and with minimum collaboration with the local community. This is a contrast to how the Hultsfred festival used to involve everybody from local sports clubs to students and freelancers. The question is how this affects the complex system of creativity that evolved over several decades.

More than a festival

If you come to Hultsfred at a time other than during the festival, there lies a great silence over the city centre as well as around the lakeside area where the festival takes place. There are no major cities nearby and the region is mostly made up of spruce forest and smaller cities with about 10,000 residents.

It is hard to imagine that for a few days every year since 1986, tens of thousands of people wander around here. It is crowded but mostly festive. Sounds boom, not just from the music but also from people who are cheering, laughing and talking. It smells of food, sweat and dust.

But there are also activities going on not far away at Rock City, even at times other than during the festival. In association with the festival activities, something was built up that most small cities can only dream about: an entertainment and tourism industry with operations throughout the year, a creative mini cluster with an influx of young people and civil society involved in the community and wanting to work for the greater good of the municipality.

Rockparty, with its festival activities provided the fuel, the building and environment that is still called Rock City today, was the hub. During its time in the spotlight it housed higher education programmes, researchers, small businesses associated with music and IT, a concert and conference hall, the restaurant Metropol, a small rock museum in the form of an open archive, as well as business and community development activities. In addition, it was the location of the actual association and festival organization, who even lobbied for a year-round concert operation.

Many of the activities remain, in particular the educational programmes, and many of those who worked with the festival and associated activities are now self-employed with offices in Rock City. As a result concerts are still arranged there.

When you come to the building, which is biking distance from city centre, there's a message on the wall that is impossible to miss.

It's all entertainment folks! The best food and music around.

It's true that the basis for the activities has been culture and entertainment, but they were made possible by a deliberate strategy and system of thinking to contribute something important to the Hultsfred district. At most, about a hundred people were employed. In Sweden's capital, Stockholm which has a million residents, it would correspond to 20,000 employed.

Over nearly ten years, several initiatives were implemented that can be regarded as cluster approaches or as proactive policy approaches, especially in the form of deliberate attempts to portray common visions and future images with the help of systematic models (Nielsén 2008; Power and Hallencreutz 2005). We can also regard these models as an effort to create good conditions for the promotion of creative processes and transactions in a particular place. In order to understand how it was attempted to stimulate these processes – as well as what happens with a new, non-present ownership structure – we will first examine which building blocks are necessary.

A place for creativity

During the Romantic Period creativity was seen as a matter of feelings and inspiration, instead of knowledge and skill. The artist – the genius – was considered to be above the demands and triviality of everyday life as well as society's laws and regulations. Based on the idea of the advanced creative person an image grew forth that it is the lone individual's efforts that lead to the best that can be achieved.

We can also easily imagine 'the creator' sitting at a grand piano, at a desk or in his or her art studio. Focused individuals in secluded places in dedicated concentration of innovation.

This image, however, must be supplemented – and greatly modified. Creation is also built on experiences with other people and from other environments. Creativity is always born out of a particular context. It comes from individuals, but is developed through a process dependent upon other people and environments. Since creativity grows out of a context, its conditions can also be influenced. So what controls this context?

Let us summarize with four factors (Eliasson and Eliasson 1997; Landry 2008; Nielsén 2008; Sahlin 2001; Törnqvist 2004):

(1) *Expertise and educational tradition.* Expertise exists within individuals which mean that it is mobile. If many experts within an area move then a great deal of the expertise disappears. However, every place can have a more permanent educational tradition founded on research, educational programmes and specific, often well-known work activities. This should be regarded as a virtuous circle: the more experts in a particular place, and the more knowledge, the greater the chance that more people with expertise will move there. This is one reason why you often see how creativity varies in cycles in places. Florence may have been the centre of the world's cultural development 500 years ago but it is hardly that today.

(2) *Capital.* Without money there can be no wages or investments. In that way culture is never self-sufficient. This is nothing new. One of the conditions for the cultural prosperity in Athens 400 BC. and in Florence during the Renaissance was a concentration of capital and economic surplus. Money in and of itself, however, is not enough to foster creativity. These places were also cultivated by competition and competent buyers who were both demanding and challenging in their orders. In addition, the money had to be distributed to people whose purpose was to produce creative results and environments. If potential funders are not made aware of these individuals or ideas, then they cannot be financed, or for that matter be influenced and consequently drive the creative processes themselves. This is related to the next point regarding communication.

(3) *Communication and the physical environment.* Isolated businesses and individuals are rarely creative. When ideas develop it is more about *evolution* than *revolution*. The individual creativity needs to be supplemented with a collective creativity. In a creation process it is therefore the meeting and communication between individuals and different areas of expertise that is strategically important. Are there places that serve as natural meeting places? Do people exchange ideas outside of their own small circles? An important part of communication is all about travelling to and from the place. First, in order to be able to get an influx of new ideas, and second in order to create collaborations (and business) with people from other places.

(4) *Diversity, variation and structural instability.* Creativity benefits from new approaches, that is to say a variation and diversity of perspectives and competencies. New approaches, however, are not enough – creativity also benefits from original competencies and the actions of experts. In addition, innovativeness is stimulated by a sense that things are not complete or finished. The influx of young people to a place therefore often works as a good engine; they are, to a much lesser degree, locked into a set of ideas, and are, particularly because of a need to provide for themselves, forced to look for new roads.

Deliberate investment

Large urban areas and capital city regions dominate the creative and cultural industries. Creativity and cultural innovation, of course, can happen in many different types of regions, but it seems that 'the business of creativity' takes place in large urban areas (Power and Nielsén 2010).

Cities have several advantages. If we start with the four above named factors about what influences the conditions for creativity then it is obvious that the cities to a greater degree accumulate expertise, can offer public transport, meeting places and capital as well as a greater diversity.

In that way smaller communities have more difficulty asserting themselves within the culture sector or the cultural and creative industries. First, bigger cities benefit to a greater degree from the fact that there is a larger range of projects, activities and people; partly because that means many jobs and assignments, partly because there is opportunity for more contacts and thereby potential for even more activities. Second, many individuals work within these sectors on a project basis and seek out places where there are continuously enough assignments. Thus, size creates continuity.

Consequently, one conclusion is that the same strategy to utilize the power of culture does not work for both small communities and big cities. The former needs to work on fundamental functions that the latter takes for granted. The Hultsfred example shows an attempt to create and promote such a system.

Around Rockparty's music and entertainment operations in Hultsfred, community planning and regional development began to take a more prominent role with the EU-funded project that started in 1997. The goal was to increase employment. Systematic and descriptive models of how activities fit together began to be developed and with this began the work on what would become Rock City. A kind of 'mini cluster' began to take shape. The results after the five-year run of the project included the following increases: from ten to seventy employed, from two to twenty businesses, from zero to five higher educational programmes, from 21,000 visitors to 27,000 visitors at the Hultsfred Festival and more live music year round.

The basis for these results was in place however much earlier. Though for that matter it was not self-evident that more activities could be built around the festival. Earlier the focus had been on arranging concerts. Therefore, many people in the association saw the expansion as a threat, particularly since the bigger the size the bigger the costs.

How much can be planned out?

The Rockparty association's journey has been dependent on people and timing, and that as such is an important conclusion: the kind of development that took off cannot be planned out.

For Hultsfred's part it was just luck that the founders of Rockparty chose to channel their energy into doing something in Hultsfred – and continue to do so – instead of moving to bigger cities like most like-minded people. Support from other associations or politicians didn't exist then. In fact, quite the opposite.

It all began in a cramped basement location on a street called Oskarsgatan in Hultsfred more than twenty years ago. There sat a group of young people who were born at the end of the 1950s or during the early 1960s. Hultsfred was a sleepy and traditional industrial community. Almost every family was dependent on the wooden house factory that had over 1,000 employees. In addition there were other large industrial factory jobs. For most of the young people life was mapped out. When they were finished with school they went to the factory where their parents worked and got a job. Club activities existed, but almost entirely connected to sports.

When punk rock emerged at the end of the 1970s, some of the young people took matters into their own hands, inspired by the do-it-yourself attitude. In

December 1981 the Rockparty association was established and the young founders immediately began calling interesting bands, booking concerts and setting up posters. It turned out that Hultsfred's geographical location in between Malmö and Stockholm was a clear advantage, since many bands preferred to travel three hours per day and play two shows, rather than to travel six to seven hours directly. The idea was that it would be possible for people to live in Hultsfred and still get to see their favourite bands, or just to be able to feel like something was happening.

The board meetings were mostly about discussing which bands should be booked. Nobody had any real knowledge about economy – receipts and other papers were put in a plastic bag and the accounting was done by one of the members' mother. Since the association didn't have any money, voluntary involvement was necessary. Those that were active in the association were on unemployment benefits or had other jobs, and tried to get as much time as possible to devote to their real interests. Two years after its establishment an early important collaboration with the municipality happened when Rockparty took over the People's Park rent free. The park was in decline and poorly taken care of and the municipality thought it was good that it would be used.

The mini cluster

The story of the Hultsfred Festival and Rock City has always stood as an example of success. This is interesting in hindsight particularly if one closely studies their history which shows that the situation was never entirely positive, not even before the bankruptcy. 'Hultsfred' is sooner a story about recurring failure. There's a motto that captures the spirit: 'If it doesn't work, we'll make it work.' The feeling was that over and over again they were forced to do something that seemed impossible.

The first Hultsfred Festival was held in 1986 and already the second year the results were catastrophic. Since then the association has been regularly plagued with financial difficulties, however through personal loans, restructuring and a big dose of volition, the association has been able to continue. Another problem emerged in 1990 when Rockparty was no longer allowed to use the sports arena for their activities. The reason the municipality gave for this was that the floor was being destroyed. This was the background to the association getting their own building, that would later become Rock City. They bought a car showroom, but budgets burst and again voluntary involvement became necessary. People volunteered in their free time as construction workers. Four hundred people participated in the work and in 1992 the building was completed. After a grand opening ceremony even more budgets burst. The first enterprise proved to be too optimistic before a more functional business model was put into place (see Table 19.1).

Moreover, Hultsfred is a small municipality and certain factors meant limitations for development, for example a lack of special expertise and people

Table 19.1 The history of Rockparty, Rock City and the Hultsfred Festival

1981	Rockparty starts up as a non-profit organization.
1986	The Hultsfred Festival is held for the first time.
1992	Metropol is built for 10 million SEK – a car showroom is transformed into a restaurant, concert hall and offices.
1997	The EU-project "Puzzel" begins. Educational programmes are initiated. A small business network is established. Microsoft begins a collaboration with the Festival.
1998	The Digital Media Distribution programme begins. Puzzel is recognized for its "good practice" by the EU.
2000	A higher education programme in Music Management starts in conjunction with the Linnæus University in Kalmar. Over 700 applicants apply for 35 places. Industry-owned IUC Musik- & Upplevelseindustri (IUC Music and Creative Industries) is formed with its headquarters in Rock City.
2002	Rock City opens after the Metropol building is expanded to a total of 5,000 square metres at a cost of 27 million SEK, with spaces for businesses, education and training, the festival offices, concert venues, rehearsal spaces and music studios.
2002	Rock City is nominated as a creative meeting place within Sweden's creative industries sector by the Knowledge Foundation.
2003	Rock City is the cause of growing pains. A shortage of accommodation occurs in Hultsfred as the number of students grows 170, now attending 5 different courses. The number of employees is now 70. An additional 5 million SEK is invested in infrastructure.
2004	The music association Sheena for the promotion of the musical interests of young women and girls, and Popkollo (a popular music camp for girls aged 12–16) are kicked off. Rock City's managing director Putte Svensson is named Entrepreneur of the Year. He holds hundreds of lectures around Sweden.
2005	The Swedish Rock Archive in Rock City creates a unique new database. All the information on 16,000 records is added to the database. The festival sets a new visitor record and attracts more media coverage than any other event in Sweden in all categories.
2006	Sweden's Audio Migration Centre is located in Hultsfred and Västervik. Sweden's audio heritage is to be safeguarded and made accessible for coming generations. New education and training initiatives are started, for example Rock City's GYRO upper secondary school. Rock City receives the EU commission's prize for best entrepreneurship in Europe. There are now more than 100 employees.
2007	Through Business Lab, over 60 businesses have been started since the beginning. Sweden's Rock Archive has over 100,000 records in its collections. Rock City prepares a national growth proposal for the music industry based on the ERIBA model and play an important role for the Swedish Creative Industries, with Putte Svensson as chairman.
2008	Campus Hultsfred is formed in association with Hultsfred Municipality and has 350 students. Popkollo is now being run at eight locations around Sweden.
2009	Rockparty also arranges the Sonisphere Festival with Metallica. Restructuring takes place because of some difficult years and financial crisis. The municipality takes over Rock City.
2010	Rockparty is declared bankrupt. The German corporation FPK Scorpio buys the assets after the bankruptcy and later receives help in the form of a loan from the municipality.
2011	The "new" Hultsfred Festival takes place in the same location but with a scaled down format. The Festival office was moved from Hultsfred to Stockholm.
2012	The Festival in its new fashion continues and the owner emphasizes his long term plans.

who could directly launch themselves into Rockparty's activities – in other words there was a need for an increased proximity to education and research.

Those in charge had noticed that the music industry in general lacked educational programmes. There were a lot of programmes for musicians, but none for the intermediaries and organizers such as promoters and managers. By the same token research was rarely conducted that the music industry or its promoters felt was for them.

Insights into these general needs triggered both contact with researchers and an investment in educational programmes, among others a university degree in Event and Music Management in the form of a subsidiary programme. A model called ERIBA was developed to emphasize that, (E) education and training, (R) research, (I) industry, (B) business, and (A) arts/culture, need to start collaborating. A national foundation funded the further development of the model in order to address all cultural and creative industries – and again Hultsfred served as an example of success (Nielsén 2008).

The activities in Hultsfred received additional public funding for various projects, even if it was the leaders in Hultsfred and Rock City that painted the visions and stood for the ideas. However, the organization was primarily self-funded with regard to the rock festival. When Power and Hallencreutz analysed the Hultsfred example from a cluster perspective they emphasized that the emergence of the cluster was primarily driven by non-public forces:

> The Hultsfred case is then an interesting example of a cluster based initiative in a rural area that is primarily driven by private sector actors who have attempted to turn success in occasional events (though admittedly large scale ones) into a more permanent industrial and educational base for the host area. The cluster approach used here did not start from the basis of an extensive and rigorous analysis of the industrial base but rather was essentially a wish list arrived at and driven by a set of cluster 'visionaries' and 'lead actors'; or more precisely a group of quasianarchistic youths bored with their locality and the economic and cultural activities its existing development strategy offered them.
>
> (Power and Hallencreutz 2005: 8)

The result after a few years was a kind of system for stimulating creativity, with Rock City as a base for more than 100 people in the little community. If we return to the building blocks that create the conditions for creativity we get a picture of this system. It is of course impossible to shut creative processes into a locked 'system', as if they can be completely controlled, but the layout can give some idea of networks and processes.

(1) *Expertise and educational traditions.* Expertise remained and in addition was attracted there thanks to the educational programmes and the impression that it was an 'exciting' place. The educational tradition was preserved after decades of promotion.

(2) *Capital.* The influx of money constituted of the traditional revenues associated with concerts, such as ticket sales, sponsorship, food and drinks. Besides, Rockparty tried to collaborate with the region's business world in other ways, which led to a few examples of product innovation and new companies; some companies even as a part of 'the Rockparty group'. Some activities were educational programmes and specific consultant projects. The big festival also had many spillover effects in the form of tourism as well as knowledge transfer and inspiration for other businesses; the last named confirms other research, among others Bakhski *et al.* (2008) who claim that such knowledge circulation that is not commercialized is relatively more derived from 'creative businesses' (see also Rammer *et al.* 2009).

(3) *Communications and the physical environment.* Rock City is said to have been built in order to facilitate meetings, with a restaurant and many common spaces. When it comes to communication, however, Hultsfred has a disadvantage. Even though the district is in between and only 300 km from three of Sweden's largest cities, it is still thought of as disconnected, particularly in terms of public transportation. Taking the train from these districts is not always easy and the daily flight connections were cancelled several years ago.

(4) *Diversity, variation and structural instability.* The different activities – particularly the educational programmes – and the constant influx of guests have contributed to Rock City getting a stream of new impressions and different perspectives. Variation has existed thanks to people who have worked with many different activities, from the restaurant industry to IT development and research archives. The structural stability can be seen from two perspectives. On the one hand continuous development has existed and there have been many challenges. On the other hand the structure has always relied on the festival activities, from scheduling to how to prioritize.

Other impacts

In order to understand the Hultsfred Festival's and Rock City's contribution to the place, it is crucial to understand how different impacts have been created. Measuring the sales and results from the festival activities is easy. It's just a matter of adding up the revenues from sponsorships, ticket sales, food and drink. The direct impacts for the municipality are tax revenues, revenues for local subcontractors and the employment of residents.

It is also easy to see how those who are attracted to the events also spend money on other things. They buy food, fuel and newspapers, and they stay in hotels or rent houses or apartments from residents. One year the financial value of the impacts that can be associated with Rockparty's activities were calculated to be almost 77 million SEK spent in the municipality of Hultsfred, of which 70.6 million SEK can be derived from the festival (Beijer 2009). This influx of money also means employment and tax revenues for the municipality.

Other impacts are not as easy to identify especially in the short term. Other indirect impacts are not as easy to identify especially in the short term. What, for example, is the value of having restaurants and event promoters in the district, in terms of the residents' quality of life? What is the value of the fact that Hultsfred in many cases is held up as a good example and that the district has become known thanks to the festival? A CEO of one of the region's biggest companies, and hence employers, gives his view:

> I for one have always benefited from the fact that people are familiar with the Hultsfred Festival. It has always been popular and an interesting topic of conversation in general discussions with customers and suppliers, primarily those from Sweden, but even with those from other countries.
>
> (Karlsson 2009)

The total economic value for the municipality means that all the values, market as well as non-market values, must be added together (Armbrecht and Andersson 2010; Bille 1996; Throsby 2000). Note that market values also include flow-through effects to innovation processes in other industries via for example diffusion of creative ideas and skill transfers (Bakhshi *et al.* 2008; Throsby 2000). Research even shows that the biggest potential of the cultural and creative industries lies outside these sectors (Bille and Lorenzen 2008). Hence, a holistic approach is needed.

Moreover, the question of value depends on whose perspective is taken. For an individual cultural business the situation can be perceived as warped in relation to who is doing the creating and enticing, and who is reaping the financial benefits. A musical or a museum can attract many visitors, but the money that the visitors spend is primarily accrued by others, for example hotels, restaurants, shops and transportation.

With Rockparty, as a non-profit organization with goals other than economic profits, it was a little special. In that way it means that certain activities ran at a loss because they aimed to meet the association's goals. In the bylaws it was stated that the work should give young adults meaningful leisure and increase the supply of live music in the surrounding area.

At the same time the business was dependent on economic realities. That means that activities should be evaluated from, above all, two dimensions: *objectives* and *cash flow*. Objectives refer to how much the activities contribute to achieving the established non-profit goals. Cash flow refers to exactly that, cash flow: the financial, operational outcome.

Who pays for the impacts?

In August 2009, Sweden's largest daily newspaper *Aftonbladet* published a long article with the headline, 'Secret documents expose Hultsfred' (Granström 2009). The question was: how can it be that Sweden's most legendary festival is constantly forced to struggle in order to survive? The answer, according to the article, was that the side projects were eating up all the money. The article can be interpreted as though Rockparty should stop doing anything other than the festival (and become a profit driven organization?).

Given the following year's bankruptcy the question is of course inevitable: would it have been better to keep the organization small, with small fixed costs and only concentrate on the festival and maybe a few other events? The question is not new but rather has existed since the association's beginning, for example when the car showroom was purchased and renovated.

It is possible that a smaller format would have been better for Rockparty businesswise – at least in a strict, business economy held analysis where the organization's results are weighed against the risks. One of the founders and the driving force behind both the Rock City building and the side projects, says in retrospect that it would have been better for the festival if the surplus had only gone back into the operation. He continues, however, that it would not have been better for Hultsfred as a place. In that case the educational programmes would not have been implemented to the same extent, and the district would have missed out on Rock City with its restaurant, business centre, concert hall and on-going entertainment activities.

Let's look at the effects that these different activities contributed to other organizations, residents and the municipality. Besides the financial effects of tourism which equal almost 80 million SEK per year, tax revenues have increased thanks to students and new employees who are now registered in the municipality. In addition, value that can be described with words like image, branding, diversity and quality of life can be perceived. To repeat an earlier line of reasoning, a calculation must therefore be based on the sum of all the different named impacts. Each individual impact cannot be isolated, but rather the tax revenues must be added to the other impacts.

Thus, the question becomes: who is going to pay for what? Table 19.2 illustrates how the entrepreneur takes business risks while other stakeholders take no, or at least very little, risk; on the contrary, their development is also a function of the entrepreneur's risk: if it goes well for the entrepreneur, it also goes well for the stakeholders and vice versa. It is a recurring question within cultural economy, just how risk and revenues should be distributed.

Table 19.2 Risks and effects, entrepreneurs and other stakeholders

	ENTREPRENEUR	OTHER STAKEHOLDERS
RISK	Business risk.	No risk with regard to own investments, but affected by the entrepreneur's business risk.
EFFECT	Return from the operations.	Return from various effects such as tourism, positive image and other spillover effects.

What then is the value for the stakeholders? By rephrasing the question some answers are revealed; what would it cost to create that value? Take away thirty years and consider what it would have cost to create that which came about in Hultsfred. What would this little district pay for an experience and visitor industry with year round activities, a creative mini cluster with a constant stream of young people and an association involved in the community that wants to work for the greater good of the municipality?

The question arose in connection with the fact that the association and thereby the festival were facing bankruptcy. Should the municipality save Rockparty? Subsequent discussions with Rockparty's leaders reveal that it would have been too late toward the end. The municipality should have been included earlier and taken responsibility for that which Rockparty perhaps should not have had to bear. 'Infrastructure' is a word that is mentioned and which captures everything in the Rock City building and the management of the mini cluster that was created. In addition to the responsibilities of their own activities, Rockparty also took on the role of cluster motor. Many cluster activities and projects were operated within the frame for Rock City, of which the municipality owned 49 per cent the year prior to the bankruptcy, but it was still 'Rockparty people' who were the visionaries and the driving forces.

The development went in the direction that the municipality took bigger responsibility toward the end, even if it didn't seem to help. Rockparty owned only 9 per cent of 'the property' Rock City at the time of its bankruptcy and only paid nominal rent. Of course there is no reason to keep the activities going just for the sake of doing so. However, if the conditions had been developed so that jobs, tax income and tourism revenues were generated then the question becomes something else. It's about comparing with what it would have cost to achieve the same impacts from scratch. Look at the many cities that are trying to start up events and educational programmes. Seen in that light it is much cheaper to take care of an existing legacy. Nobody is saying that it is easy or uncomplicated to arrange big events and to create good conditions for creativity in a small district. But the question remains, can Hultsfred's 'system for creativity' be saved?

A new chapter

Now the Rockparty association is gone, but the Rock City building is still standing with several educational programmes and many small businesses. In addition a new version of the festival has continued, even though it no longer is operated from Hultsfred, but rather only takes place there. The German corporation FKP Scorpio acquired the assets after the bankruptcy and immediately began their own version of the festival. It is clear that the German owner, Folkert Koopmans, has a different – more economically focused – approach than Rockparty. In an interview he said that 'the previous festival promoters were lazy, the organization was way too big and the profits ended up in a bunch of side projects' (TT Spektra 2011). What is rarely remarked upon – either by him or in other contexts – is that there is of course a difference between running a business for profit and doing so with a non-commercial association's altruistic goals in focus.

It does not prevent the new festival from contributing indirect impacts to the municipality. The leading politicians have demonstrated an understanding of this and have declared their viewpoint. In an interview the Municipal Commissioner said: 'There is a strong connection between the festival and the educational programmes. That was a powerful argument for entering into the agreement. We suffer a great deal from the fact that many young people move after their secondary education' (ibid.). Now the municipality supports the new owner with the argument that the new festival is establishing a new business and as such can receive public funding. The terms are even better than what they were during Rockparty's time. The municipality has – unlike earlier – approved the serving of alcohol in the entire festival area. The politicians even went against their own administrators and the police. In addition, the German owner, Folkert Koopmans, received help from the Hultsfred municipality with a rent-free loan totalling 2.7 million SEK for 2011, 2012 and 2013 which will be paid back – if possible. According to the agreement the loan has a fifteen-year term of payment. What is more, the municipality is not charging rent for the land (Silberstein 2012; TT Spektra 2011; P4 Kalmar 2012).

If we return to the line of reasoning regarding the stakeholders' risk, then the question is how they are affected by the new owner. On the one hand the politicians believe that the new owner will succeed. On the other hand, the owner is not locally rooted, which is in stark contrast to earlier. If the previous promoters had shut down the Hultsfred Festival in favour of a festival in another place it would have gone against what the association was all about, namely to be able to work in their own district.

Is there a risk that the new owner might rather choose other places and shut down the Hultsfred Festival? Koopmans has been careful in declaring that the new investment is long term and that his corporation FKP Scorpio has succeeded with a considerable increase in the number of visitors already from their first year to their second year in Hultsfred. The new Hultsfred Festival has even begun to get recognition for a functioning form (Pettersson 2012). It raises the question of what the operation's significance for the music festival will be. That subject lies outside the frame of this text, but an observation is that the visitors and the media do not care about whether or not the promoters operate with a commercial or non-commercial purpose.

The conditions ahead

The new festival, in any case, lives its own life without contact with that which previously was the hub of the mini cluster, namely Rock City, and with no relation to most of the people and organizations that used to be connected to the festival.

Let us return to the layout of the four building blocks that affect the conditions for creativity. The new ownership structure is so new that it is impossible to do a true analysis of how things have gone, but let us discuss it from a present day picture.

(1) *Expertise and educational tradition.* Many within the previous operation are still in the district and are primarily self-employed. Others have moved and do similar things in other directions in Sweden, but still as a part of the network in Rock City. There is risk for a lack of development and rejuvenation in the future, since the locally based promoters only work in-house, with smaller and fewer events, thereby decreasing the possibility of hiring. What remains is the Music and Event Management education that attracts new students to the place. The question is if they will stay when the place no longer has the same employment opportunities.
(2) *Capital.* The new promoter describes himself as a strong financial actor that can take losses in the early years. In addition the municipality is supporting the festival while at the same time actively working – on another track – with Rock City operations. One difference compared to earlier is that the new promoter does not have his office in the district and thereby makes use of fewer local subcontractors.
(3) *Communication and the physical environment.* Rock City with its meeting environment remains. However, there is no interaction between the big festival operation and the smaller, local actors. The fact that the district has landed outside of the spotlight means there is a risk that it will attract fewer visitors.
(4) *Diversity, variation and structural instability.* The structural stability is broken which has forced the need for new collaborations and solutions. Many actors that previously were connected to the festival continue to work with the event in different forms and the sense is that a lot is happening. When Rockparty existed, as the dominant actor they demanded a lot of strength from employees and other, related businesses. This affected idea development and other organizations not only in a good way. The new corporation runs the festival in its own way and thereby contributes variation. However, based on the above point, on the whole there is no place for informal exchanges and creativity such as the common, open process that existed earlier. The fact that the educational programmes remain in the district is important in order to supply the place's actors with new people, contacts and impressions.

Conclusion

Taken together 'the system for creativity' lives on, but on a smaller scale. The biggest risk is that expertise will not develop, especially if it's not rejuvenated in order to live on. The fact that the veterans remain creates a continued momentum for the time being, but it can only last for a limited time. Long-term sustainable clustering is based on the people working and surrounding the industry in question.

What made Hultsfred's mini cluster special is that it didn't grow from a large agglomeration of firms, which otherwise is a typical dimension of cluster building. Instead, it was one actor, namely the Rockparty association, with some charismatic and passionate people in the lead, that worked like a tree, from which other branches – other actors – could grow. This made it easier for a common view of the future, but it also involved risk that turned out to be fatal with the bankruptcy. Clusters that emerge and are dominated by a single actor are thus more vulnerable than clusters with a large number of actors.

Today there is no clear cluster motor in Hultsfred. The municipality has taken over responsibility for making sure that both the festival and the educational programmes live on in the district, but without a clear or common description of their direction. A cluster is a 'vision thing', to quote Power and Hallencreutz (2005). Rock City lives on, but without the biggest activity within the area that put its name on the building (i.e. 'rock' as in rock music). There is a risk that the Hultsfred Festival will become a brand only for the new owner, instead of a place-based operation that involves local businesses to any great degree.

At the same time the question is if it didn't become too much to handle for the Rockparty circle – especially for individual people – to both prioritize their own business and to be community builders. One conclusion is therefore to not allow the passionate entrepreneur to be drawn too much into discussions about community planning and clusters, or at least not to let them to work alone as the engine in cluster building. This is because of two risks that also *reinforce* each other. First, the entrepreneur risks neglecting his or her own business. And second, the cluster risks failing without that core business; a lesson from Hultsfred is that nothing lasts forever.

Such an approach, where the entrepreneur plays a smaller role in the cluster, may in the short term generate less lustre, particularly since the cluster cannot be personalized to the same extent. But in the long run it is a more sustainable approach since finances, risks and responsibilities are better distributed between stakeholders – and above all: the right person is at the right place and those who eat at the table also share the bill.

References

Armbrecht, J. and Andersson, T.D. (2010) 'Kultur och värdeskapande. En ekonomisk analys av Vara Konserthus och Nordiska Akvarellmuseet', in L. Lindeborg and L. Lindkvist (eds), *Kulturens kraft för regional utveckling*, Stockholm: SNS förlag.

Bakhshi, H., McVittie, E. and Simmie, J. (2008) *Creating Innovation: Do the Creative Industries Support Innovation in the Wider Economy?*, London: NESTA.

Beijer, L. (2009) 'Hultsfredsfestivalen en vinst för kommunen', *Barometern*, 5 September 2009, p. 27.

Bille Hansen, T. (1996) *Kulturøkonomiske studier: Økonomiske metoder vedrørende ressourceallokering til kultur- og fritidsaktiviteter*, København: Universitetet.

Bille, T. and Lorenzen, M. (2008) *Den danske oplevelsesøkonomi: Afgrænsning, økonomisk betydning og vækstmuligheder*, Frederiksberg: Samfundslitteratur.

Eliasson, G. and Eliasson, U. (1997) *Företagandets konst: om konstproduktionen i renässansens Florens*, Stockholm: City University Press.
Granström, K. (2009) 'Hemliga dokument avslöjar Hultsfred', *Aftonbladet*. Available at: www.aftonbladet.se/nojesbladet/article11969531.ab (accessed 3 August 2012).
Hultsfredsfestivalen.se (2012) 'Tack från en lyckad Hultsfredsfestival', *Hultsfredsfestivalen*. Available at: www.hultsfredsfestivalen.se/nyheter/tack-fran-en-lyckad-hultsfredsfestival (accessed 3 August 2012).
Institutet för tillväxtpolitiska studier *et al.* (2008) *Kultur i regionala utvecklingsstrategier och program: en lägesrapport*, Stockholm: Institutet för tillväxtpolitiska studier.
Karlsson, B. (2009) 'Festival för kommunen och industrin', *Kindaposten*. Available at: www.kindaposten.se/article/articleview/33786/1/88 (accessed 3 August 2012).
Landry, C. (2008) *The Creative City: A Toolkit for Urban Innovators*, London: Comedia.
Nielsén, T. (2008) *The ERIBA Model: An Effective and Successful Policy Framework for Creative Industries*, Stockholm: Knowledge Foundation.
P4 Kalmar (2012) Festivaljätte får räntefria lån. *Sveriges Radio*. Available at: http://sverigesradio.se/sida/artikel.aspx?programid=86&artikel=5073151 (accessed 3 August 3 2012).
Pettersson, T. (2012) 'Hultsfred 2012 – Hultsfred med i matchen igen', *Zero Magazine*. Available at: www.zeromagazine.nu/art.asp?id=348 (accessed 3 August 2012).
Power, D. and Hallencreutz, D. (2005) 'Cultural Industry Cluster Building in Sweden', in A. Lagendijk and P. Oinas (eds), *Proximity, Distance, and Diversity: Issues on Economic Interaction and Local Development*, Aldershot: Ashgate.
Power, D. and Nielsén, T. (2010) *Priority Sector Report: Creative and Cultural Industries*, European Cluster Observatory.
Rammer, C., Müller, K. and Trüby, J. (2009) 'The Role of Creative Industries in Industrial Innovation', *Innovation: Management, Policy & Practice*, 11(2): 148–168.
Sahlin, N.-E. (2001) *Kreativitetens filosofi*, Nora: Nya Doxa.
Silberstein, M. (2012) 'Hultsfredsfestivalen spänner musklerna', *Östran*. Available at: http://ostran.se/NYHETER/Kalmar/Hultsfredsfestivalen-spaenner-musklerna (accessed 3 August 2012).
Throsby, D. (2000) *Economics and Culture*, Cambridge: Cambridge University Press.
Törnqvist, G. (2004) *Kreativitetens geografi*, Stockholm: SNS förlag.
TT Spektra (2011) 'Ödessommar för Hultsfredsfestivalen', *Svenska Dagbladet*. Available at: www.svd.se/kultur/odessommar-for-hultsfredsfestivalen_6210745.svd (accessed 3 August 3 2012).

20 'Where the roads begin'. A northern renaissance around the Barents Sea

The Barents Euro-Arctic Region

Lisbeth Lindeborg

Prologue

> The Barents Region is a unique area in terms of both its history and its culture. It is a region with numerous cultures and languages. The wealth of the region is its cultural diversity... The cultural and creative sectors contribute substantially to regional, social and economic development in the Barents.
>
> (New Horizons in the Barents Region. 3rd Programme of Cultural Cooperation 2011–2013)[1]

The history of the Barents Euro-Arctic Region began on a cold, dark and snowy morning in the little town of Kirkenes in the Norwegian Finnmark region close to the Russian border. It was 11 January 1993. As the citizens of Kirkenes woke up that morning, they knew that the day would be of historical significance. Here the 'birth ceremony' of one of the most challenging *cross-border* regions in Europe would take place.[2] Some important politicians had already arrived – the Foreign Ministers of Sweden, Norway, Finland and the Russian Federation as well as a representative from the European Commission. They, however, were not the principal actors of this day; they just constituted the back-up for the delegations from seven regions in four states – from Norway: Nordland, Troms and Finnmark regions, from Sweden: the region of Norrbotten, from Finland: Lapland region and from Russia: Murmansk and Archangelsk Oblast.[3]

On this day, 48 years after it was totally destroyed in World War II and two years after the end of the Cold War, Kirkenes was to be made a symbol for a new kind of peaceful cooperation in Europe. Having survived 1,000 air-raid alarms and 320 air attacks during the World War II, having survived the worries and tensions along the only NATO-Soviet border in Europe, no other place could more deserve to be a focal point for peace and security.

In the Kirkenes local assembly hall the lights were on when the politicians gathered on the podium. After greetings had been exchanged and other ceremonial procedures had taken place the moment had come to sign the 'Kirkenes Declaration', thus establishing a formal cooperation around the

Barents Sea, called the Barents Euro-Arctic Region (BEAR). In the declaration the general aims with regard to cooperation within different sectors were drawn up.

In order to handle the cooperation a Barents Euro-Arctic Council (BEAC) and a Barents Regional Council (BRC) were established. BEAC was to be an intergovernmental forum with biannual meetings on the ministerial level and the BRC was to be the representative body for the seven regions as well as for its eighth member – a spokesperson for the 70,000 Samis, the indigenous people living in the seven regions.

In his speech, on this particular day, the Norwegian Foreign Minister Thorvald Stoltenberg concluded: 'A common regional identity in the North can build on a rich historical heritage. We know that there have been prolonged contacts between groups in the region. In many ways the Barents Region was a common cultural region before the European nation states erected borders in the area.'[4]

In search of a Northeast Passage in order to shorten the voyage to China and America, the Dutch seafarer Willem Barents (1550–1597) made three expeditions in the Northern seas between 1594 and 1597. He came as far as the archipelago near Novaya Zemlya and on his last expedition he discovered and named the islands of Spitsbergen (Svalbard) and Bear Island (Björnöya). He himself died on the expedition in 1597, but some of his surviving crew reached the Kola Peninsula. In 1598 a part of Willem Barents' diary was printed, but his log book was not found until 1875. The name Barents Sea first appeared on a chart in 1853. In the south its border is the Norwegian and Russian mainland. To the east it is bounded by the Novaya Zemlya, in the north its border is Svalbard and Franz Josef Land and to the west it borders the Greenland Sea. The Barents Sea is 1,300 km long and some 1,100 km wide and it has an average depth of 230 m. It was not until 1878 that the Northeast Passage was mapped out by the Swedish explorer Adolf Erik Nordenskjöld (1832–1901). In 2009 two commercial cargo vessels travelled the 'Northern Sea Route' as it is now called. Because of global warming the route is now more accessible. In 2010 the first freighter made the voyage from Kirkenes to the Pacific without stops in Russian ports and the following year 34 commercial ships used the route.

Twenty years after the first Kirkenes Declaration, leading national and regional politicians will gather in Kirkenes again – in June 2013. As the location for the Barents Secretariat the town has gained in prominence. A Kirkenes II Declaration will be signed; this time the declaration will include the increasingly important off-shore cooperation. During the twenty years of its existence the Barents Region has grown into thirteen member regions. The additional six regions are: Västerbotten in Sweden, Oulu and Kainuu in Finland and Nenets, Komi and Karelia in Russia (Figure 20.1).

In relation to the situation before 1993 the cooperation in the Barents Region is a 'success story' in spite of many difficulties and problems. The cultural cooperation is paving the way for other collaborations. More than 2,000 cultural initiatives have appeared on the 'regional stage'; they have

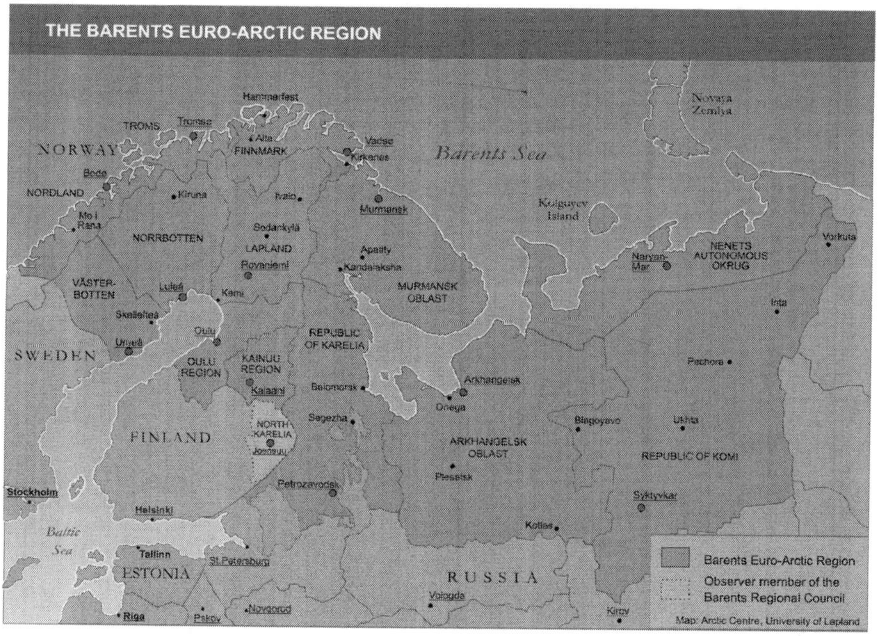

Figure 20.1 Map of the Barents Euro-Arctic Region.
Source: Arctic Centre Lapland.

been seen, heard and enjoyed before withdrawing in order to make room for ever new endeavours. One of them that takes place every other year is the *Li Biennale of Northern Environmental and Sculpture Art* in Kulttuuri Kauppila Art Centre in the Finnish Oulu Region. In 2012 artists gathered for the third time to show their works of art in the forest along the Li River. In the catalogue of the Li Biennale, its organizer Leena Vuotovesi grasped the essence of the cultural cooperation in just a few words: 'Here nature and people get strength from each other, support each other. North as such is art.'[5]

Just twenty years after its start the Barents Euro-Arctic Region could serve as a model for other regional cross-border cooperations. In order to understand its development process and the role of arts and culture in building the region, there are several questions to be answered. What is the fabric of this region, its physical prerequisites? This is an important issue. The geography and topography of a region is a basic criterion for its identity. What is its historical background? Another issue to be analysed is how the regional cooperation came about at all; what theory and experience leads up to it? What would the mental map (Gould and White 1992) of the Barents Region be like? Is there an Arctic identity? A further issue to be delved into is: what kinds of arts and culture do prosper up North? Is there a special Barents culture? These are the main issues addressed in this chapter.

Polar days and polar nights: the northern periphery of Europe

> The farther north one goes, the more objects and beings lose their fixed shapes and contours, and the Universe loses its boundaries in time and space. Space melts away and disappears. Time slows down as well and in its inability to reach the ultimate boundary it stops completely and leads into eternity.
>
> (Nikolaj M. Terebikhin)[6]

When studying cross-border cooperations the knowledge about their physical prerequisites, e.g. the geographical and topographical equipment, the demographic features, natural resources and politics of the territory in question, are essential. The 'fabric' of the regions involved determines the kind of cross-border region to develop. Empirical studies show that there are as many cross-border cooperation models as there are cooperations (Lindeborg 1995; Weihe-Lindeborg 2001/2005). There is no master plan to be copied or transferred. In order for a cooperation to be successful the exclusive and driving moment of original creativity and innovation must not be ruined through the lapse into a transfer situation.

When a cooperation is about to start, the regional partners have to define the kind of cooperation they want. There are three different basic categories: territorial cross-border cooperations; cooperation around specific issues; and different kinds of either public and/or private institutional cooperations, including people-to-people initiatives. One of their common denominators is the cultural and arts cooperation as a platform. When corresponding to all three categories a full-fledged cooperation evolves – like the Barents Euro-Arctic Region.

Besides the Baltic Sea 'mega region' the BEAR as a *cross-border macro region* is the largest regional cooperation in Europe.[7] Its 1,755,800 km^2 are equivalent to the area of France, Spain, Germany, Italy and the Netherlands together. 75 per cent of the area belongs to the five Russian regions. The Barents Region, however, is sparsely populated – with not quite six million people; four million inhabitants live in the Russian regions. In addition there are three minority populations 70,000 Sami in the eight Scandinavian regions and in the Kola Peninsula, there are 7,000 Nenets in the Nenets Region and 6,000 Veps in the Russian Karelia Republic.

Nature and environment

The natural environment of the Barents Euro-Arctic Region is harsh with barren land and wide tundras (taiga), wetlands and ice in most of its northern regions. In its southern regions there are mountainous areas with large boreal forests of conifer trees. Whereas the summer north of the Arctic Circle delights in a midnight sun from mid-May to the end of July with the Midnight Sun Film Festival in Sodankylä (Finnish Lapland), as a world famous highlight, the winter from mid-November to the end of January is dark. The climate and the topography in the region with long distances between people is but one problem to tackle.

Common to all parts of BEAR is the vulnerability of its nature. Within its borders there is one of the largest remaining intact natural ecosystems on Earth. Since the cooperation started, several groups work on preserving the natural ecosystems, the biodiversity and water quality.

At the same time BEAR is suffering from serious environmental problems. As a periphery – far away from the national centres – and thus considered of little value, it was used as a dumping ground for all kinds of waste. According to an early report (Bröms 1994) most of the problems stemmed from the Kola Peninsula, where poisonous gas and radioactive waste with its high dioxin levels have been dumped. One positive result of the BEAR-cooperation is the coordinated effort to get rid of the environmental problems in the region.

The centre-periphery issue

Not only nationally, but also from a European perspective the peripheral regions around the Barents and White Seas had a low standing until recently. With strong centralist systems in most European states, national border areas were neglected territories all over the continent. Between France and Germany the border regions were used for military purposes. In Britain the so-called Celtic fringe (Hechter 1975) fell victim to internal colonization just as the northern regions of Scandinavia. These areas were considered to be generally backward, and unattractive.

Hechter distanced himself from the so-called diffusion theory, emanating from the notion of a homogenizing/assimilating process between the centre core and its periphery. Thus, according to Hechter, a peripheral area could only be exploited (as dumping ground, for military purposes, etc.) by the core, either through a governmental ban of the genuine culture of the periphery or by employing a tactic in order to make it seem inferior. At the same time the core culture was given the highest priority in the region (Lindeborg 1991). For the inhabitants in the periphery there were only two alternatives, either to leave the periphery and join the core, which caused a brain drain, or to stay put and fight for the culture of their own group. In an interview the Scottish literary scientist Cairns Craig emphasized:

> Very often the peripheral culture has as much – or even more – to contribute as the core culture. ... Recognizing the vitality of the periphery is the first step towards overthrowing the dominant conceptions of core culture tradition. ... That will release the vitality of the peripheries.[8]

With the Europeanization and regionalization processes, however, the widespread difficult and undemocratic relations between core and periphery in any country are changing. The 'centralizing' of peripheral areas became a frequent topic in regional politics as well as in culture geographical research (Pierret 1978; Gidlund *et al.* 1988; Lindeborg 1995).

According to Alfred Mozer (1973) the borders are the scars of history. And another pioneer in European regional cooperation research, Viktor von Malchus, emphasized in 1975, that the Europeans living in the border regions still stand with their backs to the borders facing the capitals and centres of their states – no matter how far away these were (von Malchus 1975). With the cooperations in the European border regions that have been established in order to find solutions to shared predicaments caused by their peripheral location, the situation has changed.

Today several studies of some 200 cross-border cooperations in Europe show that culture and arts projects constitute a first common platform between cooperating regions – not to mention that these projects pave the way for other kinds of collaborations (Eisenhammer 1992; VRE 1992; Lindeborg 1995; Östhol 1996; Blatter 2000; Weihe-Lindeborg 2001/2005).

Democracy and oil

The peripheral location, however, is not the only obstacle for the cooperation within the Barents Euro-Arctic Region. There are also the different political set-ups in the region. Whereas the regions in the three Scandinavian states have very similar political structures, the Russian regions have been curtailed in their activities through the strong Russian centralist system with its weak democratic development. In order to democratize the cooperation on a local level the Organization of Local Councils in Norrbotten initiated the project *Icebreaker* with local communities in the region of Murmansk. The project which ran from 2004–2009 has had several positive effects including an increase of cultural cooperations.

For the past ten years the rich natural resources of the region have come into focus. In the region itself and in the Barents Sea waters outside, extremely rich deposits of gas, oil and minerals (iron, nickel and diamonds) have been found. Other resources are fish and timber. Although the Arctic area covers just 10 per cent of the earth, it has 25–30 per cent of its natural resources. According to professor Kefeli at the University of Archangelsk there is a new expression: 'Who owns the Arctic owns the World.'[9]

With regard to the off-shore wealth there have been several controversies between the two coastal states, Norway and Russia, as to how to divide the riches. Because of the good partnership in the Barents Region, however, a compromise was able to be reached in 2010 when on a state visit to Oslo the Russian president Medvedev and the Norwegian Prime Minister Jens Stoltenberg signed an agreement. This delimitation deal divides the 175,000 km^2 large area into two equally big parts. According to the agreement the deal 'would strengthen neighbourly relations, secure stability and promote cooperation in the Barents Region and the Arctic Ocean'.[10]

Historical backgrounds: hidden pasts

> On Midsummer's Day in 1518 there was a lively atmosphere of merchandizing and exchanging of goods in the harbour of Torneå. There were many ships from far away countries, carrying wine from Portugal and textiles from Germany. Finnish and Russian people, Swedes, Portuguese and Germans gathered around the merchants. Bargaining and trading in their different languages they tried to understand each other.
>
> (Fjellström 1991)[11]

For hundreds of years the most northern parts of Scandinavia were generally considered as backward and burdensome. Except for mountaineering enthusiasts and other lovers of spectacular sceneries in 'uncivilized' contexts, there was little or no interest in the history or culture of the north. As late as the 1960s with regard to the northern regions the spirit of the Venetian cartographer Giovanni Leardo still lived on. In 1448 he had drawn a map of Scandinavia writing just one sentence: *Dexerto, desabitato pel freddo*, e.g. a wasteland uninhabited because of cold. Historically and culturally that was as inaccurate a description of Scandinavia in the fifteenth century as it was of the northern regions of the twentieth century. Archaeological and other historical sources show the north to be anything but *dexerto*, or *desabitato pel freddo*. Until recently, however, it was in the interest of central government politics to dismiss the north as valueless. Thus we can talk about a hidden past.

To trace it, the thrilling journey back in history could start with the remains of the 14,000-year-old Stone Age cultures that have been found in the Archangelsk region. And 3,500 years before the Cheops' pyramid was built, Stone Age people, hunters and fishermen, lived in settlements dating back to 6,000 BC in Vuollerim in the Swedish region of Norrbotten. Remnants of their huts with fireplaces have been found (Lundholm 1993). Later on, the Roman historian Cornelius Tacitus wrote about a northern people called Fenni, probably the Sami population. It is also known that the Vikings sailed to the White Sea in order to catch fish.

During these times no borders divided the North. This was a situation serving the needs of the Sami population who constantly crossed the present borders in search of good pastures for their reindeers. But they were not the only travellers – from the Middle Ages and onward we know of a flourishing transit trade from the Atlantic in the west to Russia in the east and vice versa.

One reason for the open borders in the north was that the governments did not primarily bother about national borders. Their main interest was to divide the area into tax revenue districts in order to get the income from taxes and trade. Not until the peace of Stolbova in 1617 was a settlement reached regarding the national borders between Sweden and Russia. At this time and until 1809 Finland belonged to Sweden – for 700 years. Thereafter Finland became a part of Russia for 108 years until 1917.

Westwards the Swedish and Norwegian governments declared and fought several wars over the centuries. In 1751 the borders between the two neighbours were finally outlined. After additional warfare between Sweden and Norway, the two states agreed on a union under the reign of the Swedish king in 1815. This union lasted until 1905.

On the Russian side the founding of Archangelsk in 1584 was of significance – the town was the only Russian trading centre and port westwards. In the seventeenth century the trade between Norway and Russia increased. The inhabitants of Archangelsk, called Pomors, gave name to the trade with Norway – the Pomor trade (Henriksson *et al.* 2001). According to a ship's register from 1840, 400 Russian ships anchored in the Norwegian ports of Troms and Finnmark that year. The trade came to an end with World War I and the Russian revolution in 1917.

With the 'internal colonization' of the northern Scandinavian peripheries in the nineteenth century a kind of peripheral consciousness started to grow in the regions around the Barents Sea. In the Swedish region of Norrbotten, for example, silver and iron were found. But the minerals from Norrbotten were not allowed to be further transported on Norrbottnian ships south of Stockholm. Between 1614 and 1765 all export and import trade was under the control of the Swedish central government. The consequence for Norrbotten was poverty and stagnation.

The history in contemporary art and education

Confronted with a hidden past it is essential for the people in the Barents Region to get acquainted with their history. Several cultural cooperation projects focus on the historical heritage. Between 2003 and 2006 the goal of the project *Rock Art on the Edge of Europe* was to show the relation between Stone Age carvings, the White Sea Petroglyphs, and cultural activity in the prehistoric society. It was a multi-lateral project involving museums and universities in seven regions and with some national participation.

Of particular significance are the projects for youths. In *Living Stories* in 2004 the history of the Barents Region was performed by puppet theatres with school children as the target group. The project also brought the puppeteers together with teachers and librarians in all regions with the aim of showing the role of the puppet as an artistic tool in education. It is projects like these that make the Barents people aware and proud of their history in contrast to the negative view they used to have of themselves. At the same time it shows the outside world the uniqueness of the region.

With the publishing of encyclopedias and history books the missing historical heritage comes to life again. Under the aegis of the Northern Arctic Federal University in Archangelsk there are several volumes of *The Pomor Encyclopedia* being published, so far on biology, economy and history. In 2012 another volume on culture is envisaged like the two books *The Barents Encyclopedia* and *The History of the Barents Region*, a joint Swedish–Norwegian production with authors and experts from all thirteen regions. The purpose of these two books is to discuss the roots of the present developments and review the cultural, socio-economic and political prerequisites for a continued and intensified cross-border cooperation. In an earlier *Encyclopedia of the Arctic* published in 2005 there is a lot of unique information which cannot be found anywhere else. In the foreword it is stated: 'Rather than resulting in a confused definition of the Arctic, the material presented in the Encyclopedia of the Arctic demonstrates the beauty, power and incredible diversity of the northern regions of the globe.'

The North Calotte cooperation

Until World War I and the Russian revolution the relations in the regions around the Barents Sea went on more or less 'as usual'. In the twentieth century however big politics intervened, and with the emergence of the Soviet Union the relations cooled down. The border traffic weakened and a climate of animosity spread. The central governments decided that the relations now had to be south-north-south instead of west-east-west. This changed in 1970 with the North Calotte cooperation between the regions in the Scandinavian states and the revival of the old relations.

The reason for the initiative was clear. In the northern peripheral regions of Scandinavia the economy had gone down and people left. In this situation the Nordic Council started to analyse the possibilities for a formalized cross-border regional cooperation as a means to revive the regional economy. In order to coordinate these efforts a commission was founded in 1970 – a trilateral North Calotte commission with regional representatives, governmental civil servants and experts (von Malchus 1975).

They found the communication on all levels to be very poor. There were still passport controls, visa rules, hard customs legislation, high telephone costs and very few border crossings. In addition there were language problems, even between Swedish and Norwegian; although they are dialects of the same language, the understanding was insufficient. In order to start a cooperation, the commission recommended cultural cooperation and education as first priorities. Another field of activity was the yearly sports competition between Arctic municipalities and regions. In 1959 the Russian region Murmansk participated for the first time.

A most important recommendation from the Nordic Council was to further a common peripheral identity through cross-border cooperations. In addition the commission tried to break through the Iron Curtain with smaller local cooperation initiatives. In 1987 the Russian president Mikhail Gorbachev allowed the region Murmansk to develop international contacts of its own. In a speech that year Gorbachev suggested, that the North Pole should be a Pole of Peace.

In 1992 the Scandinavian North Calotte regions met with representatives of Murmansk and Archangelsk regions for a strategic conference in Norwegian Tromsö. There the first definite steps for a Barents Euro-Arctic Region were taken to strengthen the northern peripheral identity, to further the attractiveness of the region, to promote cultural diversity, to develop new networks, to strengthen the administrative capacities and to secure peace and political stability.

A few months later the Barents Euro-Arctic Region was established.

'North as such is art': the formal organization of Barents culture

In 1993, when the Barents Euro-Arctic Region was established, *Europe of the Regions* was an acknowledged concept. And it was well known that investments in culture and arts in regions and the establishing of cultural infrastructures also had positive financial spin-off effects. As early as 1978 the Standing Conference of Local and Regional Authorities of Europe – within the framework of the European Council – had issued its Bordeaux Declaration. There the significance of arts and culture for regional development was emphasized (Weihe-Lindeborg 2001/2005).

Likewise the experience from other cross-border regions had shown that a well-functioning organization was essential for an up-and-coming region. The responsible national and regional politicians knew that they had to find a good body structure for their new Barents Region. Just to have a vision was not enough – you had to get down to brass tacks. From the first moment it was thus decided that the cooperation in Barents Euro-Arctic Region takes place on different levels, the political, e.g. the national, regional and local level, the institutional level and between different socio-economic and society-based initiatives.

Cultural declarations

The first Conference of Ministers of Culture was held in Kirkenes on 31 August and 1 September 1993. In the first Declaration on Culture, the close historical and cultural relations between the people in the region were emphasized as well as the significance of cultural cooperation for regional development. In this context – it was declared – 'culture is to be understood in the widest sense of the concept', for example including sports. One important aim of the cultural cooperation was to increase knowledge about each other. Furthermore the cultural cooperation should be initiated and managed in close cooperation with regional cultural authorities.

In the second communiqué by the Ministers of Culture in Archangelsk (September 1998) the promotion of cultural identity was particularly underlined and the cultural policy was given the name of *Northern Renaissance*. An exchange of experts, art students and teachers was also recommended on a long-term basis.

Since then there has been a third ministerial conference, in Oulu, in Finnish Lapland in September 2002. As a first priority it was agreed to promote local and regional cultural identity and inter-regional cultural production based on the historical tradition in the Barents Euro-Arctic Region. Likewise the strengthening of cultural identity and the preservation of cultural heritage of the indigenous populations was stressed.

These three declarations on a ministerial level lay down the ultimate aims of the cultural cooperation. On the regional level a Barents Cultural Committee was set up in 1993, followed by the Barents Regional Working Group on Culture in 2001, which in 2007 was replaced by a Joint Working Group on Culture (JWGC) which works under the support of both the BEAC and the BRC. These groups constitute the framework for the real work being done (Figure 20.2).

In 1995 a special working group on the indigenous peoples was set up – Working Group on Indigenous Peoples (WGIP). Apart from its operational tasks it has also an advisory role for both the Barents Council and the Regional Council. The Barents Indigenous Peoples Office, established in 2003, is connected to the University of Murmansk. The Samis have a Sami Council with a Secretariat in Utsjoki in Finnish Lapland.

When reading the national and regional declarations we observe that their contents and language are getting more and more self assured and internationalized. The enhancement of the historical heritage and the culture of the indigenous populations show the Barents' mental map changing as well as the image and profile of the region.

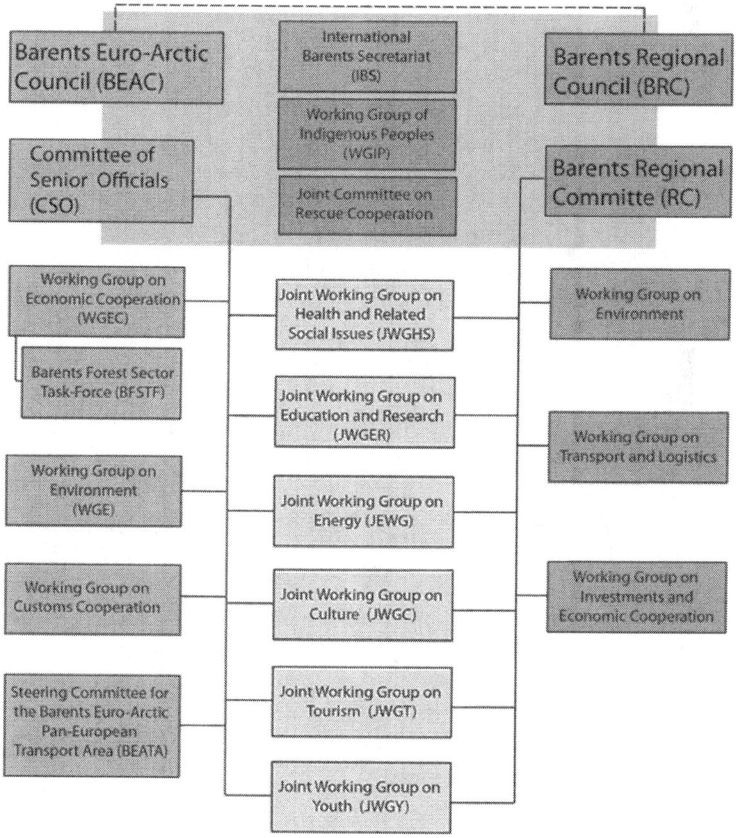

Figure 20.2 Structure of the Barents Cooperation.

A new Barents generation: cultural cooperation as a strategy of modernization

> The Barents Region's cooperation started a complete new period in the North. ... From the start culture has been one of the most active sectors... one was forced to adapt to the different cultural activities. ... For the first time in all of the history of the northern area, the cultural situation could be observed as a whole.
>
> (Laine 2001)

Eight years after it was founded the Barents Euro-Arctic Region had come into its own as an important cross-border region in the EU with a particularly successful cultural cooperation. Invited by the Council of Europe in Strasbourg, Kari Laine, from the Arts Council of Finnish Lapland, had been asked to give a talk on the significance of this cultural cooperation on 26 October 2001. In his talk 'Culture and Conflict Prevention. Experiences from Intercultural Cooperation in the Barents Euro-Arctic Region', Laine emphasized that the Barents cultural cooperation should be strengthened and integrated in a European and Baltic dimension. In that way it could serve as a model and inspiration for other parts of the world.

When Laine gave his talk in Strasbourg he had just received the first Report on the Barents Cultural Cooperation, which had been presented a week earlier at a conference in Norwegian Bodö. The report, that was written by the Barents Cultural Committee, focused on the period 1994–1999 recording that there had been some 600 projects; 10 per cent of them were multilateral, the rest were mainly bilateral. Quite a number of twin-city projects were not counted. During 1994–1999 the number of projects increased by 40 per cent – during 1998–1999 they increased by 15 per cent. Most of the projects involved sports activities (18 per cent) and library and literature projects (18 per cent). Surprisingly few involved museums (2 per cent) and theatre (2 per cent).

During this time there was one multilateral project gaining a lot of attention, the Barents Euro-Arctic Diploma for Cultural and Cultural Tourism managers. This was a one-year-long training and seminar programme run by the Barents Cultural Committee in 1993, 1994, 1996 and 1998. The aim of the project was to study how cultural activities can be part of regional development and how geo-cultural east-west traditions can be revitalized and contribute to the future of the region. During the course six participants from each of the 24 countries were trained as project leaders and entrepreneurs doing individual projects. Four seminars lasting one week each took place in one region of each country. It was underlined that although there are many differences between northern Scandinavia and Russia there is a mutual interest in developing the regions through cultural management, diversity and a strong regional identity.

One of the most spectacular Barent events in the 1990s was *Breaking the Ice* – a number of artistic events taking place in Stockholm for one week in 1998 during the European Cultural Capital year. The programme was made up of five cross-border and 17 regional performances and exhibitions attracting a public of 6,000 people. Special attention was paid to the Barents Dance Ensemble and to the exhibition *The Land of the Circle*. Since the start of the cultural cooperation dance as art has been one of the priorities.

Project organization and funding

Most of the Barents cooperations are either bi- or trilateral. Because of the long distances, insufficient infrastructure and other obstacles there are relatively few multilateral projects – so far. The bilateral cooperation between the Norwegian and Russian regions are particularly intense. Thus the Barents Secretariat in Kirkenes has spent 300 million Norwegian crowns for 2,300 bilateral projects with Russia – a majority of them on culture, youth and education. External evaluation processes have found that these projects have been successful. This has led to an increase of people, cars, trucks and buses crossing the borders.

The activity of the Barents Secretariat also includes the BarentsKult programme between professional artists, musicians, actors, theatre directors, film-makers and festival organizers. In addition the Secretariat supports the Barents Press Network for journalists working in the Barents Region. It is important that the journalists in the 13 regions travel to the other regions and report on them. There is also an exchange between schools and teachers through the network Barentsplus.

Most projects in the Barents Euro-Arctic region are on culture and identity, which are the most successful ones. The costs of the cooperation are carried by the nation states, different Nordic authorities, like the Arts Councils, the EU and to a lesser extent by the regions and local authorities themselves. It is important to explore new types of financing like the European Neighbourhood and Partnership Instrument (ENPI) from the EU. In order to stabilize the whole Barents endeavour, the EU founded the initiative the Northern Dimension in 1999. It not only encompasses the Barents Region but also the Baltic.

The organizing of the cultural cooperation, the programming of it and the aims envisaged, could not be better. Still there are some problems of a financial kind. Whereas the Norwegian, the Finnish and even the Russian governments guarantee the financing of their regions and projects in the Barents Region the Swedish side is less generous. Applicants from the Swedish regions have to go to their regional or local councils. At the same time the Swedish Institute and the Swedish Culture and Arts Council (Kulturrådet) has cut its financing. According to Jan Henriksson, a pioneer of the Barents cultural cooperation and a regional and local civil servant, there is no obvious reason for the cuts.[12]

Programmes and people-to-people cooperation

After the report from 2001 a planning programme was needed in order to be able to handle the increasing amount of cultural projects and to prevent them from overlapping each other. *Voices in the Barents Region* from 2003 was the first programme with a mandate period of three years until 2006. It was followed by another two programmes: *New Winds in the Barents Region*, 2008–2010, and *New Horizons in the Barents Region*, 2011–2013. The main goals of the three programmes are very similar:

- to make the Barents Region and its cultural dimension more visible in an international perspective and thus contribute to economic development;
- to further cultural diversity;
- to raise the consciousness of the inhabitants concerning the region's identity.

It was seen as particularly important to create a partnership between the cultural sector and other sectors such as business, industry, research and education. Thus the film industry and cultural tourism were singled out as important sectors. Since 2004 the Barents Region is being marketed in Europe and the rest of the world under the name of Arctic Europe. Most intense is the tourism traffic between Finnish Lapland and the five Russian regions. Between 2010 and 2011 the number of Russian tourists going over to Finland increased by 8.3 per cent. In the first half of 2011 there were almost half a million Russian tourists. In the other direction there was a greater increase of Norwegian tourists (13 per cent) than there were Finnish people crossing the border to Russia (4.5 per cent).

It is considered as one of the greatest achievements of the Barents cooperation that ordinary people on different sides of the borders can meet and get to know each other. Although many stereotypes and prejudices have disappeared in the twenty years of cooperation, there is still more work to do. In March 2012 a new programme for better intercultural communication was introduced through a conference at the University of Archangelsk: *Breaking Stereotypes in the Barents Region.*

In this context the people-to-people cooperation beside the regional cooperation between politicians and officials and the national cooperation between ministers 'is extensive and can be called a third pillar in the Barents cooperation' (Alnes 2012). The projects involving young people are particularly high on the agenda: 'They lay the foundation for future cooperation and for the formation of a Barents generation' (Alnes 2012).

'The land of icy terror': in search of an Arctic Identity

> We define regional identity as the positive image which individuals and groups of a given region adopt in their relations with other regions. This self image can be more or less complex.
>
> (Bassand 1990)

Field studies of culture as a location factor in cities and towns as well as studies of regional development in different areas of Europe have shown, that a strong identity – a sense of belonging to a certain place – is a great asset. A strong identity has a market value. It was not always like that; the awareness of identities as positive is a fairly new phenomenon and has a lot to do with the development of our globalized societies.

At the present time cities and regions have to show themselves off in order to be able to compete. Even if an identity of place is not a *deus ex machina* it could be an efficient instrument in order to give a place a distinct profile. Through the identity a region gets its personality. A strong and positive identity leaves a positive imprint on politicians of a region and on its citizens. That means that they can speak up for their region in a much better way. In order to utilize the endogenous potential of a region, this potential has to be defined and activated by the inhabitants identifying themselves with their region. The cultural identity fosters creativity and this in turn leads to innovations. For the economy, for the tourism industry, and for R&D activities a strong identity gives positive signals to the outside world (Lindeborg 1993; Weihe-Lindeborg 2001/2005).

As could be seen from the programmes and the organization of Barents Culture the identity of the region has highest priority. Although some of the thirteen regions have a strong individual identity there was no expressed cross-border identity because of the general negative image of the region. For the Barents Region the task is to rediscover its identity and to communicate about it. That implies a learning process which is similar to that of regions with weak identities. They too have to find methods to strengthen their identities or to change and renew them. That is where the identity creating factors are being called upon. Culture and arts are particularly prominent identity-shaping devices giving places their attractiveness and a good image, but they are not the only building blocks as we can see (Lindeborg 1993):

(1) Geographic-topographic-climatic conditions
(2) Historical heritage incorporating the past in all its facets
(3) Cultural-historical heritage, based on all kinds of cultural and socio-cultural production including all past artistic creations
(4) Language
(5) Contemporary culture and arts, e.g. the creation of artworks and culture in a wider sense
(6) Present ways of life – lifestyle – everyday living
(7) The political dimension could entail tensions between the region and the central power but could also mean a special political harassment and negligence
(8) Economic life – work and labour
(9) Projective identity encompassing planning future strategies

The question is how these factors relate to the Barents Region.

Identity creating factors in the Barents region

As regards the geography-topography-climate factor this has a strong bearing on the Barents Region. Beside its extraordinary peripheral location on the top of the globe, the ice and snow are the most outstanding and prevalent identity-shaping denominators in the Barents Euro-Arctic Region. The inhabitants of the region are always surrounded by ice and snow in their living environment. They have always had to fight their environment. Only lately they started to use ice and snow as material for art works. That means that ice and snow is part of the mental map of the Barents Euro-Arctic citizen.

Ice and snow are beautiful materials serving as inspiration for the imagination. But ice and snow also cause fear. It was the Norwegian explorer Fridtjof Nansen (1831–1930) who first called the Arctic around the Barents sea the land of icy terror'.[13] In 1893 his ship *Fram* got stuck in heavy masses of ice and he and another explorer had to continue the search for the North Pole with dogsleds, kayaks and on foot. In 1895 they reached the highest latitude ever reached by Homo sapiens.

According to Professor Lukin (2012a) the word arctic derives from the Greek arktos, which in Russian means bear. In his essay 'Arctic and Social Fears' he underlines that there are several common arctic social fears. The arctic *Terra incognita* is a basin for human fears, he writes, fears of different kinds like natural fears: of the immense and empty space, of the cold and of ice. A biological fear is the fear of dangerous animals, whereas situational fears imply fear of ice compression, fear of the darkness but also fear of the Northern Lights (*Aurora Borealis*). During the last decade another fear has developed – fear of global warming, with its devastating consequences: rise of the sea level, melting permafrost, flood, rain and a new ice age and not being able to master the ecological and environmental problems of the region any longer.

> The history of arctic exploration is full of human tragedies, severe efforts that befell many polar expeditions in the waters of the northern seas. Some of them have become widely known and have contributed to shaping the image of the Arctic as an inaccessible, harsh space relentlessly taking the lives of people. ... the development of severe huge arctic space has always required personal courage solidarity and human decency... Arctic solidarity is the basis on which it is possible to build a partnership Arctic.
>
> (Lukin 2012a)

In order to come to terms with their challenging environment artists and architects of the Barents Region started to relate to their environment of ice and snow in another and creative way – using the ice for their artworks. Prominent examples are the ice sculpture exhibitions in different places, the ice Globe Theatre a few years back in Jukkasjärvi, and in the same village there is still the world famous ice hotel. The ice dome concert hall in Piteå (see Chapter 16) are as spectacular as the Indigenous Peoples Film Festival in the Northern Light theatre, an Arctic theatre made of snow and lit with candles. It is in Skabmagovat in the Finnish Lapland region close to the Sami museum situated in a forest. The coldest performances took place in minus 40 degrees.

It is evident, that the climate and the peripheral geography of the Barents Euro-Arctic Region is much stronger as an identity creating factor than the geography and climate is of a town in Denmark. Mainly physical hardship makes people feel solidarity and togetherness within a region. That is why inhabitants in remote places – in peripheries – express a strong regional consciousness. It is one part of the identity which cannot be changed; what can be changed, however, is the perception of it. Today more and more people in the Barents Region emphasize that they live in a 'peripheral centre'. Another unchangeable identity factor is the historical and cultural–historical heritage. Again the perception of it can be changed as we have seen, when this heritage is being worked on as an object for contemporary art and other creative processes.

In order to create or rather renew and change an identity, there are the other factors to be used. The most essential one is the contemporary creation of art, which is a platform for the Barents cooperation. Lifestyle, economic structures and a projective future identity are other factors as is the political dimension. The fact that the Barents regions were neglected, exploited and met with contempt by their central governments for hundreds of years is uniting them today. They want to succeed.

'Where the roads begin': cultural diversification in the Barents region

Three months after the signing of the Kirkenes Declaration (April 1993) a seminar was held in the Swedish iron-mining town of Kiruna, north of the Polar Circle in the region of Norrbotten. People crowded in the local Peoples Park among them some Sami in their colourful costumes. The topic for the seminar was 'Arts and Culture as Development Factors for Regions'. In the discussion after the seminar there was one particularly important statement coming from a Swedish Sami representative:

> The focus on culture in order to strengthen the regional identity here up North and the right of regions to decide on cultural matters would mean that the Sami population will be officially recognized as a kind of region in its own right. We are now a part of the Barents Euro-Arctic Region.

Hitting the nail on the head, the Sami spokesman made it clear to the audience that the essence of the Barents Region, its heterogeneity and cultural diversification, would now be displayed.[14] Decentralism implies pluralism and diversification as opposed to centralist uniformity. Experience shows that homogeneous and monostructural systems are not only anachronistic but anti-creative and against innovation (Törnquist 1993).

But being a region in its own right like the other thirteen regions of the Barents cooperation does not mean a distancing from the larger Barents Euro-Arctic Region. Just as the diversification is essential this must not lead to fragmentation. A common Barents culture, a common Arctic culture is a condition in order for this immense periphery to survive. For the Barents Region as for any other big region there is a balancing between its smaller parts and the whole context. Barents could be seen as a mirror of the European principle of *unitas multiplex* (Morin 1987). One of the assets of the Barents Region is its polycentricity – there are several cities and towns of significance.

Ice belt universities with cultural profiles

Another asset of the Barents Region are its many universities. At the same time as they develop individual cultural profiles they come together under an Arctic shield – they market themselves under the heading of Universities of the Arctic.[15] The goal is to make the Arctic space a creative one. As opposed to the Sun Belt Universities in Southern Europe or the USA they could be called Ice Belt Universities. One of the most successful universities is the University of Lapland in Rovaniemi. Their Faculty of Art and Design organizes the most northern *Design Week* in the world every February. In 2012 the theme was *Lightness and Darkness*. With exhibitions, fashion shows, company presentations, international seminars and networking events, the ultimate goal was to focus on the environment, infrastructure and attractiveness of Rovaniemi. There was also a snow show full of Arctic light, sounds and ice sculptures in three snow domes. It was the fourth ever Design Week in a campaign to make Rovaniemi a city of design.

In the Northern Arctic Federal University (NarFU) in Archangelsk the cultural focus is on film. In September 2012 the film festival Arctic Cinema took place here at the same time as the international scientific conference *History of the Discovery and Exploration of the Arctic*. Another focus on film related to Archangelsk is the collection of some 35,000 early documentary films. Within a special Barents project they are now being saved and restored as a unique historical source.

With the negative image of the most northern regions in Scandinavia and Russia and the attitude from the governments that diversification is a threat to the unity of the nation state it is most important for the Barents Region to turn this image and these prejudices upside down. In this context it should be remembered that the language of the indigenous peoples, for example, the Samis, was strictly forbidden and was punished in Swedish schools a hundred years ago. One early project was a book with the participation of poets and authors from most regions using their seven languages. As opposed to the southern perception that all roads end up north, the Barents inhabitants emphasize that the Barents periphery is the beginning of the world – hence they called their book, *Where the roads begin*.

From the beginning of the cultural cooperation literature has been one of the most favoured forms of art. Libraries went together in networks and in projects and in 2010 the Norwegian Barents Secretariat and other funds decided to give 3 million Norwegian crowns for translation. For more than ten years the *Barents Literature Centre* in Kalix in Swedish Norrbotten was the hub of all literary projects in the Barents Region. In an old yellow wooden house the lights were on and people came and went for many years. It was the place for seminars, for meetings of the Barents authors, for courses for young writers, literature camps for youth, for children's book reading, for the discovery of new authors, etc. The Barents Region has always been a hot bed for creative writing. Lately, however, many of the activities have slowed down. New people took over and finally the financiers cut the money. In 2010 the centre closed down. Lately there have been new literature initiatives and events in other places for example in the Russian region Komi. With meetings between authors, library conferences, and a literature festival the focus is kept on Barents literature.

The Barents Region has an extremely diversified and rich culture. Some 20 per cent of new small enterprises are in the creative sector. There is a growing cultural mass (Harvey 1993) which is also attracting artists and cultural workers from other parts of the world to visit or settle down in the Barents Region – a slow rising of a creative class.

Summary, conclusions and perspectives

- With its abundance of natural resources and its quantitatively small but qualitatively high human capital the Barents Euro-Arctic Region has a great future potential. The formalized cooperation gives this cross-border cooperation a satisfying framework for a still fairly slow development process. The texture of the region is still coarse – much of the potential still lies fallow.
- Without the European regionalization processes as back-up the Barents cooperations would not have not been possible.
- The mental map of the Barents region is changing. After decades of negative and pessimistic status quo, and a bad image outside and inside the region, the formalized cooperations with possibilities to confront and tackle image problems has inspired the Barents people to view themselves from a new perspective resulting in a growing feeling of self esteem.
- Paving way for the cooperations as such are the hundreds of cultural cooperations as a platform giving rise to a growth of cultural infrastructures. The cultural cooperations are satisfying – they are easily handled and financed and they are open to all.
- There is a growing Arctic or Barents identity. It is based on century's old shared predicaments being a periphery, neglected by the core, as well as the fearful natural environment and climate. Historically the Arctic identity is also based on the open borders and the trade along the coast. Today the Arctic identity has additional pillars of strength like the cultural cooperations and the cooperation between the universities.
- There is a Barents Culture with unique art works in ice and snow and a region specific literature, design, film and dance.
- After twenty years of existence we can observe that the cooperations has had and still has its ups and downs like some cultural initiatives. Some of them

which were started by very enthusiastic people, like the Barents Chamber Music Youth Orchestra and the Barents Choir do not exist any longer. They stopped when there were no other people to take over the responsibility.

- A difficulty is the uneven funding. Whereas the Norwegian Barents Secretariat and the Norwegian regions are very generous with their financing of projects, the Swedish regions have not the same possibilities to go on with cultural projects; there is less money coming from central government.
- Barents has developed a cooperation which could be used as a conflict prevention model for other parts of the world. So far representatives from the Baltic area, the Balkan and Caucasus have visited the region. In this work cultural cooperations play an important role.
- With the great natural resources the Barents Euro-Arctic Region will be in focus for global attention. The question is how this will affect the region. Will it be a Klondyke-like development with all the negative consequences or could it make an example as a region with a cultural imprint?

Notes

1 See www.beac.st.
2 See the paragraph on Regional Diversity in the Introductory Dialogue in this book.
3 Oblast is Russian for region.
4 Quoted in Bröms *et al.* (1994), p. 32
5 Quoted in http://barentsculture.com.
6 Quoted in *Breaking the Ice* programme, 1998.
7 See note 2.
8 In an interview with the author of this chapter, Edinburgh 1984.
9 See Barents Review 2012, *Barents Borders. Delimitation and Internationalization*, p. 11.
10 Quoted in Arctic and North 2012b, No 6. in Lukin: 'Conceptual Approaches to the definition of the internal borders and the development of the Russian Arctic in the changing world'.
11 Own translation of Fjellström.
12 According to a telephone conversation August 2012.
13 Quoted in Lukin (2012a).
14 I was myself giving a lecture at the seminar.
15 There are 60 universities of the Arctic including the North American and Canadian ones.

References

Alnes, M. (2012) 'A Multitude of Projects Made Possible', in A. Staalesen (ed.), *Barents Borders*, Kirkenes: The Norwegian Barents Secretariat.

Bassand, M. (1990) *Culture et régions d'Europe*, Lausanne: Presses Polytechniques.

Blatter, J. (2000) *Entgrenzung der Staatenwelt*, Baden-Baden: Nomos.

Bröms, P. (1994) 'Manufacturing Sustainability' in P. Bröms, J. Eriksson and B. Svensson (eds), *Reconstructing Survival. Evolving Perspectives on Euro-Arctic Politics*, Stockholm: Fritzes.

Eisenhammer, D. (1992) *Handbuch der grenzüberschreitende Zusammenarbeit in Rheinland-Pfalz*, Mainz: Staatskanzlei Rheinland-Pfalz.

Fjellström, P. (1991) 'Det norrbottniska kulturområdet', in *Norrbottensakademien Årsskrift*, Boden: Ord och Bildskräddaren.
Gidlund, J.E., Ekman, A.-K., Lagergren, M., Lidström, B., Rudebeck, K. and Wigren, R. (1988) *Periferins Renässans*, Stockholm: Allmänna Förlaget.
Gould, P. and White, R. (1992) *Mental Maps*, London: Routledge.
Harvey, D. (1993) 'From Space to Place and Back Again' in J. Bird, B. Curtis, T. Putnam, G. Robertson and L. Tickner (eds), *Mapping the Futures*, London and New York: Routledge.
Hechter, M. (1975) *Internal Colonialism: The Celtic Fringe in British National Development 1536–1966*, London: Routledge and Kegan Paul.
Henriksson, J., Modvar, A., Laine, K., Badendyck, N., Vostriakov, L., Augustinsson, S. and Lind, T. (2001) *Report on the Barents Cultural Cooperation*, Luleå: Arra.
Laine, K. (2001) *Experiences about Intercultural Cooperation in the Barents Euro-Arctic Region*, Strasbourg: Council of Europe.
Lindeborg, L. (1991) 'European Identity as a Cultural Objective', in J.E. Gidlund and G. Törnquist (eds), *European Networks*, Umeå: CERUM, Centre for Regional Science.
——— (1993) 'Kultur och regional utveckling', in NUTEK (Närings- och teknikutveck-lingsverket), *Tretton aspekter på regional utveckling*, Stockholm: Gotab.
——— (1995) *Regionalt Samarbete i Europa*, Rapport 87, Stockholm: Expertgruppen för forskning om regional utveckling.
(Weihe-)Lindeborg, L. (2001/2005) *Zum regionalen System. Stellenwert der Versammlung der Regionen Europas*, Marburg: Tectum Wissenschaftsverlag.
——— (2006) 'Zusammenarbeit im Zeichen einer Philosophie des arktischen Nordens – Die Barentsregion und ihre globale Bedeutung', in Europäisches Zentrum für Föderalismus-Forschung Tübingen, *Jahrbuch des Föderalismus 2006*, Baden-Baden, Nomos.
Lukin, Y. (2012a) 'Arctic and Social Fears', *Arctic and North*, No. 5.
——— (2012b) 'Conceptual Approaches to the Definition of the Internal Borders and the Development of the Russian Arctic in the Changing World', *Arctic and North*, No. 6.
Lundholm, K. (1993) *Norrbotten i den svenska historien*, Luleå: Norrbottens museum.
Malchus, V. Freiherr von (1975) *Partnerschaft an europäischen Grenzen: Integration durch grenzüberschreitende Zusammenarbeit*, Bonn: Europa Union Verlag.
Morin, E. (1987) *Penser l'Europe*, Paris: Gallimard.
Mozer, A. (1973) 'Entwicklungspolitik zu Hause', *Entwicklungsregionen in der EWG*, Bonn: Schriften der Bundeszentrale für politische Bildung.
Östhol, A. (1996) *Politisk integration och gränsöverskridande regionbildning i Europa*, Umeå: Umeå universitet, Statsvetenskapliga institutionen.
Pierret, G. (1978) *Mai Breton*, Rennes: Euregio.
Törnquist, G. (1993) *Sverige i nätverkens Europa*, Malmö: Liber.
VRE, Verammlung der Regionen Europas (1992) *Les Régions Frontalières et l'Intégration Européenne*, Saragossa: Livre Blanc.

21 The role of arts and culture in regional cooperation

Mid-Scandinavian regions Jämtland and Tröndelag

Stig Westerdahl and Wilhelm Skoglund

Introduction

This chapter highlights the role of culture in cross-border cooperation. In order to do so the authors take a closer look at the Mid-Scandinavian regions Jämtland and Tröndelag, located in Sweden and Norway, respectively. Jämtland is 600 km from Stockholm and Tröndelag is 500 km from Oslo.

These two regions are parts of two nation states, and thus separate entities. But this border area also has a long common history making it reasonable to regard it as a coherent region. This tension between constituting a border region and simultaneously having loyalties to the capital of the nation state is an undercurrent throughout this chapter. Border studies is a scholarly field attracting increasing interest (Anderson *et al.* 2003a; Zimmermann and Janschitz 2004). This growing attention must be regarded against the background of forces such as globalization, integration of markets and an increased focus on regions in general. The formation of the EU is part of this process, and the EU is also instrumental in many respects. It appears to be a common understanding of this development, whilst the role of culture in this context has been overlooked (Anderson *et al.* 2003b). The tension between the nation state and allegiance to long traditions of border cooperation is thus not new, but the viewpoint raised here on the role of culture and experience industry and its dependence on public funding is not commonly seen.

The chapter describes projects in this border region where culture and the cultural industry are more or less prominent. Some of them are explicitly border-oriented, others are not but have the potential to become so. From these examples the role of public intervention in general is discussed and the relation to everyday border contacts is viewed.

In the conclusions, the possibilities for further exchange and liaisons over the border are screened. With concepts differing between more utopian projects on the one hand and those with a more down-to-earth orientation on the other, the role of culture is identified. There has to be an increased focus on what concrete steps can be taken to increase cooperation and make use of traditions and the historical legacy of everyday interaction across the border.

A long winding history of cooperation

The history of this border region Jämtland-Tröndelag is rich and vivid. 1905 serves well as a point of reference in the following historical briefing; that was the year that the Swedish–Norwegian union stemming from 1814 was dissolved. In one stroke Norway became independent from Sweden. The occasion was much celebrated in Norway, including Tröndelag. Across the border in Jämtland however, the citizens worried that it would deeply weaken the long history of common culture and strong trade connections. The fear was that the province would now become a periphery to Stockholm instead of remaining a central province on the Scandinavian peninsula (Larsson 1999). These worries can be traced to the long history of cooperation over a border that has been disputed and negotiated and consequently fluid in character.

Going long back in time, Jämtland was Norwegian (and Norway part of a Danish–Norwegian union) until 1645. The ties in Jämtland have historically always been closer to its Norwegian neighbours in the west, than the ties to the east or south (Rumar 1991). Some historians further claim that language and customs as well as ancestry in Jämtland are more connected to Norway than Sweden (Ekerwald 1994).

> The natives of Jämtland are as Norwegian as the people who live in Norway.
> (County governor of Jämtland in 1657) (in Ekerwald 1994)

This long tradition of connections starts with geographical conditions and how those facilitated transport, trade and farming. The strength of the ties over the mountain ridge, separating today's Jämtland and Tröndelag, originated partly in ancient pathways. People walked and travelled from the Baltic coast to the Atlantic coast where the Scandinavian mountain range is at its lowest. That part of the mountain range happens to be located in this region, also characterised by rich and fertile soils on both sides of the range. The search for better land and trade of goods thus became the main reasons for the interconnections over the mountain range. According to folklore stories of Snorre Sturlasson, the thirteenth-century Icelandic poet, another element of the background is the 800 AD escape from vicious rulers in Tröndelag. The fleeing people settled in Jämtland, named after their leader, Kjettil Jamte. On the other hand, people from Jämtland emigrated to Tröndelag in the sixteenth and seventeenth century (Rumar, 1991). The many ways people of Jämtland and Tröndelag are connected have also left traces in village names and the language on the Swedish side, with dialects showing many similarities, often less related to Swedish than Norwegian (Ekerwald 1994).

When Jämtland became Swedish in 1645, measures were undertaken in order to 'Swedify' the population. This was achieved through education, better infrastructure on the Swedish side of the border and beneficial rules for farmers. In this transition period for the now Swedish Jämtland, the Swedish king also sent soldiers from the southern parts of Sweden to keep the province under control –

with brute force if necessary (Ekerwald 1994; Rumar 1991). Another measure was to fortify the province by settling more people and establishing the city of Östersund, which today is the capital of the province (Rumar 1991).

In spite of all these initiatives from Swedish authorities, the connections between Jämtland and Tröndelag remained strong during the seventeenth and eighteenth centuries. Trondheim in Tröndelag continued to compete with Stockholm for trade with Jämtland. Jämtland therefore maintained two roles of being both a border area and a region within the Swedish state.

A new phase in this history evolved when a union between Sweden and Norway was created. When established in 1814, industry and infrastructure were further improved and a railway intensified connections between Jämtland and Stockholm. This led to lowering prices of goods and made trade with Norway less important. The ancient affinity across the mountain range declined as a result (Rumar 1991; Rolén and Thomasson 1990).

The historical connections between Jämtland and Tröndelag took yet another beating when the union was dissolved in 1905 and resources were instead put into the further improvement of strengthening infrastructure and cultural strings north-, south-, as well as eastbound as opposed to strengthening the bond with Norwegian Tröndelag.[1]

The last century has continued directing Jämtland towards Stockholm, and today no one seriously considers the province to be Norwegian, even though many citizens still jokingly refer to Jämtland as East-Tröndelag. University students from Tröndelag have an annual event when they display signs on the border indicating that travellers are entering ‘East-Tröndelag’ instead of Jämtland, Sweden (Adresseavisen 2004). This is one example of the amicable atmosphere along the border, with lots of cultural exchange. As this stretch of border contains many of the cross-border routes along the two nations, these connections are easily maintained. The ventures and projects initiated with the aim of more cross-border cooperation east-west instead of north-south confirm this and some of them also build upon the ancient common traditions.

Cross-border cooperation today

The initiatives to increase or enable benefits from cross-border cooperation take place both along the border itself and elsewhere in Jämtland and Tröndelag. They range from issues regarding social development to tourism and business development. Education is also important in this interaction. To give evidence of how cross-border exchange is alive, some of the more important examples are presented in the following.

The two provinces are most sparsely populated in the very northern part. This is also where the distance to the capitals, as well as to province capitals, has created an interdependent culture with a long history:

> Relations to the west were natural. The people on both sides of the border have consistently been friends and mates. One went to marry

> along both sides of the border, hence family relations occurred both ways.
>
> (Blom 1964)[2]

However, this culture has become successively weaker the stronger the bonds with the respective government has become. In order to reverse this decline, politicians from both sides of the border decided on reinventing old functioning ways, a borderless municipality. In 2008, with the common cultural heritage of the region as the foundation, the project, 'Grensefjell i Midtnorden' was granted €2.5 million from regional, national and European funds. Through ventures into common schools, police, medical care, infrastructure, culture, environmental management, church integration, tourism and business development, the municipalities in this part of the region started on a path towards cross-border dependency rather than national dependency, which is still a work in progress (Brandum 2010).

In the southern part of the provinces, the cooperation is more oriented towards a common market for tourism. In a joint work, Röros municipality in Norway and Funäsdalen in Sweden, are on the move to establish a common tourism destination, starting with the development of an already running air traffic and charter tourism (Länsstyrelsen i Jämtlands län 2011). Another curiosity from this part of the region is the mobile library travelling the roads across the border in recent years. This initiative is directed towards the Sami population, illustrating another example of an often invisible border (Gaaltije 2011).

In terms of higher education, the cooperation level is high among the institutions in the provinces. The most striking example is the entrance of the North-Tröndelag University College into the Swedish higher education system. They are now offering programmes and courses in green entrepreneurship and agriculture for both Norwegian and Swedish students. These projects all serve to illustrate how cross-border initiatives maintain cooperation between Jämtland and Tröndelag, over the border. They depend on traditions, but also have to adjust to national interests. Some are funded by the InterReg project resources, an EU-initiative to encourage border interaction. Compared to other connections to the national capital of Stockholm they are still marginal, but indicate a growing awareness of how the nation state is not taken for granted. In terms of initiatives, the national capitals, Stockholm and Oslo, are not the only potential partners available to Jämtland and Tröndelag respectively. This is also true when it comes to cultural projects, which is the focus in the next section.

Culture as the glue?

The present day Swedish region of Jämtland and its Norwegian counterpart Tröndelag have a long joint background, which has not always been without problems, but that still links the two areas together over the national border. The communalities are there and manifest themselves in many ways, including public projects. Some examples of projects with a cultural emphasis are presented in the following, where the difference between initiatives oriented toward the capital of the nation state, on the one hand, and initiatives grown out of cross-border traditions and a long joint history on the other hand, is examined. The idea is to contrast them, with these different perspectives as the dividing line. What do cross-border cultural projects entail, and why is their cultural character significant?

This question is raised regarding different kinds of initiatives that differ both in terms of scale and duration. First, Färgfabriken Norr, an art gallery, mainly managed and curated from Stockholm, is presented as an example of outbound initiatives exported to the region. The global art scene was exhibited to the visitors in Jämtland: vivid and experimental. The initiative did not survive however after the three-year project period. After that smaller-sized projects were introduced, where the cross-border idea has been more viable. The traditions they build on are somewhat longer and the regional anchoring has proved to have a more profound role. We describe the Mid-Nordic Film commission, cooperation between museums on both sides of the border and several sports events that draw on the traditions. Those projects point to the potential in cross-border initiatives built on culture.

An art gallery at the border

In April 2008 a new art gallery, Färgfabriken Norr (The Paint Factory North) opened its doors in Östersund. On the premises of one of the former regimental garrisons contemporary art was introduced to the visitors – a type of art never previously shown in the region. Some of it was labelled 'relational aesthetics' entailing that viewers coproduce the art by their presence and participation. This art intends to create a social interaction as opposed to merely passive viewing. Video films of the Russian artist Kulik showed when he imitated dogs at an exhibition and physically attacked visitors. People in Östersund could consult the virtual oracle, Miltos Manetas and have their queries answered, as well as be fascinated by carp swimming in a pond creating patterns on the water surface. Another more challenging work was 'Happy Easter', a compilation of snapshots from brutal murder-scenes in horror movies. All this was art 'teleported', as the term was coined, from earlier exhibitions at the original Färgfabriken in Stockholm.

This new art gallery in Östersund was the result of a project financed jointly by public regional actors and EU Regional Funds. The real estate company, as owners of the premises, financed the renovation of the building and voluntarily donated the rent for the three-year period that the project lasted. The project's origin can be traced to the town's recent history of events, and the possibilities created by these events in combination with EU-funding. The background is the town's long-standing demand for a larger public art gallery to supplement an existing vibrant art environment with many small local private galleries and regional artists working to sustain their living.

When an exhibition of the region's most well-known artist, the former nativist Primus Mortimer Pettersson (1895–1975), was on display in Östersund at one of the small private galleries together with one of Sweden's more prestigious contemporary artists, the idea of a public art gallery was given new energy. Some influential actors in the Stockholm art scene got involved, meetings were called in town and public politicians and civil servants began working on the idea again. The real estate firm which had newly acquired the large facilities where the recently closed infantry regiment had resided, was a driving force. Their interest in an attraction coincided nicely with the old discussion of an art gallery.

In a following step, contacts were established with one of the, at the time, few private large art galleries in Stockholm: Färgfabriken ('The Paint Factory'). It was originally financed by a public donation in 1996 which consisted of renovation costs and free use of a large building and which further relied on private and public financing for their activities. Apart from, for the most part, being privately financed, the art gallery was also known for blending their exhibitions with laboratories for discussing planning issues in general and architectural aspects in particular. Färgfabriken in Stockholm constituted an unconventional combination of an art gallery, a contemporary laboratory and a consultancy firm. Many of the necessary conditions for a new art gallery in Jämtland were hereby in place: a building to use, an interested local real estate company, and an art gallery in Stockholm in search of projects and finances. A looming crisis due to the closure of regiments proved to be another important factor.

While the closure of the regiments paved the way for renovation and use of the building for the art gallery, the abandonment of all military activities in Östersund in 2004 created a major blow to employment in the region. The county has around 120,000 inhabitants, of which roughly half live in the city of Östersund. In one strike, the national government erased 1,400 jobs in the military sector; including indirect jobs among subcontractors the numbers totalled around 3,500 employees. Taking into account all the people who were affected, such as teachers and so on, estimates point to 7,000 jobs. In a region where depopulation has been a trend since the 1950s, this was a serious situation. The private sector has never really grown strong in this rural region. No major industries have grown here and the service sector is not very strong. Tourism in winter is a major source of employment, but the main stronghold is the public sector. But even here problems have grown over the last twenty years, as many governmental jobs have been eliminated of which the military employment cuts were the most severe. The closure of regiments announced by the Secretary of Defence on the streets of Östersund in 2004 caused a sense of despair and negativism: what was to become of this? But several initiatives from the government and the regional authorities were launched to counter these feelings. A large rescue-package was announced with new jobs and funds for fresh initiatives, projects and financing of venture capital funds. The overarching idea was to turn the pessimistic mode into a sense of confidence in the future.

A number of slightly opposing ingredients were hereby at hand: closure of a major employer in a region with low employment, a sense of defeatism in need of hope and large public funds for different activities. Money in search of initiatives, to put it bluntly. The idea of a public art gallery vibrated in the background. These were the conditions when the art gallery Färgfabriken Norr was established in the old drill building at the garrison. The EU-funding, the privately funded renovation, the money from local municipality and county council all together funded three years of art exhibitions, amounting to 20 million SEK (around €2 million). The intention was to have new funding after this period and hereby establish the art gallery as a permanent institution. The stated ambition was to become not only a regional but a national stronghold for contemporary art. Where conscripted soldiers over many years had trained to perform their military duties, the most advanced modern art from all over the world was about to replace the drill and the repeated dismantling of weapons.

The opening was actually three openings, all taking place in April 2008. The first was a conference on a 'New World Bank', built on ideas as opposed to money. The next opening was the Teleport-exhibition with the challenging artworks involving relational aesthetics. The third and final opening was a 'Contemporary laboratory' where the planning challenges in the town were tackled with the help of external consultants and experts, a large aerial photo about the size of a villa plot, and school children who were bussed in from all over the county. They were all spectacular and expensive openings of the art gallery one opening in three. Or three in one?

The initiative 'New World Bank' collected people from all over the world, to discuss global matters such as inequality, pollution and bad housing. No concrete measures or initiatives were taken, the idea was to allow the flown-in experts, consultants and artists to merge ideas with local people from authorities and companies. One of the more remarkable appearances was the now deceased Malcolm McLaren, better known as manager for the Sex Pistols. He advocated the idea of 'Majestic failures', where the premise is that any major success in order to be accomplished requires a complete fiasco beforehand. Changes need failures, a suggestion some of the audience perceived as a wink to the event itself, others regarded it as a mysterious thought. The symposium 'The New World Bank' also consisted of workshops intended to foster material for the alternative global bank to be started, and the day wound up with a dinner with local specialities.

The art gallery with its works opened up on day two of the seminar. The renovated drill building housed installations, video films, paintings and other works. Most of it had been shown previously in Stockholm, thus the term 'Teleport' which was the title of the exhibition. Some of it was however original art, such as the sound from the depth of the local lake 'Storsjön' which also claimed to include the cry of the monster in the lake: 'Storsjöodjuret'. At the opening, local business people, politicians, artists and civil servants mingled and tried to hide their wonder. They slowly sipped their wine served in this extravagance of light and sound and other effects accompanying modern art.

The third opening took place a couple of weeks later, and was less spectacular. This 'Östersund at large' proved to be a remake of 'Stockholm at large' where the planning problems of the capital were discussed. A huge aerial photograph was scrutinised and discussed at the first event by external architects, planners and an anthropologist. They held lectures, led and participated in workshops that developed plans for a future city. The result was a focus on communication within the city (such as a skateboard bridge over the railway that separates city centre from the lake) and rail links to Norway (Trondheim) and Sundsvall (the neighbour town eastward). The ideas were artistically illustrated on the huge aerial photo which covered the floor, and after two days of workshops its presentation was accompanied by a smoke and laser show. With this event, new dimensions were to be introduced in the planning of the city, setting the place in a global setting and initiating debate. Following the three-day workshop schoolchildren, first from Östersund and then from all over the region, came by bus to look at the map and discuss their future in the region. These discussions with the coming generation of the county took several weeks and involved many pupils.

The openings of the art gallery attracted lots of attention and were immense in character, but the financial consequences were severe. Much of the funding was consumed early in the process, and the efforts to establish and sustain contacts with a new audience were affected. Another factor was the global rather than regional focus at the openings, with some exceptions. Few of the remaining exhibitions received that much attention after the openings, and the numbers of visitors diminished. Also, it proved that the local actors who initially were very positive, became more critical of the gallery over time. The prospects for new initiatives, links between art and commerce and a climate where new ideas could be aired – none of these expectations were met. In the midst of this mood, the cross-border initiatives also got lost. Many regional painters and visual artists active on the Swedish side of the border were educated at the Norwegian Trondheim Academy of Fine Art. Another reason for closer cooperation in art is of course the geographical proximity and the traditions. In spite of these and other possibilities at the gallery for art projects with Swedish–Norwegian emphasis, the Stockholm focus took the upper hand. According to some of the people interviewed[3] in studies conducted, Färgfabriken Norr was too modest in its marketing and did not try hard enough to attract the interest of local people. A lot of criticism was directed at the responsible parties in Stockholm. The critics in Jämtland claimed Färgfabriken did not have sufficient ambitions to make the regional connection strong enough. The undercurrent of the criticism was that the project adhered to the ideas and interests of the capital, instead of the local region.

After three years of exhibitions, Färgfabriken Norr ceased to exist in the drill building at the former garrison. No more funding was available, the public financiers lost interest and no EU-money was at hand. Varying culture is still displayed in the building, but under another name and organisation. This initiative proved to not be viable after the project period, and the reasons for this closure are manifold, as described above.

The Mid Nordic Film Commission

> The Mid Nordic Film Commission covers the areas of Central Norway and Central Sweden. Though the region is small in size it is one of the most diverse you will ever find. It covers locations from the rugged Norwegian Atlantic Coast to the wide open alpine landscapes of Sweden. We can offer fantastic unused locations, professional crews, financing opportunities + a very film friendly environment.
>
> (Source: http://midtnorskfilm.no/mnfc/)

More than most cultural expressions, film is a product of the Modern Age. Art has 'always' existed, literature has been known for ages and theatre also has a very long tradition. The history of film, however, covers only a little more than a century – the first official film ever to be shown is said to be the one performed by the Lumiere Brothers in Paris 1895. The development of the film industry as we know it, soon followed. A more advanced cutting method created masterpieces such as Potemkin, silent film was followed by sound film, and along the lines of Henry Ford and his assembly methods a huge plant in Hollywood followed. We have now become accustomed to multichannel sound, 3D films and digital cinemas where we can follow opera at the Met or a Stockholm theatre live. This has shifted the focus from one single industry shooting films in an American or Swedish studio to the film-sector becoming a question of regional politics. Following this trend, the location of film production is attracting interest. One expression of this is an explicit cross-border initiative: the Mid Nordic Film Commission established in June 2008 by the counties of North Tröndelag and South Tröndelag in Norway, together with the counties of Jämtland and Härjedalen in Sweden. The Commission has two offices, one in Trondheim, Norway and one in Östersund, Sweden.

There are several aspects of linking film to regional aspirations and policies. One of which is the actual showing of films, where the availability of cinemas or other venues for new films is important. A relatively new aspect is one where the actual shooting of films is of interest and this is where the 'Mid Nordic Film Commision' (also referred to as 'Film Commission Jämtland-Tröndelag') comes in. The aim of this EU InterReg Project 2008–2011 with a budget of roughly €1 million is to create regional growth by attracting twenty film productions (feature film/short film/documentary) to the border region. In a following step and still according to the original application for EU-funding, two production companies are to be established, with a number of subcontractors under them, all with a focus on film production. But the ambitions do not end here. By the extension, this will make the region attractive for other purposes, of which tourism is the most salient. In the end it boils down to image and branding, with the goal of making Jämtland and Tröndelag attractive regions for visitors. Previous examples of this strategy already exist, the most talked about of which is the production of *Lord of the Rings* in New Zealand. In Sweden the productions about detective Wallander for both film and TV have initiated a small industry in the very south of Sweden. The most active film commissions apart from those behind *Wallander*-productions in the south, are located in the very north (Norrbotten) and in the western parts close to Gothenburg.

Apart from the more long-term objectives on growth in terms of industry-specific companies and visitors, one argument focuses on short-term revenues. A film production is a costly exercise, where a substantial amount of the money is spent locally: be it catering, transport, manufacturing of milieu both inside and outside, lighting, sound and many other necessary ingredients. The rationale for the film commission is thus to show how this money can be spent in the region and benefit local companies – most of them small and specialised. Finally, according to Lundström (2011), one of the main opportunities of the Mid Nordic Film Commission is to further strengthen regional identify and pride as well as the shared cross-border identity.

As the Film Commission project now is about to be finalised, some preliminary reflections can be made. It has been possible to attract film productions to the area, even some more spectacular ones with prominent Hollywood actors involved, for example *The American* featuring the actor George Clooney (Lundström 2011). According to a study by Lundström (2010), film production can also be lucrative on a short-term basis. For example, the filming of one Swedish movie in the northern parts of Jämtland-Tröndelag gave a return on investment of 1:5. The problem seems to be the more long-term objectives in terms of increasing the number of visitors and forming a brand and image based on the films. There must be a kind of 'tourism infrastructure' at hand to take advantage of the productions on site, and the film has to reach a wide audience. There are not that many *Lord of the Rings*-type trilogies that can gain such widespread attention. Such shortcomings, however, must not minimise other benefits gained from the Film Commission. In view of cross-border cooperation, several advantages are revealed. The project has tried to make use of some of the region's strengths, including a reliable winter climate, beautiful scenery, and many creative small-scale entrepreneurs coupled with old cross-border traditions. The film project is not large scale in character, but draws on many smaller capacities in the region and hopes that flexibility and speed can replace size as a competitive factor. It is far too early to make any final assessment but a lot of potential has been demonstrated by the productions that have already been filmed in the border region.

Museums and sports connections

In more traditional 'cultural terms' the inter-museum cooperation in the region is strong and consists of several longer- and shorter-term ventures. The county museum Jamtli in Östersund cooperates in different ways with Tröndelag's Folk Museum, Sverresborg. Their joint work encompasses traditional handicrafts from both regions as well as pre-school teacher education that focuses on the region's cultural heritage. This work is conducted together with universities and authorities on both sides of the border (Länsstyrelsen i Jämtlands län 2011; Jamtli 2011). Another example of joint efforts is that when a visitor pays the entrance fee at either Jamtli or Sverresborg, it gives free entrance also to the other museum.

One reason for this museum cooperation is of course to attract more tourism to this cross-border region. Common stakes in tourism can be seen from many directions in the region, and also encompass cultural perspectives. There are several cooperative gastronomy projects that include tourism visits to production sites and participation in the production traditions of different communities (Länsstyrelsen i Jämtlands län 2005). The intersection between the cultural perspective and tourism can also be seen in jazz music projects used to strengthen the region with joint concerts (Länskulturen i Jämtlands län 2011).

Sport is perhaps the field where cross-border connections is most vivid and ranges from exchanges between individual associations to larger events. The most well known on the Swedish side is St Olavs relay, which stretches 300 km along the St Olav pilgrimage. St Olav was a Norwegian king who Christianised Norway, had to flee to Sweden, and on his way back to Sweden travelled along the very stretch of land discussed here (Rumar 1991). Every year, thousands of participants, representing over 200–300 teams, compete on levels ranging from friendly to highly competitive, running between Östersund in Jämtland to Trondheim in South-Tröndelag. The end of each of the race's four days includes prize ceremonies and festivities where participants dine, drink and interact, especially on the final day. The race is a mutual arrangement between organisations in Tröndelag and Jämtland (Okstad *et al.* 1994; www.st-olavsloppet.com 2011).

On the Norwegian side of the border, Flyktingloppet, a 42 km ski marathon that stretches from Nordli on the North-Tröndelag side to Gäddede on the Jämtland side, is the most prestigious cross-border sports event. The race, as well as the following dance, is a tribute to the Norwegian refugees who fled over the mountains to Jämtland during World War II. The race follows the path the refugees used and is arranged by sports associations in Jämtland and Tröndelag. Every year it attracts around 2,000 skiers with the vision to 'continuously maintain the Swedish-Norwegian fraternization' (www.flyktningerennet.no 2011).

There are also other examples of similar cooperation and ventures between the two provinces ranging from common football leagues to exchange traditions in ice hockey and tennis, most of them youth oriented. Even if the attraction level of these types of cross-border events is high, the sports sector and its associations is deeply rooted and affiliated with the National Sports Association, based in Stockholm. This entails structure, funding, education, ranking, etc., based on a Swedish system, and that cross-border activities become regarded as curiosities of less importance in more serious and competitive terms. On the other hand, the cross-border events in the sports sector are based on culture and fraternisation, and their survival can be seen as an indication of the closeness across the border in this region.

Between neighbour and capital: on the dual loyalties of a border region

The 'projectification' of some Swedish regions in the wake of EU membership is illustrated in this exposé on cross-border projects. The cultural content differs in the initiatives, but some features stand out. Progress seems to require linkages to the traditions outlined earlier in this chapter. The regional connection is also essential, and an over-dependence on Stockholm can have dire consequences, as shown by the example from Färgfabriken, where many of the stakeholders expressed a lack of regional anchoring and foothold.[4] The projects emanating not only from historical legacies, such as the sport events, but also drawing on more down-to-earth advantages, such as the Film Commission have a better track record. This fits well with other studies in this field, as will be shown later. The discussion on loyalties to the national capital and border cooperation is part of a wider picture that will first be explored.

Border studies are on the agenda again

The nation state is commonly derived in its European history from the treaty of Westphalia in 1648. The reigning view was one where the state had a supreme authority over the territory, and is the natural problem-solver. The state not only provided security, but also catered to the welfare and management of socio-economic affairs (Burgess and Vollaard 2006). In the seventeenth century, the border region studied in this chapter also reflected these tendencies. Only three years prior to this treaty, the region of Jämtland became Swedish and this area came under a clearer national mandate. The legacy of the Westphalia treaty on the European continent was not only the creation of authorities capable of controlling territories, but rather an important consequence of this treaty was also how connections over a border became problematic. Shifting to our own time the situation is different. Many contemporary trends seem to marginalise the state, whilst notions of regions and cities are becoming increasingly influential. This change of perspective is also affecting the general perception of border regions.

When nation states were strong, borders were a chronic source of concern and often an origin to war. The inherent logic in the idea of a nation state required that something outside the territory was visible. It was impossible to determine the specifics of what was inside the border and constituted the national, if the opposite did not exist. This demand for 'otherness' made border regions controversial. But in many border regions the links and contacts still remained for several reasons. Anderson, O'Dowd and Wilson (2003a) point to how borders facilitate problem-solving, how many people in border regions have seen the devastating effects of national conflicts (particular in the twentieth century) and seek to avoid them. A third reason is how inhabitants in border regions also see the potential for development in cross-border contacts.

For these and other reasons, connections over national borders are regarded as precious among international institutions. The EU is a project where borders by definition are marginalised and regions rather than states are emphasised. Those ambitions have become materialised in projects such as InterReg and Phare, where funds are financing different types of cross-border activities and initiatives. Another trend in the same direction is urbanisation, where cities for different reasons have become major entities. The joint result of globalisation, regionalisation and urbanisation is thus the de-emphasising of the nation state, and a consequence of this is how border regions are seen in a new light. Rather than being problems, they have become a focus of scholarly interest and are seen as attractive for their potential to make cooperation beyond states more concrete and also more local.

Bring border projects down-to-earth

In line with this thinking, cultural aspects have been identified. Border regions have a lot in common particularly in terms of their cultural heritage. Culture, however, is a broad concept, said to be one of the most complicated words in the English language. It can be referred to in broad terms as the general state of mind among a group of people, but also in more narrow terms of the aspects of identity. In our account, these general perspectives are de-emphasised and culture is studied in a more concrete way. It is the manifestation of culture in different forms and the formation of a cultural industry we look into. Culture can hereby be seen as expressions such as sport, handicrafts, film-making and art as well as folk dance. These aspects along with culture and its broadest connotations have been overlooked by studies in border regions (Anderson *et al.* 2003b) and our contribution can be seen in that context.

In a study of cross-border regions, Löfgren (2008) shows how peripheral border regions tend to move towards the nation state with a centripetal force. All his examples share many of the characteristics with Jämtland–Tröndelag in our account. The Öresund region, with the bridge between Sweden and Denmark as a link, as well as Torne Valley in the north of Sweden/Finland and his third case, Svinesund between Sweden and Norway all have Sweden as one nation state, share a history of border disputes and have lately been interesting for EU-funding on differing collaboration projects.

Löfgren starts with the differences between the regions. Some of them are EU 'flagships': political projects aimed at creating cooperation. Others are characterised by 'regionauts', where actors on both sides of the border make use of the differences with a market perspective. The latter thus makes use of differences in prices on goods, services and vacationing. According to the author these differences lead to unintended outcomes, as the political ambitions are hard to realise but the market-driven regionauts achieve more and faster progress. The flagships contain grand ideas, but tend to be utopian and farfetched and Löfgren is consequently critical of them.

This line of reasoning on cross-border cooperation in practice follows Perkmann (2003) and his claim that much of the literature has a strong normative flair. He further states EU impact is often exaggerated and shows how ideas on cross-border emancipation from the nation state often remain an unattainable dream. The main conclusion that one can draw from his studies is that municipal cooperation tends to be more successful, as it is less burdensome from an administrative perspective and it also poses less of a threat to the nation state. These projects are simply more down-to-earth. Anderson, O'Dowd and Wilson (2003b) also draw attention to everyday life and cross-border initiatives. The authors claim there is in general an emphasis on grand EU projects, and consequently a negligence of the role of culture and the way ordinary cross-border activities are constituted, in other words how life is lived in cross-border regions.

The Färgfabriken example shows how a lack of regional grounding and a cross-border perspective, which in that case were often related concepts, became a problem. The smaller projects with their history of cooperation have an advantage, not only with their legacy but also with their more concrete approach. This is especially clear with the sports projects where crossing the border is concrete and manifested in the event as such. This is also true in the case of the film project, as it makes use of the natural preconditions in the area and their similarities and differences. This poses a natural advantage for cooperation.

Finally, the most interesting example in relation to the discussion on flagships, regionauts and the risk of fostering too grandiose projects without context and focus on everyday border life, is the municipal perspective described above. Interacting with the EU and EU-funding, does have the potential to bring cultural perspectives into the cross-border work, however whilst Färgfabriken Norr was more cultural than cross border, other cross-border municipal initiatives involving sports, museums and film illustrate how culture and the down-to-earth perspective it entails can be pushed to the forefront in the attempts to bring border regions closer and less dependent on the nation state.

Notes

1 The story and history of Jämtland and Tröndelag is of course part of a larger context, political strategies as well as wars fought here and elsewhere. The accurate version of historical events is, like everywhere else, also debated (Bull 1970). One ongoing debate regards the first settlers in a wider north Scandinavian perspective: many claim the Sami people constitute the aborigines. A more complete picture of these issues is, however, beyond the scope of this chapter.

2 Directly translated from Brandum (2010).

3 For more extensive information, see Skoglund and Westerdahl (2009) and Skoglund (2010).

4 For more information on this, see Skoglund (2010).

References

Adresseavisen (2004) 'Her er öst-fronten'. Available at: www.adressa.no/nyheter/article7075.ece.

Anderson, J., O'Dowd, L. and Wilson, T.M. (eds) (2003a) *New Borders for a Changing Europe. Cross-border Cooperation and Governance*, London: Frank Cass.

——— (2003b) 'Culture Co-operation and Borders', *European Studies A Journal of European Culture, History and Politics*, (19): 13–31.

Blom, Z. (1964) in Brandum, M. (2010) 'Att återvinna ett kulturarv', in B. Johannisson and D. Rylander (eds) *Entreprenörskap i regioners tjänst. Ingångar till nya näringar genom design, upplevelser, kulturarv*, Jönköping: Jönköping International Business School.

Brandum, M. (2010) 'Att återvinna ett kulturarv', in B. Johannisson and D. Rylander (eds), *Entreprenörskap i regioners tjänst. Ingångar till nya näringar genom design, upplevelser, kulturarv*, Jönköping: Jönköping International Business School.

Bull, E. (1970) *Jemtland og Norge* (first published 1927), Östersund: AB Wisénska bokhandelns förlag.

Burgess, M. and Vollaard, H. (eds) (2006) *State Territoriality and European Integration*, London: Routledge.

Ekerwald, C.-G. (1994) 'Folkstämningen i Jämtland vid övergången till Sverige', in S. Rentzhog (ed.), *Jämten 1995*, Östersund: Jämtlands läns museums förlag.

Flyktningerennet. Available at: www.flyktningerennet.no. (accessed 25 September 2011).

Gaaltije (2011). Available at: www.gaaltije.se (accessed 20 September 2011).

Jamtli (2011). Available at: www.jamtli.com (accessed 20 September 2011).

Länskulturen i Jämtlands län (2011) 'Kulturplan för Jämtlan ds län 2012–2014', Östersund: Länskulturen i Jämtlands län.

——— (2005) 'Projektbanken Interreg IIIa', Östersund: Länsstyrelsen i Jämtlands län. Available at: www.interreg-sverige.norge.com (accessed 20 September 2011).

——— (2011) 'Projektbanken Interreg IIIa', Östersund: Länsstyrelsen i Jämtlands län. Available at: www.interreg-sverige.norge.com (accessed 20 September 2011).

Larsson, H. (1999) 'Seklets krönika', in S. Rentzhog (ed.), *Jämten 2000*, Östersund: Jämtlands läns museums förlag.

Löfgren, O. (2008) 'Regionauts: The Transformation of Cross-border Regions in Scandinavia', *European Urban and Regional Studies*, 15(3): 195–209.

Lundström, C. (2010) *I spåren av varg*, Ås: JiLU. Available at: www.regionjamtland.se/dokument/verksamhet/cat_view/80-verksamhet/82-publikationer/83-utveckling-och-forskning (accessed 10 September 2011).

——— (2011) *I spåren av Clooney och Stormare*, Ås: JiLU.

Mid Nordic Film Commission. Available at: http://midtnorskfilm.no/mnfc/ (accessed 20 September 2011).

Okstad, A., Nyborg, J. and Solli, E. (1994) *St Olavsloppet. Lokaløkonomi og forbedringsforslag*, Steinkjer: Nord-trøndelags-forskning 1994:6.

Perkmann, M. (2003) 'Cross-border Regions in Europe: Significance and Drivers of Regional Cross-border Co-operation', *European Urban and Regional Studies*, 10(2): 153–171.

Rolén, M. and Thomasson, L. (1990) *Jämtlands och Härjedalens historia. Femte delen 1880–1980*, Östersund: Jämtlands läns museums förlag.

Rumar, L. (1991) *Historia kring kölen. En bok om Jämtland, Härjedalen och Tröndelagen.* Östersund: Jämtlands läns museums förlag.

Skoglund, W. (2010) *Färgfabriken Norr – konst eller näringsliv?* Östersund: Regionförbundet i Jämtlands län. Available at: www.regionjamtland.se/dokument/verksamhet/cat_view/80-verksamhet/82-publikationer/83-utveckling-och-forskning (accessed 10 September 2011).

Skoglund, W. and Westerdahl, S. (2009) *Relationell estetik möter gammal militärstad. Historien om Färgfabriken Norr*, Ås: JiLU. Available at: www.regionjamtland.se/dokument/verksamhet/cat_view/80-verksamhet/82-publikationer/83-utveckling-och-forskning (accessed 10 September 2011).

St Olavsloppet, Available at:www.st-olavsloppet.com. (accessed 25 September 2011).

Zimmermann, F.M. and Janschitz, S. (eds) (2004) *Regional Policies in Europe. Soft Features for Innovative Cross-border Cooperation*, Graz: Leykam.

Index

References are to paragraph numbers.